*Eisenhower Center Studies on War and Peace*

# John F. Kennedy and Europe

# John F. Kennedy and Europe

*edited by*
Douglas Brinkley and Richard T. Griffiths

*foreword by*
Theodore Sorensen

Louisiana State University Press *Baton Rouge*

00  02  04  06  08  07  05  03  01  99
1   3   5   4   2

Designer: Glynnis Weston
Typeface: Galliard
Typesetter: Coghill Composition
Printer and binder: Edwards Brothers, Inc.

Library of Congress Cataloging-in-Publication Data

John F. Kennedy and Europe / edited by Douglas Brinkley and Richard T.
Griffiths : with a foreword by Theodore Sorensen.
    p.   cm. — (Eisenhower Center studies on war and peace)
Includes index.
ISBN 0-8071-2332-3 (cloth : alk. paper)
  1. Europe—Foreign relations—United States.  2. United States—
Foreign relations—Europe.  3. United States—Politics and
government—1961–1963.  4. United States—Foreign
relations—1961–1963.  5. Kennedy, John F. (John Fitzgerald),
1917–1963.  I. Brinkley, Douglas.  II. Griffiths, Richard T.
III. Series.
D1065.U5J59   1999
327.7304—dc21                                    98-56145
                                                    CIP

*for*
Kerry Kennedy-Cuomo
*and*
Charles U. Daly

# Contents

# Foreword

John F. Kennedy, as a United States senator, presidential candidate and president, initiated a new relationship with Latin America, the Alliance for Progress; took a special interest in Africa, encouraging the transition from colonialism; devoted enormous time and worry to Southeast Asia, where multiple communist insurgencies threatened to escalate into full-scale war; and recognized the growing importance of Japan as an emerging economic and political power. He paid special attention to troubles in Cuba, China, India, the Congo, Algeria, Egypt, and elsewhere. He traveled to Canada, Mexico, and several Latin American states. He wanted to know more about every country in the world, to do more for the less developed countries, to build more U.S. ties with Third World countries hesitating on the choice between communism and democracy. He was proud of his inauguration of the Peace Corps, sending volunteer teachers and technicians to virtually every corner of the globe except Europe.

But Kennedy's remarkable sense of objectivity and rationality gave him in all aspects of public policy a strong sense of priority—which programs and places merited the most money, which crises required the strongest response, which issues required the greatest time and attention. In foreign affairs he knew that he must accord top priority to Europe. And he did—not for sentimental reasons stemming from his youthful travels there, not for political reasons arising from the American electorate's dominant ancestral and cultural ties with that region, not for economic reasons reflecting our closer trade and investment links at that time, not even for historical reasons, though his love of history embraced his acknowledgment that America, in Charles de Gaulle's phrase, was "the daughter of Europe." He simply recognized that Europe, during his days in the White House, was the key to America's success, security, and survival in a dangerous world.

On Inauguration Day 1961, the Cold War between communism and the West was at its height. The Soviet Union's menace and reach were global, and its opportunities for expanding and exploiting its influence were greatest in the new and poorer countries of the Third World. But its massive armies and nuclear weapons were targeted primarily toward the West. In Eastern Europe Soviet power had achieved its greatest and most brutal successes. In Western Europe the United States and its traditional allies had mobilized their own mighty military organization to deter a Soviet-led invasion or nuclear attack. And in the heart of Europe West Berlin—an island of freedom in the middle of Soviet-controlled East Germany, geographically cut off from the rest of the West by the fortunes of war but politically and economically linked to it—represented in his mind the single most likely detonator for what he had termed in his Inaugural Address "mankind's final war."

It was in this context that President Kennedy gave top priority to Europe—more meetings with its leaders than those of any other region, more time to its problems, more trips to its capitals. He was not as Euro-centered as his Department of State, and he did not always see eye-to-eye with his European allies. But he was determined to prevent an East-West military conflagration and to preserve the essential unity of the Western Alliance, despite obstacles created as much by Allied stubbornness as Soviet pressures; and he succeeded in doing so. He believed that Western unity and resolve would do more in the long run to discourage Soviet aggression and ambition than American arms and propaganda, and he proved to be right.

Prophecy, to be sure, was not John Kennedy's style. He believed in setting goals—as distinguished from deadlines ("all this will not be finished in the first 100 days")—and he knew enough about the uncertainties of a difficult world to avoid specific predictions. The monstrous Wall that divided Berlin, Germany, and all of Europe symbolically as well as physically could not, he knew, be talked down by the West during a seemingly endless Cold War or knocked down without the hot war he strove to prevent. He rejected the temptation to predict the Wall's early demise in the speeches he delivered to beleaguered West Berliners during his final trip to Europe in the summer of 1963, despite their desperate need for some hint of hope, because he rejected hypocrisy and demagoguery in his speeches as well as prophecy.

Yet his careful mix of optimism, realism, and patience that day produced a formulation that nearly three decades later would prove to be a remarkably prophetic vision: "A united Berlin in a united Germany, united by self-determination, and living in peace. . . . When all are free, then we can look forward to that day when this city will be joined as one."

That day *will* finally come, he said, and it did. The peaceful fall of the Berlin Wall and the triumph of "the cause of freedom on both sides of the Wall" (to which he had offered a toast at lunch inside West Berlin's City Hall) would have given John F. Kennedy, had he lived to witness them, a sense of exultation and satisfaction unlike any he had ever experienced. Not because he would have claimed credit for winning the Cold War, as some American politicians have. On the contrary, he would have given most of the credit to the vitality and resistance of Berliners on both sides of the Wall, to the determination and persistence of dissidents and playwrights and scientists from Potsdam to Vladivostock who refused to be silenced, and to all the people in every corner of Europe and the alliance who remained steadfastly united and dedicated to freedom through more than four decades of peril. He would not have needed to exaggerate the importance of his own role to have been justifiably proud as well as happy when the Wall came tumbling down.

Would that sense of exultation and satisfaction be replaced today by dismay and scorn over NATO's inability to agree on a clearly defined peacetime role, the West's disarray over the breakup of Yugoslavia and the brutality in Bosnia, or continuing economic and other squabbles within the European Union and between Europe and the United States? I do not believe so. It was JFK's nature to take the long view, to recognize the frailty of political leadership, the difficulty of international alliances, and the value of incremental, evolutionary progress.

As a champion of West European union who believed that it was a necessary precondition to the true and interdependent Atlantic partnership for which he called, he would have admired with enthusiasm the steady (yet, in total, spectacular) progress that has been made by European integrationists since his days in the White House. Having encountered frustrating delays and complaints from several European capitals in his effort to forge a common position on Berlin (and having quoted Napoleon's remark that his successes came when he fought with his allies and Winston Churchill's that the history of any alliance is the history of mutual recrimination), he would not have been surprised, much less permanently disheartened, by today's lack of perfect harmony among Konrad Adenauer's, Harold Macmillan's, and de Gaulle's successors. "The fact is," he once said, "You can't possibly carry out any policy without causing major frictions . . . we are prepared to have everybody mad if it makes some progress."

Nor would he be turning away from Europe today, now that the Cold War is over and the economic power and potential of the Pacific Rim nations dominate that newly important economic arena. The words he spoke upon his arrival in Europe in 1963 did not refer to our military forces alone: "In a larger sense, the United States is here on this continent to stay. So long as our presence is desired and required, our . . . commitments will remain. . . . Out of necessity as well as sentiment . . . our fortunes are one." And he told his audience in Frankfurt two days later: "Today there are no exclusively German problems or American, or even European problems. There are world problems—and our two countries and continents are inextricably bound together in the tasks of peace as well as war." Remarkable insights from a remarkable man. But, alas, with respect to Europe as with so many other items on his agenda, John Kennedy is remembered today more for what he began than for what he completed. (He had been unintentionally prophetic in concluding the previously quoted sentence from his Inaugural Address: "All this will not be finished in the first 100 days . . . nor even perhaps in our lifetime on this planet. But let us begin.")

With the peaceful resolution of the Cuban Missile Crisis, the reduction of tensions over Berlin, the signing of the Limited Nuclear Test-Ban Treaty, and other breakthroughs in 1963, Kennedy had just begun by November 1963 to lay the groundwork for an East-West détente and a stabilization of the arms race. Having learned more about the uses of power, the leadership of NATO, and who among his fellow Western leaders could be depended upon and should be listened to (and who should not), he had just begun to build the framework for a closer and more creative alliance and for an eventual Atlantic partnership with a unified Europe. He had plans for an official state visit to Italy and a possible tour of the Soviet Union, for new arms limitations proposals, and for new approaches to Berlin.

On 22 November, he was at the "top of his game," moving, healthy, happy, respected, confident. That morning he told a Texas audience that "because we are stronger . . . our chances for security, our chances for peace, are better than they have been in the past." On that day, his presidency, to his countrymen and most of the world, represented—indeed, exuded—hope for a better, safer future.

Unfortunately, that future was not to be. France's president Charles de Gaulle, having broken one of his customary rules by coming to Kennedy's funeral, broke another by speaking in English upon his arrival—only three words: "What a tragedy!"

THEODORE SORENSEN

# Preface

To most observers John F. Kennedy's European policy means the June 1961 Vienna Summit, when Soviet premier Nikita Khrushchev demanded that West Berlin be transformed into a "demilitarized free city." It would be "a cold winter," he threatened, if the United States did not meet his demands. Kennedy refused, countering with a proposal to boost the military budget and other martial steps should Khrushchev's belligerence persist. In a television address on July 25, 1961, Kennedy made his tough stance public, saying, "I hear it said that West Berlin is militarily untenable. And so was Bastogne. And so, in fact, was Stalingrad. Any dangerous spot is tenable if men—brave men—make it so."

Three weeks later, Soviet troops in East Berlin began blocking all travel from East Germany into the Western sector and began building the Berlin Wall. Again Kennedy harshly denounced the Soviet action but refused to take military steps. On August 13, 1961, the East German government closed the border between East and West Berlin. When the wall dividing them was completed, seven crossing points remained.

The Berlin Wall's barrier to freedom of movement would become the symbol of communism's failure. A year later, in a moving speech near the Wall, Kennedy pronounced: "Ich bin ein Berliner" (I am a Berliner). Meanwhile, Khrushchev quietly abandoned his threats to take over West Berlin if the Western allies did not surrender power by December 1961.

Because of the high drama of the Berlin crisis, monographs on Kennedy's presidency tend to pay less attention to other significant aspects of U.S.-European relations. To rectify this omission, as well as to capitalize on newly opened Kennedy-era archival collections in the United States and Europe, a major international symposium was held at the European University Institute in Florence, Italy, to discuss "Kennedy and Europe." The three-day event, in October 1992, cosponsored by the John F. Kennedy Foundation in Boston, brought together a stimulating array of academics and former government officials from ten countries to discuss U.S.-European relations between 1961 and 1963. Besides the scholarly contributions included in this volume from historians, journalists, economists, and political scientists, distinguished Kennedy administration alumni—Robert Bowie, McGeorge Bundy, John Kenneth Galbraith, Arthur Hartman, Arthur Schlesinger, Jr., Theodore Sorensen, John Tuthill, and William J. vanden Heuvel—offered illuminating eyewitness testimony on topics ranging from NATO's nuclear program to the president's friendship with British prime minister Harold Macmillan. European diplomats who worked with President Kennedy on transatlantic policies also offered fresh anecdotes and insights into the era. Founders of the European Union—including former secretary-general Emile Noel—shared evidence of President Kennedy's wholehearted admiration for Jean Monnet. Publishing transcripts of these voluminous insights under a single cover would have been impossible, but they are available at both the John F. Kennedy Library in Boston and the European University Institute in Florence.

What emerged from the conference—and these papers—is just how activist the Kennedy administration's European policy truly was, how open JFK was to new approaches aimed at further cementing the Atlantic alliance. Kennedy was a true believer in European unity; it was, for example, the underlying theme of the Trade Expansion Act, to which he committed a great deal of his own political capital in 1962. Kennedy consistently spoke of the desirability of a true partnership between the United States and Europe as two pillars of democracy of equal weight with leaders of equal voice.

*John F. Kennedy and Europe* presents a collection of original essays, written by seventeen distinguished scholars using the latest documentary evidence available to evaluate U.S. policy toward Europe from 1961 to 1963. Included in the volume are thoughtful pieces by British historian Alistair Horne ("Kennedy and Macmillan"), journalist John Newhouse ("De Gaulle and the Anglo-Saxons"), policymaker Walt W. Rostow ("Kennedy's View of Monnet and Vice Versa"), and arms control specialist Carl Kaysen ("The Limited Test-Ban Treaty of 1963"). And for the first time appear essays on such important topics as the Kennedy administration's Italian and Portuguese policies that use archival evidence from recently declassified material in Lisbon and Rome.

Taken together, the essays in *John F. Kennedy and Europe* make a balanced contribution to Cold War historiography, a landmark study of the dynamics of what is still today called the Atlantic partnership. By focusing on security and trade issues—while keeping a watchful eye on the role personalities play in international affairs—the authors provide a singular service, emphasizing Kennedy's accomplishments rather than his persona.

It is our hope that anyone doing research on Kennedy's foreign policy approach will find in this book a more realistic view of those dynamic thousand days in the early 1960s when the Cold War was at its chilliest. No doubt future monographs will focus on the great crises of the Kennedy administration—Berlin and Cuba—but it is our hope that this volume will inspire a new generation of historians to look more closely at the larger features of American strategy toward Europe developed during those tumultuous years.

DOUGLAS BRINKLEY
RICHARD T. GRIFFITHS

# Abbreviations

| | |
|---|---|
| ACDA | Arms Control and Disarmament Agency |
| AEC | Atomic Energy Commission |
| APAG | Atlantic Political Advisory Group |
| CAP | Common Agricultural Policy |
| CBTB | Complete Test-Ban Treaty |
| CEA | Council of Economic Advisors |
| CIA | Central Intelligence Agency |
| DC | Democrazia Cristiana [Italian Christian Democratic Party] |
| EC | European Community |
| EDC | European Defence Community |
| EEC | European Economic Community |
| EFTA | European Free Trade Association |
| ENDC | Eighteen-Nation Disarmament Committee |
| Fed | Federal Reserve Bank |
| GATT | General Agreement on Trade and Tariffs |
| GDR | German Democratic Republic |
| ICBM | Inter-Continental Ballistic Missile |
| IDA | International Development Association |
| ILO | International Labor Organization |
| IMF | International Monetary Fund |
| IRBM | Intermediate-Range Ballistic Missile |
| JCS | Joint Chiefs of Staff |
| LDC | Less-Developed Countries |
| MAAG | Military Aid and Advisory Group |
| MSAG | Military Aid and Advisory Group |
| MAP | Military Aid to Portugal (Program) |
| MFN | Most Favored Nation |
| MLF | Multilateral Force |
| MRBM | Medium-Range Ballistic Missile |
| NATO | North Atlantic Treaty Organization |
| NSAM | National Security Action Memorandum |
| NSC | National Security Council |
| NTB | Non-Tariff Barrier |
| OECD | Organization for Economic Cooperation and Development |
| OEEC | Organization for European Economic Cooperation |
| OSS | Office of Strategic Services |
| PCI | Partito Comunista Italiano (Italian Communist Party) |
| PSAC | President's Science Advisory Committee |
| PSI | Partito Socialista Italiano (Italian Socialist Party) |

| | |
|---|---|
| PTBT | Partial Test-Ban Treaty |
| SAC | Strategic Air Command |
| SACEUR | Supreme Allied Commander, Europe |
| SALT | Strategic Arms Limitation Talks |
| SHAPE | Supreme Headquarters Allied Powers Europe |
| START | Strategic Arms Reduction Talks |
| TEA | Trade Expansion Act (1962) |
| TNC | Trade Negotiations Committee |
| UPA | União das Populações de Angola |
| USIA | U.S. Information Agency |

# John F. Kennedy and Europe

# Part One

*Kennedy and the European Leaders*

# 1

# Kennedy and Macmillan

*Alistair Horne*

∽

When one looks back on the history of the twentieth century, one is struck by how brief the Kennedy era was and how many events and crises were packed into those three years. A good example is his association with Harold Macmillan, prime minister of Great Britain, around which gravitated most of both countries' dealings in foreign affairs during the period. Never afterward and probably only once before, during the World War II years of Franklin D. Roosevelt and Winston Churchill, was the association with Great Britain so great. But, additionally, by the grim fall of 1963, when both men were to be removed unexpectedly from office within a month of each other, it could be reckoned that no other statesmen, including Churchill and Roosevelt, had ever become so close personally within the "special relationship."

The association began with Khrushchev's play for Berlin, and ended, in the summer of 1963, with the partial nuclear test ban. In this essay, I give preponderance to the Cuban Missile Crisis of October 1962 because it shows the two leaders working closely together in what was clearly the most dangerous crisis of their administrations—indeed, it would be hard to think of any more potentially dangerous episode in the entire postwar era of the Cold War. (On a recent visit to Los Alamos, I was interested to discover, in the small museum commemorating the development of the first atom bomb, a wall to which were pinned newspaper front pages of historic events marking the development of nuclear weapons, beginning with Hitler's *Anschluss* with Austria in 1938 and running through Pearl Harbor to Hiroshima. The last date to be earmarked in this way was 22 October 1962.) The Cuban Missile Crisis marked the flash point in

This essay is partly based on a lecture delivered in September 1990 to the Soviet Institute of Military History in Moscow, I have also endeavored to include here some of the Soviet reactions that emerged from the (very friendly and uninhibited!) discussion that ensued. The subject, I should perhaps add, was selected by the Institute itself. It appended, as its own subtitle, "Anglo-American Strategy in the Cold War." I deliberately stressed the theme of "Danger through *Miscalculation*," referring back to Kaiser Wilhelm in 1914 and Hitler (in the specific context of the Non-Aggression Pact with Stalin) in 1939—coupled with the name of Saddam Hussein in August 1990, which was topical at the time.

Khrushchev's challenge to the West, though—always in Macmillan's opinion—it was closely linked to the threat to Berlin, which, to him, was possibly even more menacing and which I deal with at length here also.

## *Harold Macmillan*

The three main players in October 1962 were President John F. Kennedy, Prime Minister Harold Macmillan, and Chairman Nikita Khrushchev.

Harold Macmillan was born in 1894, of a Scottish father and a strong-willed American mother, and lived to 1986. His American blood was to have an important bearing on his later relationship with Kennedy. As far as Macmillan was concerned, his "special relationship" with the Americans began in December 1942, when Churchill sent him to be his ministerial representative in Algiers, attached to the headquarters of General Dwight D. Eisenhower, the Allied supreme commander. The contacts and opinions formed at this time—and over the ensuing two and a half years in the Mediterranean—were to be among the most fundamental influences in Macmillan's life.

In World War I, Macmillan was wounded no less than five times, leaving him with a certain wariness about Germans, with or without machine guns—and a lasting horror of war. Yet when in office following World War II, he came to be regarded as "soft" in domestic policy but a "hard-liner" in foreign policy. (During the Suez crisis of 1956, he was, of course, the leader of the Conservative "Hawks.") In 1932, as a Conservative member of Parliament (MP), he made a first visit to the Soviet Union, which left him with a lasting admiration and affection for the Russian people. He was the best-read prime minister in British history, and one of his favorite books was *Anna Karenina*, which—to the end of his life—he regularly reread every year. All this had its influence on him when dealing with Khrushchev. He became a leading supporter of the nuclear deterrent—but also of the "graduated response"; to modify Teddy Roosevelt's famous dictum, he believed in waving a big stick in public but speaking softly in private.

## *The Berlin Crisis, 1958–1961*

Macmillan became prime minister in 1957, following the Suez debacle of 1956 and the fall of Anthony Eden; he retained the post until ill health forced him to resign in October 1963. Following the disastrous rift in the Anglo-American alliance caused by Suez (and doubtless influenced by his American blood), Macmillan made the restoring of the special relationship, first with President Eisenhower, then with President Kennedy, his first consideration.

On 10 November 1958, Khrushchev suddenly demanded the withdrawal of Allied troops from Berlin. Ten days later he announced that he intended "to liquidate the Occupation Statutes concerning Berlin." The Western allies saw this threat as a direct breach of the Potsdam Agreement of 1945. Macmillan seriously feared that it might be in Khrushchev's nature to miscalculate. But he was almost equally fearful of the Americans overreacting. Of a Washington plan to force the road to Berlin open, he wrote in December 1960, "The whole art of dealing with an opponent who is indulging in 'brinkmanship' consists of not allowing him to get into a position in which he has to choose between war and humiliating retreat. This would be precisely the choice which would be imposed on the Russians under the American plan."[1]

This statement was a keynote of his philosophy, and eventually Macmillan's moderation came to be accepted by President Eisenhower, his friend from wartime days.

In February 1959, Macmillan visited Moscow, the first British peacetime prime minister ever to do so. In the existing state of Soviet nuclear power, he was terrified of the world returning to the dangers of the 1930s—of war by miscalculation, on one side or the other—and he felt it was incumbent on him (because Eisenhower and the Americans were unreceptive to his initiative) to try to break the "logjam" of the Cold War with Khrushchev. The visit was not a success, the two leaders coming to an angry impasse over the future of Germany. But it was an opening in personal relations, and it also helped Macmillan win his reelection later that year with a record majority of a hundred seats.

In 1960, under strong pressure from Macmillan, a "summit" conference was scheduled to take place in Paris in May. But, rashly, the Central Intelligence Agency (CIA) continued high-altitude "spy" flights by American U-2 planes, a grave miscalculation. On 7 May, Macmillan wrote in his diary: "The Americans have created a folly. . . . One of their machines has been shot down by a rocket (it is said, a few hundred miles from Moscow). . . . Worse still, the pilot . . . did not poison himself (as ordered) but has been taken prisoner (with his poison needle in his pocket!) The Russians have got the machine; the cameras; a lot of the photographs—and the pilot."

Khrushchev's reaction was extreme. He broke up the Paris conference almost before it began, in May 1960. Rightly or wrongly, Macmillan concluded that Khrushchev was then acting under the influence of the Soviet military.

The collapse of the 1960 summit marked the end, in effect, of Eisenhower as a negotiating partner with Khrushchev. The U.S. presidential election of that November brought in the unknown John F. Kennedy. Macmillan was extremely nervous about the new incumbent, following the departure of his contemporary and old friend Dwight D. Eisenhower; "this cocky young Irishman . . . how am I going to deal with him?" he remarked to Henry Brandon, the longtime *Sunday Times* correspondent in Washington. It is all the more remarkable that, despite the twenty-five-year age gap, the special relationship between these two very different men was to blossom into something astonishingly close and warm.

1. Macmillan to Caccia, 6 December 1958, quoted in Alistair Horne, *Harold Macmillan, 1894–1956,* and *1957–1986,* 2 vols. (London, 1988–90), II, 118.

The friendship was perhaps first bonded in June 1961, when Kennedy came to London after his first meeting with Khrushchev, in Vienna. Kennedy had found Khrushchev at his toughest and most menacing—over Berlin. A rearmed Germany, he declared, signified the threat of a third world war; whatever the West did, he intended to sign a peace treaty with East Germany by December. Kennedy reached London, in Macmillan's words, "stunned and shocked by the almost brutal frankness of the Soviet leader. The Russians are (or affect to be) 'on top of the world.' They are now no longer frightened of aggression. They have at least as powerful nuclear forces as the West. They have interior lines. They have a buoyant economy and will soon outmatch Capitalist society in the race for materialist wealth. It follows they will make no concessions."[2]

Macmillan took the battered young president up to his private rooms and gave him a strong whiskey; he offered sympathy and total support, which Kennedy never forgot.

## The Wall

Then on Sunday, 13 August 1961, Khrushchev shook the world by building the Berlin Wall. In public, Macmillan was tough, warning the British people that the lessons of appeasing Hitler in the 1930s and of not standing up to "acts of force" were not to be repeated. But in private, he took a line of pragmatic realism, urging that Kennedy adopt a policy of "flexible response." To him, the Allied rights to West Berlin were simply "an agreement between generals" and the division of Germany an artificial postwar creation. He reckoned that Western populations—especially the British—would not face the prospect of nuclear war for the sake of Berlin. He was severely critical of de Gaulle of France and Adenauer of West Germany for assuming militant postures, when, with no nuclear forces at their disposal, it was not *they* who would be responsible for a nuclear holocaust.

Just as he had cautioned Eisenhower about "being what is called 'tough' over Berlin," so, in September 1961, he warned President Kennedy "that this policy would lead either to a nuclear war or to a great diplomatic defeat. If we continued to be 'tough' there was a risk of war. If we shrank back from a nuclear war at the last moment and made some kind of accommodation, the more we had talked up 'no surrender' the greater would be the loss of dignity when it was clear that some concessions must follow. I think President Kennedy has accepted this."[3]

The Berlin Wall was a most disappointing personal setback for Macmillan, representing as it did one more failure in his attempts for détente with Khrushchev; the Berlin Crisis was also to become inextricably bound up with what was to follow over Cuba.

2. See *ibid.,* 303. All this makes for curiously dated reading in the 1990s.
3. Letter of 15 September 1961, Macmillan Archives, Bodleian Library, Oxford.

Going against the tide of Pentagon advice, by the end of the year Kennedy, too, had come to "accept" Macmillan's advice on "playing it cool." In October there was an ugly alarm when U.S. and Soviet tanks moved up to the Wall in Berlin and faced each other muzzle to muzzle. Khrushchev now began testing some of the most powerful hydrogen warheads ever exploded; persuading a thoroughly reluctant president, the U.S. military followed suit with a new escalation in nuclear tests. Macmillan, extremely unhappy, did all he could, with both Kennedy and Khrushchev, to counter the trend. Meanwhile, he had had lengthy talks with de Gaulle at his home, Birch Grove, that November, noting acridly in his diary: "He [de Gaulle] does not want war. He does not believe there will be war. But he wants to pretend to the French and the Germans that *he* is the strong, loyal man. . . . If de Gaulle thought there was a real danger of war, he would be in a panic."[4]

At the Bermuda conference in December, there was some plain speaking within the special relationship. In December Macmillan wrote Kennedy a pessimistic letter (which assumes, perhaps, a new relevance in the 1990s), warning that, ultimately, nuclear weapons would turn up in the hands of all kinds "of dictators, reactionaries, revolutionaries, madmen. . . . Then, sooner or later, and certainly I think by the end of century, either by error or folly or insanity, the great crime will be committed."[5] He begged the president to make one more personal overture to Khrushchev for a nuclear test ban.

### Khrushchev Backs Down on Berlin: The Cuban Crisis Begins

Khrushchev's December deadline, however, passed without his threats against Berlin being carried through. Why, having made these terrifying menaces, he then appeared to back down remains one of the many mysteries of the period; I found little enlightenment here in Moscow. Nevertheless, Macmillan heaved a sigh of relief, and for most of 1962 the Berlin Crisis seemed to slip onto the back burner. But there remained a very tense feeling in the West at large that, for whatever reason, Khrushchev was out to force a confrontation. Where?

In October 1962 the answer came. A crisis broke out far away at the other end of the Atlantic, which at once threatened to eclipse Berlin. Since the disastrous failure of the Central Intelligence Agency's (CIA) Bay of Pigs operation against Fidel Castro of April the previous year, the United States had established a trade embargo against Cuba (in which Britain had declined to join). Castro was becoming increasingly authoritarian and oppressive as the economy slumped—despite large Soviet subsidies—and relations between the two coun-

---

4. Macmillan Diaries (unpublished), 29 November 1961, quoted in Horne, *Harold Macmillan,* 316.
5. Letter of 5 January 1962, Macmillan Archives.

tries had correspondingly worsened. Castro affected to believe that the United States was planning a new invasion of Cuba. But if this was the basis of his decision to install missile systems on the island, Khrushchev seems to have been misinformed. Certainly hard-liners in both the Pentagon and the CIA, smarting under the humiliation of the Bay of Pigs, desired intervention, but the president had no such intention. Equally, if Kennedy's refusal to back up the Cuban exiles' landings at the Bay of Pigs in 1961 was taken as a sign of irresolution, then Khrushchev also seems to have been badly advised.

Some time in April 1962, so it was believed in the West, Moscow decided to install missiles in Cuba of its own volition and not in response to any request from Castro. On Sunday, 21 October, Macmillan received an urgent, top-secret signal from Kennedy: U-2 photographic intelligence had "established beyond question" that the Soviets were planting medium-range missiles in Cuba. Six sites had already been identified, two of which possibly were in operational readiness. The U.S. government had decided, he informed Macmillan, "to prevent any further build-up by sea and to demand the removal of this nuclear threat to our hemisphere. . . . This extraordinarily dangerous and aggressive Soviet step obviously creates a crisis of the most serious sort in which we would have to act most closely together." Kennedy went on to stress: "What is essential at this moment of highest test is that Khrushchev should discover that if he is counting on weakness or irresolution, he has *miscalculated*."[6]

It is important to note here that the first, crucial, decision had been taken on Kennedy's own responsibility, before consulting Macmillan or any other ally. De Gaulle had been informed, most courteously, by the veteran diplomat Dean Acheson, secretary of state under Harry Truman, who flew personally to Paris to see him, but he was *not* consulted. De Gaulle declared himself prepared to accept Kennedy's word, without examining the photographic supporting evidence, telling Acheson, "A great nation like yours would not act if there were any doubt about the evidence, and therefore I accept what you tell me as a fact without any proof of any sort needed."[7]

Macmillan, however, to Kennedy's disappointment, insisted on having the photographs for publication. His point was valid; for the sake of British (and world) public opinion, it was essential to publish the U-2 photographs as incontrovertible proof. He also reminded Kennedy that Europeans had lived for so long in close proximity to the enemy's nuclear weapons that they had got "accustomed to it, so European opinion will need attention."

## Did Khrushchev Hope to Trade Cuba for Berlin?

Kennedy's message did not take Macmillan by surprise; already in the diary for 3 October, he had recorded his judgment that "the Russians are clearly using

6. Signal of 21 October 1962, Macmillan Archives; emphasis added.
7. Dean G. Acheson, recorded interview, 22 October 1962, John F. Kennedy Library Oral History Program; in Horne, *Harold Macmillan*, 667.

Cuba as a counter-irritant to Berlin." Macmillan's immediate fear was, and remained all through the ensuing tense week of crisis, that Khrushchev's real purpose "was to trade Cuba for Berlin. If he was stopped, with great loss of face, in Cuba, would he not be tempted to recover himself in Berlin? Indeed, might not this be the whole purpose of the exercise—to move forward one [chess] pawn in order to exchange it for another?"[8]

One has to remember that, strategically, Berlin was close to Britain, which had fought six long years for the right to be there. But Cuba was a faraway island. Yet to America the reverse was true: Cuba was ninety miles from Florida; the United States still had considerable superiority over the Soviets in long-range missiles, but short-range missiles placed in Cuba would upset the balance of terror because they could escape the North American early warning system. Thus Washington saw its security, if not its survival, profoundly set at risk. Macmillan recognized this, but equally his abiding fear throughout was simply that "Khrushchev might have suggested a swap of Cuba for Berlin—how could the Americans have resisted?"[9]

## Britain's Role, 22–25 October

On the night of the 22 October, Kennedy telephoned Macmillan, in the first of a remarkable series of uninhibited conversations initiated by the president, which continued each night of the crisis.[10] Macmillan reminded the president, gently, that Europeans had lived so long in close proximity to Soviet nuclear weapons that they had "got accustomed to it . . . if you live on Vesuvius, you don't bother much about eruptions!" The meaning of this last remark—don't fuss so much— did not delight Kennedy. While Kennedy took full responsibility for decisions that specifically concerned American security, Macmillan's calmness (known to his British electorate as "unflappability")—and far-ranging support— undoubtedly helped bolster the young president in the lonely isolation of responsibility at this time.

That first night, to Macmillan, Kennedy "seemed excited, but very clear." He said that there were plans for a naval blockade of Cuba and that he was "building up his forces . . . to seize Cuba, should that become necessary."[11] It subsequently became clear that Kennedy was under strong pressure from the Pentagon either to invade or to "take out" the missile bases with an air strike, which, of course, carried with it the serious risk of killing Soviet personnel. At various times in the crisis, Macmillan urged caution against this danger.

The British ambassador in Washington, David Ormsby-Gore, was a close

8. Macmillan Diaries, 22 October 1962, quoted in Horne, *Harold Macmillan,* 366.
9. Conversation with the author.
10. They make extraordinary reading, and I have published them extensively in my biography.
11. Macmillan Diaries, 22 October 1962, in Horne, *Harold Macmillan,* 367.

personal friend of both Macmillan and Kennedy, and—as an indication of just how close Britain and the United States were throughout the crisis—he was accorded the unprecedented privilege of sitting in on sessions of the White House National Security Council (NSC), and contingency arrangements were even made for the Ormsby-Gore family to be brought into the safety of the presidential fallout shelter deep beneath the Appalachians.

On the twenty-third, after Kennedy backed away from the air-strike option, Ambassador Gore, acting entirely on his own but with Macmillan's full support subsequently, made a crucial suggestion: that the proposed "quarantine line" of the U.S. naval blockade be modified from eight hundred miles to five hundred miles off the Cuban coast. This would give the Soviet ships approaching from Europe more time to react and provide Khrushchev with a face-saver. Kennedy agreed; the blockade went formally into effect.

At the UN, the Soviet representative, Zorin, had the effrontery to deny that there were either missiles or launching pads in Cuba. Nevertheless, off Florida the United States was assembling the most massive seaborne invasion force since World War II, including 100,000 army troops, some 45 ships, and 240 aircraft deployed to enforce the blockade.

## Penkovsky

Britain's second important contribution took the shape of the intelligence double agent Colonel Oleg Penkovsky. Although there are elements that, to the West, remain far from clear, the colonel's defection from Soviet military intelligence was apparently motivated chiefly by fear that Khrushchev's bombastic threats might spark off a sudden nuclear war. Penkovsky was regarded by both the British (who recruited him) and American intelligence operators as having been the most important Western agent since 1945 (a view Macmillan strongly endorsed). His most valuable material included details on the installation of the Soviet missiles in Cuba, as well as information suggesting that the state of Soviet rocketry was far less advanced than Khrushchev boasted. It was this intelligence that helped strengthen significantly Kennedy's resolve to confront Khrushchev over Cuba.[12]

Penkovsky was arrested by the KGB on 22 October, the day Kennedy publicly revealed the existence of the missiles; this might have been coincidental or a direct consequence of the intelligence delivered under extreme pressure. Penkovsky was not a cautious man. The following May, he was reported to have been shot.

12. For some years KGB disinformation—falling on fertile ground in the Western media—to a notable extent was extremely successful in spreading the notion that Penkovsky had all along been a treble agent of Moscow and that the intelligence he supplied was worthless. This is certainly not the impression to be gained in Moscow today.

A few years ago, a senior Soviet foreign official admitted to me that the chief value to the Soviet Union of the three British spies was that they "told us [the Soviets] just how weak the West was—and so we knew we could take risks." Something similar, in reverse, could perhaps be said of Penkovsky. At the Soviet Institute of Military History during my lecture in 1990, I was surprised to discover among the audience not only those who admitted to having known Penkovsky personally but were also prepared to corroborate (with Macmillan) the importance to these events of the information (down to specific details) which he provided as a double agent.

## A Trial of Will, 24-26 October

Wednesday, 24 October, the world held its breath, waiting to see whether any of the Soviet ships would turn around. Twenty-five were reported on their way to Cuba; fourteen were believed to be carrying missiles. The Americans were all set to launch a conventional, preemptive attack. That night, Kennedy, on the telephone, asked Macmillan, "Should he take out Cuba?" Macmillan replied that he would like to think about it and would send back a considered message.

The next day, after mulling it over all night, Macmillan sent Kennedy his answer. As regards "taking out Cuba," he felt that "events have gone too far. . . . I think that we are now all in a phase where you must try to obtain your objectives by other means."[13] But, with firmness, he recommended that the military buildup be continued as important for maintaining pressure on Castro.

Just how dangerous the crisis had come within Britain itself is indicated by some recent research which suggests that, almost incredibly, Britain did go to the brink of mobilization—as it were, by mistake. On 24 October, when America's Strategic Air Command (SAC) had moved onto "Alert," Britain's Royal Air Force (RAF) Bomber Command was itself already in the midst of an "alert and readiness" exercise, completely unrelated to events in the Caribbean. As that crisis worsened, the C-in-C Bomber Command, a relatively lowly air marshal (lieutenant general) decided to prolong and increase the alert even further. At this stage, British nuclear forces were capable of being launched within fifteen minutes, or less, against 230 targets in the Soviet Union and Warsaw Pact nations. The decision appears not even to have been referred to the Ministry of Defence; the White House was never aware of it—nor, almost certainly, was Macmillan. (There is no reference to this alert in the otherwise detailed Macmillan diaries for the period.) He would have been horrified, had he known.[14]

The United Nations now entered the scene, in the shape of the secretary general, U Thant, who proposed that Khrushchev keep his ships out of the quaran-

---

13. Quoted in Horne, *Harold Macmillan,* 372.

14. For this information I am indebted to Professor Scott D. Sagan of Stanford University and Air Vice Marshal Stewart Menaul, *Countdown: Britain's Strategic Nuclear Forces* (London, 1980).

tine area and asked Kennedy to avoid a confrontation. Backed by Macmillan, Kennedy responded with a wisdom and adroitness that the older statesman found "extremely ingenious" and accepted—though still under strong pressure from the Pentagon to attack.

On Friday night, the twenty-sixth, Macmillan had "two *long* telephone talks with the President. The situation is very obscure and dangerous. It is a trial of will."[15] At the back of Macmillan's mind was the nagging fear that Kennedy was being influenced by the Bay of Pigs; "just as we were by Suez—he couldn't have risked another failure."[16]

Next came a Soviet proposal to "bargain" the missiles they had placed in Cuba against the U.S. Jupiters in Turkey. Macmillan thought this was "dangerous and specious"; acting under unacceptable pressure, it would demoralize North Atlantic Treaty Organization (NATO) allies, not only the Turks.

## The Crisis Ends, 27-28 October

Saturday, 27 October, was filled with deadly menace; in Britain as well as in the United States, it was remembered as the most frightening day anyone could recall. An American U-2 was shot down over Cuba; the Pentagon was poised to launch a retaliatory air strike on the SAM bases that had killed their pilot; almost certainly Soviet personnel would have been killed.

Two conflicting signals then arrived from Khrushchev. The first proposed that if the United States would not "participate in an attack on Cuba and that [if] the blockade would be lifted," he would agree to send in no more weapons and allow those already in Cuba to be withdrawn or destroyed. The condition was that Kennedy should promise not to invade Cuba. This was, in Macmillan's opinion, "a complete capitulation,"[17] because it met Kennedy's demands in full. But this first, conciliatory signal was followed up by a second, couched in more formal and harsher terms and much less accommodating.

Then, after an evening of intolerable suspense, the president's younger brother Robert Kennedy came up with "a thought of breathtaking simplicity": why not ignore the second Khrushchev signal and reply to the first? The message was sent off at noon; an hour or two later news came over the radio that the Russians had given in. "So it was all over!" Macmillan wrote in his diary, in a state of complete nervous exhaustion; "It was a complete climbdown."[18]

## Macmillan's Influence

Just how great had Prime Minister Macmillan's influence been in "crisis management" over Cuba? No one was better able to judge than the late Lord Harlech,

15. Macmillan Diaries, 26 October 1962, quoted in Horne, *Harold Macmillan,* 373.
16. Conversation with the author; Horne, *Harold Macmillan,* 373–74.
17. Horne, *Harold Macmillan,* 376; Arthur M. Schlesinger, Jr., *A Thousand Days: John F. Kennedy in the White House* (Boston, 1965), 757.
18. Quoted in Horne, *Harold Macmillan,* 377.

David Ormsby-Gore, who admitte
from London that changed the U
JFK."[19]

Macmillan himself confessed, ma
the cards above their face value." K
however (who was seldom one to
both the Cuba and Berlin crises, on t
himself "a pretty tough guy."[20] Did t
those remarkable transatlantic teleph
*formation*? If it was not, strictly speaki
to it.

Recently a distinguished Israeli sch
ing suggestion to me: namely, that, fo
had deliberately played down the "cor
or offending President de Gaulle; by cc
simply been "informed" at the beginni
the fact that several highly delicate Fra
time, notably, on the nuclear front, purs
of "nonproliferation." De Gaulle was c
October 1962, the United States needec
the forthcoming decision, crucial to Har
European Economic Community (EEC)
to which Kennedy was highly sympathet

What was indisputable was the lastin
won from Kennedy. Even if de Gaulle mi
private boast that he had "helped keep th
phone calls—to which he had not been p
source of some aggravation and one mor
*Saxons*" in a crisis. It was, at any rate, less
devastating "*NON!*" to Macmillan's appl
would occur.

The rest is now history. In Berlin, the c
backed down over Cuba. In June 1964, he
many, but it tacitly accepted the West's co
months later, Khrushchev too had disappea

19. Lord Harlech, interview with author in 1980–
20. On BBC1, 1 June 1972; McGeorge Bundy, rec
tory Program.
21. In this context, it is perhaps worth noting th;
sometimes found among French commentators—the a
Jean Lacouture makes no mention of Macmillan's role i
in his pages.
22. Macmillan Diaries, 4 November 1962, quoted i

The world had
from revelation
Armageddon i
the time. But w
deal at the tim
to be tacitly he
rial safety of C;
from short-ran

The glimps
ing summer,
ban. The enha
was testified, j
to help Macm
missile projec
laris missiles c
litical coup. T
ill health; a
Khrushchev a
Macmillan al
his seven yea
we—Presider
gone on?"[23]

Here may
As it was.
agreements
Kennedy ha
a reluctant C
(and perhap
duction Talk
deed, the en

Returnin
the West's
Macmillan
firmness, w
Soviet aims
motivation
man who v
umph abro
nuclear su
Speakin

23. See F

13

*Alistair Horne*

## *So, What Was Achieved?*

come closer to the brink of nuclear war than ever before or since;
s emanating subsequently from post-Glasnost Russian sources,
October 1962 may have been far closer than anyone realized at
hat had been achieved? For the socialist bloc, in what was a secret
but which (though excoriated by the American right) continued
nored by both the Reagan and Bush administrations, the territo-
stro had been guaranteed; for America, the safety of her territory
ge rockets was assured. But was it all worth it?
of the abyss did seem to open a new era of détente. The follow-
963, it led the three powers to sign a first (partial) nuclear test
nced closeness which Cuba had brought in the special relationship
st two months after the crisis, when Kennedy bent over backward
illan out of a most awkward spot over the collapse of the Skybolt
. Acting against the advice of his advisers, he handed Britain Po-
n highly beneficial terms, giving his friend a notable personal po-
he following October, Macmillan was forced to resign because of
month later Kennedy was assassinated—dangerously leaving
stride the world scene. Reflecting on this double loss to the West,
ways claimed the Test-Ban Treaty as the greatest single success of
s as prime minister. He speculated, many years later, "What might
t Kennedy and myself—have achieved with Khrushchev, had we

be a line for revisionist historians to work on!
Macmillan regarded the Strategic Arms Limitation Talks (SALT)
of the 1970s as stemming directly from that 1963 treaty (which
accepted under strongest pressure from Macmillan, in the teeth of
ongress); were he alive today, he would almost certainly also claim
s not totally without reason) some share in the Strategic Arms Re-
s (START), the Gorbachev era, the fall of the Berlin Wall, and, in-
ding of the Cold War itself.
g, finally, to Berlin and Cuba: when Khrushchev, in 1964, accepted
ights to Berlin—and then fell from power four months later—
onsidered that his policy (which he had urged upon Kennedy) of
th flexibility, had been thoroughly vindicated. As regards what were
in this enormously dangerous game—and particularly Khrushchev's
—we can still only speculate. Did he think that Kennedy was a weak
ould cave in under pressure? Did he feel he needed a prestigious tri-
d for domestic reasons? Did the USSR really feel threatened by U.S.
eriority, back in 1962?
g to me, years later, Macmillan reckoned that Khrushchev's ploy over

orne, *Harold Macmillan,* II, chap. 15; conversations with the author.

Cuba could be seen as a brilliant, if dangerous, démarche which, had it succeeded, would have drastically altered the nuclear strategic balance. Why, then, did he finally withdraw and cut his losses—very considerable, both in prestige and money? Macmillan thought it was "probably owing to the same pressures that brought him down,"[24] meaning it was the forces of "conservatism" in Russia, notably the "Old Guard" in the Red Army, which disapproved of Khrushchev's "adventurism" over Cuba, much as it had disapproved of his attending the (aborted) summit of 1960. (They are the same forces within the party which, one sensed in Moscow in 1990, were then poised to bring down Mikhail Gorbachev.)

Macmillan remained puzzled as to why Khrushchev never made a "countermove" on Berlin, which he had fully expected, even after the maximum danger of missiles week was past. On balance, he came down on the side of the argument that Khrushchev accepted that Kennedy really would invade Cuba on either 29 or 30 October but that the Soviets were not prepared to face being the first to squeeze the nuclear trigger. Sooner or later, an answer to all these questions will probably come out of the Kremlin archives. Meanwhile, of some passing interest may be the revelation I picked up, in 1990, from the then Soviet ambassador in London, Zamyatin (who fell from grace during the 1991 Moscow coup), that in October 1962, when he himself had been in charge of contingency planning, preparations for nuclear conflict were at top alert level in the Kremlin: "Our fingers were on the button." If so, the danger could hardly have been greater.

In the words of my friend Hugh Thomas, the historian of Cuba: "Small powers can often begin a world crisis; great powers always end them." This is perhaps as relevant to the perpetual state of crisis in the Persian Gulf in the 1990s—and Yugoslavia today—as it was over Cuba thirty years ago.

24. Conversations with the author.

# 2

# Kennedy and Adenauer

*Roger Morgan*

~

President John F. Kennedy was born in 1917; Chancellor Konrad Adenauer was born in 1876. There was thus a difference of nearly forty years in the ages of the two men, and this in itself goes far to explain the differences in the ways they looked at the world of the early 1960s.

Their official relationship got off to a bad start. At the time of the West German election of October 1957—during a period when Adenauer enjoyed the almost boundless support of the Eisenhower administration and in particular of Secretary of State John Foster Dulles—the young Senator Kennedy published an article in *Foreign Affairs* in which he dismissively wrote, "Whatever the elections show, the age of Adenauer is over." The cool personal relationship between the two men, indicated by remarks such as this, persisted until the end: in October 1963, on Adenauer's retirement from the chancellorship, forty-three world leaders agreed to a request from the German magazine *Der Spiegel* to write farewell tributes, but the American president declined to join in this public event, indicating that "he would prefer to mark the occasion by a personal letter to the Chancellor."[1]

As well as the personal distance between the two leaders, there was a striking difference between their respective teams of advisers. The young president's leading officeholders (mainly young, like himself, or relatively young) reflected his message that "the torch has passed to a new generation," and they were restless, as he was, not only to regenerate American society but also to explore new ways of overcoming the stagnation and deadlock of the Cold War. Adenauer's

This essay includes material from the author's book *The United States and West Germany, 1945–1973: A Study in Alliance Politics* (London, 1974), which is reproduced by kind permission of the Oxford University Press and the Royal Institute of International Affairs. I am also grateful for information provided by several participants in the European University Institute conference of October 1992.

1. Kennedy and his staff may not have intended this refusal as a slight, but it was taken as such in Germany. See Walter Stützle, *Kennedy und Adenauer in der Berlin-Krise, 1961–1962* (Bonn-Bad Godesberg, 1973), 15. On Kennedy's *Foreign Affairs* article, see ibid., 19.

advisers, in contrast, were mainly elderly and in every sense conservative; the old chancellor's election-winning slogan "No Experiments!" perfectly expressed their concern that the Federal Republic's hard-won stability, respectability, and security should not be placed at risk.

This contrast between the mind-sets of the national leaderships in turn reflected a structural contrast, or even conflict, between the national interests of two significant states in the international system. Kennedy's America was the global superpower, preoccupied with world stability and the global military balance, with Latin America, Southeast Asia, and Africa, as well as the problems of Europe. Adenauer's Federal Republic, by contrast, was a state whose main political interests centered almost exclusively on Europe; a state that was essentially on the defensive because its geographical exposure to pressure from the Soviet Union, particularly in Berlin, made it fear for its security. This fear was all the more acute because the exposed and threatened West German state insisted on maintaining a claim in principle to carry out a change to the map of Europe—the incorporation of an East German communist state which Bonn refused to recognize—and Adenauer's government was aware that this claim was not unreservedly backed by Germany's allies, despite their repeated public commitments to the German right to self-determination.

These differences in perspective between Washington and Bonn, and some others, had already become fairly clear during the late 1950s; even John Foster Dulles, in his last months, gave Adenauer cause for considerable concern when he appeared to vacillate in his support of Germany. All the sources of German-American conflict, however, were to be accentuated during the period of just over a thousand days for which Kennedy was president. The way in which German-American tensions developed and were resolved, and in which they reflected both differences of personality and style and also underlying differences in national interests, may be illustrated by a consideration of three specific issues of that period: the Berlin Crisis, the organization and management of the Western Alliance, and the attempt to promote and manage détente between this Western Alliance and the Soviet bloc.

## The Berlin Crisis, 1961–1962

The problem that came to a dramatic climax with the building of the Berlin Wall in August 1961 was already on the agenda when Kennedy took office. The Kennedy administration inherited a situation created by Khrushchev's ultimatum of November 1958, which stated that the Western powers must give up West Berlin by a certain date (originally within six months) or else the Soviet Union would hand over its responsibilities for Berlin to the German Democratic Republic (GDR). East-West negotiations on this question had been interrupted by the fiasco of the 1960 summit conference in Paris, but as the Soviet demand had not been withdrawn, it was clear that negotiations would one day have to be resumed. The incoming administration reviewed the Berlin problem in the context of the broader perspective of an improved East-West relationship, which was a major goal of the new president and his advisers. In the early weeks of the administration, in March 1961, Kennedy's ambassador-at-large, Averell Harriman, announced that the negotiating positions taken up by the Eisenhower administration in 1959 and 1960 were no longer valid and that "all discussions on Berlin must begin from the start."[2]

When Kennedy and Khrushchev met for the first time, in early June in Vienna, Khrushchev presented the president with a forceful reminder that the situation of West Berlin was "abnormal" and had to be normalized and pressed on him a written statement repeating the essence of the demands made by the Soviet Union since 1958.[3]

Kennedy was able to base his reply on a document worked out by Dean Acheson in April, which indicated that in the American view the essential elements of a Berlin settlement must be the following: freedom for the West Berliners to choose their own political system; the continued presence of Western troops in West Berlin as long as the Berliners wanted them there; and unimpeded travel between West Germany and West Berlin along all the existing land and air transport routes. Kennedy reminded Khrushchev that the United States had been present in West Berlin for fifteen years and continued firmly that "he had not assumed the office of the Presidency to accept arrangements totally inimical to American interests."[4]

Khrushchev's demands, however, required a more detailed response, which was intensively discussed in Washington in July and early August. There were fairly deep differences of opinion between the various groups of Kennedy's advisers. Not surprisingly, the working paper produced by the State Department on 18 July appears to have consisted essentially of a reiteration of the well-established Western view that any Western weakening on Berlin would demoralize the Federal Republic and would encourage the Soviet Union to make further demands, whereas some of the president's less conventional advisers urged the need to explore ways of preventing the conflict from escalating. For instance, three Democratic members of the Senate, Senators J. William Fulbright, Hubert Humphrey, and Mike Mansfield, pressed for an accommodation with the Russians (Mansfield suggested placing the whole of Berlin under United Nations control as a "free city"), while Kennedy's academic advisers in the White House, Carl Kaysen, Henry Kissinger, and Arthur Schlesinger, Jr., also favored what the last-named described as "a more aggressive canvas of diplomatic possibilities."[5]

---

2. Arthur Schlesinger, Jr., *A Thousand Days: John F. Kennedy in the White House* (Boston, 1965), 341.

3. *Ibid.,* 380–84; Theodore Sorensen, *Kennedy* (New York, 1965), 584.

4. Sorensen, *Kennedy,* 583–84.

5. *Ibid.,* 587, 596; Schlesinger, *A Thousand Days,* 383–84.

One important point in Kennedy's approach to the Berlin problem, as indicated in his statement to Khrushchev, was the status of West Berlin. The Kennedy administration appeared to concentrate on preserving the position of the western part of the city, both its links to West Germany and also the presence of the Western allies. The Federal Republic, quite naturally, wished to keep the way open for German reunification, and for Bonn this meant that the legal unity of the *whole* of Berlin should be stressed as strongly as possible. This had indeed been the normal posture of the Eisenhower administration, though John Foster Dulles had shown occasional signs of weakening in his last months in office. Adenauer's view of the Berlin problem, indeed, was influenced by his belief that the ultimate disappearance of the GDR would be facilitated by a firm refusal to have any official dealings with this illegitimate regime, and he feared that any negotiations with the East Berlin government would strengthen its position by implying diplomatic recognition and hence harden the division of Germany into two states.

The moment at which these differences between Kennedy's approach and Adenauer's were to come sharply to the surface was the building of the Berlin Wall separating East from West Berlin on 13 August 1961. The Kennedy administration (and still more Macmillan's government in London) took the view that negotiation with the East—including at some stage the GDR—was a logical and necessary way to "defuse" the situation, whereas for Adenauer, any negotiation with or concerning the GDR as a government would only have the consequence of hardening Germany's division.

President Kennedy's confidential correspondence with Khrushchev that began in September 1961 thus led to considerable concern on the part of Adenauer and his government. The existence of this correspondence was known in Bonn, but its contents were secret, and this secrecy led some of Adenauer's advisers to believe that the U.S. government had had previous knowledge of the East German intention to build the Wall and had perhaps even tacitly encouraged it. Kennedy's letters to Khrushchev appear to have attempted to dissuade the latter from signing a peace treaty with East Germany (which, he argued, would provoke violent resentment in Bonn), but at the same time the Kennedy administration made numerous suggestions for changing the status of Berlin so as to reduce tension. These suggestions included the idea of establishing East-West technical commissions on access and contacts between Berlin and the outside world (a revival of part of the "Western Peace Plan" of 1959); a proposal that the Berlin issue should be submitted for adjudication to the World Court; a suggestion that the whole of Berlin should be declared a "free city"; a suggestion that the status quo in and concerning Berlin should be preserved by mutual agreement for a fixed term, for instance five or ten years; the idea that the headquarters of the United Nations Organization might be transferred to Berlin; the notion of a security plan for all of Central Europe; and the idea of setting up an international access authority controlling the routes between West Berlin and the West.[6]

This last-mentioned proposal particularly antagonized Adenauer and his government because every possible variant of the scheme included East Berlin or the GDR as a partner in the proposed international authority, and such an upgrading seemed to threaten any future possibility of reunification. One of Kennedy's close advisers has reported that the president realized, in retrospect, that he was making a serious mistake in committing "the folly of pressing upon the Germans and other allies solutions which were not really negotiable anyway" (i.e., not negotiable with the Russians); but his approach at the time—characteristically—was to believe that by trying out a wide variety of ideas, an acceptable compromise for the Berlin problem might be found, as it had been for the problem of Austria a few years earlier. For Adenauer and his administration, however, such an approach instilled a sense of horror, which became more acute as Washington embarked on detailed negotiations with Moscow at the end of 1961.[7]

Kennedy had discussed the question of internationalizing the access routes to West Berlin with the Soviet foreign minister Andrei Gromyko in September and with Khrushchev's son-in-law Alexy Adzhubey (the editor of *Izvestiya*) in November. Both he and his secretary of state, Dean Rusk, appeared to have accepted the view expressed by Adenauer's new foreign minister, Gerhard Schröder, that the forthcoming talks should be limited to the Berlin question alone, without extending to the broader questions of European security, which would inevitably have brought a risk of upgrading the status of the GDR.[8]

After a first round of Soviet-American talks on Berlin, carried out early in 1962 in Moscow by Foreign Minister Gromyko and the U.S. ambassador Llewellyn Thompson, it was agreed that they should be continued by Rusk and Anatoly Dobrynin (the new Soviet ambassador to Washington) in mid-April. With this timetable in mind, the U.S. administration worked out two position papers, which were presented to Bonn via Ambassador Wilhelm Grewe on 11 April, with a request that any German comments be made within forty-eight hours. Adenauer insisted on more time, called a meeting of the leading figures of his party, and then on 12 April declared his agreement in principle with the American suggestions (apparently assuming that the Soviet government would in any case turn them down).[9]

After anxious discussions between Adenauer and his party colleagues, one of the latter (either Heinrich von Brentano or Adenauer's closer associate Heinrich

6. Bruno Bandulet, *Adenauer zwischen Ost und West: Alternativen der deutschen Aussenpolitik* (Munich, 1970), 161, 282. Cf. Hans-Peter Schwarz, *Adenauer: Der Staatsmann, 1952–1967* (Stuttgart, 1991), 683–85; Sorensen, *Kennedy*, 599.

7. Sorensen, *Kennedy*, 598, 600; William E. Griffith, "Die Bundesrepublik in amerikanischer Sicht," *Aussenpolitik*, XIII, no. 3 (1962), 157–64.

8. Herbert von Borch, "Anatomie einer Entzweiung," *Aussenpolitik*, XIII, no. 6 (1962), 357–60.

9. *Ibid.*; Bandulet, *Adenauer*, 166; Schwarz, *Adenauer*, 743.

Krone) leaked the essential points of the American paper to a group of Bonn journalists, and they were published the next day.[10] This revelation unleashed the worst storm in German-American relations since the war. The State Department complained of the "flagrant breach of diplomatic usage," charging that it had caused "incurable harm" to relations between the two countries, the more so as this was not the first German indiscretion of this kind: indeed, Adenauer's earlier leaks of German-American negotiations were well known in Washington. Secretary of State Rusk sent a telegram of protest to Bonn, which, according to one account, Adenauer wished to return unanswered because of its violent tone, and the text of the counterprotest which Adenauer finally sent is said to have been diluted by his embassy in Washington before transmission to the State Department.[11]

The American document that had caused this unprecedented rift between Washington and Bonn contained three main proposals: that the United States and the Soviet Union should not hand over nuclear weapons to third parties; that NATO and the Warsaw Pact should exchange formal declarations of nonaggression; and that several all-German committees should be established to deal with technical contacts and agreements between the two parts of Germany. These points, together with the particularly delicate suggestion of an international control authority for Berlin (its membership to include neutral states and also the German Democratic Republic), were the substance of the German leak to the press in mid-April.[12]

Despite Bonn's indiscretion, the Rusk-Dobrynin talks began on 16 April and were still in progress when Rusk met Schröder at the NATO ministerial meeting in Athens at the beginning of May. Schröder apparently expressed no misgivings at the continuation of the Rusk-Dobrynin talks (it is said that not even his French colleague Maurice Couve de Murville took exception to them), and American diplomats were still congratulating themselves on the "reasonableness" of Adenauer's foreign minister when the old chancellor made a series of public statements in Berlin which were unprecedentedly critical of American policy. It seems that he had brooded for three weeks in his Italian retreat at Cadenabbia, then flew to Berlin, and, in the words of one well-informed German commentator, "smashed as much alliance-political china as he possibly could." Adenauer's Berlin statements dismissed Kennedy's idea of a Berlin access authority as unworkable; poured open sarcasm on Rusk's attempts to negotiate an agreement with the Soviet Union; urged the United States to break off these talks before any more harm was done; and finally gave an indication of a Gaullist

10. Schwarz, *Adenauer,* 744, follows Bandulet (*Adenauer,* 282) in blaming von Brentano for the indiscretion; see also Roger Morgan, *The United States and West Germany, 1945–1963: A Study in Alliance Politics* (London, 1974), 113. Further direct information from a participant, however, has identified Krone as the source of the press briefing.

11. Schwarz, *Adenauer,* 687; Borch, "Anatomie einer Entzweiung," 359.

12. Bandulet, *Adenauer,* 167, 283; Schwarz, *Adenauer,* 743–44.

kind that British membership in the EEC—on which Kennedy set great store—was not necessarily desirable.[13]

In explaining his action, Adenauer told the American journalist James Reston that the text of Rusk's complaint to Schröder was more "wounding" than anything he had encountered in his entire experience as chancellor. The Kennedy administration also took the matter very seriously: on 8 May, the day after Adenauer's outburst in Berlin, it was announced that Ambassador Grewe—with whom the administration had refused to communicate since the indiscretions of April—was being recalled to Bonn at Washington's request.

During the spring and summer of 1962 the exchange of views between Washington and Moscow on the Berlin question continued, though with no tangible result. The Cuban crisis of that October—which involved the two superpowers in an "eyeball-to-eyeball" confrontation, followed by a mutual desire for overall détente—led to a reduction of Soviet pressure on Berlin, with the result that none of the controversial suggestions for Berlin access arrangements were to be discussed in any detail. The Kennedy administration's notion of nonaggression agreements between NATO and the Warsaw Pact was to be revived only in connection with the negotiation of the Test-Ban Treaty a year later, and even then it was not to be implemented.

The Berlin Crisis of 1961–62 had clearly indicated the potential for conflict between the young American president and the most senior of the European leaders who were his allies, a conflict rooted not only in the contrasting personalities of the two men but also in the divergent interests and perspectives of the two states they governed. Similar differences were also to appear in connection with the broader issue of how the Western Alliance, of which the United States and the Federal Republic were leading members, should be organized.

### The Politics of the Western Alliance

It was no surprise that the Kennedy administration, as part of its reappraisal of America's domestic priorities and foreign policy, undertook a critical reassessment of the structure and functioning of the alliance that had now become a central part of U.S. foreign policy. The first stage of this reassessment of American security policy, which was carried out by Kennedy's secretary of defense, Robert McNamara, and his colleagues, concerned the needs and capabilities of the United States itself. A well-informed observer, remarking favorably on this strategic review undertaken in the first eight months of the new administration, commented: "Exactly what it [i.e., the reassessment] would mean for NATO would become apparent only when America's long-term military program had

13. Borch, "Anatomie einer Entzweiung," 360; Bandulet, *Adenauer,* 168; Schwarz, *Adenauer,* 748–49.

gained sufficient scope and momentum to permit a range of new decisions and initiatives concerning allied strategy and capabilities."[14]

This meant, among other things, that the important proposal submitted to the NATO Council in December 1960 by Secretary of State Christian Herter, on behalf of the Eisenhower administration, was shelved until further notice. This was the idea of making NATO a "fourth atomic power" by establishing a new force of five submarines with a total of eighteen Polaris missiles, as well as one hundred further land-based missiles. This suggestion, which corresponded with the wishes of NATO's supreme allied commander in Europe, General Lauris Norstad, was warmly received by the German government. Adenauer's minister of defense, Franz Josef Strauss, had been pressing for a larger German say in nuclear defense since his appointment in 1957, and he now proposed a NATO summit conference for spring 1961 to work out the details.[15]

Strauss, clearly with Adenauer's approval, continued to make further favorable references to the so-called Norstad-Herter proposal during 1961. In a broadcast talk at the end of the year, he insisted that this proposal to make NATO into a fourth atomic power "absolutely must" be decided in the course of the year 1962.[16]

The determination of Adenauer's defense minister to go ahead with this plan ran into some difficulties, in view of the Kennedy administration's doubts about the proposal and its espousal of the new nuclear doctrine of "flexible response." Whereas the idea of creating a new atomic power including the European members of NATO had made some sense in the context of the overall doctrine of "massive retaliation" propounded by John Foster Dulles in 1954, the concept of flexible response required the broadest possible span of retaliatory measures by the United States to any conceivable level of Soviet threat: a small conventional incursion should be answered by slightly superior conventional forces, and a scale of deterrence should proceed by graduated steps up to all-out nuclear retaliation. These views, set out in an important book by General Maxwell Taylor, Kennedy's appointee as chairman of the Joint Chiefs of Staff in July 1962, reduced the significance of nuclear retaliation in Western strategy and led to considerable misunderstandings between the Kennedy administration and the Adenauer government.

Although American spokesmen, from Secretary McNamara downward, tried to reassure their European allies that their security was not in any way diminished, the German view was not so optimistic, especially after the building of the Berlin Wall. Whereas the American view was that the Soviet government had no aggressive intentions, the Federal Republic under Adenauer feared that the exposed outposts of the Western Alliance, in particular Germany, were in greater danger of a Soviet attack in a situation in which the two superpowers were ap-

14. Robert E. Osgood, *NATO, the Entangling Alliance* (Baltimore, 1962), 356.
15. Bandulet, *Adenauer,* 157.
16. *Ibid.,* 152.

parently moving toward a tacit agreement not to use nuclear weapons against each other.

Adenauer's close ally Charles de Gaulle (they had become ever closer since their first official meeting in 1958) was not slow to remind the Germans that the new American strategic doctrine potentially created a serious distinction between the security of the United States and that of its European allies. De Gaulle, while redressing what he saw as an imbalance in the Western Alliance by building up an independent French nuclear force, argued that it was necessary to avoid a dangerous division of labor within the alliance, by which America produced the nuclear forces and Europe the conventional ones. When Kennedy met Adenauer in April 1961 and assured him that he intended to strengthen America's commitment to NATO, he left no doubt that the European partners were in return expected to bring their own conventional forces up to the levels Washington considered necessary. Regarding German participation in the control of NATO nuclear weapons—the objective that was dear to Strauss and also supported by Adenauer—the view of the Kennedy administration remained fairly negative. In November 1961 Kennedy took an initiative which the Germans regarded as tactless, if not insulting: true to his policy of seeking a dialogue with the Soviet Union on world security, he gave an interview to Khrushchev's son-in-law Alexy Adzhubey in which he went out of his way to say that West Germany "for the moment" represented no threat to the Soviet Union because it had no nuclear weapons and its conventional forces were firmly integrated within NATO. He did, however, go on to tell his interlocutor that "if this situation changed, if Germany developed an atomic capacity of its own, if it developed many missiles or a strong national army that threatened war, then I could understand your concern and I would share it."[17] This indication of common American and Soviet interest in an implied cooperation against German military development aroused some disquiet in the Adenauer government.

The Norstad-Herter plan for a NATO nuclear force was finally buried at the ministerial meeting of the alliance in May 1962. This put an end to the hopes of Adenauer's defense minister Strauss that nuclear deterrence would remain an essential pillar of NATO doctrine: he now had to accept that the Kennedy administration was firmly committed to flexible response.[18] A month later, Secretary McNamara made an important speech at Ann Arbor (16 June 1962), stressing Washington's determination to maintain centralized control of all the nuclear forces of the alliance and inviting its European members to concentrate on contributing conventional forces. This challenging declaration of a new strategic doctrine enhanced Adenauer's feelings of insecurity; neither his government in Bonn nor his embassy in Washington at that time had the necessary understand-

17. Konrad Adenauer, *Erinnerungen, 1959–1963* (Stuttgart, 1968), 92–93; D. C. Watt, ed., *Survey of International Affairs, 1961* (London, 1965), 49; *Public Papers of the Presidents of the United States: John F. Kennedy, 1961* (Washington, D.C., 1962), 751.
18. Bandulet, *Adenauer*, 159–60.

ing of strategic theory to follow the sophisticated logic of the "McNamara Doctrine" in all its detail.[19]

In any case, Adenauer had for some years been perturbed by an apparent decline in America's concern with Western Europe—he and de Gaulle were in the habit of exchanging lengthy reflections on the subject and for the old chancellor McNamara's speech did no more than confirm the painful impressions created by American behavior on Berlin and other issues.

The first eighteen months of the Kennedy administration were thus a period when several factors within the Atlantic Alliance—of which disagreements about nuclear strategy and the challenge presented by de Gaulle were the most obvious—added a new degree of tension to the German-American relationship. By the autumn of 1962 it had become clear that there were two quite divergent views about the future of the alliance. On the one hand, the so-called Grand Design presented in Kennedy's Philadelphia speech of 4 July 1962 foresaw an "Atlantic Community" with an American and a European pillar—the latter strengthened economically and politically by British entry into the EEC, though preferably not endowed with any nuclear weapons independent from those of the United States.[20]

The rival conception to this Anglo-American vision (which Prime Minister Macmillan largely shared with Kennedy, although they differed on the desirability of independent nuclear deterrents for European states) was the one presented by President de Gaulle. For him, British entry into the EEC was becoming ever more suspect as an American device for preserving the "hegemony" of the United States over Europe, and the future West European structure had to be firmly based on cooperation among the six states of the existing European Community, particularly France and Germany. Chancellor Adenauer, indeed, was being drawn ever more closely toward de Gaulle's conception of the Western Alliance as the year 1962 came to an end. A series of dramatic events in December 1962 and January 1963 was to bring the conflict between these two opposed concepts of the alliance to a head and was to have profound repercussions on the relations between Adenauer's Bonn and Kennedy's Washington.

In mid-December Macmillan, having received from de Gaulle at a meeting at Rambouillet a fairly clear warning that Britain's attempt to enter the EEC was doomed to failure, flew to Nassau in the Bahamas to engage in critical talks with Kennedy on the future of the British independent deterrent. As the American administration had decided not to proceed with the Skybolt missile, on which the future of Britain's deterrent was based, Macmillan persuaded Washington to return to an earlier commitment to make available a substitute in the form of Polaris missiles for British submarines.

19. This opinion was expressed by Berndt von Staden, at that time counselor of the German Embassy in Washington (interview, June 1966); the text of the Ann Arbor speech is in *Survival* IV–V (1962), 194–96.

20. Sorensen, the author of Kennedy's Philadelphia speech, has described the idea of the "Grand Design" in his *Kennedy,* chap. 20.

This Anglo-American agreement, prolonging both the British deterrent and the apparent special relationship between Washington and London, was one of the reasons given by de Gaulle for his statement in a press conference on 14 January 1963 that the negotiations for Britain's entry into the EEC could not continue. In the same press conference (of which, incidentally, his ally Adenauer had not been given any advance warning) he denounced Kennedy's notion of an Atlantic community as an ideological mask for American domination of Europe and insisted yet again that Europe must be free and independent.[21]

By January 1963 the main elements of Kennedy's "Grand Design" were thus in ruins: British membership in the EEC had been rejected, and France insisted with redoubled force on getting its own way in the alliance, complete with its own nuclear force independent of American control. All this had a dramatic effect on Washington's thinking about the alliance. What would happen if Adenauer followed the example of his friend de Gaulle in demanding a nationally controlled nuclear deterrent for Germany? What if, at the very least, German feelings of discrimination and unfair treatment should surge to the top in German politics, perhaps bringing Strauss or some even more nationalistic figure to the chancellorship? Such fears of what came to be called "German Gaullism" were widespread in Washington, and they led to what one eminent critic called an "ardent wooing" of Bonn in an attempt to prevent its following the pernicious example of Paris. This situation allowed the group of "Europeanists" in the State Department to win high-level support for their idea of a multilateral nuclear force, which they saw as a tranquilizer for Germany and cement for the alliance. The German government meanwhile had welcomed this plan for the same reason that it had welcomed General Norstad's scheme of 1960—as a way of gaining access to NATO's nuclear decision making through part-ownership and shared control of some of the alliance's "hardware." This prospect was confirmed in German minds when Kennedy's national security adviser McGeorge Bundy, in a speech in Copenhagen in September 1962, intimated that the American administration might ultimately, if the multilateral force developed as planned, remove the American veto on its use, thus effectively "Europeanizing" it.[22] By this time, the proposal had been modified from the original idea of a submarine force—which the U.S. Navy had vetoed—to a plan for a fleet of surface ships equipped with Polaris missiles. This change weakened the earlier interest of London and other European capitals (France had rejected the scheme from the beginning), with the result that Germany emerged as one of the main partners of the United States in the multilateral force (MLF) discussions.

The Franco-German treaty signed on 22 January 1963, in which Adenauer

21. Charles de Gaulle, *Major Addresses, Statements and Press Conferences, May 19, 1958–January 31, 1964* (New York, 1964), 208–22.

22. Henry A. Kissinger, *The Troubled Partnership* (New York, 1965), 235, 74; Schlesinger, *A Thousand Days*, 851ff.; Dieter Mahnke, *Nukleare Mitwirkung* (New York, 1972), 133; Alastair Buchan, *The Multilateral Force: An Historical Perspective* (London, 1964).

and de Gaulle committed their countries to close bilateral consultation and collaboration in all matters of foreign policy, increased the feeling in Washington that decisive countermeasures were necessary against this apparent evidence of German Gaullism. The Kennedy administration strongly encouraged those politicians in Bonn (including Adenauer's vice-chancellor Ludwig Erhard) who wished to add a preface to the new Franco-German treaty specifying that it would not affect Germany's existing commitments to NATO. In addition, high-level pressure from Washington on the German government to accept the MLF plan was stepped up.[23]

By the autumn of 1963, when a study group representing several Allied governments was set up to give more detailed analysis to the MLF proposal, a close harmony of interests appeared to prevail between Washington and Bonn on this issue. In the event, both Kennedy (in his last weeks in office) and his successor Lyndon B. Johnson were to discover that European enthusiasm for the MLF was less than they had expected, and the scheme was to be quietly shelved by the Johnson administration before the end of 1964.[24] That so much American effort had been invested in the MLF was, however, a clear indication of the concern felt in the Kennedy administration at the consequences that would follow if German policy under Adenauer were to go in the direction that France was taking under de Gaulle.

In the summer of 1963 Kennedy took another important step, his visit to Western Europe. The time he spent in Germany in June 1963 is chiefly remembered for his Berlin speech with its dramatic phrase "Ich bin ein Berliner" ("I am a Berliner"). A more significant aspect of his message, however—given particularly clearly in a speech in the Paulskirche in Frankfurt—was that the Germans should not automatically count on American support for German reunification along the lines conceived in the past by Adenauer and Dulles.[25] This warning was clearly in line with the policy pursued by Kennedy since the building of the Berlin Wall two years earlier and embodied in the abortive negotiating position of spring 1962: the United States would certainly maintain its own rights in West Berlin and with them the city's political and other links with West Germany, but an extension of West German influence to East Berlin, or to East Germany more generally, would not receive the backing of the United States. Kennedy was in effect telling the Germans that German reunification could be envisaged only as part of a long-term and much more complex process involving the coming together of the two rival power blocs in Europe as a whole. It was to achieve this aim, as well as to control and limit nuclear weapons at the global level, that the Kennedy administration now intensified its efforts to seek an over-

23. Adenauer, *Erinnerungen, 1959–1963,* 214–15; Bandulet, *Adenauer,* 218; Schlesinger, *A Thousand Days,* 872–73.

24. Morgan, *The United States and West Germany,* 151–52.

25. *Public Papers of . . . John F. Kennedy, 1963* (Washington, D.C., 1964), 525, 520–21. For the background, see Charles R. Planck, *The Changing Status of German Reunification in Western Diplomacy, 1955–1966* (Baltimore, 1967), esp. 33–48.

all accommodation with the Soviet Union. It was not surprising, in view of the contrasting geopolitical situations of the United States and the Federal Republic and the contrasting perceptions of their respective leaders, that this bid for global détente on the part of Kennedy was to produce further friction between the American president and the German chancellor.

## The Pursuit of East-West Détente

The American position paper of April 1962 on East-West negotiations, whose leaking to the German press caused such a furore, contained ideas not only concerning Berlin and the possibility of technical negotiating committees in which both German states would be represented, but also on much broader issues such as a Soviet-American agreement on nuclear nonproliferation and a nonaggression pact or declaration to be signed by all the members of the Warsaw Pact and NATO.

Even though Adenauer and his government were somewhat reassured, as the year 1963 opened, by the way the Cuban crisis of late 1962 had unexpectedly reduced Soviet pressure for an agreement on Berlin, they remained wary of possible moves by the Kennedy administration which might in one way or another compromise the national interests of Germany, as these were perceived in Bonn. Even parts of the 1962 negotiating paper that did not directly concern Berlin or the formal aspects of relations between the two German states were liable, in the German point of view, to be of concern to Germany because they involved a degree of recognition of the GDR and therefore threatened to weaken the possibility of German reunification.

The Kennedy administration's pursuit of nuclear nonproliferation and a test-ban treaty in 1962–1963 was indeed used by the Soviet Union to promote the idea of a comprehensive nonaggression pact between the two alliance blocs. This would automatically have the effect of upgrading the status of the GDR—hitherto not recognized by any of the Western powers—and thus of consolidating a "European settlement" on the lines desired by the Soviet Union.

Early in June 1963, shortly before his celebrated visit to Europe, Kennedy delivered a major foreign policy speech at the American University in Washington, in which he indicated the general lines on which East-West détente would be sought by his administration. Later that month, while Kennedy was reassuring America's West European allies, Averell Harriman went to Moscow, accompanied by Carl Kaysen, McGeorge Bundy's deputy, to negotiate the details of a test-ban treaty.[26] The details of this agreement were worked out in time for its signature on 5 August, but not before fairly serious differences of opinion had developed between Washington and Bonn. These disagreements, although in no

---

26. *Public Papers of . . . John F. Kennedy, 1963,* 459–64; Schlesinger, *A Thousand Days,* 903ff. I am very grateful to Carl Kaysen and McGeorge Bundy for information on this and related matters.

way as acute as the explosions of April–May 1962, indicated three fundamental divergences between American and German views about negotiations with the Soviet Union. First, the German government was concerned that the link between arms negotiations and German reunification, established in the 1950s, was now being broken. An agreement on nuclear testing without a corresponding one to change the political status quo in Germany, it appeared to Adenauer, could only consolidate the latter. Second, the negotiations were being conducted by the two superpowers (and to some extent by Britain) without any effective consultation with Bonn. This meant, for instance, that it was relatively easy for the Soviet Union to introduce the demand that the GDR be accepted as a signatory of the treaty—a demand not too troubling for the United States but in 1963 profoundly unwelcome to West Germany. Third, some of Kennedy's advisers were inclined to accept the Soviet demand that the proposed test-ban treaty should be followed by a general nonaggression pact, or series of pacts, signed by all the members of NATO and the Warsaw Pact (including, again, East Germany).

In June 1963, when Harriman and Kaysen saw Kennedy before setting off for Moscow, the president instructed them to explore with Khrushchev the prospects of a general understanding with the Soviet Union, which would of necessity include at least some discussion of the Soviet wish for a nonaggression pact. When Harriman remarked that any American reticence on this point (concentration on the test-ban treaty alone) would require "something to sweeten the package," Kennedy replied, "I have some cash in the bank in West Germany and am prepared to draw on that if you think I should."[27]

In the end, the Test-Ban Treaty was signed on 5 August without the Soviet demand for a nonaggression pact being met first, but this demand persisted in the aftermath of the treaty. One of the American diplomats concerned in the negotiations described the mood of some of his superiors as one of "millennial optimism," and it was clear in Washington that one of the purposes of Schröder's visit there in mid-September was "to block the search for a non-aggression arrangement between NATO and the Warsaw Pact."[28]

Walt Rostow, in 1963 chairman of the State Department's Policy Planning Council, later confirmed that West German resistance had been responsible for the fact that "we resisted in Moscow all pressures to link the nuclear test-ban to a non-aggression pact between NATO and the Warsaw powers."[29] The pressures, however, had been strong, and the temptation to give way to them had been and remained strong too.

In the end the West German government signed the Test-Ban Treaty, but its

27. Schlesinger, *A Thousand Days*, 904. Kennedy was referring to Washington's possible acceptance of the Soviet demand for a nonaggression pact, despite the deep-seated objections of Bonn.

28. Herbert von Borch, "USA setzen Hoffnung auf Schröder," *Die Welt*, 2 September 1963; Planck, *The Changing Status of German Reunification*, 44–48. Schwarz reports Adenauer's bitter complaint to McNamara: "The United States is selling everything so cheaply" (*Adenauer*, 851).

29. W. W. Rostow, *View from the Seventh Floor* (New York, 1964), 75.

signature was delayed for a few days while Bonn made it absolutely clear that West Germany would not sign the same copy of the agreement as East Germany. The West German signature was deposited in Washington and the East German in Moscow; Dean Rusk even agreed, on 12 August, after a long and difficult discussion in Bonn, that the United States would officially take no notice of the East German signature, thus denying East Berlin anything that could be construed as recognition.[30]

It should not be thought that the United States had a monopoly, during the summer months of 1963, on considering transactions with the Soviet Union which might alarm its alliance partners. Adenauer, in his last few months in office, revived a project he had submitted to the Soviet Union in June 1962 for a ten-year "truce" on the subject of German reunification, by which the status of the two German states would be tacitly recognized even by Bonn, in exchange for some improvements in the situation of the East German population. The Soviet response in 1962 had been very negative (the plan was seen as a trick to bring about reunification, and Adenauer had indeed proposed free elections for all Germany at the end of the ten-year period), but in the summer of 1963 Adenauer appears to have mentioned both to Kennedy and to de Gaulle the possibility of reviving it. It appears that when Adenauer informed Kennedy of the idea in June 1963—as he tells us, "not in so much detail" as he gave de Gaulle—the president had at first "not seemed keen" on the proposal, though he later encouraged Adenauer to try it out.[31]

Adenauer decided against a further démarche toward Moscow on the question. His main aim in East-West relations was to reaffirm the standard West German position on reunification, and these relations during 1962–1963 were thus characterized essentially by American dealings with the Soviet Union, which aroused more or less sharp feelings of alarm in West Germany. It was a period in which Washington had tried, though not always very attentively, to live up to the precepts laid down by Dean Acheson as the period came to an end:

> My thesis is that in making political and military judgements affecting Europe a major—often *the* major—consideration should be their effect on the German people and the German government. It follows from this that the closest liaison and consultation with the German government is an absolute necessity. . . . Unexpected or unexplained action nearly always causes consternation in Bonn. Sensible action after careful consultation, even when there has been some difference of view, rarely does.[32]

30. H. Bechtoldt, "Deutschland und das Moskauer Abkommen," *Aussenpolitik*, XIV, no. 19 (1963), 579–82.

31. Bandulet, *Adenauer*, 232–34; Schwarz, *Adenauer*, 844–51; Adenauer, *Erinnerungen, 1959–63*, p. 226.

32. *New York Times Magazine*, 15 December 1963.

How well did Kennedy and his administration live up to the standards implied by this warning, which was published, incidentally, a mere three weeks after the president's assassination? The record shows that there were indeed cases of "unexpected or unexplained action" but that on the main lines of policy affecting American and German interests, Kennedy and his advisers, after some early blunders, learned how to undertake "sensible action after careful consultation."

# 3

# De Gaulle and the Anglo-Saxons

*John Newhouse*

∿

General Charles de Gaulle was acutely aware of his prestige in America and Britain. He exaggerated when he regarded himself as a factor in American presidential politics, but his calculation that, whatever the political weather, he would hold a wide Anglo-American following was valid throughout the larger part of his tenure.

In an age of uncertain priorities, de Gaulle was a leader who knew what he was about—summoning France's sense of past glory and of great trials overcome by exemplary Frenchmen. This sureness, combined with the granitic character and brilliant style of the man, inspired trust. In Britain and America, as in France, de Gaulle found support among ordinary people, politicians, civil servants, and in the academic community. Because Washington treated him with skepticism and hostility for much too long during the war, many Americans swung to the other extreme and gave him the benefit of every doubt in his innumerable disputes with their government. And the British, who followed Sir Winston Churchill in sticking with de Gaulle from start to finish—no matter how difficult this was—could not easily disabuse themselves about a man who seemed to them to measure up to his own self-portrait.

Many Americans and Britons who think seriously about relations with France suspect that de Gaulle was "lost" to the Anglo-Saxons during the war, thanks chiefly to President Franklin Delano Roosevelt. But this implies that de Gaulle might have been "available" as an ally in the conventional long-term sense. He never was available in those terms. De Gaulle's wartime conflicts with his overburdened colleagues at 10 Downing Street and the White House affected his attitude toward the Anglo-Saxons, but they did not define it. They fed the Gaullist bias, but the effects of his tenure in the Elysée Palace were anticipated by a set of attitudes that had been formed much earlier.

De Gaulle arrived in London in June 1940, a fully formed French nationalist of a familiar breed, a product of the bourgeois, pious, intellectual milieu deeply marked by France's capitulation to Prussia in 1871 and her diplomatic retreat before Britain at Fashoda. World War I made the lesson of 1871 indelible: Ger-

many must be confined, if not dominated, by a combination of diplomatic encir-
clement and military force. The application of these traditional methods, de
Gaulle believed, would require a great and solitary chief, whose qualities he set
forth in his book *The Edge of the Sword*, written in 1932. The book still offers the
sharpest single glimpse of de Gaulle's thoughts, while the three volumes of his
war memoirs—longer but richer in precise clues—provide another path to understanding the man. Together, the early and later works establish the essential
distinction between de Gaulle and his contemporaries—his mystical sense that
France's destiny was his own.

Churchill established a lasting pattern when he sought to mediate Free
France's difficulties with the United States (though usually, but not always,
yielding to Washington in the end). At a time when everyone would have liked
to scuttle de Gaulle in the winter of 1942–1943, he and Eden perceived that
there was nobody else to build up. Thanks largely to Britain's efforts, de Gaulle
was an established figure in France and, perhaps more important, controlled
many of the resistance "nets" established there. For Churchill he may have been
the "monster of Hampstead," but he was also the "constable of France." On the
American side, only the Office of Strategic Services (OSS) and the army appeared to accept this view. The White House and State Department—that is,
Roosevelt and Cordell Hull—went on resisting, somewhat willfully, to the end.
In backing General Henri Giraud, a simple soldier and political innocent—a man
who, unlike de Gaulle, could claim no support in France—the Americans lost de
Gaulle's respect. He could understand their earlier support of Admiral Jean Dar-
lan, who, after all, was the link to Vichy France. Never Giraud.

The wartime conflicts between de Gaulle and the Anglo-Saxons arose from
the difference in their ultimate purposes. Washington and London were ab-
sorbed in winning the war, de Gaulle in restoring France, France's "rank," and
France's influence in her dependent territories. In de Gaulle's view, the outcome
of the war had been settled on 7 December 1941.

While it is true that the Churchill government did not always resist the temptation to exploit France's enfeebled position, especially in Lebanon and Syria,
Churchill and Eden performed notable services of lasting value to de Gaulle and
to France, unfailingly backing de Gaulle's political claims and, later, France's demand for a position in Germany as one of the victorious occupying powers and
for permanent membership on the United Nations Security Council. (Washington also backed France's membership on the council.) At the Teheran Conference, Joseph Stalin surprised Roosevelt by observing that it was Henri Petain,
not de Gaulle, who represented "the real physical France." Stalin also did not
consider that France could be trusted with any strategic positions outside its
own borders after the war and doubted that de Gaulle was a factor. Then, at
Yalta, Stalin at first refused to allow French participation in the occupation of
Germany, and Roosevelt sided with him throughout most of the conference.
But as Harry Hopkins noted, "Winston and Anthony fought like tigers for

France."[1] Yet de Gaulle, while formally acknowledging his debt to the British, seemed, or chose, to remember only the dark side of his association with them.

His return to the helm in 1958 meant that relations between Washington, London, and Paris would be directed by three worldly men and wartime confederates. As chief custodians of the Alliance, de Gaulle, Eisenhower, and Macmillan made an auspicious troika. Although Macmillan had not been nearly as grand a figure as the other two, he knew de Gaulle and Eisenhower very well—better than either knew the other. But Macmillan uncharacteristically chose to believe what he wanted to believe about de Gaulle's intentions, a lapse for which he later paid dearly.

Eisenhower had always found de Gaulle more sinned against than sinning during the war. Also, he was better able than most to see things from the French point of view. "In fairness to de Gaulle," he once told General Lauris Norstad, "we would react very much as [he] does if the shoe were on the other foot."[2] Most important, Eisenhower considered de Gaulle the strength of France.

Eisenhower and Secretary of State John Foster Dulles knew that de Gaulle would press French claims and interests with greater force than any predecessor and, in general, be a more persistent and demanding interlocutor. Just how much more demanding and difficult they would soon discover. But they may also have reckoned that ridding France of the Algerian incubus would keep him more or less fully occupied for some time.

If so, they were wrong. For de Gaulle, settling the Algerian issue would be a squalid prelude to a far more exalted task: ridding France of Anglo-American domination and molding the states of Western Europe into a French-led coalition (*un rassemblement des vieux pays autour de moi*). He was uncomfortable as a member of the alliance system. Whatever its obvious advantages to France—and these he always relied on—he saw it as robbing individual members of their freedom of maneuver, if not their sovereignty. He rightly saw the system as dominated by America, with support from its special ally, Britain. De Gaulle's own preference was for a restoration of a concert of powers, the system he understood better than any contemporary. Although a sworn enemy of what he called "bloc politics," de Gaulle began in September 1958 by proposing an inner Western leadership bloc of America, Britain, and France—the so-called tridirectorate.

"The years since 1945 had not filled de Gaulle with confidence in the wisdom of the Anglo-Saxons," wrote McGeorge Bundy in his book *Danger and Survival*; he went on to cite episodes in which Anglo-Saxon leadership could have reasonably been seen as badly flawed from de Gaulle's perspective.[3] From time to time de Gaulle felt obliged to deny the charge that he was anti-American or anti-

1. Robert Sherwood, *White House Papers of Harry L. Hopkins: An Intimate History* (London, 1948–49), 775, 781–82.

2. Stephen E. Ambrose, *Eisenhower*, Vol. II, *The President* (New York, 1984), 434.

3. McGeorge Bundy, *Danger and Survival: Choices About the Bomb in the First Fifty Years* (New York, 1988), 477.

British. Strictly speaking, he was probably right. He was a French nationalist whose devotion was borne up by a total commitment to the "certain idea" of France he set forth in the opening passage of his memoirs. France's interest, as he defined it, might one day require close relations with America. Thus anti-Americanism, although a useful chord to strike from time to time, was not to be formalized as policy.

The unsentimental part of de Gaulle feared American power because it seemed to block realization of a great role for France. And he claimed to see an imperial design in most American purposes. Britain was a threat only insofar as it was a stalking-horse for Washington. Thus Britain had to be denied a continental role until it had shed its heavy American baggage and given up any claims or pretensions to power that might jeopardize France's preeminence in Western Europe.

There may have been no room for anti-Americanism per se in the Gaullist vision of France, but it had an explicitly anti-German content. America might threaten to stifle French civilization, to prevent its light from radiating throughout the world, but America was not a primordial threat to France or a real rival for the leadership of Western Europe. Germany was and is. One day America would go back to being a Western Hemisphere and Pacific power, leaving Europe to the Europeans. Then, as before, Germany might well be the most powerful state in Western and Central Europe. Therefore, Germany must remain subordinate to France.

Since World War II, Britain and France have struggled with the problem of how to maneuver American power to support their national goals. They adopted different strategies. The British worked at sustaining their role as America's privileged ally, whereas the French, by and large, kept their distance and relied on traditional diplomacy. They reckoned that the special relationship Britain had built with the other and greater "Anglo-Saxon" power was actually a junior partnership and neither available to them nor desirable. An aversion to being *demandeur* runs deep in France. Best to drink from one's own glass while touching glasses all around, de Gaulle used to say. He agreed with Lord Palmerston that a nation does not have friends, only interests. Relations between the three countries were for years largely shaped by nuclear issues—by the determination in London and Paris to deploy their own nuclear weapons rather than relying entirely on America's. But each wanted American help; without it, the path to a nuclear deterrent would be longer, much more costly, and laden with uncertainty.

"Schizophrenic" best describes Washington's attitude toward assisting the British and French programs. The Eisenhower administration, like Truman's, initially tended to keep both at arm's length, even though Eisenhower himself fully understood and sympathized with Britain's interests. In 1950, the British began working on their own gaseous diffusion plant but got no help even though the technology had originated with them.[4] In 1952, the British asked

4. John Newhouse, *De Gaulle and the Anglo-Saxons* (New York, 1970), 14.

Washington if they could test a bomb at one of the American test sites in the Pacific. The Americans were standoffish and tried to discourage the British, who then got permission from Australia to test their first atom bomb at Monte Bello Island; the date was 3 October 1952.

American support for France's nuclear program at this time was precluded, if only because French facilities were thought to be deeply penetrated by the Communist party. In 1956, Washington cut the price of enriched uranium sold abroad for industrial use, mainly to discourage France from building a plant for the production of fissile materials. Not long afterward, the problem of French security procedures had disappeared, and these were blessed by America's CIA and Atomic Energy Commission (AEC).[5]

The Suez crisis of 1956 did more to damage France's relations with the Anglo-Saxons, especially the Americans, than any other episode in postwar history. It forced France's latent mistrust of the Anglo-Saxons to the surface. Washington was seen to have betrayed its chief allies and Britain abjectly to have deserted France at the first sign of disapproval in Washington. What further proof for de Gaulle, who had supported the Suez action, that only the boldest and most independent spirits could avoid becoming hostages to American power?

Among the lessons of Suez drawn by the Conservative party's hierarchy, not least by Macmillan, was that never again could Britain permit itself the luxury of a basic policy conflict with the United States. But the effect of Suez in France was even more profound and pervasive. Whereas the affair divided Britain, it tended to unite France, and, far from reaching the same conclusion as the Tory hierarchy, the prevailing French attitude was the belief that Europe must find a way to manage its affairs without reference to the superpowers. The Suez crisis had much to do with encouraging the creation of the Common Market and animating France's nuclear program.

Politically, that program dates in a sense to a left-of-center icon, Pierre Mendès-France, although French scientists had been working on nuclear fission for as long as any. As prime minister in 1955, Mendès-France tried but failed to promote world support for a test ban. He then acquiesced in a French program, giving two reasons: "One is nothing without the bomb in international negotiations . . . [the bomb] would be the main difference between France and Germany."[6] The Mendès-France government fell a few weeks later, and for a time the program's fortunes rose and fell as the revolving door of France's Fourth Republic briskly ushered successive governments in and out. But Suez and the prospect of a British bomb—an Anglo-American stew in French eyes—anchored the French program. The detonation of the first French atomic bomb in April 1960 was authorized by Prime Minister Felix Gaillard more than two years earlier.

5. *Ibid.,* 12.

6. *L'Aventure de la Bombe,* transcript of meeting organized at Arc et Senans, Université de Franch-Comté and the Institut Charles de Gaulle, 27, 28, and 29 September 1984 (Paris, 1985), 81.

De Gaulle expected less from Washington than his predecessors had, at least on issues concerning Europe and the Third World. And perhaps he never held high hopes for creating a French-led Western Europe that would become the arbiter between America and Russia—those greater powers but lesser societies. De Gaulle was a realist and sensitive to the limits of French power and the restraints on French ambition. But for the figure to whom history confided French legitimacy in June 1940 and had embodied it ever since, nothing less than a great enterprise could restore France.

Washington's ambiguous, often contradictory policy on aiding France's weapons program marked both the Eisenhower and Kennedy years. Few issues in the period between 1958 and 1963 preempted more of the time and thought of high officials, including the two presidents. And perhaps none stimulated so much division, even bitterness, within the American government as the question whether to put American relations with France on the same footing as those with Great Britain. Major agencies, including the State Department, were split. Since France was sure to have nuclear weapons one day, the argument was why not help and thereby spare France part of the huge investment in time and resources the task would require; in return, France would presumably play a stronger role in NATO and become more supportive of American policy. Other advocates, mainly in the Defense Department, wanted to offset the heavy pressure on America's balance of payments arising from its NATO commitments.

Resistance was strong. America's duty, said some officials, was to discourage the spread of nuclear weapons, not help to spread them about—even to a close ally. Admittedly, the British horse was out of the barn, but that was all the more reason to draw the line before the next aspirant.

Even more persuasive to many was the "German argument." "Never do for France what you are unwilling to do eventually for Germany," said Jean Monnet, the architect of the European Community, to numerous American officials (in successive administrations) who sought his sensible advice. France's political instability also seemed to argue against accelerating its entry into the nuclear fold.

One thing that de Gaulle did want from Washington was the help with nuclear weapons that had been denied his predecessors. To have access to Anglo-American expertise in inertial guidance systems, isotope separation, warhead technology, and so on would be vastly beneficial to the French program. But de Gaulle was not willing to trim his principles to gain access to advanced technology. He never told his government not to seek this aid from America or Britain. He merely established that he would never pay a political price for it; that being the case, he told his ministers and generals that they were free to seek the aid but stood little chance of succeeding.

De Gaulle's initial meetings with Eisenhower and Dulles in Washington in July 1958 established an enduring pattern. He noted France's position as continental leader with a global vocation. His hosts replied that a world directorate of the sort de Gaulle had in mind was unrealistic and would be resented by other

Western and nonaligned countries.[7] The U.S. leadership stressed joint activities and the NATO mechanism. It saw the communist countries as a menacing bloc forged by a common ideology. De Gaulle observed that the deeper reality was the existence of nations with different personalities and histories; their social systems were less important, he felt, and in any case not lasting. He conceded the threat of Soviet Russia but felt that more and more it would become a matter of traditional Russian interests being asserted, as opposed to the insidious spread of the doctrine of a new church militant. De Gaulle saw the world as an ensemble of nations; Washington saw a system of two alliances, the one designed to check the malign purposes of the other.

Just one day before this meeting, Britain and the United States had signed an agreement establishing closer nuclear cooperation; following passage of the amended U.S. atomic energy law—amended in Britain's favor. For the meeting with de Gaulle to occur on the following day could have been—and was—considered inopportune. But the coincidence probably served to sharpen the tone of the talks—to point up more clearly the gulf between the parties.

Little time was spent on the nuclear issue. Both sides knew it was central, but they understood that it would always be more of a tacit than a current piece of business between Washington and Paris (or between London and Paris). Washington recognized that de Gaulle's France, like Britain, would never support a ban or limitation on nuclear testing until its own weapons program was far enough along to do without tests. De Gaulle's message was plain: he was not asking for help, but he was telling the Anglo-Saxons that French support of test-ban talks and related projects would have to be paid for in the coin of technology. Washington was also put on notice that the United States would not be given the right to deploy nuclear weapons on French territory.[8]

Eisenhower and Dulles did not underrate de Gaulle's obdurate style or France's place at the geographic heart of NATO. But they were more sensitive to the problem of Germany. West Germany had to be anchored to the Western system and kept immune from nuclear temptation. De Gaulle wanted to check the German impulse with French strength, whereas the Americans were fearful that French power would arouse the impulse; they sought constantly to reassure the West Germans about American guarantees, the reality of interdependence, the virtues of European integration, and so on.

De Gaulle was looking ahead to a quadripolar world system, the four power centers being Washington and Moscow, joined eventually—perhaps in the 1980s—by Peking and Paris. The Atlantic Alliance would be superseded; Great Britain, weakened by economic pressure and declining political fortune, might remain in the American orbit or might shift its allegiance to a French-led Eu-

7. George W. Ball, *The Discipline of Power* (London, 1968), 128–29.
8. Newhouse, *De Gaulle and the Anglo-Saxons*, 58–59, 61.

rope. Before returning to power, he said, "As soon as France has a policy she will follow another path and take the Continent with her."[9]

~

Between 1959 and late 1962 most events were seen in relation to Berlin. It was the longest period of high tension and great danger in the Cold War saga. Eisenhower entered his lame-duck period still embroiled in this, the greatest of Nikita Khrushchev's gambits. And Kennedy, within four months of taking charge, found himself and his untested administration with an even graver crisis over Berlin than the one that faced Eisenhower. Berlin was a test of the will, determination, and coherence of the West's Big Four—Washington, London, Paris, and Bonn.

Eisenhower mainly wanted to maintain a firm Western position while minimizing the risk of nuclear war and making certain that the issue of war and peace was clearly set forth in political terms. This meant that Washington would not, say, declare war if Moscow delegated to East Germany the right to stamp Western passports.

Great Britain was chiefly concerned with defusing the situation, and to accomplish this Macmillan was willing to pay a higher price than the others. In the end he held firm, but he wobbled often. The role of peace broker attracted him strongly—and not just because it suited the British political climate. So in December Macmillan arranged to have himself invited to visit Khrushchev in Moscow, and he notified Bonn, Paris, and Washington of his plans without specifying his intentions.

West German policy was paradoxical. Adenauer's real concern was to preserve Bonn's sovereign preeminence vis-à-vis East Germany; he was in no case prepared to risk a war over the status of Berlin. Franz Josef Strauss, his defense minister, was equally reluctant to risk war notwithstanding his strong rhetoric. Strauss lacked confidence in the Americans' judgment and frankly feared they might use tactical nuclear weapons on German soil. He felt that maintaining a position in Berlin, a city far from Western defenses, suited an offensive strategy but not the defensive strategy imposed by geography. Together, Adenauer and Strauss sought to harden the Western position while discouraging plans to keep open by force the autobahn linking Berlin to the Federal Republic, as Washington was prepared to do if it became necessary.

De Gaulle seemed never for a moment to have doubted that Khrushchev was bluffing. De Gaulle took the hardest public line of any of the Western leaders vis-à-vis Moscow's demands and ultimatums on Berlin. Although he was also withdrawing French units from the NATO command at this time, he nonetheless managed to enlarge Adenauer's concerns about the supposedly unreliable

9. Charles de Gaulle, interview with United Press, 10 July 1950.

Anglo-Saxons. Throughout these four troubled years, de Gaulle did his best to turn Adenauer away from Washington and to start a process that would end with Bonn looking to Paris for its security. In a sense, Berlin was an opportunity: in return for Adenauer's support for French policies favoring limits on the development of the European Community (EC), de Gaulle appears to have backed Adenauer's position on East Germany.[10]

De Gaulle's policy was abetted by Britain's. Macmillan was bent on achieving an agreement of genuine importance with Khrushchev in Moscow. He arrived with a hastily improvised proposal for an inspected freeze, or limitation, on nuclear and conventional arms within an agreed zone on either side of the Iron Curtain. Eisenhower, de Gaulle, and Adenauer did not know that Macmillan was going to make such a proposal. Since the Americans had just consented to a revival of Anglo-American nuclear weapons cooperation, this bit of evasiveness did not go down well in Washington. In taking final leave of Macmillan, Dulles, who was terminally ill, had admonished: "I see nothing to negotiate over Berlin."[11]

Macmillan achieved nothing by his solitary maneuver in Moscow other than to strengthen the Franco-German diplomatic axis and to deepen Adenauer's doubts about British intentions and their pernicious effects on the Americans. Adenauer's long and unconcealed anti-British bias had been fortified by London's refusal to join the Common Market and then by its creation of a rival organization, the European Free Trade Association (EFTA). And now Macmillan seemed to be playing into Khrushchev's hands by undermining the unflinching line set forth by Adenauer and de Gaulle. For Adenauer and others around him this was more than just mischievous; it was anti-"Europe", an attitude arising from an impulse (common to both the Tory and Labour parties) to play the dual role of Washington's junior partner and the catalyst of a great power dialogue.

10. Alfred Grosser thinks the understanding was reached in their first meeting: "Without being able to prove it in any way, I believe that as early as Sept. 14, 1958, there was a sort of gentlemen's agreement between the General and the Chancellor—not explicit, unsigned, undrafted, based on reciprocity: the Federal Republic would aid France in her Atlantic and European ambitions, and France would give firm support to the Eastern policies of the Federal Republic. On reunification and Berlin, France was never to take any initiatives that did not first emanate from Bonn. Since no initiatives ever emanated from Bonn in this domain, likewise none emanated from Paris" (*French Foreign Policy Under de Gaulle* [Boston, 1967], 66).

11. My understanding of events associated with de Gaulle's rejection of Britain's bid to join the European Community is based in large measure on documents and private conversations. Late in 1967, I was allowed to read British records of the three meetings, including the one at Rambouillet, that de Gaulle and Macmillan held in 1962. These records, which were prepared by the late Sir Philip de Zulueta, who served as Macmillan's private secretary and interpreter, were always transcribed and typed promptly; at Rambouillet, the British record was ready before Macmillan and his party left the chateau. It was judged the authentic version by various French officials, who conceded that the Elysée's record was less reliable. De Gaulle's interpreter, Prince Andronikov, took no notes in these meetings. My knowledge of these events and those that transpired at Nassau was further enhanced by numerous conversations with de Zulueta, the late Lord Harlech, and others on both the British and French sides.

This British attitude contained the seeds of future difficulties not just for Macmillan but for his successor.

In 1959 and 1960, the Berlin Crisis inspired Allied contingency planning conducted in Washington by the American, British, and French ambassadors. This working group managed to present all sides with the same factual evaluation of the threat. In July 1961 the group was enlarged to include West Germany and then was split into several subgroups dealing with the various political, military, and economic aspects of the Berlin problem. Special military arrangements for handling a Berlin crisis were established outside NATO in a little-known command called Live Oak. Its chain of command ran through the Big Three governments, and the commanding generals—one each from Britain, France, and the United States—were responsible to NATO's supreme commander *only* when a military contingency plan had been set in motion by the governments. Live Oak worked alongside Supreme Headquarters Allied Powers Europe (SHAPE) but had separate communications and so on.

All these arrangements suited de Gaulle perfectly. They offered him precise and reliable estimates of the various problems but committed him to nothing. It would remain so. Never during the anxious weeks and months of the 1961 Berlin Crisis did de Gaulle agree to a predelegation of authority to an Allied military commander. His real concern lay in the possibility that Berlin would in the end draw Washington and Moscow closer together bilaterally. That would have conflicted with de Gaulle's own plans, and it reinforced his hostility to any Soviet-American contacts on Berlin. He appeared to feel that the United States should provide forces for Europe's defense, along with a nuclear guarantee, but should not otherwise meddle in Europe's affairs.

Within the four-power group, Britain's position was usually the most flexible, while the West Germans were the least flexible on any point that even remotely touched on the issue of East Germany's legal status. De Gaulle appeared to sympathize with Bonn's sensitivity to the less rigorous Anglo-Saxons, while siding with Britain on the issue of predelegations of military authority. These tactics irked many in Washington. In a military sense it mattered little; the United States supplied the bulk of the force, and the British provided a good deal more than the French. But de Gaulle got credit for the hardest declaratory position.

Remarkably, the Berlin planning group, however, chafed by the dissonant voices of the governments, managed to play its role with distinction. Indeed, the group performed a historic, possibly unprecedented, function. Besides doing much to stabilize the Berlin situation, its continuing efforts taught the governments much about joint crisis management.

Nuclear weapons became a doctrinal issue that created difficulties for Eisenhower and Kennedy with de Gaulle and with most other NATO members as well. America's nuclear stockpile had begun to pyramid in the late 1950s. These weapons were put in Europe to help NATO defend itself against superior Soviet non-nuclear forces. Eisenhower had been uneasy about the buildup but did nothing to stop it. Kennedy and his advisers felt that a credible defense required strong non-nuclear as well as nuclear forces in Europe. They wanted a higher nuclear threshold. It was one thing to rely on nuclear weapons in the 1950s, when America had a near monopoly and faced little risk of retaliation (Khrushchev's bluster notwithstanding). It was quite another in the 1960s, when the Soviets were in a position to respond in kind.

Europe's reaction was hardly enthusiastic. Having endured two devastating wars in a short span, Europeans were opposed to any strategy that might make war—non-nuclear or nuclear—less unlikely. They complained that Washington's new line signaled a retreat from the commitment to use America's strategic weapons in their defense. Lurking sensitivities were aroused. Why, asked continentals, was Britain the sole beneficiary of America's nuclear largesse? And why should Europe be asked to run the risk of becoming a battlefield yet again but forgo possession of the weapons that would decide the outcome of a war? Europeans were, they felt, being asked to risk everything so that America might remain a sanctuary.

A project—a dubious one in my view—called the multilateral force (MLF) became a point at which the doctrinal issue converged with the nuclear sharing dilemma. The MLF amounted to creating a fleet of surface ships armed with Polaris missiles jointly owned and operated by several NATO members, each of which would have a veto over the use of the nuclear weapons. The MLF's purpose was to give the Germans a sense of participation in such matters. But since the missile warheads were to remain in American custody, not to mention decisions regarding their use, the MLF would change nothing; it was akin to taking clothes out of one closet and putting them in another. The project dated to the late Eisenhower period, when the Defense Department, backed by some members of State, wanted to deploy ballistic missiles on barges and railroad cars in Western Europe. A variant of this idea was to offer ballistic missiles to several European countries, either for purchase or manufacture under American license. The navy was pushing its Polaris at the Europeans, with little regard to questions of control. (It had installed a small model of the Polaris system at NATO's former headquarters in Paris, and any curious delegate, by pushing a button, could witness a miniaturized missile takeoff.) And an air force colonel was simultaneously hawking the Minuteman, then hardly out of the design stage.

The MLF was strenuously opposed by de Gaulle; however transparent and implausible, the project might have blurred an essential difference between France and Germany—the right to a place in the nuclear club. De Gaulle's strong position sharpened the tension with Washington and put the Germans between the upper and nether millstones. The MLF acquired some momentum as well as notoriety during the Kennedy administration. It survived Kennedy's skepticism but not Lyndon Johnson's, who shelved it in December 1965 but not before it had divided and seriously weakened the government of Adenauer's successor, Ludwig Erhard, the MLF's only genuine supporter in Europe—and a reluctant one at that.

As the 1960s began, Britain's relationship with the United States had entered a slow, if barely perceptible, decline. Numerous State Department officials wished the British deterrent would disappear, and they strongly opposed abetting de Gaulle's plans. At the Pentagon, many senior officials—civilian and military—appeared to favor lifting the embargo on aid to France's nuclear weapons program. Serious pressure developed to help France in return for better cooperation from de Gaulle. Britain, after all, was a nuclear power and not likely to give up this role. France was also establishing a claim and moving as rapidly as possible. France could not be ignored; one day it would be essential, whether in political or strategic terms, to link French nuclear forces as tightly as possible with America's and Britain's. The problem of a West German claim would thus require some solution other than a ban on aid to France. Such was the thinking of quite a number of traditionalists in the government, many of whom were officials in the State Department with "country" responsibilities, or intelligence specialists.

The French were seeking nuclear submarine technology and inertial-guidance components. Some elements in the State Department who had earlier supported aiding de Gaulle put forward a plan to supply France with a nuclear propulsion system for submarines, an offer that had been the victim of many false starts in the preceding two years. Around this time, the Kennedy administration decided to make inertial-guidance components and technology available to the West Germans, who were procuring and manufacturing under license advanced tactical American combat aircraft. This distinction in Bonn's favor was carefully noted—and resented—in Paris, where it was also known that once, and possibly twice, during 1961 Macmillan had tried unsuccessfully to sell de Gaulle certain technology and material that Washington continued to embargo.

As before, the proposal to sell France what it wanted failed. Kennedy sided with opponents of the move, accepting their argument that by taking political risks to help France he would not be helping himself; de Gaulle was unlikely in return to become a more obliging ally.

In the weeks that followed, matters became clearer still and edgier. Bob McNamara anathematized "weak national nuclear forces" in the commencement speech at Ann Arbor in which he unveiled America's "no cities" nuclear strategy. Such forces, he said, "are not likely to be sufficient to perform even the function of deterrence . . . [and] are dangerous, expensive, prone to obsolescence and lacking in credibility as a deterrent." Any doubt that France was McNamara's target was removed a few days later when he issued a clarification excusing Britain from his broadside because its deterrent was coordinated with America's.

Kennedy appeared to have been leery of schemes intended to discourage either the British or French nuclear claims. Britain was unlikely to give up its deterrent when France was about to acquire similar status. Also, while just as leery of doctrine and bold designs, Kennedy, like Macmillan, had attached himself to one known as the Atlantic partnership that ran counter to de Gaulle's. It amounted to promoting British membership in a politically cohesive European Community. Then as now, Europe was a collection of small and middle-sized states, no one of them capable of assuming its own well-being and each dependent for its security on American guarantees. A more closely knit structure of the sort envisaged by the EC's pioneers (mainly French) would gradually allow Europe to overcome centuries of strife and disunity and also do more for itself, thus lightening America's burden. De Gaulle's contempt for this notional scheme became legendary, even though it was no more implausible than his own.

Kennedy and Macmillan underestimated de Gaulle, possibly because their attention was often elsewhere. The Cuban Missile Crisis, after obscuring other problems, changed everything. The Cold War in its crudest and most unstable form was over. Overnight, Kennedy's status as leader of the West was clearer and hardly disputable. His rising stock threatened Gaullist policy. For de Gaulle, restoring a more balanced situation would require a *coup de théâtre* of his own. Events helped.

In November, while Kennedy's people were trying to get Khrushchev's IL-28s out of Cuba, another crisis erupted, this one in Anglo-American relations. It began with Britain's discovery that Washington was about to cancel a missile called Skybolt, then being developed. Skybolt was a thousand-mile, two-stage ballistic missile designed for release from beneath the wing of a large airplane; it would allow bombers to stand off and attack an enemy well beyond the range of its air defenses. For the air force, Skybolt was the "Polaris of the sky." It would extend the life of America's B-52 force. For Britain, Skybolt was vastly more important and, indeed, vital; it alone could save a deterrent composed of 180 elderly bombers from obsolescence. Or so it seemed. In 1960, Eisenhower had agreed to sell Skybolt to Macmillan; in return he got an informal assurance that a naval base at Holy Loch, in Scotland, would be available to American nuclear submarines. To pay for Skybolt, the British canceled a missile of their own called Blue Streak. The decision was an act of faith in the special relationship; Britain's future as a nuclear power became dependent on a still-to-be-built American weapons system.

Macmillan's government was shocked, or pretended to be, by the cancellation, although it had received fair warning from the outgoing Eisenhower administration, as well as its successor, that Skybolt was in trouble. It was the most complex missile system yet undertaken by anyone; its costs and technical problems were expanding rapidly. McNamara finally concluded that Skybolt did not justify all the expense and uncertainty; America did not need it. But since Britain did, some parts of the Washington bureaucracy spotted clear profit in the missile's demise. Macmillan would have to withdraw Britain from the nuclear club.

At that point, Macmillan urgently needed support from Kennedy and de Gaulle. Only Kennedy could keep Britain's deterrent alive. Only de Gaulle stood between Britain and membership in the EC—Macmillan's priority goal at this point. As it happened, two meetings within two days of each other in December 1962 would settle both questions. First came Macmillan's talks with de Gaulle on the fifteenth and sixteenth at a château in the forest of Rambouillet. It was their third meeting in just over a year to discuss Britain's "European" bona fides and whether they justified admission into the Community of Six. Washington wanted Britain inside playing its old role of balancing unsteady continentals, thereby becoming an even more useful American partner. Kennedy was optimistic; he would know more when he saw Macmillan at Nassau on the eighteenth, but, meanwhile, he and his advisers were relying on deceptively bullish reports from the British and the French about the two earlier de Gaulle–Macmillan meetings. In fact, de Gaulle had not tipped his hand.

De Gaulle's political position in December was much stronger than it had been during the earlier meetings. A month before, legislative elections had strengthened him and his party. The Algerian war had been settled, and his hands at last were entirely free. At Rambouillet, he gave Macmillan the bad news: their two countries could cooperate but only bilaterally. There was no place for Britain in Europe. Macmillan left the château beaten, his foreign policy in ruins.

The communiqué disguised the abject failure of the meeting. Two days later, at Nassau, Kennedy expressed concern about Britain's European hopes. His advisers had warned him that another Anglo-American nuclear arrangement might give de Gaulle a pretext for vetoing Britain's entrance into the Community. Without telling Kennedy that he had just heard the veto pronounced, Macmillan said the two issues were not connected. He had come to Nassau to obtain the Polaris missile system as a substitute for Skybolt; if possible, Britain's deterrent would be deployed beneath the waves. Most of Kennedy's advisers were opposed to selling Polaris, but they were overruled. Macmillan had been made politically vulnerable by the dark cloud hovering over Britain's deterrent. It had been put there by the Skybolt decision. His friend Kennedy would not accept the responsibility for bringing him down. Furthermore, unlike some of his advisers, Kennedy was unwilling to toss aside the special relationship, something he knew and understood, for what seemed the will-o'-the-wisp of a federal Europe.

With Macmillan's problem disposed of, the question became what to do about de Gaulle. Should Kennedy offer him Polaris, too? In publicly offering the Polaris missile system to de Gaulle, Kennedy did not seem to be risking much. Since France, unlike Britain, had neither the thermonuclear warheads for the missiles nor the submarine technology, de Gaulle was hardly likely to be tempted by an offer of a submarine-launched missile. He would need much more. At Palm Beach, shortly after Nassau, Kennedy said to his old friend David Ormsby-Gore, "If de Gaulle accepts this deal—and I don't think he will—warheads lie at the end of the road—yours."[12] Kennedy meant that de Gaulle would require warheads and that he, Kennedy, was not going to take on the thankless task of seeking the Joint Atomic Energy Committee's approval of such a transaction.

Kennedy told Charles Bohlen, his ambassador to Paris, to open negotiations

12. Author's conversation with Lord Harlech, 1967.

with de Gaulle at once. Bohlen's British colleague, Sir Pierson Dixon, got similar instructions from Macmillan. Each saw de Gaulle separately in early January and gave him to understand that he was being offered a good deal more than the unarmed Polaris missile system.[13] Accepting would have allowed de Gaulle to deploy a secure subsurface and fully modern nuclear force years sooner than planned and at a great saving in French resources. Accepting would have moved France close to the *directoire à trois* with America and Britain that had once appeared to be a priority goal. But the implicit price—being obliged to admit Britain into Europe and link his forces to those of the Anglo-Saxons—was too high. De Gaulle did not want parity with Britain or a comparably special relationship with a dominant American partner. He wanted supremacy in Western Europe.

On 14 January, in one of his semiannual press conferences, de Gaulle produced the *coup de théâtre*. Britain was rejected. So was the Kennedy temptation—nuclear partnership. Occasionally, de Gaulle wrapped an event in myth, using the myth to justify a step he had already decided to take. A few days after the press conference, the myth appeared: the meeting in Nassau had provoked his veto of Britain's bid. By creating a new and stronger defensive link with the Americans, Macmillan, like British leaders before him, had shown that America mattered more to his country than Europe. Britain was not and could not be European.

After de Gaulle put paid to Washington's grand design, Kennedy's skeptical instincts took tighter control. He did not give up trying to strengthen the tie with the general, nor did he wholly abandon the design. But he did work harder at improving relations with his adversary, Khrushchev, and with another difficult ally, Konrad Adenauer.

⁓

In June 1965, France suddenly began a boycott of the EC institutions (despite private assurances to the West Germans that a crisis would be avoided). The early days of the boycott coincided with rumors that de Gaulle was planning to disengage France, whether entirely or partly, from NATO. The EC crisis was settled in January. Some French diplomats felt that de Gaulle had settled on terms less favorable than he had sought because he was ready to make his move against NATO and that trying to manage two intra-Western crises at the same time would have been difficult even for him. On 21 February, de Gaulle referred to NATO in a press conference as an "American protectorate," and he made reasonably clear his intention to leave it eventually, although he was vague about timing.

13. My understanding of what went on at Nassau and just afterward in Paris is, once again, based on conversations with the men cited just above and various American counterparts; among the latter was the late Charles E. Bohlen, with whom I had numerous conversations on these matters during his tenure as ambassador in Paris.

Shortly after that press conference, de Gaulle instructed his ministers to have memorandums prepared dealing with the implications of extricating France not just from NATO but from the alliance itself. This posed a tough question. Was de Gaulle actually on the verge of removing the distinction between alliance with the other Western powers under the North Atlantic Treaty and participation in the military command structure? To quit everything, his ministers warned, could prejudice France's position in Berlin as one of the victorious powers. Theoretically, these rights would not have been affected by withdrawal from the Atlantic Alliance, but in practice they probably would have been. If de Gaulle had justified denunciation of the treaty on the grounds that circumstances had changed, so then could the others have ignored his privileged place in German affairs on the grounds that he had unilaterally changed the conditions on which this position was based. Other NATO members would have been able to say that he had, in effect, opted for a fully neutral position between the blocs.[14]

It was unclear whether de Gaulle had been tempted to withdraw from the Atlantic Alliance at this stage or was merely testing the internal reaction to that prospect. He chose, of course, to remain a party to the treaty while removing France from the command structure.

The reaction in Eastern Europe to de Gaulle's move was far from simple. He would visit the Soviet Union in June. His people had warned him that France's usefulness to the Russians would decline with the decline in his nuisance value, obviously greater inside the alliance, where he could block, alter, or otherwise influence Allied policy. Although the pluses of the move doubtless outweighed the minuses from the Soviet point of view, de Gaulle was rocking the system on which Europe's stability was based. Briefly, his assertion of independence from America struck responsive chords in some parts of Eastern Europe and aroused concern in others. *Le Monde*'s André Fontaine described a conversation that he had at the time with an East European diplomat. " 'France's decision,' he said in effect, 'disappoints us. We were hoping she would manage a reform of NATO which would have allowed us to obtain some redistribution of roles within the Warsaw Pact. In showing there is no middle ground between integration and withdrawal, she risks perpetuating the situation which currently exists in our pact, where all the commands are held by the Soviets and where there is no question that any of us could withdraw as long as the German problem is unsettled.' "[15]

De Gaulle's dealings with the United States and Britain during the balance of his tenure were minimal, negative, and notable chiefly for a second rejection of Britain's effort to join the EC. The tacit understanding between him and the Anglo-Saxons—that they were fated to disagree—was based to a considerable

---

14. My knowledge of what transpired between de Gaulle and his administration on NATO withdrawal is based mainly on conversations with closely involved French diplomats and to some extent on conversations with two Western ambassadors who were in Paris then.

15. *Le Monde,* 12 March 1966.

extent on his petition for a veto over America's strategic deterrent. His proposed tridirectorate was mainly about that and could not have been accepted by any American president. In *Danger and Survival*, Bundy makes that point while also explaining why de Gaulle felt obliged to insist: "To say that de Gaulle's demand was unacceptable is not at all to say that it was without justification. His argument has great strength. Who can wish his country's survival to be dependent on the good sense of others? Who can wish to increase his country's danger by accepting dangerous weapons on his territory without any control over the decisions that might bring them under attack?"[16]

It also seems fair to say that had de Gaulle been willing to take just a little water in his wine he could have maneuvered eventual acceptance of something reasonably close to the tridirectorate. He might also have had his French-led coalition of states organized on something approaching his own terms. The Europe he left behind is unlikely to resemble the integrated structure against which he thundered and fought—certainly not for a long time—but still less will it be the French-led coalition of states for which he struggled. De Gaulle once compared the effort to build Europe with the time, patience, and dedication required to construct a cathedral. It was not a bad metaphor. The realist in de Gaulle saw as clearly as anyone that Europe's organization would emerge only slowly, painfully, and in stages. But the romantic in him made claims for France for which the realist could entertain no real hope.

A great many sensible and well-intentioned Americans and Britons—presidents and prime ministers among them—tried unsuccessfully to meet de Gaulle partway. The tension all that created, along with a heavy residue of bitterness, all but obscured what de Gaulle did for France. Twice he restored a sense of honor and self-respect, and once perhaps he averted a civil war. He probably understood better than those against whom he tilted that promoting continuities in France, especially workable political institutions, would before very long obscure both his disputes with Anglo-Saxon notables and their causes.

In the case of one such notable—John F. Kennedy—on the morning after his death in Dallas, de Gaulle said to the British ambassador, "At heart he was a European."[17] This was perhaps the highest tribute that de Gaulle could pay to the star-crossed young colleague and rival, who for a time had wanted few things more than good relations with de Gaulle's France.

16. Bundy, *Danger and Survival*, 479.
17. Andre Fontaine, *History of the Cold War from the October Revolution to the Korean War* (London, 1968).

# Part Two
## Kennedy, NATO, and the Grand Design

# 4

# The MLF Debate

*Lawrence S. Kaplan*

∽

There is a striking similarity in the roles played by the European Defense Community (EDC) in the early 1950s and the multilateral force a decade later in NATO's history.[1] Both were experiments in the integration of national forces which, if successful, would have been powerful agents in advancing the cause of a United States of Europe. Both concepts would have served multiple purposes for their American sponsor. The EDC would have facilitated the tapping of German resources for service in NATO and was intended as well to resolve permanently the destructive rivalry between Germany and France. It would also have been the instrument for keeping West Germany in the NATO camp without having to make the Federal Republic a formal member of the alliance. The MLF was designed to serve even more numerous functions—dispatching needed medium-range ballistic missiles (MRBMs) to the SHAPE command, satisfying German ambitions for equality in the alliance, and demonstrating the solidity of U.S. nuclear guarantees.

Both projects failed, in large measure because the elements of deception in their design ultimately outweighed the more noble objectives that they professed. Implicit in both projects was a streak of American idealism, no matter how arrogantly expressed, that underlay plans to reshape Europe. Their function was not just to frustrate the development of European nuclear weaponry systems or to appease German ambitions but to make Europeans worthy partners of Americans. An EDC or MLF would help to break down antiquated and dangerous nationalist passions and pave the way for a united Europe, following a path opened by the French economist Jean Monnet. Such was the thinking of such true believers in the State Department as Robert Bowie, Gerard Smith, and

1. Abbreviations used in the notes:

| | |
|---|---|
| JFKL | John F. Kennedy Library, Boston |
| LBJL | Lyndon B. Johnson Library, Austin |
| LC | Library of Congress |
| NDUL | National Defence University Library |
| NSF | National Security Files (JFKL/LBJL) |
| OSD | Office of the Secretary of Defense |

Henry Owen in the Eisenhower administration. They were joined in the Kennedy administration by George Ball and Walt Rostow. The MLF's survival from 1960 to 1965 was a tribute to the devotion of these officials.

The MLF never won such dedicated adherents in the Defense Department. The most notable exception was Admiral John S. Lee, director of the Pentagon's Policy Planning Staff, whose interest was sustained by the prominence given to surface ships in the projected MLF. Although General Lauris Norstad, Supreme Allied Commander, Europe (SACEUR) was a fellow traveler for part of the way, his was essentially a different route built on a multinational rather than multilateral force. The MLF owed its initial momentum to the support of Secretary of Defense Thomas Gates in 1960. His goal was the extension of a land-based medium-range missile system that would provide a sense of security for Europeans which the obsolescent Jupiter missiles had failed to do. When the Polaris missile turned out to be the only MRBM readily available, he accepted the establishment of a seaborne force using a submarine program already under way. Defense interest, however, did not center on mixing of NATO nationalities but on the urgency of dispatching MRBMs to European allies. Moreover, whether the ships were to be on or below the sea, Defense officials anticipated a considerable European contribution to any multilateral buildup. But lurking behind the variations on a multilateral force was a doubt that only increased with time. It was based on what General Lyman L. Lemnitzer characterized as the incompatibility between a mixed-manned multilateral force, as opposed to multinational units under a single commander, and the actual implementation of this force in combat.[2]

## JFK and the Ottawa Signals, Spring 1961

Notwithstanding the many caveats that accompanied the origins of the MLF, the Kennedy administration had no choice but to pursue lines laid down in the Eisenhower administration. At the NATO ministerial meeting in Paris in December 1960, Secretary of State Christian A. Herter had recommended that the United States commit to NATO an interim MRBM force of five nuclear submarines, armed with eighty Polaris missiles, on condition that the Europeans come up with some system to manage them. The MLF contained too many potential answers to NATO's problems to be discarded as unwise or impractical without further investigation. Even when the inherent weaknesses in the MLF became glaring as efforts were made to translate the concept into concrete proposals, the prospect of exploiting the MLF to resolve intractable differences between the United States and its major allies continued to attract American support.

The MLF's opportunities for growth were limited from the outset. The Ken-

---

2. Lyman L. Lemnitzer notes, n.d., L-1364-71, in Folder 39 (Atlantic Nuclear Force), Lemnitzer Papers, NDUL.

nedy administration had other priorities in foreign relations to grapple with before it could come to grips with the MLF. Obviously in a Eurocentric administration Europe would not be neglected. But the issues would be Berlin in crisis or the conventional force buildup rather than a complicated plan for nuclear sharing with the allies. There was not even a consensus within the government on its contents. Questions immediately arose: was the MLF essentially a method of strengthening NATO defenses with IRBMs until intercontinental ballistic missiles (ICBMs) were in place? Or was it an instrument to create a new relationship with the European powers as Robert Bowie sought? Or was it a means of appeasing Europeans who might otherwise follow the Gaullist model? Or was it a fraudulent effort to make Europeans believe they would have equal status with Americans in the MLF?

No answers emerged from the infighting between State and Defense and between the secretary of defense and SACEUR. Nevertheless, other questions were apparently answered before Kennedy took office. First, the nuclear weapon of choice would be the Polaris, which was available. Second, it would be employed on submarines. Third, the United States and Germany would assume 70 to 80 percent of the burden. The national costs of the MLF would be no more than 1 to 5 percent of any nation's military budget. The United States would provide the first fifty missiles as grant aid, with the allies sharing the remaining costs.[3]

If the European response to this initiative was muted, it may have been because heavy European expenditures would be necessary. The suggestion of linkage between the European contribution of one hundred additional missiles in exchange for the U.S. commitment of its five Polaris submarines was disturbing. It suggested unintentionally that failure to respond might mean that U.S. troops in Europe would be withdrawn along with the offer of five submarines. The Europeans could not help but notice American concern over an unfavorable balance of payments.

Such was the unsettled state of the MLF in January 1961. There were distinct differences between the Defense outlook on sale of missiles under strict U.S. control and Norstad's emphasis on SACEUR's authority over whatever missile system was developed. And both differed from the more grandiose vision of the Europeanists in the State Department who looked ahead to a new entity completely owned and controlled by the participating nations. It would take time for the new administration to sort out the nuances.

The MLF coalition faced a combination of divided counsels, each representing a separate constituency. The Pentagon sensed a growing conflict between the push for conventional forces and the continued reliance on nuclear weapons, as implied in the MLF; and within the Pentagon the Joint Chiefs of Staff separated from the secretary of defense on this subject. Both sides agreed to oppose an independent MLF complete with control over nuclear warheads, and both worried over nuclear proliferation through development of national nuclear forces.

---

3. Robert E. Osgood, *The Case for the MLF: A Critical Evaluation* (Washington, D.C., 1964), 7.

In Brussels, General Norstad doggedly pursued his own agenda. He would accept the pledge of the five submarines but insisted that they could not take the place of mobile land-based missiles. Norstad felt that the president was apparently unaware of many of the factors bearing on the role of IRBMs as replacements for fighter planes and light and medium bombers. It was this aspect of the MLF that Norstad reiterated at every opportunity, and it fitted (absent the air force) more closely the Office of the Secretary of Defense views on the end product of nuclear sharing than did the ideological image of the State Department enthusiasts. Norstad's projection of a multinational force involved no erosion of presidential authority over the use of nuclear warheads.[4]

Because of these distinct points of view emanating from different parts of the Kennedy administration, the MLF adherents could make little headway. The most that they could extract from the president was a statement in favor of nuclear cooperation in Ottawa on 17 May 1961. Speaking to the Canadian Parliament, the president formally committed to the NATO command five Polaris submarines in the spirit of the Herter proposal. This was no longer a controversial issue; all factions in the MLF debate had assumed that this commitment would be the first step. But Kennedy went on to say, "Beyond this, we look to the possibility of eventually establishing a NATO sea-borne force, which would be truly multi-lateral in ownership and control, if this should be desired and found feasible by our Allies, once NATO's nuclear goals have been achieved."[5]

Although the last clause might have put a damper on the expectations of the MLF enthusiasts, the general tone of the president's message renewed their energy. His statement was far stronger than his earlier cautious and vague references in February, when he announced the appointment of Dean Acheson to head an advisory group on NATO's future.[6] Despite the blocks erected in the Pentagon and at SHAPE, the MLF supporters could take pride in the initial results of their efforts. Their center was in the Policy Planning Staff, chaired by Walt Rostow, and where Robert Bowie, former chairman and now consultant, and Henry Owen could develop the partnership with Europe.[7]

Nevertheless, there was a distance between the concept of Atlantic partnership and the concept of European unity, two antithetical ideas that could coexist comfortably as long as no effort was made to give them real substance. Despite his good intentions, Kennedy resisted any action that would weaken American control over nuclear weapons. Exhilarating as the Ottawa statement was to believers in the MLF, there were no widespread reactions abroad or activity within the Defense Department to justify their optimism.

4. Robert S. Jordan, "Norstad: Can the SACEUR Be Both European and American?" in *Generals in International Politics,* ed. Jordan (Lexington, 1987), 86–91.

5. Address before the Canadian Parliament in Ottawa, 17 May 1961, *Public Papers of the Presidents: John F. Kennedy, 1961* (Washington, D.C., 1962), 385.

6. The president's news conference of 8 February 1961, *ibid.,* 67. In *The Cybernetic Theory of Decision: New Dimensions of Political Analysis* (Princeton, 1974), John D. Steinbruner interprets Kennedy's accompanying comments to be similar to those in the Bowie report (222).

7. Steinbruner, *Cybernetic Theory,* 223.

The only genuine appreciation of the president's consideration of a multilaterally owned and controlled NATO naval or military force came from Germany. German endorsement, however, was a mixed blessing. On the one hand, that nation's involvement would be a vital element in deflating the German appetite for a national nuclear capability. The Berlin Crisis in the summer of 1961 had given rise to a host of German doubts about the direction of American policy, and the promise of a new multilateral force was one way of alleviating them. On the other hand, there was concern among the allies that the Germans might press too hard for immediate action on the MRBMs. The possibility of nuclear weapons winding up in German hands was unsettling to Britain as well as to the smaller members of the alliance. If Germans were the only Europeans embracing the MLF, attention would focus not on a new NATO nuclear entity but on potential German control of that entity.

## MLF at Athens, May 1962

But Germany was not the focus of the American debate on missiles for Europe. The MLF was a distant prospect because of the implied caveat in Kennedy's Ottawa speech that non-nuclear, or conventional, forces, had to be given priority over the MRBMs for Europe. This was not an aside, as was made evident at the North Atlantic Council meeting in Athens in May 1962.

By furnishing the allies with adequate information on the problems of organization and control of nuclear warfare, the United States would win their support of U.S. military policies and programs for NATO. The administration intended to use the Athens meeting to educate the allies to the facts of nuclear life.

Only a small part of the Athens meeting was taken up by MLF affairs, and this was done with apparent reluctance on the part of the NATO partners. McNamara repeated the earlier statements that the United States was prepared to enter into detailed discussion of an MRBM force if this was what the allies wanted. But his words of support were belied by the "many complicated questions to be dealt with," including the lack of a military necessity and the burden of heavy costs which the United States had no intention of bearing alone.[8]

The allies initially avoided reacting to McNamara's central commentaries on independent nuclear forces and on conventional forces. But they did react to his statements on the MLF, and with no more enthusiasm than the secretary himself had shown. There was nothing new in McNamara's approach to the MLF or in the response of the allies. The MRBM issue was marginal to all parties at the May meeting. The central themes remained McNamara's elevation of conventional weaponry and his concurrent deprecation of nuclear forces, particularly

8. Secretary of Defense statement at ministerial meeting of the North Atlantic Council at Athens on 5 May 1962, sanitized, in OSD Historical Office files, the Pentagon, Washington, D.C.

national nuclear forces. These themes did not receive full attention until they were restated publicly in his Ann Arbor address a month later.

The MLF supporters in the State Department felt let down by the obvious indifference to European integration displayed by the administration at Athens. No gains were visible. And the attention given to withholding control of weapons from the allies would lead inevitably to their loss of interest. The outcome, then, could be precisely what McNamara had warned against at the North Atlantic Council session: namely, development of national nuclear capabilities along the lines set by France.

General Norstad was also displeased by the course of events, although for different reasons. The prescription that the United States would support MRBMs for NATO only if they were part of a multilaterally owned, financed, and manned sea-based force ruled out his plans for land-based missiles. But Norstad felt that the U.S. position even diminished the military importance of an MRBM, and this attitude could destroy the centerpiece of his and the Joint Chiefs' plans for NATO.

Norstad's most influential opponent was in the Pentagon, not in the State Department. It was McNamara, after all, who believed that preference for nationally manned missiles would set a dangerous precedent for future allied nuclear efforts and in particular would create divisive strains through German participation in the Norstad program. Moreover, Norstad's stance represented a veiled criticism of conventional forces and was a deviation from the administration's recommendations to the allies.[9]

As a result of dissension in Washington and its reverberations across the Atlantic, the administration authorized Thomas K. Finletter, the U.S. ambassador to NATO, to deliver a major speech in June 1962 which cast doubts on any military requirement for a multilateral MRBM and directed attention to its political and military value. Finletter rejected the Norstad proposal for land-based missiles but opened the way for the naval version. Initial reactions showed that allied confusion over U.S. intentions had not ended. According to Finletter, the American deferral of requirements for development of an MRBM for assignment to NATO led Germans to feel that this action removed the possibility of an MLF.[10]

Nevertheless, the very uncertainty surrounding the American attitude toward the MLF gave the MLF enthusiasts an incentive to intensify their evangelizing. Bowie, Owen, and their colleague in the Pentagon Admiral John Lee, director of the Policy Planning Staff, circulated among all the constituencies telling each what it wanted to hear. The Joint Chiefs of Staff would be told that the NATO MRBM had military usefulness; State would be assured that national nuclear

9. Rusk and McNamara memorandum for the president, "Your Interview with General Norstad," 14 July 1962, Folder 104B, Box 37, in Maxwell Taylor Papers, NDUL.

10. Legere memorandum for record, "Meeting with the President on MRBM Instructions to Ambassador Finletter," 13 June 1962, in National Security Archive, Box 35, LBJL; Colonel Burris memorandum to the Vice President, 20 June 1962, Vice President Security File, *ibid.*

capabilities would be thwarted; and even McNamara, in the midst of a cost analysis study, was to be satisfied by pointing to Europe's shouldering a large share of the expenses. The navy's sympathies were influenced by the role it would play in a seaborne force. Guided by Lee, a study was arranged in the summer of 1962 under Rear Admiral Frederick H. Michaelis, supported by Deputy Chief of Naval Operations Admiral Claude N. Ricketts, both surface fleet officers, which would assure the centrality of a surface fleet in the MLF program.[11]

By the end of the summer of 1962, however, there seemed to be no obstacle in the way of the MLF's success. Gerard Smith, now working as a consultant to the State Department, traveled over Europe in August, briefing allies on the virtues of the MLF, as defined in the Michaelis study. Using the language of the president's Ottawa speech and Rusk's affirmation of it in Athens, the Smith team of State and Defense representatives won over both departments to the concept of a multilateral seaborne MRBM force. Despite repeated professions of American unwillingness to appear to impose the MLF on Europeans, the Smith group was not unwilling to take the initiative.[12]

They achieved the legitimization of National Security Action Memorandum (NSAM) 147, approved by the president on 18 April 1962, which stated American willingness to join its allies in developing a modest-sized MLF. The plan, originating in the Defense Department and edited by the Smith team, would create a NATO MRBM agency headed by a civilian director, of ministerial level, subordinate to the North Atlantic Council. The commander of the MRBM force would serve under the agency. The missiles of choice would be the Polaris A-3 with improved guidance. The assumption was that they would be available before a competitive Missile X by about two years, and they would be mounted on merchant ships. The report provided details that had been lacking in the past.[13]

A constituency still favored land-based missiles, although its numbers had diminished. As long as Norstad remained SACEUR, he continued to argue the case. To the very end of his career in NATO Norstad pressed for modernization of airborne missile forces as prescribed in MC 26/4. The seaborne force, along with the MLF itself, were diversions from the main goals. But this was Norstad's last hurrah. Had the Cuban missile crisis not broken out in October, his designated successor, General Lemnitzer, would have been SACEUR throughout the fall of 1962. Instead, Lemnitzer did not assume command until January 1963, leaving both men in Paris, uncertain about their respective roles.

A more powerful brake on the momentum developed by the supporters of the MLF was the uneasiness of both the secretary of state and the secretary of defense. McNamara in particular was disturbed about the message Smith and Lee were delivering to Europeans. He wanted assurance that the allies were fully

---

11. Steinbruner, *Cybernetic Theory*, 229–31.

12. *Ibid.*, 232–33.

13. State telegram to American Embassy, Paris, TOPOL 344, 15 September 1962, in NSF/Box 216, JFKL; Steinbruner, *Cybernetic Theory*, 216.

aware of conditions required by the United States before a new entity came into being: namely, that they would have to bear a large share of the costs of the MLF and that no action would be taken until conventional forces were sufficiently increased. He hoped that the MLF could be kept off the agenda of the forthcoming North Atlantic Council meeting.[14]

## Impact of Nassau, December 1962

Any objections McNamara may have had about the rapid evolution of the MLF were silenced for the moment by the events at the Kennedy-Macmillan meeting in Nassau, where the Skybolt controversy held center stage. After Nassau there was no way of avoiding a central role for the MLF. It became a major focus of NATO diplomacy in a fashion that none of the principals, Americans or Europeans, had anticipated. To compensate Britain for the loss of the Skybolt missile, the United States promised to substitute Polaris, with the understanding that it would become part of NATO's multilateral force. The MLF was now an imperative. The Nassau agreement of 21 December specifically identified a "NATO nuclear force" targeted in accordance with NATO plans. In paragraph six of the agreement both U.S. Strategic Forces and the U.K. Bomber Command, as well as tactical nuclear forces in Europe, would be part of this new entity.[15]

This was a solution that the British welcomed after the Nassau conference. But there was potential confusion involving the concepts of "multinational" and "multilateral." Paragraph seven of the agreement specifically noted that the purpose behind the provision of Polaris missiles to the United Kingdom was "the development of a multilateral NATO nuclear force in the closest consultation with other NATO allies." But this was not the message conveyed in paragraph six. The "immediate start" mentioned in that paragraph was essentially a multinational action, closer in spirit to General Norstad's conception of a NATO MRBM force than to the multilateral mixed-manned force advocated by the State Department. NATO would receive allocations from the U.S. Strategic Forces and from the U.K. Bomber Command as well as from tactical nuclear forces already in Europe. Europeans might see this as a continuation of a special relationship that would coexist with a lower-level MLF.

The Nassau Agreement exposed the ambivalence of the U.S. position on the MLF. The president would not oppose a purely European MLF in the future, but he did not wish to appear to initiate a "made in U.S." solution. This posture did not imply hostility. Paragraph six became a fallback in the event the more ambitious multilateral approach faltered. But given the impetus of the Nassau

14. Steinbruner, *Cybernetic Theory*, 233–34.
15. "Text of Nassau Agreement—United States Offer of POLARIS Missiles to the UK . . . ," 21 December 1962, in *American Foreign Policy: Current Documents, 1962* (Washington, D.C., 1966), 636.

Agreement, contradictions notwithstanding, a more benevolent image of the MLF prevailed in White House if not in Pentagon circles.

There were, however, some puzzling ambiguities in the position on the MLF in 1963, particularly in the attitude of Secretary McNamara. Given his emphasis on the importance of conventional forces and his equal emphasis on the need for centralized control over nuclear weaponry, his new initiatives in promoting MRBMs in Europe require explanation. Part of the explanation may lie in his responsiveness to pressures by the Joint Chiefs of Staff and SACEUR for MRBMs. John Steinbruner found an answer in the primacy McNamara gave to budget considerations over the risks to centralized control in extending Polaris to Britain or France. The costs of Skybolt were the first reason for its cancellation. Moreover, the need to repair relations with Britain and to bolster European integration through the MLF were his pragmatic responses to specific problems stemming from the cancellation of Skybolt.[16] But McNamara's support of the MLF was never more than a tactical move, unlike his concerns over conventional forces. His actions in 1963 did not represent a conversion to the ideologists' conception of Monnet's Europe.

Because of the Skybolt controversy, the momentum for action in the winter of 1963 remained with the advocates of the MLF. Plans that had been little more than vague concepts earlier were given substance by an interdepartmental steering group, which proposed assigning such national forces to the MLF as twenty B-47s, their equivalents in British V-bombers, and the Polaris missiles stationed in the Mediterranean. The commander of the projected force would report to SACEUR, and its command headquarters would be manned by representatives of each NATO nation. The United States, however, at least initially, would maintain custody of the warheads and exercise a veto over their use. The cost of the fleet and its weapons would be shared by participating nations. Individual ships of the twenty-five assigned to the MLF would be commanded by officers of different nationalities, allocated roughly according to the nation's share of the financial burden. It was estimated that the MLF would cost from 1 to 5 percent of the participating nation's military budget.[17]

To prove the seriousness with which the United States now looked at the MLF, the administration was prepared to seek approval from the North Atlantic Council for bilateral discussions within the foregoing framework. Moreover, it would appoint a person of the rank of ambassador or under secretary to head the negotiating team. Apparently, the only controversy within the administration was over the placement of warheads on surface vessels or submarines. Political opposition to sharing Polaris submarines as well as anticipation of greater costs of a submarine force helped to resolve this controversy in favor of a surface fleet.[18]

16. Steinbruner, *Cybernetic Theory*, 245.
17. Osgood, *The Case for the MLF*, 6–7.
18. Admiral Rickover was the leading opponent of placing Polaris submarines into an MLF. "Summary Record of the NSC Executive Committee Meeting No. 41," 12 February 1963, in NSF/ Executive Committee Meetings, JFKL.

Supporters of the MLF in the State Department took full advantage of this decision. Prospects for action in Congress to loosen its control over nuclear warheads, which appeared to be "a long way off" in November, were considerably brighter in January 1963. Their hopes were further enhanced by the general reaction to President de Gaulle's press conference on 14 January at which he announced France's veto of British entry into the EEC, its rejection of the U.S. offer of Polaris missiles, and its refusal to participate in a NATO nuclear force.[19] De Gaulle's actions, though hardly unexpected, added a sense of urgency to the MLF planners, especially because of the impact they would have on Franco-German relations.

## The Merchant Team, Spring 1963

These concurrent activities in January 1963 led to the appointment of a State-Defense negotiating team under the direction of Livingston Merchant, a close associate of Robert Bowie. The senior Defense member, Rear Admiral Lee, was a firm ally of State. On 21 February the president instructed the Merchant team to investigate "as a matter of urgency the possibility of an international agreement."[20] It was expected that the mission would be completed by July 1963.

Despite the president's endorsement, there were reservations in the White House about just how enthusiastically the Merchant team should go about its work. Kennedy needed assurance that he had alternatives in the event the MLF either failed to materialize or produced embarrassing results. Foy Kohler, ambassador to the Soviet Union, warned that the Soviets were in "deadly earnestness" in their distress over the possibility of eventual German control of nuclear delivery systems that could reach the USSR. The MLF touched a sensitive Soviet nerve, according to Kohler, even though the MLF itself would dilute German involvement.[21]

Just what Merchant would present to the Europeans had to be resolved before his team left for Europe. He urged the president to leave open the question of control of the multilateral force, "including the possibility of no US veto over the firing of the missiles." The question of submarine versus surface vessels was easier to manage. Kennedy not only had the benefit of Admiral Hyman Ricko-

19. James T. Ramey, AEC Commissioner, memorandum to Jeffrey Kitchen, Deputy Assistant Secretary of State for Political Military Affairs, "Possible Basis for Amendment to Atomic Energy Act concerning Multilateral NATO Nuclear Arrangements," 22 January 1963, in NSF/Box 217, JFKL; State Circular telegram 217, 16 November 1963, in NSF/Box 218, JFKL; *American Foreign Policy: Current Documents, 1963* (Washington, D.C., 1967), 443–45.

20. JFK memorandum for members of the MLF Negotiating Team, 21 February 1963, in NSF/Box 217, JFKL.

21. Kohler memorandum for Ambassador Bruce, "Soviet Reactions to Multilateral Forces," 8 February 1963, in Folder JFK-LBJ Trips and Missions—Test Ban Treaty Background, in Box 560, W. Averell Harriman Papers, LC.

ver's strong views against use of Polaris submarines, but he also realized that there could be trouble with the Congress should that route be followed. Secretary of Defense McNamara favored a surface fleet in light of both cost and survivability factors.[22] Merchant could begin his tour with backing from the NSC Executive Committee and with an understanding that a surface fleet was on the agenda but no decision had been made.

Merchant's travels to Rome, Bonn, Brussels, and London appeared to have been a success, according to Thomas Finletter, the U.S. permanent representative on the North Atlantic Council. He felt that the British and Germans were close to agreement on most aspects of the MLF, while the Italians were favorably disposed, even though there was uncertainty about the survival of the present government. If the Belgians came along, the Dutch, Greeks, and Turks would follow.[23]

This positive account of the Merchant mission, however, found little resonance in the European press. The reaction to his first visit ranged from open antagonism in France, to mounting skepticism in Germany and Britain, to a qualified endorsement in Italy and Scandinavia. The U.S. approach to an MLF thus far had failed to impress most Europeans on its intrinsic merits. While there was a general willingness to continue the search for solutions, too many Europeans were convinced that the end game was to punish de Gaulle for his *force de frappe* by offering the allies the illusion of possessing their own strike force.[24]

These warnings from abroad did not faze the Merchant team. Its mission was to win over European governments as quickly as possible. And despite some disappointment over Macmillan's lack of knowledge about the MLF, Merchant was confident of ultimate success. His hopes rested primarily with the Germans. He was gratified to learn that they were willing to spend hundreds of millions annually, at least in principle, despite U.S. retention of the veto over use of the warheads. "This government is prepared to bear a share," Merchant claimed, "of the costs of the force equal to that borne by the US, on the understanding that no state participating in the force shall bear more than forty percent of the costs."[25]

The ambassador noted that in supporting the MLF German leaders recognized that "the use of weapons should be controlled according to the principle of unanimity among the participating states." At the same time they hoped that "the voting formula would be 'reviewable'" after the allies had gained sufficient experience in operating the force. Although Merchant did not commit himself on this issue, he did not rule out that majority voting might be accepted in the future. After the MLF was in effect, the allies would come to understand the facts of nuclear life. His colleague Robert Bowie later in that year made it clear

22. "Summary Record of NSC Executive Committee Meeting, No. 41," 12 February 1963.

23. Finletter telegram to Rusk, POLTO 1163, 16 March 1963, in NSF/Box 218, JFKL.

24. Briefing Item—USIA, "Initial West European Assessment of Multilateral Force Proposals," 7 March 1963, in NSF/Box 217, JFKL.

25. Merchant telegram to Secretary of State, No. 2316, 7 March 1963, in NSF/Box 217, JFKL.

that he would welcome a genuine second pillar in a nuclear force freed from American control. But for the immediate future the value of the MLF lay not in an alternative to the British or French nuclear forces but, as Robert Osgood projected, in its limited role "fostering a constructive place for Germany in Europe."[26]

By directing their attention to the German problem, MLF propagandists could dispel doubts about the success of their efforts. West Germany, it seemed, had accepted the principle of a viable multilateral force. They enjoyed the backing of U.S. Navy leaders. Admiral Claude Ricketts, under instruction from Secretary McNamara, was dispatched to Bonn to convince the German government of the superiority of surface missile warships over the submarine.[27] It was a mission that a senior naval officer could carry out with zeal.

The tone as well as the substance of Adenauer's letter to Kennedy contained almost everything Americans would want from a European partner. It seemed that the forthcoming meeting of the North Atlantic Council in Ottawa would be the occasion to crown the Merchant and Ricketts missions with NATO's blessings on the MLF. Whatever reluctance the president may have expressed earlier, Adenauer's response moved him to push the British into the MLF club. The president urged the prime minister to join Germany in making a definite commitment to participate. Its decision would demonstrate to the Germans that theirs was a responsible choice and put an end to the possibility of Franco-German cooperation in nuclear weapons systems in a narrow Gaullist spirit.[28] It was obvious that in the spring of 1963 the president was making a major effort to keep alive the flame ignited by Adenauer. Everything should have been in place for Under Secretary Ball to initiate congressional consultations with hopes for a final agreement in September.

### Slowing the Pace

But there was to be no final agreement. The Ottawa meeting produced a cautious communiqué, similar to those in the past when vague endorsements were made in favor of some kind of MLF. The council did approve assignment of V-bombers and Polaris submarines to SACEUR and created a deputy SACEUR

26. *Ibid.;* Robert R. Bowie, "Tensions Within the Alliance," *Foreign Affairs,* XLII (October 1963), 49–69; Osgood, *The Case for the MLF,* 53.

27. Merchant (Bonn) telegram to Secretary of State, No. 2316, 7 March 1963, in NSF/Box 217, JFKL; Steinbruner, *Cybernetic Theory,* 276. The telegram contains details of Germany's MLF intentions. Ten days before, the president sent William R. Tyler, assistant secretary of state for European affairs, to Bonn with instructions regarding German participation in a multilateral force. See JFK memorandum for William R. Tyler, 29 March 1963, in NSF/Box 217, JFKL.

28. Steinbruner, *Cybernetic Theory,* 277; Rusk memorandum to JFK, "Proposed Reply to Prime Minister," 27 May 1963, in NSF/Box 174, JFKL; "Suggested Letter to Prime Minister Macmillan," 6 May 1963, *ibid.*

for nuclear issues, but these steps were in harmony with a British-inspired multi-national force, not an MLF.[29]

What happened to the momentum that had been moving so fast in the spring of 1963? A variety of factors dampened the enthusiasm. Recognition of the costs of the enterprise chilled the atmosphere. France's negativism remained. But the principal problem was that Britain had not advanced beyond the multinational idea expressed at Nassau. British refusal to make a commitment to an MLF would make the project an American-German affair, which would be as undesirable to the Germans as it would be to the Americans. So instead of the Ottawa meeting paving the way for an early agreement, it became an occasion for pause. The president's advisers, including the MLF teams, agreed to pull back slightly and to work more cautiously toward a draft treaty. Deadlines were no longer valid.

Not an inconsiderable factor in slowing the momentum was the attitude of the Joint Chiefs of Staff, who continued to be decidedly unenthusiastic. At a meeting on 1 May 1963 the Joint Chiefs addressed directly the military advisability of the MLF and were unable to say that it was either militarily advisable or inadvisable. The prudent response then was to "proceed with arrangements involving the nuclear capability of NATO-committed national forces rather than the irrevocable commitment of the United States, at this time, to a multilaterally owned and manned sea-based surface MRBM force which, in itself, is but one of several long-range options available to the United States and NATO." After discussion with Secretary McNamara, the Joint Chiefs recognized the "political judgement that there is no alternative to the MLF." They then agreed on its military feasibility as long as the NATO partners fully supported it. This endorsement seemed no less halfhearted than their previous stand.[30]

The president's closest advisers were clearly relieved over the interruption in MLF negotiations. Bundy, whose interest in the MLF was never strong, warned Kennedy against expending excessive capital on the program. Further activity would antagonize the French, he felt, arouse the Soviets, and expose friendly governments to charges of subservience to U.S. pressure. On the eve of the president's visit to Germany, Bundy noted how fast and how far the MLF project had proceeded in the United States and blamed himself for not having reined in the "passionate MLF staffers." "They had pressed the case more sharply and against a tighter schedule," Bundy told the president, "than either you or the Secretary would have chosen. I myself have not watched them as closely as I should have, and more than once I have let them persuade me to support them where I might well have been more skeptical."[31]

29. Meeting of the North Atlantic Council, 22–24 May 1963, *Texts of Final Communiques, 1949–1974* (Brussels, n.d.), 150–52.

30. W.Y.S. memorandum for General Taylor, SPCOL-S-068-87, 1 June 1963, in MLF folder, Box 39, Taylor Papers, NDUL.

31. Bundy memorandum to the President, "The MLF and the European Tour," 15 June 1963, in NSF/Box 214, LBJL.

The experience at Ottawa and the words of his advisers had revived Kennedy's long-standing skepticism over the MLF even before he embarked on his European tour. On that visit he discovered that without American prodding there would be little response from the Europeans. Realizing this problem, the president was careful in his inspiring address at the Paulskirche in Frankfurt to speak out on behalf of an Atlantic partnership and of a "new Atlantic force" but also to emphasize that it would not be in the American or European interest "to try to dominate the European councils of decision." He returned home leaving the Germans and British with his reaffirmation of the MLF concept but with no wish to do more than continue discussions without deadlines and "without prejudice to the question of British participation in such a force."[32]

Yet the MLF was still alive. Even Bundy had admitted that after Nassau the United States had no choice about taking the initiative on the MLF whether or not there was real support for it in Europe. A hasty reversal of American support would be as undesirable as too eager an embrace. Since the MLF was still open to debate, the president suggested that an effort be made to begin the mixed-manning process and accepted a plan to use a ship from the Sixth Fleet as a test case. It would also be an earnest of the American commitment to the MLF. In accepting the demonstration, Defense attached a caveat to the effect that it would not consider the demonstration to be a signal to press for progress in MLF negotiations.[33]

Despite McNamara's warnings, it was understandable that Merchant's group and its followers in the State Department would be heartened by a mixed-manned experiment. Simply putting a concept into action was itself encouraging. The plan was to have one or two ships, such as a guided missile destroyer with its sophisticated weapons systems, to enable MLF participants to become proficient in the maintenance and operation of complex missiles, fire control, and electronic systems. The ship would operate as part either of the U.S. Sixth Fleet in the Mediterranean or of the Second Fleet in the Atlantic and participate in U.S. and NATO exercises as appropriate.[34]

Kennedy seemed intrigued with the idea. It found a willing constituency not only among MLF enthusiasts but also in the U.S. Navy, which would play a central role in the demonstration. From the administration's perspective, the plan would demonstrate U.S. seriousness of purpose at little cost or commitment. If the MLF failed, the onus for failure would not fall on the United States.

The experiment succeeded, although not until after Kennedy's death. But what did success mean? The MLF collapsed in the Johnson administration, re-

32. Address in the Assembly Hall at the Paulskirche in Frankfurt, 25 June 1963, *Public Papers of the Presidents; John F. Kennedy, 1963* (Washington, D.C., 1964), 517–18; New York *Times,* 1 July 1963.
33. Bundy memorandum to the President, "The MLF and the European Tour," 15 June 1963; Bundy memorandum for Secretary of Defense, 13 July 1963, in NSF/NASM 253, JFKL.
34. Steinbruner, *Cybernetic Theory,* 283–84.

moved from sight as irrelevant or as an embarrassment in late 1964 or sometime in 1965. Even the date of its passing is not clear.

The shortcomings of the MLF were always far more visible than the strengths. Lip service was offered but not much more. In the United States the military, including important segments of the navy, had continuing doubts over the viability of such a force. And while the major figures of the administration—from the president to the secretary of defense—spoke positively about the MLF from time to time, their position never went beyond acceptance of the principle that if the allies were willing to pay for it, the United States would participate. Obviously their expectations were low. And if the MLF had actually come into being, it is doubtful that the administration would have been pleased with its implementation. The new entity might inhibit proliferation of nuclear weapons in the alliance, but it would continue to emphasize the primacy of nuclear weaponry at a time when McNamara was working to direct the allies' attention to conventional rather than to nuclear forces. Aside from its devotees, there were few mourners over the fate of the MLF.

# 5

# Kennedy and the Test Ban: Presidential Leadership and Arms Control

*Bernard J. Firestone*

∾

On 5 August 1963, representatives of the United Kingdom, United States, and the Soviet Union assembled in Moscow to sign the Treaty Banning Nuclear Weapons Tests in the Atmosphere, in Outer Space, and Under Water, also known as the Partial Test-Ban Treaty (PTBT) or Test-Ban Treaty. The agreement, climaxing close to five years of tortuous, multilateral negotiations, stimulated widespread anticipation that the Cold War was about to enter a new, more benign phase. Reflecting that expectation, the highly respected *Bulletin of Atomic Scientists* set back its "death watch"—an imaginary clock signaling the approach of nuclear disaster—from 11:52 to 11:48. While others, opposed to or more skeptical about these developments, warned of the dangers inherent in peace "euphoria," elements of the American public gained the impression that the East-West relationship was moving in a new and possibly more favorable direction.[1]

Thirty-five years later, the Test-Ban Treaty can be placed in more sober perspective. The accord ended the deadly production of radioactive fallout that atmospheric testing inevitably produced, but it did little to abate either the quantitative or qualitative pace of the superpowers' accumulation of nuclear weapons. Nor did it arrest the proliferation of nuclear weapons to the so-called nth countries, as President John F. Kennedy had hoped. To be sure, more than one hundred governments have signed the Test-Ban Treaty since 1963, but the list of those who have not is potent enough that the world is still a dangerous place. Finally, the expectation that the treaty would usher in a new era in political relations between the United States and the Soviet Union soon gave way to more routine Cold War pessimism, as the Vietnam conflict escalated into a major war, the arms race accelerated, and an uninterrupted series of crises continued to roil

---

1. *Newsweek,* 7 October 1963, p. 29; see the testimony of General Maxwell D. Taylor, chairman, U.S. Joint Chiefs of Staff, U.S. Congress, Senate Committee on Foreign Relations, *Hearings: Nuclear Test Ban Treaty,* 88th Cong., 1st sess., 1963, pp. 275–76.

the East-West conflict. It took another twenty-five years and a dramatic transformation in Moscow finally to end the Cold War.

What, then, was the significance of the Test-Ban Treaty? I contend that the accord provided the American public with its first opportunity to face the fundamental ambivalence in Washington's Cold War stance—an ambivalence born in the exigencies of nuclear politics and sustained through the presidencies of Kennedy's two postwar predecessors, but, until Kennedy, not yet confronted in so direct and systematic a fashion. By the time Kennedy assumed the presidency, the basic contours of the American approach to the Soviet Union had been well developed, if not well defined. The doctrine of containment implied a balance between restraining communism and forestalling nuclear war, and both Harry Truman and Dwight Eisenhower had shown themselves to be respectful of the constraints that the threat of nuclear war placed on America's resistance to Soviet expansionism.[2] By pressing for a test ban, a policy initiated by his immediate predecessor, Kennedy did not strike out in new policy directions as much as he challenged the various actors in the political system—from the executive branch to Congress to the public—to locate a formal balance between anticommunism and avoidance of nuclear war. For Kennedy, achieving that balance meant not only exercising restraint in America's effort to curb communism but in developing policies that deliberately sought to integrate these core aspects of the national interest into a single foreign policy program.

If seeking a balance between anticommunism and avoidance of nuclear war was the inevitable presidential position during the Cold War, the exercise of presidential power was indispensable for its implementation. No issue better illustrates the ambivalent nature of America's Cold War interest and the requirements of presidential leadership than arms control. Theory concerning arms control, as it developed during the early 1960s, assumed that the superpowers, no matter how intense their political differences, shared a mutual interest in limiting the outbreak and extent of nuclear war and that areas of mutual interest could be identified and codified in agreements or integrated into each side's strategic policy. Whereas disarmament assumed that war is prevented by "the eradication of military establishments, military tradition and military thinking," arms control rested on the belief that mutual deterrence formed the bedrock of a stable relationship between the superpowers.[3]

A multiplicity of government agencies were involved in the formulation of arms control policy, each with its own sphere of expertise and assumptions about international politics. The military, in particular, typically viewed arms

2. In a 1963 press conference, Kennedy said about Truman and Eisenhower: "The reason the action wasn't taken was because they felt strongly that if they did take action it would bring on another war." See *Public Papers of the President of the United States: John F. Kennedy, 1963* (Washington, D.C., 1964), 152.

3. The most influential statement of arms control theory was a product of the 1960 Harvard-M.I.T. Arms Control Seminar, Thomas C. Schelling and Morton H. Halperin, *Strategy and Arms Control* (New York, 1961), 143.

control with suspicion, seeing it as isolated from and even antithetical to the development of a strong strategic posture. The fissile tendencies of the policymaking system placed a premium on presidential leadership as the only way to reconcile divergent policy positions, bargain to win over the skeptical, and act independently to circumvent the recalcitrant. As President Kennedy's national security adviser McGeorge Bundy wrote shortly after the president's death:

> Unless the President uses these powers with energy, arms control agreements are improbable. The momentum of the arms race . . . is enormous. Military men in all countries find it hard to approve any arms control proposal which is not either safely improbable or clearly unbalanced in their favor. In the United States only a strong Commander-in-Chief with a strong Secretary of Defense is in a position to press steadily for recognition that the arms race itself is now a threat to national security. Only the President can ensure that good proposals are kept alive even after a first rejection, and that new possibilities are constantly considered—so that there may always be as many proposals as possible on the table waiting for the moment of Soviet readiness. [4]

Politically, arms control was distinguished by the interest it mobilized outside the executive branch, a rare occurrence in the realm of foreign policy. The test ban had emerged as a partisan issue during the 1956 and 1960 presidential campaigns and had attracted the regular interest of important congressional committees and individual members of Congress. The test-ban issue went to the heart of the ambivalence in the American approach to the Soviet Union, for while it promised to lessen the chances of nuclear war it also raised dark anxieties about the dangers of negotiating with communists. And while public opinion, in general, seemed to permit policymakers some latitude within the poles of anticommunism, on the one hand, and avoidance of nuclear war, on the other, among the informed public sharp differences existed regarding the priority that should be attached to one or the other of these objectives. Ultimately, then, it was the president who had to calibrate what could or could not be sold to the American people as consistent with a national interest that demanded a balance between anticommunism and avoidance of nuclear war. And in Kennedy's time, that meant challenging a strong and prevailing anticommunism in Congress and among substantial elements of the population.

Kennedy's success in promoting and winning approval for the Partial Test-Ban Treaty represented, therefore, no decisive departure in either the political or strategic dynamics of the Cold War. It did, however, serve as a precedent for presidential leadership in defining the fundamental ambivalence in American

4. McGeorge Bundy, "The Presidency and the Peace," *Foreign Affairs,* XLII (April 1964), 362–63.

policy toward the Soviet Union. As Kennedy said in a speech at the University of Maine in the fall of 1963: "There is nothing inconsistent with signing an atmospheric nuclear test ban, on the one hand, and testing underground, on the other; about being willing to sell the Soviets our surplus wheat while refusing to sell strategic items; or about exploring the possibilities of disarmament while maintaining a stockpile of arms."[5] His successors, to one degree or another, would repeat the lessons gained from the test-ban debate as they too sought to steer a path through the fundamental poles of the national interest.

## The Setting

The search for a test ban originated in the Eisenhower administration. Eisenhower, according to Herbert York, who under Kennedy was a member of the General Advisory Committee of the Arms Control and Disarmament Agency, "just like President Kennedy, was very much concerned about where the world was heading and that something ought to be done." Eisenhower's concern, however, was not immediately expressed in the form of support for a test ban. Convinced that the Soviets could not be trusted to observe a ban and that the United States would have to test nuclear weapons to maintain the strength of its strategic deterrent, Eisenhower long resisted both international and domestic pressure to separate the issue of a test ban from the larger issue of disarmament.[6] But in the late spring of 1957, his secretary of state, John Foster Dulles, was signaling a shift to a pro-ban stance, and Eisenhower began to explore the possibilities of negotiating a test-ban treaty. In April 1958, he proposed to the Soviets the convening of a Conference of Experts to examine the technical feasibilities of policing a test ban, and in October 1958, after the Conference of Experts reported favorably on the technical issues, test-ban talks involving the United States, the Soviet Union, and Great Britain opened in Geneva.

The talks initiated under Eisenhower did not produce a test ban during his presidency; in fact, when Kennedy assumed the presidency, negotiations were in a state of complete deadlock. But developments under Eisenhower were important to Kennedy's subsequent efforts in several ways. First, despite Eisenhower's initial uncertainties, the United States and the Soviet Union, by the late 1950s, had effectively separated the issue of disarmament from that of a test ban so that progress on a test ban was not necessarily connected to the far more elusive issue of disarmament. Second, negotiations during the Eisenhower presidency served to highlight the issues dividing East and West, particularly the question of inspections. The Soviets, while insisting that inspection was unnecessary, offered

5. *Public Papers of . . . Kennedy, 1963,* p. 796.

6. Herbert York, recorded interview by Steven Rivkin, 16 June 1964, p. 18, in John F. Kennedy Library Oral History Program; Robert Divine, *Blowing on the Wind: The Nuclear Test Ban Debate, 1954–1960* (New York, 1978), 150.

at Geneva to accept an inspection system modeled after the report of the Conference of Experts. That report, known from then on as the "Geneva System," outlined an intricate system for detecting underground nuclear blasts, involving, among other things, a vast array of control posts, on-site inspections, and the formation of an international control organization to monitor compliance with the treaty. But a subsequent series of American underground nuclear tests, labeled "Hardtack," indicated that the Conference of Experts had based its conclusions on too optimistic an assessment of the Geneva System's ability to distinguish lower-yield underground blasts from earthquakes. That evidence, combined with questions about the ability to detect high-altitude explosions and the possibilities of exploding nuclear weapons in huge underground cavities, a process known as "decoupling," prompted the United States and Great Britain to insist that negotiations would have to proceed on the basis of the newest scientific data.[7]

But the Soviet side refused to consider seriously any of the latest technical information. That refusal led Eisenhower, in April 1959, to propose an atmospheric ban as a first step toward a comprehensive ban, a proposal rejected by Soviet leader Nikita Khrushchev. In the early spring of 1960, following Premier Khrushchev's successful visit to the United States, the two sides exchanged new proposals, and the Soviets accepted some number of on-site inspections and the Western side agreed to accompany a policed ban on those explosions that could be detected under the Geneva System with a moratorium on those that could not. But though prospects for an agreement appeared strong, the negotiations fell victim to the May 1960 collapse of the Paris Summit. From that point until Kennedy assumed office, the Geneva talks were stalemated.

The inspection issue was not only a source of East-West disagreement but also a point of contention between those in Washington opposed to or in favor of a test ban. To be sure, a major factor in shaping the American negotiating position, under both Eisenhower and Kennedy, was the objective evidence gleaned from scientific experimentation. But the interpretation of the data and the relative weight attached to different strands of scientific information were more often than not attributable to each agency's subjective position on the test-ban question. Under Eisenhower, those most resolutely opposed to a test ban were the Atomic Energy Commission, first under the leadership of its influential chairman Lewis Strauss and later under his successor John McCone, and the Joint Chiefs of Staff (JCS). In May 1957, JCS chairman Admiral Arthur Radford summed up what was to become the standard military position on the test-ban question: "We cannot trust the Russians on this or anything. The Communists have broken their word with every country with which they ever had an agreement."[8] More favorably disposed toward the test ban were the president's

---

7. The "decoupling" argument was advanced by Professor Albert Latter, a strong test-ban opponent. He and Edward Teller wrote an influential attack on the test ban, *Our Nuclear Future: Dangers and Opportunities* (New York, 1958).

8. Divine, *Blowing on the Wind*, 144.

science adviser, a position created in the aftermath of the Russians' Sputnik launching; the Central Intelligence Agency, which viewed inspection as a means to penetrate Soviet secrecy; Eisenhower's disarmament adviser Harold Stassen, who was forced to relinquish his post in 1958; and, most important, Secretary of State Dulles, whose conversion to the pro-ban position was a key factor in Eisenhower's shift.

Eisenhower, once convinced of the value of a test ban, helped push the negotiations in Geneva along, but critics faulted him for allowing administration opponents of the test ban either to delay or significantly to dilute his negotiating initiatives.[9] Those opposed generally seized on the inspection issue and the inconclusive scientific evidence regarding detection of underground explosions to combat the pro-test-ban sentiment in other areas of the administration. Upon entering negotiations, the administration, in virtual contravention of its move to separate the test ban from other disarmament issues, warned that any agreement would be contingent on the success of other disarmament negotiations. Similarly, in offering its April 1959 partial test-ban proposal, the administration, without indicating specifics, insisted on techniques for control. At no point did the Western side, with Eisenhower as American president, table a draft treaty in Geneva; under Kennedy a full treaty was tabled fewer than three months after the new president took office. As Robert Divine has written about Eisenhower: "Yet in the long run the failure to negotiate a test ban treaty was due primarily to his own lack of leadership. For two years, he had permitted a difference of opinion between his diplomatic and scientific advisers and his military and national security experts to paralyze the negotiations at Geneva. One may well question the sincerity of the Soviet advocacy of a comprehensive test ban treaty, but American indecision meant that Russian intentions were never fully probed." Kennedy shared this assessment of Eisenhower's test-ban policy. As Kennedy's AEC chairman Glenn Seaborg has written of his first business meeting with Kennedy, the new president regarded his predecessor's "efforts as insufficient."[10] But whatever the character of Eisenhower's performance, there is no question that the policymaking process that began during his presidency significantly shaped the way policy would be made under Kennedy. To be sure, important differences existed, both in the personnel who filled key positions and in the decision-making styles of the two presidents. But the constellation of actors involved and their institutional stands and methods of operation were well in place when Kennedy took over. Moreover, new institutions created by Eisenhower, such as the White House science adviser and the Committee of Principals, the latter a high-level interagency decision-making body devoted exclu-

9. For a critical account of Eisenhower's test-ban policy, see Harold Karan Jacobson and Eric Stein, *Diplomats, Scientists, and Politicians: The United States and Nuclear Test Ban Negotiations* (Ann Arbor, Mich.: 1966). For a more positive view of Eisenhower's role, see Robert Gilpin, *American Scientists and Nuclear Weapons Policy* (Princeton, 1962).

10. Divine, *Blowing on the Wind,* 314; Glenn Seaborg, *Kennedy, Krushchev and the Test Ban* (Berkeley, 1981), 30.

sively to arms control policy, were to play significant roles under Kennedy as well.

Another influence on American policy that began to assert itself under Eisenhower was the British government of Prime Minister Harold Macmillan. France had joined its NATO allies in early disarmament initiatives, but by the late 1950s, the French, to the consternation of the United States, had embarked on a program designed to give Paris independent nuclear striking power. From that time forward, successive French leaders, including President Charles de Gaulle, took the position that an end to nuclear testing had to be tied to a general agreement on disarmament. By the end of the decade, the Western position was, therefore, whatever the Anglo-American allies defined it to be. That position was reached through active consultation and coordination. While the British appeared more willing to take bolder initiatives, Prime Minister Macmillan enjoyed easy access to American policymaking circles, and in one dramatic instance, he flew to Washington to prod Eisenhower to be more forthcoming at the negotiating table.

A further source of influence under Eisenhower was the United States Congress, whose individual members employed the legislative machinery to press their own viewpoints on the administration. The foremost congressional test-ban advocate was Senator Hubert Humphrey (D.-Minn.) of the Subcommittee on Disarmament. Senator Albert Gore (D.-Tenn.), who visited the Geneva negotiations soon after they began, is generally credited with being the first major American political figure publicly to call for an atmospheric ban alone. With the administration unsettled about the course of American policy, these voices were accorded greater value than might otherwise have been the case. In a sense, Congress assumed a policy initiation role during the Eisenhower administration.

Thus upon taking power in January 1961, the Kennedy administration walked into a policy area that had already developed considerable momentum. In place were a voluntary moratorium on nuclear testing, begun in October 1958, and a negotiating forum in Geneva. Notwithstanding the stalemated character of the negotiations, central issues had already been drawn and interested parties, from within and outside the executive branch, mobilized. Kennedy's task was twofold. First, he had to find a negotiating formula simultaneously satisfactory to the disparate elements of his administration and capable of moving the talks off dead-center and, second, he would have to build and sustain public and congressional support for those negotiations in the face of continued Soviet obstructionism in Geneva and a general deterioration in East-West relations.

## Kennedy and Arms Control

As a moderate northern Democrat, Kennedy, during his years in the Senate, supported a nuclear test ban. His party and its standard-bearer had promoted a test ban during the 1956 presidential campaign, and Kennedy did likewise in

1960.[11] Upon acceding to the presidency, he appointed longtime establishment figure John J. McCloy to review American arms control policy, and within three months, his administration tabled a draft test-ban treaty at Geneva. Clearly, the test ban was from the start of Kennedy's presidency a high-priority foreign policy goal.

Seaborg, who has written the most comprehensive insider's account of the evolution of Kennedy's test-ban policy, has convincingly traced the president's determination to achieve a test ban to his concern over nuclear proliferation. As early as 7 March 1961, the president, in a conversation with Seaborg and other members of his national security team, cited the importance of the proliferation issue and mentioned Israel as a potential nuclear power whose efforts could be halted through a test ban. At a White House meeting some two years later, Kennedy reiterated the link between a test ban and nuclear proliferation and specifically referred to the test ban's potentially dampening effect on China's nuclear program. These private words were matched by the president's public statements. Time and again, he warned of the dangers of proliferation and the need to reach a test-ban agreement, and in a 1962 press conference, he voiced reservations about concluding an agreement that failed to include all of the world's potential nuclear powers. In the president's oft-used phrase, failure to reach a test-ban accord would let the "genie out of the bottle."[12]

Consistent with the president's concern about proliferation was the administration's attitude toward the development of independent nuclear forces in Europe. Defense Secretary Robert McNamara, in a NATO address delivered in Athens in the spring of 1962, made clear his view that Europe's defense could best be secured through a centrally controlled nuclear deterrent. In a parallel effort, the State Department seized on a plan, known as the MLF, first advanced during the last days of the Eisenhower administration, to draw the Europeans into a multilateral nuclear force and thereby discourage the development of independent nuclear programs. In general, the Europeans supported the president's test-ban efforts. An 8 July 1963 memo from Thomas Hughes of the State Department's Bureau of Intelligence and Research to Secretary of State Dean Rusk reveals that most European countries welcomed the test ban, either as a means to prevent nuclear proliferation or to relax East-West tensions. Although German leaders worried that a test ban might lead to a "softer" American stance toward the Kremlin, Hughes predicted that Bonn would "publicly welcome a test ban agreement." Only the French opposed a test-ban treaty. In a last-minute effort to convince the French to sign an accord, Kennedy suggested to Macmillan that he would release vital nuclear information to Paris in return for a French signature on the treaty. According to diplomatic historian Michael Beschloss,

11. Michael Beschloss, *The Crisis Years: Kennedy and Khrushchev, 1960–1963* (New York, 1991), 84.

12. Seaborg, *Kennedy,* 48, 182; *Public Papers of the Presidents of the United States: John F. Kennedy, 1962* (Washington, D.C., 1963), 139, 424.

Kennedy was so frustrated by French president Charles de Gaulle's refusal to commit to a test ban that he complained: "Charles de Gaulle will be remembered for one thing only—his refusal to take that treaty."[13]

It would appear, then, that what most strongly motivated the president in his striving for a test-ban accord was his anxiety over nuclear proliferation. This fear outweighed whatever concerns he might have entertained about the strategic value of continued testing, about which opinion was divided within the administration. While opponents in Congress and in the military pointed to what remained to be learned from nuclear testing, including information about missile defense and tactical nuclear weapons, the strategic arguments in favor of testing seem to have had less impact on Kennedy's test-ban policy than did the president's concern over nuclear proliferation. In fact, Seaborg observes that Kennedy "appeared, in private, to be considerably more in favor of accepting risks and making compromises in order to achieve a test ban than either he or U.S. negotiators ever allowed themselves to be in public."[14]

Underlying Kennedy's test-ban effort was a pervasive attitude among civilian elements of the administration that political and military competition with the Soviet Union did not preclude the search for an accommodation between the superpowers, particularly at the level of nuclear politics. This, in part, explains Kennedy's shift to a "flexible response" military strategy, away from the heavy reliance on nuclear weapons that had characterized Eisenhower's "massive retaliation" strategy. Kennedy reasoned that the development of multiple military options, including a much wider array of non-nuclear military responses, would not only reduce the risk of nuclear war in Europe but also more effectively deter and combat Soviet-inspired threats to American interests in the strategically important Third World, an area staked out by Khrushchev for communist advance.[15] In 1962, McNamara carried the multiple options strategy even further by unveiling a "cities avoidance" strategy, with modalities for fighting limited nuclear war, and by rationalizing the new strategy as offering a humane and more effective alternative to all-out nuclear conflict.[16] Arms control was seen not

13. Memorandum, Thomas L. Hughes to the secretary, "Allied Attitudes on Linking a Test Agreement with a Non-Aggression Pact," 8 July 1963, National Security Files, Box 265, John F. Kennedy Library; Harold Macmillan, *At the End of the Day: 1961–1963* (New York, 1973), 153; Beschloss, *Crisis Years,* 626.

14. The Committee on Atmospheric Testing, made up of high-level Kennedy administration officials, reported to Kennedy on 28 November 1961 that testing would be directed toward defense and assuring the "deliverability" of U.S. weapons. See Seaborg, *Kennedy,* 123, 129.

15. On 6 January 1961, Khrushchev delivered a speech in which he argued for the importance of wars of national liberation in the eventual triumph of communism. In a February 1962 speech to the American Bar Association, McNamara called the Khrushchev address "one of the most significant speeches of the past year." (quoted in Bernard J. Firestone, *The Quest for Nuclear Stability* [Westport, Conn., 1982], 50).

16. See William W. Kaufman, *The McNamara Strategy* (New York, 1964), 257–58. For a discussion of the evolution of McNamara's thinking on strategy, see Bernard J. Firestone, "Defense Policy as a Form of Arms Control: Nuclear Force Posture and Strategy under John F. Kennedy," in *John F. Kennedy: The Promise Revisited,* ed. Paul Harper and Joan P. Krieg (Westport, Conn., 1988), 57–70.

only as the negotiation of agreements to curtail the arms race but, in keeping with the latest theory, as a form of competitive collaboration, in which adversaries would develop military options that would support the system of mutual deterrence on which the world's existence rested or, in the worst case, limit nuclear war should it occur.

It is difficult to assay to what degree this view of arms control informed Kennedy's thinking about dealing with the Soviets. The creators of and point men for the new strategy were McNamara and several of his subordinates, although it is clear that the secretary of defense enjoyed the president's trust and respect. But if Kennedy did not himself articulate the strategic position with which McNamara has been long identified, the president apparently shared the view of the arms controllers that conflict between adversaries did not preclude the existence of areas of mutual interest between them. Notwithstanding the frequent harshness of his Cold War rhetoric, Kennedy possessed a largely nonideological view of the Soviet threat. As his adviser and biographer Arthur Schlesinger, Jr., has written: "He never took ideology very seriously, certainly not as a means of interpreting history." While he viewed the Soviets as expansionistic and opportunistic, he also believed that, given the superpowers' shared interests, there could be some reciprocation in the nuclear field. He also felt that nuclear accommodation might attenuate Soviet ambitions in other areas, but only because arms control signified Soviet acceptance of American capabilities to frustrate the Kremlin's objectives through limited and controlled military responses. He understood, though, that while arms control agreements might improve the atmosphere in superpower relations, they alone could not resolve the outstanding differences between the nuclear giants. For this reason, he pursued a test ban without pressing the Soviets vigorously for collateral political agreements on, for example, Germany and Southeast Asia. Neither did he accept the recommendation of his adviser W. W. Rostow that a test ban be made contingent on gaining political concessions from the Soviets on Cuba, Laos, and Vietnam.[17]

Kennedy's view of Soviet realism in foreign affairs appears to have been reinforced by Khrushchev's behavior during the Cuban Missile Crisis. On 17 December 1962, the president told a nationwide audience: "I do think his [Khrushchev's] speech shows he realizes how dangerous a world we live in." And in a magazine interview published in August 1963, Kennedy stated: "I am sure that the event had a sobering effect on Mr. Khrushchev." Kennedy's view that ideology invariably could be expected to take a back seat to national interest was further buttressed by evidence of an emerging split between the Soviet Union and the People's Republic of China. Asserting something equivalent to a nineteenth-century balance-of-power concept of alliance building and disintegration, the

17. Arthur M. Schlesinger, Jr., *A Thousand Days* (1965; rpr. New York, 1967), 283–84; Memorandum, W. W. Rostow to the Secretary of State, "The Viet Minh in Laos and the Harriman Mission," 4 July 1963, and Memorandum, W. W. Rostow to the President, "The Harriman Probe," 8 July 1963, both in National Security Files, Box 265, John F. Kennedy Library.

president declared at the American University in June 1963: "And history teaches us that enmities between nations as between individuals do not last forever. However fixed our likes and dislikes may seem the tide of time and events will often bring surprising shifts in the relations." And on 26 September 1963, Kennedy stated his concept of the national interest: "We must recognize that every nation determines its policies in terms of its own interests. . . . National interest is more powerful than ideology, and the recent developments within the Communist empire show this very clearly. Friendship, as Palmerston said, may rise and wane, but interests endure."[18]

His friends and associates thought Kennedy may have actually undervalued the role of ideology in foreign policy. According to Charles ("Chip") Bohlen, a longtime Kennedy intimate and former U.S. ambassador to Moscow, Kennedy didn't quite understand the ideological aspects of the Cold War because "I don't believe—I never had the impression—that President Kennedy had seriously read Marx or Lenin, or any of the Soviet theoretical writers very much . . . [to be familiar with] any of the subtleties of [the theory's] application by the Russians."[19]

British prime minister Harold Macmillan, a Kennedy admirer, appeared astonished by the president's lack of attention to the ideological aspects of Soviet behavior: "There is a marked difference between President Kennedy 'in action' on a specific problem . . . and his attitude to larger issues (the nuclear war, the struggle between East and West, Capitalism and Communism, etc.). In the first, he is an extraordinarily quick and effective operator—a born 'politician.' . . . On the wider issues, he seems rather lost."[20]

This assessment was corroborated by U. Alexis Johnson, under secretary for political affairs in the Kennedy State Department: "[Kennedy] was not what I would call of a philosophical or a subjective turn of mind . . . and if he had a weakness I would say it was a tendency to decide in the light of the immediate circumstances at the time without trying to look far ahead."[21]

And Llewellyn Thompson, the United States ambassador to Moscow when Kennedy assumed the presidency, faulted the president for allowing himself to be drawn into a futile discussion of ideology with Khrushchev during the two leaders' Vienna summit: "I think in retrospect, I'm sorry in a way that the discussion got off on ideological grounds. . . . I don't think the President quite appreciated the fact that a Communist like Mr. Khrushchev could not yield [on ideology] even if he wanted to. I mean he couldn't formally deny his own ideology."[22]

18. *Public Papers of . . . Kennedy, 1962*, pp. 796, 899; *Public Papers of . . . Kennedy, 1963*, pp. 461, 736.

19. Charles E. Bohlen, recorded interview by Arthur Schlesinger, Jr., 21 May 1964, pp. 7–8, in John F. Kennedy Library Oral History Program.

20. Macmillan, *At the End of the Day*, 147.

21. U. Alexis Johnson, recorded interview by William Brubeck, 1964, p. 12, in John F. Kennedy Library Oral History Program.

22. Llewellyn Thompson, recorded interview by Elizabeth Donahue, 23 March 1964, and by Joseph E. O'Conner, 27 April 1966, p. 36, in John F. Kennedy Library Oral History Program.

Whatever the weaknesses of Kennedy's understanding of communism, his relatively nonideological approach to the Soviets made him particularly well suited to exploit opportunities for stabilizing the superpower relationship. The test-ban initiative did not stem so much from a strategic vision about the salutary effects of a scaled-down arms race as it did from a philosophy that assumed that continued military and political competition with the Soviet Union could coexist with measures designed to stabilize that relationship. In fact, the test ban was pursued simultaneously with a massive expansion in U.S. strategic forces—one designed to give the United States clear military superiority over the Soviet Union—and by the beginnings of American military involvement in South Vietnam. By the time Kennedy became president, the test ban had, in the words of Franklin Long of the Arms Control and Disarmament Agency (ACDA), in a 12 July 1963 letter to the president, "come to represent almost an institutional barrier to improved relations between the two countries, and failure of the two countries to resolve this issue has symbolized their inability to reach agreement on the central problems of the Cold War."[23] For Kennedy, then, reaching a test-ban accord, in combination with his nuclear weapons buildup and expansion in American conventional force capabilities, was of a piece with his view that an ambivalent stance toward the Soviet Union—one that combined firmness with accommodation—was consistent with the American national interest.

## The Geneva Negotiations

In early 1961, following an intense review of the Western negotiating position, Kennedy authorized his new disarmament negotiator, Arthur Dean, to offer the Soviets a sliding scale of from ten to twenty inspections per year. That concession, proposed at Geneva in April 1961, was rejected by the Soviets, who now repudiated the principle of on-site inspection and went on to insist, in a new departure for them, that the administration of the proposed control commission should be in the hands of a troika and therefore subject to a Soviet veto. In a further provocation, on 1 September, the Soviets broke the unofficial moratorium on nuclear testing by detonating the first in a series of huge atmospheric tests. Kennedy responded, first, by offering the Soviets an agreement to ban atmospheric testing and, second, in the face of yet another Soviet rejection, by ordering the resumption of underground nuclear testing in the United States.

The moratorium was a collateral but no less significant issue. The Joint Chiefs, along with several influential members of Congress and the scientific community, had been urging the president to resume nuclear testing even before the Soviet abrogation of the moratorium. But Kennedy resisted, and when the blue-ribbon Panofsky Panel, convened under the auspices of the President's Sci-

23. Franklin Long to President Kennedy, "Political Implications of a Nuclear Test Ban," 12 July 1963, in John F. Kennedy Library.

ence Advisory Committee (PSAC), reported in August 1961 that no evidence of Soviet cheating could be documented, the president sided with those who opposed a unilateral resumption of testing. The Soviet test series forced Kennedy's hand, but, despite intense pressure from the military and the Atomic Energy Commission, the president refused to authorize a resumption of aboveground testing until early March 1962, and even then he did so only with the greatest reluctance.

In March 1962, following the collapse of the three-party Geneva talks, test-ban negotiations moved to a new venue, the UN-instituted Eighteen-Nation Disarmament Committee (ENDC). The president, sensitive to the pro-ban sentiment of the eight neutrals represented on the ENDC and responsive to pressures from Prime Minister Macmillan for a relaxation of the Western stance, urged American negotiators to adjust the Western negotiating position. In March 1962, the West offered to drop the 4.75 seismic magnitude threshold from its April 1961 proposal for a comprehensive ban, without any corresponding increase in on-site inspections. The Soviets, however, rebuffed the Western proposal, once again rejecting the principle of on-site inspection. With the neutrals appearing to back the Soviets on the inspection issue and with results from the American seismic program—Project VELA—suggesting that national detection capabilities were potentially more effective than originally thought possible, the Arms Control and Disarmament Agency, during the summer of 1962, conducted a major interagency review of the Western negotiating position. On 27 August, the United States and Great Britain tabled two new draft treaties in Geneva, one for a partial ban, the other comprehensive. The draft comprehensive treaty insisted on the principle of on-site inspection but specified no number, and Western negotiators hinted to their Soviet counterparts that the West would be willing to reduce both the number of inspections it would demand and the number of inspection stations required on Soviet territory.

Throughout this period, Kennedy demonstrated qualities of leadership on the test-ban issue that helped to keep negotiations alive in the face of repeated Soviet obstructionism. For one thing, Kennedy participated in numerous meetings of the Committee of Principals, including the three meetings of 27 and 30 July and 1 August 1962, at which key decisions leading to the tabling of the two draft treaties at Geneva were made. Seaborg's minutes of the meetings, transcribed in his book, show the president to have been an active questioner, interested not only in the broad outlines of his administration's test-ban policy but in its details as well. According to Adrian Fisher, deputy director of the Arms Control and Disarmament Agency and a key figure in the summer 1962 policy review, "[Kennedy] seemed to me about as well advised on the subject as any non-scientific person could be."[24]

Although differences of opinion existed within the administration over spe-

---

24. Seaborg, *Kennedy,* 164–68; Adrian Fisher, recorded interview by Frank Sieverts, 13 May 1964, p. 15, in John F. Kennedy Library Oral History Program.

cific details of the test-ban issue, Kennedy assembled a team whose outlook precluded the kind of disagreement on fundamentals that had stymied the making of test-ban policy under Eisenhower. According to Abram Chayes, under Kennedy legal adviser to the State Department, Kennedy chose advisers such as Jerome B. Wiesner, Arthur Schlesinger, Jr., and Carl Kaysen who were clearly committed to exploring new directions in East-West relations. Wiesner, Kennedy's science adviser, played a large role in seeking a relaxation in Western inspection requirements, and Kaysen of the National Security Council, along with John McNaughton of the Defense Department, was a key exponent of the partial test-ban proposal. Another major personnel change was the replacement of hard-line AEC chairman John McCone with Seaborg. Defense Secretary McNamara was valued not only for his ability to control the military but for recognizing that he could only "go so far in overwhelming the Joint Chiefs of Staff if he was to maintain morale and support within the Pentagon."[25] Apart from the military, therefore, there were within the Kennedy administration no strong, anti-test-ban dogmatists.

In addition to staffing his administration with officials who supported a test ban, Kennedy created institutional machinery to consider and promote arms control policy. In 1961, on Kennedy's recommendation, the Congress created the Arms Control and Disarmament Agency, an outgrowth of the Democratic Advisory Council's "Peace Agency" idea. Nominally located in the Department of State, but with its director answerable to both the secretary and the president, ACDA was designed both to direct more government attention to the problem of arms control and to give the president greater control over arms control policy.[26] The agency, which was responsible for coordinating the various arms control policies of the administration, played a large role in the interagency review conducted during the summer of 1962. Its first director, William Foster, was accorded a seat separate from the secretary of state on the Committee of Principals so that interagency deliberations, for the first time, included representation of an agency with a bureaucratic commitment to arms control.

By the late summer of 1962, the administration, despite Soviet intransigence, had fashioned a policy that satisfied major governmental interests. The hard-liners, particularly among the military, were at least temporarily reconciled by the continued American insistence on verified inspection and by the resumption of atmospheric testing. The comprehensive ban advocates in ACDA, who opposed the tabling of a partial ban, were encouraged by the simultaneous tabling of a comprehensive treaty. A middle ground was struck by the tabling of the partial ban, an alternative that the president did not necessarily favor but which

25. Abram Chayes, recorded interviews by Eugene Gordon, 18 May, 22 June, 23 June 1964, p. 226, in John F. Kennedy Library Oral History Program; Schlesinger, *A Thousand Days,* 456; Theodore Sorensen, recorded interview by Carl Kaysen, 26 March and 4 April 1964, p. 14, in John F. Kennedy Library Oral History Program.

26. Memorandum, Richard Neustadt to John J. McCloy, re: Location of the contemplated disarmament organization, 29 March 1961, President's Office Files, Box 36, John F. Kennedy Library.

he supported nonetheless as a means to respond to political pressures for a test ban.[27] Underlying his administration's efforts were Kennedy's resolve to achieve a test ban and his willingness to involve himself in the development of a test-ban policy—two attributes clearly absent during Eisenhower's presidency.

## The Road to Moscow

Any progress on the test-ban issue was temporarily interrupted by the Cuban Missile Crisis of October 1962, but the negotiating tempo accelerated dramatically following resolution of the crisis. On 19 December 1962, Premier Khrushchev forwarded a personal letter to President Kennedy in which he offered to accept a maximum of three inspections per year, a return to a position first proposed when Eisenhower was still president. In advancing this concession, the Soviet leader relied on conversations between Ambassadors Dean and V. V. Kuznetsov and scientists Wiesner and Yevgenii Federov in which the Americans were alleged to have agreed that three inspections would suffice. Khrushchev adhered to the Soviet position that internationally supervised inspections were unnecessary, instead asserting his appreciation for Kennedy's domestic political requirements, a theme that would recur throughout subsequent negotiations.

Kennedy responded by rejecting the Soviet understanding of the Dean and Wiesner comments and by insisting that Western inspection requirements were dictated by national security rather than political concerns, but he otherwise struck a positive note in his reply and recommended the convening of a high-level tripartite conference in New York and Washington.[28] He also postponed a planned underground test, pending the outcome of negotiations. The new momentum failed, however, to narrow the gap between the two sides, and, as the talks shifted once again to the ENDC, Kennedy decided to resume underground nuclear testing.

Over the next several months, negotiations in Geneva stalemated, despite a relaxation in Western inspection demands, down to seven. The Soviets, moreover, became more truculent in their assaults on Western policies, and Washington's MLF scheme came under particularly strong attack. In March 1963, Prime Minister Macmillan wrote a letter to Kennedy, suggesting, among other things, the convening of a summit conference to include Khrushchev. Instrumental in the formulation of this initiative was David Ormsby-Gore, British ambassador to the United States and a confidant of President Kennedy—a fact appreciated by Macmillan in his own dealings with the president.[29]

27. According to Adrian Fisher of the Arms Control and Disarmament Agency, the idea for a limited ban did not originate with President Kennedy. See Fisher interview, 14.

28. U.S. Arms Control and Disarmament Agency, *Documents on Disarmament, 1962,* 2 vols. (Washington, D.C., 1963), II, 1277–79.

29. U.S. Arms Control and Disarmament Agency, *Documents on Disarmament, 1963,* (Washington, D.C., 1964), 161–70; Macmillan, *At the End of the Day,* 153.

Kennedy, though not averse to circumventing his bureaucracy, was reluctant to engage Khrushchev in high-level summitry, believing that negotiations were best left to lower diplomatic levels. In answering Macmillan, Kennedy reiterated his apprehensions about summitry and in a follow-up letter added: "Memories . . . of May 1960 are very strong in this country, and . . . I believe that on the historic evidence it is not likely that Khrushchev would make major changes at a Summit from positions put forward under his direction."[30] Kennedy suggested instead that the Western leaders propose the convening of a high-level conference to discuss the test ban, a recommendation endorsed by the prime minister and acted upon with a letter to the Soviet leader. Khrushchev's reply was harsh and unyielding but did not reject in principle the convening of a high-level meeting. Despite Kennedy's discouragement at the tone of Khrushchev's letter, Macmillan persuaded the president to continue his initiative, and on 8 June, the Soviet premier agreed to the convening of a conference in Moscow.[31]

Kennedy announced Khrushchev's acceptance of the Western offer two days later at American University in a speech long remembered for its conciliatory tone. Even Khrushchev was impressed, as he observed one year later in an oral history interview: "That statement can be called courageous and more realistic than what the Soviet Union and other countries of the socialist world often heard from American leaders." The president had been contemplating a major address on peace since the early spring, but the advice of Norman Cousins, *Saturday Review* editor and peace activist, gave his intentions greater immediacy. Cousins, who for several months had been acting as an unofficial go-between for Khrushchev and Kennedy, warned the president that the Soviet leader was facing great pressure from Kremlin hard-liners and the Chinese communists to renounce his "arms control initiative" before the convening of a Chinese-Soviet summit scheduled for that summer. In a memo to Kennedy, Cousins wrote: "The moment is now at hand for the most important single speech of your Presidency. It should be a speech which, in its breathtaking proposals for genuine peace, in its tone of friendliness for the Soviet people and its understanding for their ordeal during the last war, in its inspired advocacy of the human interest, would create a world ground-swell of support for American leadership."[32]

At the president's instruction, Theodore Sorensen began assembling materials for the speech. According to Sorensen: "Unlike most foreign policy speeches— none of which was so sweeping in concept and import as this turned out to be— official departmental positions and suggestions were not solicited. . . . He [Kennedy] did not want that new policy diluted by the usual threats of destruction, boasts of nuclear stockpiles and lectures on Soviet treachery." Sorensen remem-

---

30. *Public Papers of . . . Kennedy, 1962,* p. 136; Macmillan, *At the End of the Day,* 465.

31. Macmillan remembered in his diary: "David Gore is confident that the President will agree—if only to please me." See Macmillan, *At the End of the Day,* 469.

32. Nikita Khrushchev, recorded interview, 29 June 1964, p. 2, in John F. Kennedy Library Oral History Program; Norman Cousins, *The Improbable Triumvirate* (New York, 1972), 114–16; Norman Cousins to President Kennedy, 30 April 1963, in John F. Kennedy Library.

bered that he and the president's national security adviser McGeorge Bundy were the only two presidential advisers who knew of the speech. Once Sorensen's initial draft was completed, it was circulated around the executive branch, although not through conventional channels. It was shown to the secretaries of defense and state, and on 7 June, Bundy convened a small group including Kaysen, Rostow, Schlesinger, and Sorensen to examine the draft. Llewellyn Thompson remembered that Sorensen read him a draft of the speech over the phone. Finally, at night on 9 June, Bundy's deputy Kaysen circulated the speech among cabinet-level departments for "minimum clearance." Because the president announced that the United States would not be the first country to resume atmospheric nuclear testing, those parts of the speech dealing with nuclear testing were, according to Sorensen, shown to the Joint Chiefs of Staff. His recollection did not correspond to that of the Air Force Chief of Staff, General Curtis LeMay, who told a Senate committee: "I did not have any prior knowledge of the suspension of atmospheric testing. I don't think the Joint Chiefs knew about it either." According to AEC commissioner Leland Haworth, neither the Joint Chiefs of Staff nor the AEC was consulted in advance of the president's announcement to suspend plans for the resumption of atmospheric testing.[33]

## Preparing for the Harriman Mission

To head the American delegation to the Moscow talks, Kennedy chose longtime diplomat and former governor of New York Averell Harriman. The American ambassador to Moscow, Foy Kohler, might have appeared a more obvious choice, but he was, according to Benjamin Read of the State Department, treated in effect as persona non grata by Khrushchev. Moreover, if Robert Kennedy's views on this matter accurately reflected the president's, then Kohler was not a presidential favorite either. Robert Kennedy was alleged to have said: "I wasn't too impressed with him [Kohler] at all. He gave me rather the creeps and I don't think he'd be the kind of person who would get anything done with the Russians." John J. McCloy, who had been Kennedy's disarmament adviser before the establishment of ACDA and was a Republican, might have helped to deflect criticism on Capitol Hill, but he was unavailable. William Foster, head of ACDA, was bypassed because, in his vigorous promotion of a comprehensive ban, he had, in Read's words, "stepped on too many toes" in Congress, where there was substantial opposition to a comprehensive ban. According to Schlesinger, it was Rusk who suggested the appointment of Harriman, probably at the suggestion of Carl Kaysen. Kaysen recommended that Harriman be ap-

33. Theodore C. Sorensen, *Kennedy* (New York, 1965), 730–31; Sorensen interview, 72; Thompson interview, 20; Memorandum, Pierre Salinger to Carl Kaysen, 9 June 1963, in John F. Kennedy Library; U.S. Congress, Senate Committee on Armed Services, Preparedness Investigating Subcommittee, *Hearings: Military Aspects and Implications of Nuclear Test Ban Proposals and Related Matters*, 88th Cong., 1st sess., 1963, pp. 317, 297.

pointed without delay so that State Department regulars, who did not like Harriman despite his position in the department, should not scuttle the appointment. It is also apparent that Kennedy had had his eye on Harriman, who had performed excellently in negotiations over Laos, at least since April, when the president told Cousins: "This looks like a job made to order for Averell Harriman."[34]

The selection of Harriman was of a piece with Kennedy's desire to control the negotiations, for though Harriman was a member of the State Department, he was also—by dint of his stature and years of service to individual presidents—free of its parochialism. Harriman wanted Kaysen and McNaughton, two early advocates of a limited ban, to accompany him to Moscow and was insistent on excluding the military from the delegation. Harriman had strong feelings about the need for civilian supremacy over the military: "I'm just trained by experience and knowledge of the need for domination of the military because they are trained to do certain things." At the same time, Kennedy took extraordinary measures to ensure the secrecy of deliberations at the White House. After one conversation with the president, Harriman returned to the State Department with specific instructions as to the circulation of cables from Moscow through the executive branch. According to a memorandum on the subject:

1. All substantive communications between Moscow and Washington will be designated BAN, eyes only.
2. Upon receipt in the State Department's Communication Center, incoming messages slugged BAN will be relayed automatically to the White House.
3. The message will then be sent in two copies in sealed envelopes to S/S-Mr. Read. The names of those who see the cables in the Communication Center will be written down.
4. One copy will be put in a brown envelope as a file copy. Another copy for the Secretary of State can be shown by Mr. Read to George Ball and Ambassador Thompson. Test Ban material is to be forwarded to William Foster at the ACDA.[35]

The president's precautions were directed primarily at the military, who were, by and large, hostile to his test-ban efforts. As Read remembered, "This was part of the same feeling of concern on the part of the President that cables that went to the Defense Department would inevitably get into the massive military ma-

34. Benjamin H. Read, recorded interviews by Joseph E. O'Conner and Dennis O'Brien, 22 February 1966 and 17 October 1969, p. 10, in John F. Kennedy Library Oral History Program; Arthur M. Schlesinger, Jr., *Robert Kennedy and His Times* (Boston, 1978), 501; Read interview, 11, 10; Cousins, *Improbable Triumvirate*, 114.

35. W. Averell Harriman, recorded interviews by Michael Forrestal, 13 April 1964, and by Arthur Schlesinger, Jr., 17 January and 6 June 1965, p. 87, in John F. Kennedy Library Oral History Program; State Department Memorandum on Handling BAN, in John F. Kennedy Library.

chinery and the close security that he wanted and insisted on would be jeopardized." Kennedy himself carefully drew the circle of those involved in drafting the instructions to the Moscow delegation. The original group included the president, Rusk, Ball, Foster, McNamara, and McCone (now of the CIA) meeting in the White House Cabinet Room. Included later were U. Alexis Johnson, Edward Murrow of the U.S. Information Agency (USIA), Sorensen, and Thompson. But clearly the president set the "tone for the outgoing communications," and, in Read's words, that fact soon became evident to officials in the State Department: "We had suspected before that time, but it was made explicitly clear in the Moscow discussion, that it was the President's initiative that produced the negotiations."[36]

Kennedy's struggle with the military over the test ban reflected both philosophical and political differences between civilian and military sectors of the administration. The military, and particularly the air force, which saw nuclear superiority as a fundamental requirement of American national security, suspected civilian officials in the Pentagon of pursuing what the Air Force Association called a "nuclear stalemate strategy." In truth, both the civilians and military in the Defense Department supported the maintenance of U.S. nuclear superiority over the Soviet Union. Civilians, however, believed that superiority could be stabilized through arms control measures and assumed that a military understanding between the United States and the Soviet Union carried an implicit acknowledgment on both sides of America's nuclear superiority. Harold Brown, director of defense research and engineering under Kennedy, argued in 1963 before the Preparedness Investigating Subcommittee of the Senate Armed Services Committee that a comprehensive ban would lock in American superiority by preventing the Soviets from learning all that was possible from underground testing. Military officials, in contrast, contended that though political agreements might lead to a relaxation of tensions, a political accommodation would have no impact on Soviet military decisions. The military viewed arms control as being of limited value if not an outright detriment to the strategic standing of the nation, and in congressional testimony, both before and after the Harriman mission, the JCS made clear their opposition to a comprehensive ban.[37]

Another source of friction stemmed from the military's view that McNamara, who entertained strong opinions about national security policy, was attempting both to impose his will on the military and to isolate it from the decision-making process. According to Herbert York, the military resented the secretary's intrusion into areas that were traditionally considered to be within its pale of expertise. Throughout 1963, the McNamara-JCS imbroglio captured national headlines. On 20 April, the secretary of defense saw fit to respond to his critics in the military by asserting that *he* was in the best position to determine the nation's

---

36. Read interview, 9, 3, 8.
37. See the testimony of SAC Commander General Thomas Power, *Hearings: Military Aspects,* 746; *New York Times,* 12 September 1963, p. 21; *Hearings: Military Aspects,* 864–65, 303–304.

security needs. In September, the former chief of naval operations, Admiral George Anderson, accused McNamara of downgrading military advice. On 4 October, representative, F. Edward Hebert (D.-La,), a staunch military ally, charged that civilians in the Defense Department were meddling in military af fairs. Adding to the Senate's concern over whether the military was adequately consulted was the statement of General LeMay, who, when asked why the chiefs had waited until late June to express their public disapproval of a comprehensive treaty, responded: "I think we were all caught a little bit by surprise at the seri- ousness of the administration trying to get a treaty signed, up to the point where Mr. Harriman was going over there. Up until then we hadn't recognized the seriousness of the approach to this particular treaty." Summing up what the mil- itary's friends on Capitol Hill suspected about military input into the test-ban policy, James T. Kendall, the chief counsel of the Preparedness Investigating Subcommittee, said to Franklin Long of ACDA, "I would hope that the fact that the people wore a uniform would not be a factor in your thinking that we went to the wrong place."[38]

Although McNamara was the most visible protagonist in the continuing round of civilian-military jousting, Kennedy himself expressed in private certain reservations about the quality of military advice. Kennedy's confidant Benjamin C. Bradlee quoted the president as saying, "The first advice I'm going to give my successor is to watch the generals and avoid feeling that just because they are military men their opinion on military matters is worth a damn." Whatever Ken- nedy's private thoughts, it is difficult to challenge the administration's conten- tion that it apprised the military of the progress in test-ban negotiations. The Joint Chiefs were represented at meetings of the Committee of Principals eight times between 26 July 1962 and 8 July 1963. In its 14 June meeting, the com- mittee authorized JCS chairman General Maxwell D. Taylor to solicit the opin- ions of the chiefs with regard to a limited ban. At that same meeting, McNa- mara, while expressing support for a comprehensive ban, urged, in deference to the opposition of the JCS, that Harriman not table the draft comprehensive treaty already approved by the administration several months earlier but clearly not concurred in by the chiefs. Taylor, who did not have a complete treaty in his hands until the conclusion of negotiations, nonetheless had access to all cable traffic from Moscow. In addition, other members of the Joint Chiefs, both indi vidually and collectively, met with the president twice in July to hear his case for a treaty.[39]

### The Harriman Mission

On 2 July, Khrushchev, in a speech in East Berlin, signaled his willingness to conclude a treaty banning nuclear testing in the atmosphere, outer space, and

38. York interview, 26; *New York Times,* 21 April 1963, p. 1, 5 September 1963, p. 1, 5 October 1963, p. 7; *Hearings: Nuclear Test Ban Treaty,* 382; *Hearings: Military Aspects,* 197.

39. Benjamin C. Bradlee, *Conversations with Kennedy* (1975; rpr. New York, 1976), 112; *Hear- ings: Military Aspects,* 608, 733; Seaborg, *Kennedy,* 100.

underwater. Llewellyn Thompson claimed some personal credit for this about-face on the part of the Soviet leader. According to Thompson, in a private luncheon conversation, Soviet ambassador to the United States Anatoly Dobrynin told him that, owing to the prevailing mood in the Senate, it was impossible for the Kremlin to consider a limited ban as a realistic proposal. Thompson retorted, "If the President is behind it, the Senate will fall in line."[40] Thompson surmised that Dobrynin's subsequent report to Khrushchev resulted in the new Soviet position on a partial accord.

Despite Khrushchev's offer, Harriman was instructed by the president to explore the possibility of a comprehensive ban, although no new concessions were proposed on the inspection issue. Indeed, high-level discussions in Washington indicated that serious disagreements existed within the administration over the requirements for a comprehensive ban.[41] Khrushchev, however, quickly dismissed Harriman's probe on a comprehensive treaty, retreating from his previous offer of three on-site inspections and reverting to a Soviet proposal first floated at the ENDC in December for the installation of unmanned black boxes on Soviet territory. After the first day, there was no further discussion of a comprehensive ban.

Harriman experienced equal frustration in attempting to draw Khrushchev into a serious discussion of the emerging Sino-Soviet rift and the related issue of nonproliferation. Kennedy clearly regarded the division in the communist camp as historically significant. As early as 1960, when Kennedy was still only a presidential candidate, he received a letter from Soviet specialist George F. Kennan, which offered the following advice: "The main target of our diplomacy should be to heighten the divisive tendencies within the Soviet bloc. The best means to do this lies in the improvement of our relations with Moscow." Indeed, Kennedy told Harriman and Kaysen upon their departure for Moscow that they could go as far as they wished "in exploring the possibility of a Soviet-American understanding with regard to China." In a cable to Harriman Kennedy wrote: "I remain convinced, however, the China problem is more serious than Khrushchev's comments in his first meeting. I believe you should press the question in a private meeting with him. I agree that large stockpiles are characteristic of U.S. and U.S.S.R. only, but consider the relatively small forces in hands of people like the Chinese Communists could be very dangerous to all of us. I believe that even the limited test ban can and should be the means to limit diffusion." But Khrushchev did not appear particularly eager to discuss his Chinese problem and deflected any serious discussion of a nonproliferation accord. Nevertheless, the test-ban negotiations highlighted the differences between Moscow and Peking over the issue of "peaceful coexistence," and Harriman reported to Washington that "[it] is becoming crystal clear that the Soviets have as their objective . . . an attempt to isolate the Chicoms."[42]

40. Thompson interview, 9.
41. Seaborg, *Kennedy,* 222.
42. George F. Kennan to John F. Kennedy, 17 August 1960, in John F. Kennedy Library; Schlesinger, *A Thousand Days,* 825; Read interview, 24; Beschloss, *Crisis Years,* 625.

The Soviets experienced equivalent frustration of their effort to link the test ban to a European nonaggression pact. Harriman persuaded the Soviets that a nonaggression pact would require considerable negotiation between the United States and its Western European allies and, in the final communiqué, the parties to the test-ban accord agreed to take up the issue of a nonaggression pact at a later date.

The Soviet draft treaty on a limited ban proposed only a prohibition on atmospheric, outer space, and underwater testing, without mentioning collateral issues such as a withdrawal clause or peaceful nuclear explosions. For this reason, the more comprehensive American draft treaty of 27 August 1962 became the basis for further discussion. The American side anticipated problems with the JCS and on Capitol Hill because of the absence of a withdrawal clause, especially since nuclear testing in China might compel the Americans to resume testing even without a Soviet violation. The record shows that on 17 July, Rusk cabled Harriman about the importance to Congress of a withdrawal clause.[43] The Soviets, however, countered that the principle of sovereignty implied their right to withdraw from a treaty even without specific language to that effect. The Soviets also objected to wording in the American draft permitting peaceful nuclear explosions, which would have protected the AEC's "Plowshares Program." To resolve these differences, Kennedy authorized Harriman to concede on the issue of peaceful nuclear explosions in return for the inclusion of language that would permit withdrawal in the face of third-party nuclear tests. After much wrangling, and with the president insistent that wording satisfactory to Congress would have to be included, a compromise was struck and a withdrawal clause suitable to Washington was inserted.[44]

At the eleventh hour, a new predicament developed to envelop the British and American allies in their first and only major negotiating dispute. Until then, British and American cooperation had been exceptionally strong. According to Sir Michael Wright, a disarmament expert attached to the British negotiating team in Moscow, the American and British delegations met daily in Moscow to discuss their respective instructions from London and Washington. Wright remembered that there were many different channels of communication between the two groups "on a low level to a high level."[45] The Soviets proposed that any country not then a party to the treaty but agreeing to its provisions in the future should automatically have its name affixed to the copy of the treaty kept in each of the original parties' depositories. The American delegation was apprehensive

43. "Chronological Index and Distribution Sheet on ALL BAN Messages," in National Security Files, Box 265, John F. Kennedy Library.

44. The wording was, "Each Party shall in exercising its national sovereignty have the right to withdraw from the treaty if it decides that extraordinary events, related to the subject matter of this treaty, have jeopardized the supreme interest of the country." See U.S. Department of State, *United States Treaties and Other International Agreements* (Washington, D.C., 1964), 1319.

45. Sir Michael Wright, recorded interview by David Nunnerly, 14 May 1969, p. 2, in John F. Kennedy Library Oral History Program.

that such a procedure might give the Soviets the opportunity to gain de jure American recognition of East Germany by including the communist government in a treaty to which the United States was a principal party. Harriman suggested that a stipulation be included in the treaty noting that accession to the agreement by a new government should not imply recognition by previous signatories. The Soviets, who had made the recognition of East Germany a cornerstone of their policy in Central Europe, strongly demurred. This impasse was further complicated by Soviet language in the preamble suggesting an abrogation of the right to employ nuclear weapons, even in self-defense.

The American insistence on not implying recognition of new signatories vexed the British. Macmillan wrote in his diary on 25 July 1963, ironically the day the Test-Ban Treaty was initialed: "The new American clause seemed to go back on the compromise already agreed which was quite sensible and said that no country *need* accept formal adherence from a country with which they were not in relations. The other American change was that nothing in the Treaty could be taken to prevent the use of nuclear weapons in war! That was so absurd as to be hardly credible."[46]

The impasse was partially resolved when the Soviets agreed to exclude any language in the preamble prohibiting the right to use nuclear weapons in wartime. Abram Chayes, the State Department's legal adviser, was particularly insistent on this point, although not for legal reasons. Chayes was convinced that the retention of wording outlawing all nuclear explosions—no matter how ambiguous—would raise serious problems in the Senate, where "the natural tendency would be for opponents of the treaty to try to load on to the reservation as much as they could to attenuate in this way, if not to defeat, the purpose and effects of the treaty."[47] The other outstanding issue was resolved when Fisher and McNaughton engineered a compromise whereby signatories would be required to sign only with governments that they recognized. In the late afternoon of 25 July, while Gore and Bundy were in the president's office, Kaysen called from Moscow and recommended that Kennedy approve the revised language. The president agreed immediately and phoned Macmillan with the news that the negotiations had been concluded.

With the treaty initialed, Kennedy attempted to tie all loose ends in the executive branch so that the administration could present a united front in testimony before the Senate. The Joint Chiefs, except for Chairman Taylor, were denied direct access to all cable traffic and excluded from active participation in the Moscow negotiations. Once the treaty became a certainty, however, the president and other civilian members of the administration lobbied the Joint Chiefs, both individually and collectively, vigorously and intensively. The main line of argument on behalf of the treaty was that the political value of ratification far ex-

46. Macmillan, *At the End of the Day*, 483.
47. Memorandum, Abram Chayes to Under Secretary Ball, 24 July 1963, in National Security Files, Box 265, John F. Kennedy Library.

ceeded any possible military disadvantages. Nevertheless, the Joint Chiefs calculated that the cost-benefit ratio of treaty ratification could be achieved only if four conditions were met:

1. The United States should not accept a limitation on testing if the Soviet Union could achieve a major advantage that could not be overcome by the United States under the present treaty.
2. The Test Ban Treaty is acceptable only if clandestine testing by the Soviets would not seriously affect the balance of power.
3. Withdrawal should be uncomplicated, allowing the United States to withdraw upon violation or serious jeopardy to the national interest.
4. If conditions under criteria 1 and 2 are not met, the treaty must convey adequate compensatory advantages elsewhere.[48]

Kennedy, eager to win the support of the Joint Chiefs, offered to attach safeguards to the treaty to meet these conditions. In testifying before the relevant Senate committees, each member of the Joint Chiefs stressed that his endorsement of the treaty was predicated on the enactment of guarantees that the president promised. Even so, there were still some reservations regarding the specific character of these safeguards, as LeMay testified before the Senate Foreign Relations Committee: "We are all aware of the statement by the President and the Secretary of Defense have made in regard to maintaining a test program and so forth. We have not, however, discussed with them what they mean by that—whether what we consider an adequate safeguard program coincides with their idea on the subject."[49]

## The Test-Ban Treaty and Domestic Politics

In an oral history interview conducted in 1965, George Kennan said of Kennedy: "He was very troubled about this problem [negotiating with the Soviets] because, having been in Congress, he was very sensitive to the strong anti-Communist feelings that were prevalent in a portion of the electorate and in a large portion of Congress. He wanted to handle this problem in such a way as to make progress in composing our differences . . . but not to get himself attacked at home for being soft on communism or anything of that sort."[50]

Kennedy negotiated the test-ban treaty with an eye toward the Senate ratification process. Specific items, such as the withdrawal clause, were negotiated with Senate objections in mind, and the Joint Chiefs were mollified to win their

48. *Hearings: Military Aspects*, 588.
49. *Ibid.*, 373.
50. George F. Kennan, recorded interview by Louis Fischer, 23 March 1965, pp. 43–44, in John F. Kennedy Library Oral History Program.

support on Capitol Hill. Not only did Khrushchev assume that Kennedy's insistence on on-site inspection was a function of politics, but Sir William Penney, a scientist attached to the British delegation to Moscow, told Macmillan: "It's not science but politics which holds back the President."[51]

Early in 1963, the potential for partisan division on the test-ban issue was strong. The Republican Conference Committee, in an attack echoed by the nation's leading Republicans, charged that Kennedy was leading the country into acceptance of a "risky, unenforceable pact" and established a committee, under the chairmanship of a strident test-ban opponent, Representative Craig Hosmer (R.-Calif.), to offer an alternative to the administration position. The Democratic side was far less united in support of the president. On 21 February, Senator Thomas Dodd (D.-Conn.) accused the administration of offering too many concessions to the Soviets, and, in the hearings of the Preparedness Investigating Subcommittee, two respected defense-oriented members of the party, Senators Henry Jackson (D.-Wash.) and Stuart Symington (D.-Mich.), questioned the administration's tendency to lower inspection requirements in return for negligible Soviet concessions.[52]

To combat criticism of Kennedy's test-ban policy, administration officials worked to cultivate important members of Congress. AEC commissioner Haworth engaged in extensive conversations with Senator John Pastore (D.-R.I.), chairman of the Joint Committee on Atomic Energy, and Adrian Fisher of ACDA did the same with Albert Gore. Senator Hubert Humphrey (D.-Minn.), a leading congressional supporter of the test ban, was actively consulted as well. Administration canvassing revealed that while there was substantial support for a partial ban, a comprehensive ban would be subject to considerably less favorable scrutiny.[53] That became clearer when, on 27 May, thirty-four senators, including Dodd, signed a resolution recommending that the United States actively pursue a partial test ban.

The centerpiece of the administration's lobbying efforts was the president himself. Throughout the early part of 1963, Kennedy repeatedly stressed the importance of a test ban, and on 21 March, while acknowledging the existence of opposition to his policy, he pledged to continue striving for an agreement. Although the number of interest groups favoring an accord outnumbered those opposed, the president understood that persuading the public at large of the wisdom of a test ban would require an active presidential commitment. As political adviser Fred Dutton wrote to the president in early 1963, "Most people outside of the ban-the-bomb groups are poorly informed and increasingly suspicious on the subject."[54]

51. Macmillan, *At the End of the Day*, 455.

52. *Hearings: Military Aspects*, 21–44, passim.

53. Mary Milling Lepper, *Foreign Policy Formulation: A Case Study of the Nuclear Test Ban Treaty* (Columbus, 1971), 78.

54. *Public Papers of . . . Kennedy, 1963*, p. 280; Memorandum, Fred Dutton to President Kennedy, n.d., John F. Kennedy Library.

Once the treaty was signed, however, Kennedy carefully orchestrated the activities of the pro-ban groups. On 7 August, representatives of the Citizens Committee for a Nuclear Test Ban met with Kennedy to discuss a lobbying strategy. Over the next month and a half, the president so closely monitored the efforts of the committee that he personally targeted senators such as Henry Jackson for attention by special interest groups and approved newspaper and television advertisements. The president also directed the committee to concentrate its efforts on swing states such as Colorado, Illinois, Iowa, Missouri, Ohio, South Dakota, and Washington.[55] Whatever the source of the change, public opinion moved decisively in favor of the treaty. At the 7 August White House meeting, a tally by congressional liaison Larry O'Brien revealed congressional mail running against a test ban by a fifteen-to-one margin. By 27 August, the tide began to turn, with pro-ban letters trailing anti-ban letters by a margin of three to two. By September letters in favor of the treaty took a decisive lead.[56] Paralleling the shift in letter-writing, public opinion polls indicated a demonstrable change. A Harris Poll conducted in early July showed 47 percent of the public offering unqualified approval for negotiations; a poll conducted on 1 September elicited 81 percent approval for the treaty.[57]

The public opinion trend made it unlikely that the Republican party, which had been critical of Kennedy's effort to secure a comprehensive ban, would mount a challenge to the partial ban. This reality was supported by a Harris Survey published on 26 August 1963, which demonstrated that while the president could be beaten in 1964 on economic and civil rights issues, 81 percent of the public supported him on his handling of Khrushchev. With some exceptions, Republican legislators from areas where the president's popularity was still over 50 percent such as George Aiken (R.-Vt.) and Pennsylvania senator Hugh Scott and former presidents Herbert Hoover and Eisenhower tendered immediate support. Although presidential aspirants such as Richard Nixon and Nelson Rockefeller attacked the "military and political assumptions" that underlay the treaty, even they supported ultimate ratification. Clearly, as one Republican senator told *Newsweek* on 5 August: "I don't see any political mileage in opposing the treaty. It is very likely that the Senate would approve such a treaty."[58]

The absence of any substantial political value in opposing the Test-Ban Treaty helped to forge the bipartisan consensus that ultimately produced an enormous victory, eighty-one to nineteen, for Kennedy in the Senate. The president, however, with an eye to 1964 and a commitment to achieving as near a unanimous vote as possible, did not take Republican or Democratic support for granted. Sensitive to Woodrow Wilson's personal and national defeat some forty-five

55. Cousins, *Improbable Triumvirate,* 138–44.

56. Vermont senator George Aiken noted that many of the anti-ban letters came from Texas and California, where right-wing groups were strongest. See *New York Times,* 19 September 1963, p. 10.

57. Cited in Lepper, *Foreign Policy Formulation,* 51, 54.

58. *Newsweek,* 26 August 1963, pp. 25–27; *New York Times,* 12 August 1963, p. 1; *Newsweek,* 5 August 1963, p. 17.

years earlier and convinced that his Democratic predecessor had needlessly alienated the Senate, Kennedy made certain to apprise key senators and Senate committees on developments from Moscow. Montana senator Mike Mansfield, the Democratic majority leader of the Senate, recalled that a tentative test-ban agreement was forwarded to the Foreign Relations Committee two weeks before its initialing in Moscow. In addition, the president dispatched Secretary Rusk and ACDA director Foster to speak individually with every senator while test-ban talks were in progress. On 24 July Rusk briefed members of the Senate Armed Services Committee and the Joint Committee on Atomic Energy, which had been particularly inclined to criticize the administration's previous negotiating position. From these conversations, it became clear to the administration that the treaty would have difficulty passing the Senate if it was attached to a nonaggression pact.[59]

Spurred by the president's stated desire to achieve "quick action" on ratification, Senate leaders of the Democratic party mobilized their legislative forces. At times their attempt to build broad, bipartisan support backfired as, for example, in the case of Humphrey's proposal to send a bipartisan congressional delegation to Moscow for the official signing ceremony. Republican leaders such as Bourke Hickenlooper of Iowa and George Aiken of Vermont feared that by going to Moscow, they would commit themselves to voting for the treaty even before Senate hearings convened. Arkansas Democrat J. William Fulbright, chairman of the Foreign Relations Committee, also opposed the idea on the grounds that it would create an issue that would deflect attention from the treaty itself. Ultimately this wrangle was resolved when Republicans Aiken and Leverett Saltonstall, from Kennedy's home state of Massachusetts, accompanied the delegation.

As senators gradually declared their intentions with regard to the treaty, Kennedy administered the decisive gesture in mid-September. On 28 July Senator Everett Dirksen, the Republican minority leader, had objected to the treaty on the grounds that it rested too heavily on Soviet good faith. In a meeting with Dirksen on 9 September the president assured the Republican leader of certain guarantees that would safeguard the security of the United States. These guarantees, contained in a public letter to Dirksen and Mansfield dated 11 September, included commitments to continue an underground testing program, to maintain preparedness for possible resumption of testing in prohibited environments, and to continue research in the detection of underground tests and a stipulation that the president still retained the right to employ nuclear weapons for self-defense purposes.[60]

These provisions were designed to satisfy the reservations voiced by the Joint Chiefs in their testimony before the Preparedness Subcommittee and the Foreign Relations Committee. In a larger sense, however, the commitment to main-

---

59. Mike Mansfield, recorded interview by Seth P. Tillman, 23 June 1964, p. 16, in John F. Kennedy Library Oral History Program; Read interview, 12.

60. *Public Papers of . . . Kennedy, 1963,* pp. 669–71.

tain vigilance in the face of continued Soviet hostility was designed to put the treaty in its proper perspective. Kennedy was essentially assuring the public, Congress, and the Joint Chiefs of Staff that by engaging in a nuclear test-ban treaty, the administration was merely committing itself to a course of action that had in the past enjoyed widespread and bipartisan support, that is, the balancing of the goals of avoidance of nuclear war and anticommunism. Dirksen, in supporting the treaty unreservedly, clearly associated the Republican party with the goals of the Democratic president. Items Dirksen listed in favor of the treaty included reference to the fact that the Republican party platform of 1960 had pledged to seek an early agreement to forgo nuclear tests in the atmosphere.[61] In this regard, Kennedy's policy was correctly seen as a culmination of efforts begun by his Republican predecessor.

## Assessment

The achievement of a partial test-ban accord, in conjunction with the Hot Line agreement of June 1963 and the wheat deal of October, represented a victory for Kennedy's belief that political and military competition with the Soviet Union did not preclude the achievement of agreements in areas of mutual interest. The Test-Ban Treaty, however, fell short of the president's stated goal to achieve a comprehensive accord. In part, that failure could be attributed to hesitancies on the Soviet side and the limits of seismic identification technology. Indeed, Seaborg argued that even had the numbers issue been resolved, many more logistical problems would have remained to be settled before a comprehensive treaty could be signed.[62]

Nor did the test ban appear to fit a strategic vision about the relationship between arms control and military policy. The test-ban efforts of the Kennedy administration occurred simultaneously with an expansion in American nuclear capabilities and indeed stimulated a counter-buildup on the Soviet side. Although civilian members of the administration defended the treaty as securing American nuclear superiority over the Soviet Union, there does not appear to have been a consensus about the extent to which an end to testing would indeed arrest the arms race. The test ban, therefore, was seen either as a way to curb proliferation or to create a more positive political atmosphere between East and West, but it otherwise had a negligible impact on strategic decisions made under Kennedy.

Notwithstanding the limitations of the test ban, it did display the importance of presidential leadership in the arms control area. Aside from strengthening those elements of the administration most in favor of a test ban, Kennedy took independent actions to keep the negotiations alive when they appeared least

61. U.S. Arms Control and Disarmament Agency, *Documents on Disarmament, 1963,* p. 497.
62. Seaborg, *Kennedy,* 191–92.

promising. Gestures such as the Moscow talks initiative, the suspension of atmospheric testing, and the American University address all circumvented routine bureaucratic channels. Once the talks reached the decisive point, Kennedy personally managed the flow of information within the executive branch, distanced the military from active participation in the negotiations, and presented the Joint Chiefs with what amounted to a fait accompli. This point was not lost on LeMay, who testified: "I think that the fact that it had been signed had an effect on me. . . . I think I would have been against it." The impression that the chiefs were, in fact, endorsing a treaty they opposed was strong among opponents of the agreement. On 13 September 1963, Senator John Stennis (D.-Miss.), who as chairman of the Preparedness Investigating Subcommittee had close ties to the military, charged that the military had been coerced into approving the test ban. For his part, Kennedy was not so certain that public support of the chiefs would prevent the military from lobbying behind the scenes to defeat it.[63]

The question remains as to whether Kennedy would have prevailed on the test-ban issue had the Soviets actually accepted his offer of seven inspections per year and had other logistical issues been resolved. The military had made clear its public opposition to a comprehensive ban on the eve of Harriman's departure to Moscow. Had Harriman reached an accord with the Soviets on a comprehensive ban, it is not certain that the chiefs would have endorsed the treaty after the fact, as they did the partial treaty. It is also unclear as to whether the Republican party would have supported Kennedy on an agreement that relied on what Republicans had been describing throughout the early part of 1963 as minimal inspection requirements. Even the support of the Democrats would have been questionable. The Senate resolution calling for an atmospheric ban, sponsored by comprehensive ban opponent Senator Dodd, was offered not as a means to pave the way toward a comprehensive ban but as an alternative to it. It is difficult to escape the conclusion that Kennedy succeeded in rallying support for the Test-Ban Treaty, in part, because it was so tame in comparison to what the critics had been expecting.

But it was precisely this attention to what could or could not be offered to the public that distinguished Kennedy's test-ban policy. Throughout his presidency, Kennedy was careful to cultivate congressional opinion on arms control, and his negotiating positions were clearly crafted with the Senate and the public in mind. He wanted a comprehensive ban and felt that Soviet cheating on such a ban would have minimal influence on the strategic balance, yet he dared not go below the offer of seven inspections, despite urgings from some in his administration and Prime Minister Macmillan to do so. He thus managed to locate an acceptable balance between the goals of anticommunism and avoidance of nuclear war and to set a standard for the fashioning and promotion of future arms control policy.

63. *Hearings: Nuclear Test Ban Treaty*, 373; *New York Times*, 14 September 1963, p. 4; Cousins, *Improbable Triumvirate*, 134.

# 6

# The Limited Test-Ban Treaty of 1963

## Carl Kaysen

~

On 5 August 1963, the foreign ministers of the United Kingdom, the Union of Soviet Socialist Republics, and the United States formally signed the Treaty Banning Nuclear Weapons Tests in the Atmosphere, in Outer Space, and Under Water, which their representatives had negotiated and initialed in Moscow less than a month earlier. The title of the treaty repeats its chief substantive provisions, contained in Article I, paragraph 1.[1] There are two other noteworthy points in the treaty. The first is made in two paragraphs of the preamble that proclaim the "speediest possible achievement of . . . general and complete disarmament" as a principal aim of the parties and pledge their determination to continue negotiating to achieve "the discontinuance of all test explosions of nuclear weapons for all time." The second is expressed in the oblique language of the withdrawal clause in Article IV, allowing each party, in exercising its national sovereignty, to withdraw on three months' notice "if it decides that extraordinary events, related to the subject matter of this Treaty, have jeopardized the supreme interests of its country."[2] The treaty went into force on 10 October 1963, upon ratification by the United States, the other two original parties having already ratified it. By the end of 1963, 109 states had adhered to it; at present the most important nonsignatories are China, France, Cuba, and North Korea.[3]

Despite the promise in the preamble of the Partial Test-Ban Treaty, thirty years later, a complete test-ban treaty (CTBT) has not yet been achieved. Since 1980, the United States has been the main obstacle; President Ronald Reagan

---

1. The Appendix to this chapter contains the text of the treaty.
2. See treaty text, Article IV.
3. Jozef Goldblatt, *Agreements for Arms Control* (Stockholm, 1982), table, 304–305. As of 1 January 1991 there were 118 adherents. See SIPRI 1991 Yearbook page 668, and table, pp. 670–86. China and France have never signed the treaty but renounced atmospheric testing unilaterally, France in 1975 and China in 1985; see Jozef Goldblatt and D. Cox, eds., *Nuclear Weapons Tests: Prohibition or Limitation* (New York, 1988), 10. Pakistan signed the treaty in 1963 but did not ratify it until 1988; see Goldblatt, *Agreements for Arms Control,* and SIPRI Yearbook.

reversed the policy of his predecessors from Eisenhower on, and the United States has refused to discuss a CTBT.[4]

## The Historical Background

Nuclear testing was brought to the fore as a political issue and a matter of international concern by the U.S. test series on Bikini in the western Pacific in early 1954. On 1 March, the Bravo test of a hydrogen device—at a yield of fifteen megatons, twice the predicted value—produced widespread radioactive fallout. The crew of a Japanese tuna trawler suffered severe radiation sickness and one subsequently died; nearby Marshall Islanders were also seriously affected, and a small number of American servicemen in the area were exposed as well, but less seriously. Fish contaminated by radioactivity appeared in the Japanese market. The fears and anxieties of Hiroshima and Nagasaki were revived in Japan and soon reflected worldwide. In the United States, for the first time one corner of the veil of secrecy that covered nuclear weapons was lifted and the public became aware of the enormous destructive potential of hydrogen weapons. A contentious public discussion of their desirability and necessity followed.[5]

This discussion was raised to the level of international politics at the beginning of April, when Prime Minister Jawalarlal Nehru, speaking to the Indian Parliament, called for an immediate standstill agreement between the United States and the Soviets to prohibit nuclear tests while the United Nations worked out a comprehensive disarmament agreement.

From the first, the public discussion of nuclear testing intertwined two different strands of concern. One, and perhaps the more widespread in the United States, was anxiety about the health effects of radiation from fallout. The other was concern with testing as both a symbol and an instrument of the U.S.-Soviet arms race and the consequent specter of nuclear war.

The administration tried to minimize the first concern by emphasizing the very small additional contribution weapons tests made to natural background radiation and—at first—suggesting that the new contribution was below a "threshold" level of radiation that could cause disease or genetic mutations. The

---

4. The Johnson, Nixon, and Ford administrations focused their efforts in arms control on other targets: Johnson on the Non-Proliferation Treaty, Nixon and Ford on strategic arms limitation. Discussions of a complete test-ban treaty continued episodically in the United Nations Committee on Disarmament but were not pursued with any persistence or determination. Under Carter a renewed but ultimately unsuccessful effort was made. See G. Allen Greb, "Survey of Past Nuclear Test Ban Negotiations," in Goldblatt and Cox, eds., *Nuclear Weapons Tests;* also, Herbert York, *Making Weapons and Talking Peace* (New York, 1987), chapter 14.

5. This account is drawn from Robert A. Divine, *Blowing on the Wind: The Nuclear Test Ban Debate, 1954–1960* (New York, 1978), a lively representation of the nuclear testing issue during the Eisenhower administration. See also Harold K. Jacobsen and Eric Stein, *Diplomats, Scientists, and Politicians* (Ann Arbor, 1966), a more detailed and scholarly history of the negotiations on a test-ban treaty from 1957 to 1963.

weight of scientific judgment, however, was that no threshold existed and that testing did in fact cause a very small but definite increase in cancers of various sorts, as well as genetic damage responsible for abortions, stillbirths, and deformations in succeeding generations. The second concern was more salient abroad than at home, and the administration's response to it, that nuclear weapons tests were vital to our security, was broadly accepted in the United States. Further, the small increase in health risks was simply a necessary price to pay for maintaining the U.S. strategic superiority that prevented nuclear war.

International anxiety about fallout and the arms race persisted. It was heightened by a series of large Soviet thermonuclear tests in the fall of 1955 that spread fallout worldwide. At the same time, the Soviets took up the Indian proposal for a suspension of tests, repeating it in various international forums. At the end of year, the Christmas message of the pope incorporated this call in a broader disarmament proposal, contributing to the continued pressure on the United States.

President Eisenhower was not unsympathetic to these anxieties. He respected the popular concern over fallout and worried—as his military and atomic energy advisers did not—about the possible consequences of the arms race. In early 1955, Eisenhower had appointed Harold Stassen as his special assistant on disarmament, thus providing an institutional focus for pressures on these issues. A year later the Senate, with a Democratic majority, added a subcommittee on disarmament, chaired by Hubert Humphrey, to its Foreign Relations Committee, thus providing still another channel for public discussion.

Continued testing in 1956 and 1957 by the United States and the Soviet Union—joined in the spring of 1957 by Britain, which tested its first thermonuclear weapons in the South Pacific—kept the level of fallout, international anxiety, and discussion high. In the United States, Adlai Stevenson, the Democratic candidate in the 1956 presidential campaign, called for a suspension of testing and the negotiation of a test-ban treaty. The endorsement of Stevenson's position by the Soviet leadership, followed by the Soviet invasion of Hungary, destroyed the electoral appeal of Stevenson's position. He was widely portrayed as a Soviet dupe by Republican speakers, though not by the president, who simply reiterated the necessity for continued testing on national security grounds. Nonetheless, the question of ending nuclear testing had become an issue on the public's agenda, domestically as well as internationally, and remained there. The scientific community continued to discuss the health hazards of fallout, and precisely because the issues were complex and difficult and the evidence scanty, the questions were unresolved. Discussion and public anxiety persisted.

All during this period, these issues were under consideration in the United Nations' Commission on Disarmament, specifically in the five-nation subcommittee consisting of the United States, Soviet Union, Britain, France, and Canada. Discussion was repetitive and fruitless. The Soviets repeatedly proposed an uninspected test-ban treaty as a first step in the disarmament process; the United States responded by proposing a halt to all nuclear weapons production, supervised and verified by international control machinery. Although the talks recycled old positions and made no progress, public concern remained high, and opposition to continued testing increased.


## America Changes Its Position

Three sets of events in the first part of 1958 culminated in a change in the American position. The Soviets conducted a massive series of tests in late February and March. Almost immediately following, they announced that they were unilaterally halting further tests and invited the United States and United Kingdom to do the same. Of course, if the latter two nations continued to test, then the Soviets would feel free to do likewise.

The United States was just preparing its own next series of tests, which the weapons laboratories and the military felt were indispensable. So the administration's first response was to denounce the Soviet call as cynical propaganda, announce the forthcoming U.S. test series, and repeat the U.S. position that a test ban was possible only if it were linked to a cutoff in weapons production. This position was unpersuasive to many in the United States and abroad. Protests against the proposed U.S. tests reached a new level of intensity and political support; the Soviets scored a considerable propaganda coup.

Third, and probably most important, the president had begun to receive technical advice on the issues from a source in his administration other than the weapons laboratories and the Pentagon. For the first time, he heard serious arguments in favor of a test ban from people he respected and trusted, not from critics outside the government who could be dismissed as hostile, politically motivated, and ill-informed.

The President's Science Advisory Committee, created in response to the Soviet launch of Sputnik in October 1957, consisted of a group of eminent scientists outside the government who had worked on nuclear and other weapons during and immediately after World War II, as well as the most senior scientific personnel in the Pentagon and the Atomic Energy Commission. It reported to the president through his newly appointed full-time special assistant for science and technology, James Killian, on leave from his position as president of MIT.

A PSAC panel, chaired by Hans Bethe, who had been one of the senior scientists at Los Alamos, reported that an inspected test-ban treaty was feasible, though not free of risk, and would, on balance, be in the U.S. security interest. This information reinforced Eisenhower's own feelings against the continuation of testing. He accordingly proposed to Khrushchev—who had just recently become the top Soviet leader—that the United States, USSR, and United Kingdom send teams of scientists to Geneva to seek agreement on the technical parameters of a verification system for a test-ban treaty.

## The Geneva Conference of Experts and the Opening of Negotiations

The conference met in Geneva in July and August 1958 and finally agreed that a worldwide system of from 170 to 180 land and sea control stations would have a "good probability" of detecting explosions of down to one kiloton in size. For deep underground events there would be difficulty in distinguishing between explosions of less than five-kiloton magnitude and earthquakes; for events of five-kiloton-equivalent magnitude or above, the probability of identification was estimated at 90 percent. The conference report recognized the need for inspections to determine the nature of unidentified events, without detailed discussion of how such inspections would be conducted or how many might be required.[6]

Following the agreed report, the United States proposed to the Soviets and British that the three begin negotiations on a test-ban treaty at the end of October and offered to cease further nuclear tests for a year and to continue the moratorium annually as long as progress was being made in establishing a control network and moving toward actual disarmament. For the first time, the United States accepted a test-ban treaty as a desirable goal in itself, without linking it to a simultaneous end to production of nuclear weapons.

The tripartite Geneva Conference on the Discontinuance of Nuclear Weapons Tests opened on 31 October 1958. It was preceded by a flurry of tests by all three participants: nineteen by the United States, mostly underground; fourteen atmospheric tests by the Soviet Union; four by the United Kingdom. In all three countries the weapons designers pressed to learn as much as possible before the moratorium. The Soviets even conducted two small tests on the first days of November after the conference opened. Indeed, 1958 was the peak year for nuclear tests up to that time: 111 for the three powers, compared with 178 from 1946 through 1957.[7]

The negotiations in Geneva continued for the rest of Eisenhower's presidency. They were difficult and several times appeared to reach an impasse. New analyses of the underground test series in the fall of 1958 by a PSAC panel led to a reevaluation of the control system agreed to by the Conference of Experts the previous summer. Its capacity to detect and identify underground explosions below ten-kiloton-equivalent was thought to be much less than previously supposed. Improvements and extensions to the system could make up for some of the difference, and further effort could produce more improvements in detection capability. Problems in the detection of small, very high altitude explosions were revealed by other tests conducted during this period. Finally, the possibility of concealing fairly large underground explosions by "decoupling"—conducting them in large underground chambers—was raised.

6. See Chapter 3 of Jacobsen and Stein, *Diplomats, Scientists, and Politicians,* for a detailed discussion of the Conference of Experts.

7. See SIPRI Yearbook 1991, part I, chapter 2, Appendix tables A.2 and 3, pp. 46–47.

All this produced an amplified replay of public argument in the United States between the proponents of a test ban in Congress and the public and its opponents in the AEC and the Pentagon. President Eisenhower maintained his commitment to seeking a treaty. His resolve was strengthened by the pressure from Prime Minister Macmillan, who was eager for a measure of détente with the Soviets, and the continued support of the PSAC under its second chairman, George Kistiakowsky.

In April 1959, Eisenhower offered a partial test-ban treaty, covering tests in the atmosphere below fifty kilometers, as an interim measure, while negotiations on a comprehensive treaty continued. Khrushchev rejected the proposal and pressed for renewed negotiation on a comprehensive treaty.

In early 1960, the United States and the Soviets came close to agreement in Geneva. In February, the United States had offered a treaty ending all nuclear tests in the atmosphere, in the oceans, in space up to the limits of detectability, and underground above a threshold of 4.75 on the Richter Scale, equivalent to twenty kilometers, with an annual inspection quota for events of smaller magnitude. A month later the Soviets agreed to accept the U.S. plan provided the parties also agreed to a moratorium on underground tests below the threshold.

Eisenhower, facing continued divided counsel, even more passionately expressed, decided in favor of a positive response to the Soviet proposal. In this he was again strongly supported by Macmillan, ever active in his search for détente. Two key questions remained for negotiation: how long would the moratorium on underground tests below the threshold last? What would be the annual quota of on-site inspections? These issues were left for direct negotiation between Eisenhower and Khrushchev at the forthcoming Paris summit in May.

The shooting down of a U-2 spy plane over the Soviet Union on 1 May 1960 and its consequences aborted the summit and ended the possibility of agreement on a test ban. Although the meetings in Geneva resumed over the next six months, negotiations stalled; the Soviets were waiting for a new administration.

## The New Administration

John F. Kennedy took office in January 1961 committed to a test-ban treaty and determined to show he could succeed in achieving it, as his predecessor had not.[8] One indication of the importance he attached to the treaty and disarmament questions more generally was his appointment of John J. McCloy as his special

---

8. See Glenn Seaborg, *Kennedy, Khrushchev and the Test Ban* (Berkeley, 1981), 32–33, for expressions of Kennedy's position before his campaign for the presidency. Seaborg, who had received a Nobel Prize in chemistry for his creation of transuranic elements, was chairman of the Atomic Energy Commission from 1961 to 1971. The book is a careful and thorough account of the Kennedy administration's dealings with the question of nuclear weapons testing, based on Seaborg's contemporaneous diaries. I have drawn on it heavily, supplementing it with my own recollections of some events.

adviser on disarmament and Arthur Dean as head of the U.S. delegation to the Geneva Conference. Both were centrist Republicans, who were seen as friends and respected by the previous administration. It was characteristic of Kennedy to select Republicans or nonpartisans to deal with issues in which bipartisan support was necessary: for example, Douglas Dillon at the Treasury, Robert McNamara at Defense, John McCone at the CIA.

The Geneva Conference was scheduled to resume on 7 February 1961. Shortly after his inauguration, Kennedy requested and the Soviets and British agreed to a postponement until 21 March to allow the new administration to review its position. The review, conducted by McCloy, started within a week of the inauguration. The president himself was an active participant in the discussions, and he led one White House briefing of a group of important members of Congress.

As a result of the review, the U.S. delegation returned to Geneva with several new elements in its position, all seen as moving to accommodate Soviet views. The most important were an increase in the duration of the moratorium on underground testing below seismic magnitude 4.75 from two to three years, although the Soviets had asked for four or five; an offer to allow Soviet inspections of the internal mechanisms of devices used in research and peaceful tests; an acceptance of a total ban on tests in space; a reduction in the number of detection posts on Soviet soil from twenty-one to nineteen, whereas the Soviets had set fifteen as the number they would accept, and acceptance of the Soviet request for an equal annual quota of inspections of each original party to the treaty, that is, on the U.S. formulation, twenty for the USSR, twenty for the United States, and twenty for the United Kingdom, although the Soviets, up to that time, had spoken of a quota of three inspections; and acceptance of East-West parity in the staffing of detection stations and the organs of the proposed control commission. The Soviets continued to reject the U.S.-U.K. proposals and were unmoved by an offer to make the inspection quota proportional to the number of unidentified seismic events beyond sixty, varying the annual inspections quota from ten at sixty events to a maximum of twenty.[9]

The new U.S.-U.K. position in Geneva did not end the division of opinion among the United States public and in the government. The military and the weapons laboratories were still unsympathetic to a test ban and anxiously suspicious of undetected Soviet testing in violation of the moratorium. The chairman of the AEC, Glenn Seaborg, supported the proposed treaty, unlike John McCone, his predecessor under Eisenhower. The rest of the lineup was not too dissimilar from what it had been. The president's science adviser, Jerome B. Wiesner, was a strong proponent of a treaty, as his predecessor had been. So were McCloy and Dean—Dean possibly bringing more conviction and enthusiasm to his task than James Wadsworth, the previous head of the delegation. The civilian leaders of the Defense Department, Robert McNamara and Roswell Gil-

9. Seaborg, *Kennedy,* 67.

patric, were more sympathetic to the treaty than their predecessors, but they too were sensitive to the military's concern about falling behind the Soviets. When Harold Brown came from Livermore Laboratory to replace Herbert York as director of Defense Research and Engineering—the chief technical person in the Department of Defense—in June 1961, he was much more skeptical of the desirability of a treaty than his predecessor. The decisive voice, of course, was the president's. Eisenhower had over time become a proponent of a treaty but was losing his enthusiasm after the blowup of the May 1960 summit; Kennedy had started as an enthusiast.

The continued Soviet stonewalling at Geneva raised the question of how long the United States should maintain its observance of the moratorium, giving more force to the views of those who opposed it in the first place and were hostile to the treaty. The question was further highlighted by Kennedy's meeting with Khrushchev in Vienna at the beginning of June. Khrushchev did not explicitly break off the Geneva negotiations, but he called them futile and insisted that there could be no inspections without Soviet consent. Despite his dismay, the president persisted in pushing the discussions in Geneva, but he became more concerned with the necessity and desirability of resuming weapons tests. He asked for the advice of a PSAC technical panel under the leadership of W. K. H. Panofsky on the possibility of clandestine testing by the Soviets and what they might learn from so doing, what the United States could learn from a resumption of tests, and the relative advantages to both sides of resumption.

The panel concluded that there was no evidence on whether the Soviets had been testing secretly, and there was no urgent, immediate need for the United States to resume testing. But the panel judged that if the Soviets were testing secretly, a moratorium could not be sustained in the long run without impairing the U.S. military position.

The report and discussion of it by his advisers persuaded the president to send Dean back to Geneva for another test of Soviet intentions. He was armed with a further small piece of bait, which he presented near the end of August. If improvement in the technology of identification allowed it, the threshold in underground tests would be reduced or eliminated at the end of the moratorium period of three years. The Soviets showed no interest; the reason soon became obvious.

### The Resumption of Testing

On 30 August, an intercepted message from the internal Soviet news service revealed that the Soviets were about to announce the resumption of nuclear testing; the formal announcement came later the same day. It was bellicose in the extreme, boasting that the tests would reveal super weapons and rockets that could deliver them to any spot on the globe. Over the next three months, the

Soviets conducted more than fifty tests, including a fifty-eight-megaton explosion—the largest ever made.[10]

President Kennedy was outraged; he felt both deceived and humiliated.[11] But his first public response was to propose jointly with Prime Minister Macmillan that the USSR join with Britain and the United States in signing a treaty to outlaw tests in the atmosphere that caused fallout, relying on national detection capabilities rather than international control machinery for its enforcement. The proposal was made on 3 September; it was rejected by Khrushchev, as its proposers expected, on 9 September. Even before Khrushchev's response, Kennedy announced that the United States would resume testing, but only underground, without contributing to further fallout. The first test came ten days later, on 15 September. The series lasted into the spring of the following year, constituting twenty tests in all.

Kennedy's decision was at least as much political as technical. He had to deal with the internal pressures for testing from the military and the weapons laboratories, reinforced now by the fact that the Russians were learning from their tests. Equally or more important, he felt he had to respond to the public challenge represented by the Soviet test series. A conversation with Adlai Stevenson, his ambassador to the UN, was reported as follows by Arthur Schlesinger:

> "What choice did we have? They had spit in our eye three times. We couldn't possibly sit back and do nothing at all. We had to do this." Stevenson remarked, "But we were ahead in the propaganda battle." Kennedy said, "What does that mean? I don't hear of any windows broken because of the Soviet decision. The neutrals have been terrible. The Russians made two tests after our note calling for a ban on atmospheric testing. Maybe they couldn't have stopped the first, but they could have stopped the second. . . . All this made Khrushchev look pretty tough. He has had a succession of apparent victories—space, Cuba, the thirteenth of August [the Berlin Wall], though I don't myself regard this as a Soviet victory. He wants to give out the feeling that he has us on the run. The third test was a contemptuous response to our note. . . . Anyway the decision has been made. I'm not saying it was the right decision. Who the hell knows? But it is the decision which has been taken."[12]

An American response limited to underground testing was clearly inadequate, from both technical and political perspectives. Evaluation of the Soviet test series

10. Jacobsen and Stein, *Diplomats, Scientists, and Politicians*, 342. U.S. experts estimated that the design would have been the basis for a one-hundred-megaton weapon had a uranium rather than a lead blanket been used as an outer layer around the fusionable material.

11. Personal observation.

12. See Arthur Schlesinger, Jr., *A Thousand Days: John F. Kennedy in the White House* (Boston, 1965), 482. This passage is quoted by Seaborg, *Kennedy*, 88.

led to the conclusion that Soviet capabilities in weapons design were in some respects equal to or superior to our own. This contrasted strongly with the general appraisal when the test-ban negotiations started in 1958 that the United States had a substantial technical lead. Nor was an invisible series of small underground tests the psychological and propaganda equivalent of the Soviet megaton blasts as an answer to their tactic of intimidation.

Although the U.S. delegation returned to Geneva at the end of November, the attention of the administration shifted to the resumption of testing in the atmosphere: whether, when, where, how many tests of what kind.

Once again the internal divisions became evident. The military and the weapons laboratories pressed for resumption, and on a large scale. They had support from the civilian leadership of the Defense Department and the head of the AEC. Those more concerned with ideas and opinions than military hardware, the secretary of state, the U.S. ambassador, the director of the United States Information Agency, opposed it. They were supported by several in the White House staff, by the president's science adviser, and by many PSAC members, who saw the risks of the ongoing arms race as at least as great as the risks of allowing the Soviets to learn more about nuclear weapons sooner, and they were worried about fallout. These decisions inside the government were mirrored in congressional and public discussion, although the constraints of secrecy on detailed public discussion of nuclear issues were still strong, to an extent now difficult to remember.

Prime Minister Macmillan was an important addition to the side opposing resumption, and his influence on the president—always present—was increased because the United States wanted to use the British test site in the Pacific on Christmas Island. Macmillan pressed Kennedy to renew the offer of an atmospheric test ban; he would not. Later, at the end of October, Macmillan proposed that the United States and United Kingdom announce a new six-month moratorium on atmospheric testing. Again Kennedy said no, and in early November, he announced publicly that preparations for an atmospheric test series were under way but that no final decision on whether they were to go forward had yet been made.

The Geneva Conference had its last fruitless sessions at the end of 1961 and the beginning of 1962. The day after the talks resumed on 28 November, the Soviets had a new proposal of their own. Tests in the atmosphere, outer space, and underwater would be forbidden; enforcement would be by national means of observation. Further, the parties would agree to an indefinite moratorium on testing underground while they negotiated on a control system. After a month, the conference recessed for the year-end holidays, resuming on 16 January 1962. On that date the United States and United Kingdom formally rejected the Soviet proposal: no more uninspected moratoria. After two more weeks, the conference adjourned *sine die*.

On 2 March, four months after his announcement that preparations to resume atmospheric testing were under way, four months filled with repeated discussions of its desirability, the president announced his decision to resume test-ing at the end of the following month. The announcement was hedged with the proposal that the test ban treaty the United States had offered at Geneva was still on offer; should the Soviets sign it, there would be no tests.

## Continuing Negotiations in a New Forum

Though the tripartite Conference on the Discontinuance of Nuclear Weapons Tests was dead, the discussions themselves were not. As a result of bilateral discussions between the United States and the Soviets in the summer of 1961, an Eighteen-Nation Disarmament Committee had been created under the auspices of the United Nations. Transferred to this new committee, a further discussion of a test ban began in March 1962.[13] Discussions lasted a month. Despite the efforts of the eight neutrals, the two sides essentially repeated their previous positions, and no progress was made.

The U.S. test series began on 25 April 1962 and lasted until the beginning of November. There were forty tests, with a total explosive force of twenty megatons, about one order of magnitude less than that of the Soviet test series. In July, the ENDC resumed its sessions in Geneva. Meanwhile, the United States continued to examine the problems of detecting and identifying underground tests. The analysis of new data and the reevaluation of the seismic record using evidence from experimental underground explosions led to a further modification of the U.S.-U.K. position on the number of seismic stations and number of inspections required for an effective control system.

The continuing efforts of the eight neutrals to find a position intermediate between Soviet rejection of on-site inspections and U.S. insistence on them acted as further pressure on the United States to modify its position. In April, this group had produced a draft memorandum, not conspicuous for its clarity or precision, providing for an international scientific commission drawn from nonaligned countries to review seismic data from all sources. In the case of a significant unidentifiable event, the commission would "seek clarification from the party in whose territory the event had occurred. 'The party and the Commission should consult as to what further measures of clarification including verification *in loco* would facilitate the assessment.' . . . After the commission had furnished the parties with its assessment, the parties 'would be free to determine their action with regard to [withdrawing from] the treaty.' "[14] This provision for

---

13. Jacobsen and Stein, *Diplomats, Scientists, and Politicians,* 356–60. The membership of the committee included Canada, France (which never attended), Italy, the United Kingdom, and the United States—NATO members; Bulgaria, Czechoslovakia, Poland, Armenia, and the U.S.S.R.—Warsaw Pact members; and Brazil, Burma, Ethiopia, Mexico, Nigeria, Sweden, and the United Arab Emirates—"neutrals." Discussion alternated between the full committee and a subcommittee consisting of the U.K., the U.S. and the USSR.

14. Seaborg, *Kennedy,* 148–49. The memorandum in considerable detail is in Jacobsen and Stein, *Diplomats, Scientists, and Politicians,* 370–77.

what came to be termed "invitational inspection" was unacceptable to the United States and attractive to the Soviets, who accepted it as a basis for continuing negotiations and used it to argue against the need for obligatory inspections.

At the end of August, the United States and United Kingdom offered two new draft treaties. One banned tests in the atmosphere, in space, and underwater, requiring no international control machinery at all. The second was a comprehensive treaty, requiring significantly less elaborate and extensive control machinery than earlier versions the West had presented. There would be more reliance on existing national seismic stations and fewer international control stations specially installed. But a quota of obligatory inspections remained, though neither the number of stations nor the number of inspections was specified. The United States indicated clearly that substantially smaller numbers of each than were discussed in 1960–61 would be acceptable and that inspections would be focused on areas of seismic activity and limited in a-seismic areas.

All this was to no avail. The Soviets immediately rejected both drafts. The partial treaty was unacceptable because it was partial: it "legalized" underground testing. The comprehensive treaty was merely a recycling of the same unacceptable elements, specifically the requirement of on-site inspections binding on the party on whose territory an unidentified event occurred. When the ENDC recessed in early September for the fall meeting of the UN General Assembly, expecting to reconvene in early November, the deadlock appeared as complete as ever. Nor did the discussions in the General Assembly change the situation.

## A New Soviet Initiative

The confrontation over the Soviet deployment of MRBMs and intermediate-range ballistic missiles (IRBMs) in Cuba dominated the international scene in the last half of October. The course and resolution of the crisis increased Kennedy's concern with the U.S.-Soviet military competition and strengthened his determination to complete the negotiations on the test-ban treaty. It probably led Khrushchev to a new view of Kennedy and underlined for him the true state of the U.S.-Soviet nuclear balance.[15]

Khrushchev, in his letter to Kennedy of 28 October, in which he agreed to withdraw the missiles from Cuba, wrote, "We should like to continue the exchange of views on the prohibition of atomic and thermonuclear weapons, on general disarmament and other problems relating to the relaxation of international tension." Kennedy's immediate response was that "perhaps now, as we

---

15. A play about the October crisis entitled *The Kennedy Brothers* was very popular when it showed in 1963. It was written by Feodor Burlatsky, one of Khrushchev's speechwriters, who had participated in drafting some of Khrushchev's letters to Kennedy, and may be taken to reflect Khrushchev's own attitude.

step back from danger, we can make some real progress in this vital field. I think we should give priority to questions relating to the proliferation of nuclear weapons . . . and to the great effort for a nuclear test-ban."[16]

Toward the end of December, Khrushchev wrote another "pen pal" letter to Kennedy on the test-ban negotiations. His central point was that he saw the U.S. insistence on international control and inspection as the chief obstacle to a treaty. Although he was certain that both were unnecessary, he was willing both to discuss the installation of automatic seismographs in the Soviet Union (which had been discussed at the ENDC in Geneva earlier in the month) and to accept "two to three inspections per year in the territory of each of the nuclear powers." Khrushchev explained the number by referring to a discussion between Dean and Kuznetsov, the Soviet deputy foreign minister, in New York at the end of October, in which Dean said that two to four inspections per year would suffice. Dean himself believed that the only numbers he mentioned to Kuznetsov as an acceptable quota of inspections ranged from eight to ten, a range Kennedy repeated in his response to Khrushchev.[17] In that response, he welcomed Soviet acceptance of the principle of inspection and expressed the hope that the Soviets would move up from a quota of three because the United States had moved down from a quota of twelve to twenty to one of eight to ten.

The gap between a quota acceptable to the Soviets and the tolerable minimum the United States could risk bedeviled the remaining discussion of the comprehensive treaty. In April 1963, Khrushchev granted an interview to an American publicist, Norman Cousins, then editor of the *Saturday Review*. Cousins's report of the interview quoted Khrushchev as follows:

> After Cuba, there was a real chance for both the Soviet Union and the United States to take measures together that would advance the peace by easing tensions. The one area on which I thought we were closest to agreement was nuclear testing, and so I went before the Council of Ministers and said to them:
>
> "We can have an agreement with the United States to stop nuclear tests if we agree to three inspections. I know that three inspections are not necessary, and that the policing can be done adequately from outside our borders. But the American Congress has convinced itself that onsite inspection is necessary and the President cannot get a treaty through the Senate without it. Very well, then let us accommodate the President."
>
> The Council asked me if I was certain that we could have a treaty if we agreed to three inspections and I told them yes. Finally, I persuaded them.
>
> People in the United States seem to think that I am a dictator who

16. Quoted in Seaborg, *Kennedy*, 176.
17. Quoted *ibid.*, 174.

can put into practice any policy I wish. Not so. I've got to persuade before I can govern. Anyway, the Council of Ministers agreed to my urgent recommendation. Then I notified the United States I would accept three inspections. Back came the American rejection. They now wanted not three inspections or even six. They wanted eight. And so once again I was made to look foolish. But I can tell you this: it won't happen again.[18]

Another source of Khrushchev's conviction was a conversation between Y. K. Federov, a Soviet scientist and member of the Geneva delegation, and Wiesner in Washington in October 1962, which Khrushchev mentioned to Cousins.[19] In Wiesner's own report of the conversation he said that he suggested to Federov that if Khrushchev offered three inspections, Kennedy would respond with seven or eight, and then there might be a compromise on five.

In frequent discussions within the government on the progress of the negotiations at this period, Kennedy displayed his strong sense of urgency and focused in particular on his concern over the Chinese nuclear weapons program. Yet he knew that the Chinese had denounced the Soviet-American negotiations and publicly stated that they would not join the treaty. Perhaps he felt that the pressure of criticism from Third World neutrals would focus on China if the major nuclear powers signed a treaty to which most nations adhered.

Following up on the Kennedy-Khrushchev correspondence in December, further tripartite talks were held in Washington and New York in January 1963. They were unproductive: the Soviets simply repeated their positions on three unmanned seismic stations and a quota of three inspections. The U.S.-U.K. delegates sought to discuss the mode and parameters of on-site inspections before addressing the quota; the Soviets refused. In the continuing internal discussions with his senior officials, the president had decided that he could accept an inspection quota as low as six, although the smallest number mentioned to the Soviets was seven.

The ENDC continued to meet during the spring without result. The Soviets repeated their insistence that the United States accept what the Soviets described as the U.S. proposal of three inspections; the United States continued to ask for discussion of the specifics of an inspection before negotiating on the quota; neither responded.

## The Last Mile

Frustrated by the lack of progress, Macmillan tried to stimulate Kennedy to new activity. After further correspondence, the two sent a joint letter to Khrushchev,

18. Norman Cousins, "Notes on a 1963 Visit with Khrushchev," *Saturday Review,* 7 November 1964, p. 21.
19. Seaborg, *Kennedy,* 180–81.

delivered by their ambassadors in Moscow, suggesting that they were ready to send very senior representatives to Moscow to talk directly with Khrushchev. Khrushchev, at the end of a rather polemical response, agreed to receive such emissaries. At the end of May, Kennedy and Macmillan proposed that they go in late June or early July.

On 10 June 1963, President Kennedy delivered the commencement address at the American University in Washington, D.C. Kennedy had come a long way from his inaugural address invoking the nation's resolution in pursuit of the Cold War and an early special message to Congress calling for increased spending on arms and space in the competition with the Soviet Union. The necessity of peace was the topic of his speech: the impossibility in the nuclear age of resolving conflicts by war and the futility of the arms race, hence the need for coexistence and a reevaluation of U.S. relations with the Soviet Union. He concluded with two announcements: first, that "high-level discussion would shortly begin in Moscow looking toward early agreement on a comprehensive test-ban treaty; second, that the United States would conduct no further nuclear tests in the atmosphere, so long as other states do not."[20] In his second announcement, Kennedy in effect accepted Khrushchev's oft-repeated claim that because the Americans had tested first, it was only fair that the Soviets be allowed the last round, the one they had completed by the end of 1962.

The speech was well received in Moscow. The Voice of America translation was rebroadcast in its entirety, a sharp change in the previous Soviet practice of jamming such broadcasts.

On 2 July, less than two weeks before the U.S.-U.K. delegation arrived in Moscow, Khrushchev delivered a harsh speech in East Berlin about the forthcoming negotiations. He again referred to Western demands for inspection in connection with the test-ban treaty as directed at espionage, saying the Soviet Union "would never open its doors to NATO spies." He went on to say that "since the Western Powers are impeding the conclusion of an agreement on the cessation of all nuclear tests, [the Soviet Union] expresses its readiness to conclude an agreement on the cessation of nuclear tests in the atmosphere, in outer space and under water." He tied this treaty to another agreement, a nonaggression pact between NATO and the Warsaw Pact.[21]

The U.S. and U.K. delegations arrived in Moscow on 15 July. The U.S. delegation had stopped in London on its way. In a conference with Harriman and Lord Hailsham, the heads of the U.S. and U.K. delegations, Macmillan made it plain that Hailsham's instruction was simply to follow Harriman's lead.[22]

20. *Ibid.*, 227–28.

21. Personal recollection; I was present at the meeting as Harriman's executive assistant on the delegation.

22. The delegation had received a further, characteristically Soviet message to this effect the preceding day. Frank Press, a distinguished geophysicist, then at Cal Tech, who had led the reinterpretation of the seismic data which was the basis of the drastic revision of U.S. ideas on control stations and inspection quotas, had come as a technical adviser to the U.S. delegation. When he tried to call

The process of instructing Harriman in Washington was more complicated. The discussions there revealed the continued unhappiness of the Joint Chiefs of Staff with the whole idea of the test ban, shared by the director of the CIA, and the doubts as to the readiness of the Senate to ratify the draft treaty that had been proposed in Geneva. The Chiefs of Staff were less hostile to a partial test-ban treaty that allowed continued testing underground. The Senate was also thought more likely to ratify a partial treaty. Nonetheless, Harriman was instructed initially to propose a comprehensive treaty and agree to a partial one only as a fallback.

The negotiations in Moscow were brief, lasting only eleven days, and, with three exceptions, relatively straightforward—more a matter of fussing with the precise wording of texts and the comparison of English and Russian versions than the hard, tedious, and fruitless bargaining that had characterized the preceding five years. Khrushchev made it plain at the start that he was ready to consider only a partial test ban, a treaty draft for which he tabled on the first day of the conference.[23] While Harriman continued to mention the desirability of a comprehensive ban, he did so more for the record than in the hope that it would be the subject of serious discussion.

The three items that raised difficulties were the Soviet proposal of a nonaggression treaty, the withdrawal clause (Article IV), and the question of the depositary governments (Article III, paragraph 2).

A nonaggression treaty between NATO and the Warsaw Pact had been a longtime goal of Soviet foreign policy and a focus of Soviet propaganda. For the Soviets, it represented at least a step toward the goal of accepting the results of World War II: ratifying the western boundary of the Soviet Union, the new boundaries of Poland, and the division of Germany. For the same reason, it was unacceptable to NATO, and particularly to Germany. Had Germany been willing to accept it, the rest of NATO almost certainly would have been ready and, for the Europeans, even eager to do so. But in 1963, the United States was not prepared even to discuss the possibility with the Federal Republic.

Harriman dealt with the question by sidestepping it, saying that it would be an appropriate topic for discussion after the completion of the test-ban treaty. In the final communiqué of the Moscow conference, the parties agreed to take the matter up with their respective allies in due course; this was never done. That the Soviets were content to accept this purely pro forma gesture showed how eager Khrushchev was to complete the treaty.

The withdrawal clause occasioned the most contentious and difficult part of the negotiations. The original Western draft contained both a list of reasons justifying withdrawal and a time-consuming procedure for effecting it. The first So-

---

several Soviet geophysicists he knew with whom he had worked, he found that they were all "away on vacation" and unreachable. Diligent pursuit led to the conclusion that there was not a single important Soviet geophysicist in Moscow.

23. See Theodore C. Sorensen, *Kennedy* (New York, 1965), 743–45.

viet response was to deny the need for any withdrawal clause, arguing that withdrawal was the sovereign right of any signatory. Harriman insisted that the United States could not accept a treaty in its absence. The compromise was the tortured language of Article IV, which met the Soviet desire to avoid mention of nonsignatory nations or any language that seemed to point to China. Finally, the cumbersome and unusual arrangements for three depositary nations avoided the question of accession to the treaty by nations one or another original party did not recognize: East Germany, Taiwan, North Korea, and others.

The negotiation was straightforward because it was clear that Khrushchev wanted a treaty, but two issues might have derailed the negotiations had they been led by a less adroit U.S. representative. Both the original proposal for tying the treaty to a nonaggression pact and the original Western concept for the withdrawal clause could have been sticking points had the United States insisted on its traditional positions.

The treaty, signed in Moscow on 5 August by the three foreign ministers, went into effect on 10 October, when the three signatories exchanged instruments of ratification.

Ratification by the United States meant, of course, approval by a two-thirds vote of the Senate. This came more easily than Kennedy had initially expected, and the vote for ratification was eighty to nine. Nonetheless, hearings in the two Senate committees that took testimony on the treaty and discussion on the Senate floor revealed the continued deep divisions within the government on the desirability of arms control. While the Foreign Relations Committee recommended ratification with only one dissenting vote out of seventeen, the Subcommittee on Preparedness of the Armed Services Committee (the Stennis Committee) recommended against, five to two.

President Kennedy had purchased the acceptance of the treaty by the Chiefs of Staff at a high price. He agreed to continue a vigorous program of underground testing, to stand ready to resume atmospheric testing should the Soviets violate the treaty, and to expand and improve U.S. capabilities for detecting treaty violations.

But there was a more positive side to the Senate's action. The president found that the mention of the treaty was increasingly well received by the public in the trips around the country he had begun to make in the late summer and early fall, anticipating his 1964 reelection campaign.[24] This too influenced the outcome favorably.

Kennedy was greatly pleased with the result. In his biography of Kennedy, Theodore Sorensen, the White House staff member who saw him more frequently and had served him longer than any other, wrote, "No other accomplishment in the White House ever gave Kennedy greater satisfaction."[25]

24. See *ibid.,* 740.
25. See SIPRI Yearbook 1991, note 7.

## A Retrospect: What Did It Signify?
## Could It Have Been Otherwise?

The Limited Test-Ban Treaty fulfilled some of the hopes that Kennedy had for it but badly disappointed others. It greatly reduced the poisoning of the atmosphere. The three signatories carried out no further nuclear weapons tests in the atmosphere. France and China conducted 37 and 23 respectively, for a total of 60, between August 1963 and 1990. This compares with a total of 457 atmospheric tests before August 1963, 217 by the United States, 215 by the Soviets, 21 by the United Kingdom, and 4 by France.[26]

The treaty was not the first step toward ending "all tests for all time"; quite the contrary. Kennedy had had to commit himself to maintain a vigorous test program. The U.S. weapons laboratories discovered that it was cheaper and more convenient to test underground in nearby Nevada than to mount the kind of naval expedition to the Pacific test sites involved in all but the very smallest detonations in the atmosphere. The Soviets presumably made a parallel discovery. Once testing went underground, worldwide anxiety about fallout and the consequent popular pressure mobilized against testing disappeared. As a result, nuclear weapons tests became routine and attracted little or no notice outside the relatively small groups concerned with disarmament more broadly. In the period from 5 August 1963 through 1990, the United States performed 598 tests and the Soviets 500, or about 40 tests a year together, compared with about 28 per year between 1945 and 1963.[27] Thus the treaty in no way slowed down the arms race; arguably, it allowed it to be speeded up.

Nonetheless, it was a significant first step toward arms control. Direct negotiations with the Soviet Union over weapons development and deployment were put on the agenda of Soviet-American relations and remained there henceforward. Kennedy's expectation that it would be a first step was fulfilled, if in a different way than he might have expected or foreseen. To be sure, the continuing arms control negotiations did not end the arms race and began to reverse it only with the Reagan-Gorbachev agreement calling for the removal of intermediate-range missiles from Europe. But the process itself made the competition much less dangerous than it would have been in its absence.

Could it have been otherwise? Did we in fact miss the goal of a comprehensive treaty by the difference between six and three inspections per year? I think not. If we had gone down to a quota of five—which I believe Kennedy would have done if he saw the prospect of concluding on that and the Soviets were willing to accept it as a basis for further discussion—the exploration of what was involved in an inspection and how it would be conducted would have revealed a new set of unbridgeable differences.

U.S. acceptance of the suggestion of the eight neutrals for invitational rather

26. *Ibid.*
27. *Ibid.*

than obligatory inspections seems to me to have been a more likely path to agreement. I think the U.S. negotiators and the administration more broadly were overly concerned with dotting the i's and crossing the t's of verification, seeing it more as a question of the need for certainty in assigning a moral grade, so to speak, and less as a matter of reinforcing the incentives for adherence to the treaty. It may also be true, however, that the Senate would not have overcome the stronger objections to a comprehensive test-ban treaty and ratified it with such a control scheme.

We now have the technical capacity to verify a comprehensive test-ban treaty with a very high degree of confidence. If for no other than important symbolic reasons, it would still be desirable to achieve one, to tell the world that no one needs either more or better nuclear weapons. It seems the United States government has taken an initiative in extending the current moratorium on testing in a way that appears likely to achieve this result.

Appendix to Chapter 6

## *Treaty Banning Nuclear Weapons Tests in the Atmosphere, in Outer Space, and Under Water*

The Governments of the United States of America, the United Kingdom of Great Britain and Northern Ireland, and the Union of Soviet Socialist Republics, hereinafter referred to as the "Original Parties,"

Proclaiming as their principal aim the speediest possible achievement of an agreement on general and complete disarmament under strict international control in accordance with the objectives of the United Nations which would put an end to the armaments race and eliminate the incentive to the production and testing of all kinds of weapons, including nuclear weapons,

Seeking to achieve the discontinuance of all test explosions of nuclear weapons for all time, determined to continue negotiations to this end, and desiring to put an end to the contamination of man's environment by radioactive substances,

Have agreed as follows:

### Article I

1. Each of the Parties to this Treaty undertakes to prohibit, to prevent, and not to carry out any nuclear weapon test explosion, or any other nuclear explosion, at any place under its jurisdiction or control:

(a) in the atmosphere; beyond its limits, including outer space; or underwater, including territorial waters or high seas; or

(b) in any other environment if such an explosion causes radioactive debris to be present outside the territorial limits of the State under whose jurisdiction or control such explosion is conducted. It is understood in this connection that the provisions of this subparagraph are without prejudice to the conclusion of a treaty resulting in the permanent banning of all nuclear test explosions, including all such explosions underground, the conclusion of which, as the Parties have stated in the Preamble to this Treaty, they seek to achieve.

2. Each of the Parties to this Treaty undertakes furthermore to refrain from causing, encouraging, or in any way participating in, the carrying out of any nuclear weapon test explosion, or any other nuclear explosion, anywhere which would take place in any of the environments described, or have the effect referred to, in Paragraph 1 of this Article.

### Article II

1. Any Party may propose amendments to this Treaty. The text of any proposed amendment shall be submitted to the Depositary Governments which shall circulate it to all Parties to this Treaty. Thereafter, if requested to do so by

one-third or more of the Parties, the Depositary Governments shall convene a conference, to which they shall invite all the Parties, to consider such amendment.

2. Any amendment to this Treaty must be approved by a majority of the votes of all the Parties to this Treaty, including the votes of all the Original Parties. The amendment shall enter into force for all Parties upon the deposit of instruments of ratification by a majority of all the Parties, including the instruments of ratification of the Original Parties.

### Article III

1. This Treaty shall be open to all States for signature. Any State which does not sign this Treaty before its entry into force in accordance with paragraph 3 of this Article may accede to it at any time.

2. This Treaty shall be subject to ratification by signatory States. Instruments of ratification and instruments of accession shall be deposited with the Governments of the Original parties—the United States of America, the United Kingdom of Great Britain and Northern Ireland, and the Union of Soviet Socialist Republics—which are hereby designated the Depositary Governments.

3. This Treaty shall enter into force after its ratification by all the Original Parties and the deposit of their instruments of ratification.

4. For States whose instruments of ratification or accession are deposited subsequent to the entry into force of this Treaty, it shall enter into force on the date of the deposit of their instruments of ratification or accession.

5. The Depositary Governments shall promptly inform all signatory and acceding States of the date of each signature, the date of deposit of each instrument of ratification of and accession to this Treaty, the date of its entry into force, and the date of receipt of any requests for conferences or other notices.

6. This Treaty shall be registered by the Depositary Governments pursuant to Article 102 of the Charter of the United Nations.

### Article IV

This Treaty will be of unlimited duration.

Each Party shall in exercising its national sovereignty have the right to withdraw from the Treaty if it decides that extraordinary events, related to the subject matter of this Treaty, have jeopardized the supreme interests of its country. It shall give notice of such withdrawal to all other Parties to the Treaty three months in advance.

### Article V

1. This Treaty, of which English and Russian texts are equally authentic, shall be deposited in the archives of the Depositary Governments. Duly certified copies of this Treaty shall be transmitted by the Depositary Governments to the Governments of the signatory and acceding States.

In witness whereof the undersigned, duly authorized, have signed this Treaty.

Done in triplicate at the city of Moscow, the fifth day of August, one thousand nine hundred and sixty-three.

# 7

# Turkey's Jupiter Missiles and the U.S.-Turkish Relationship

*Bruce R. Kuniholm*

The probability of nuclear war during the Cuban Missile Crisis has been variously estimated as 1:1, 1:2, 1:100, exaggerated, and next to zero.[1] The variance in estimates derives from the fact that participants and analysts have had very different assumptions about the nature of threats to security, the effectiveness of deterrents, the judgments of government officials, the logic of escalation, the capacity of responsible governments to control events, and the risks involved.[2] In this essay I focus on one of the more controversial factors in the crisis: the role of Turkey's Jupiter missiles. I will then look at assumptions about the U.S.-Turkish relationship during the Kennedy administration and speculate on the extent to which the Cuban Missile Crisis reinforced or changed those assumptions.

When the Kennedy administration came into office, U.S. policy toward Turkey was solidly based on the containment doctrine that had been enunciated in the 1940s and institutionalized after Turkey was admitted to NATO in February 1952. As a member of NATO, Turkey was important to NATO's Supreme Allied Commander Europe (SACEUR) both because it made possible a greater threat to the Soviets' southern flank and because it enhanced deterrence. With the region's military potential integrated in a security framework, the Soviet Union would have to commit significant forces to protect its southern flank and its vital oil fields around Baku. NATO's security commitment to Turkey also constituted a far more effective deterrent than previous arrangements for resisting a Soviet attack, not only along the Middle East's entire northern frontier—

---

1. Abbreviations used in the notes:
   DDEL    Dwight D. Eisenhower Library, Abilene
   JFKL    John F. Kennedy Library, Boston
   LBJL    Lyndon B. Johnson Library, Austin
   2. See Theodore C. Sorensen, *Kennedy* (London, 1965), 705; McGeorge Bundy, *Danger and Survival: Choices About the Bomb in the First Fifty Years* (New York, 1988), 453, 461; Arthur M. Schlesinger, Jr., *Robert Kennedy and His Times* (Boston, 1978), 529; David A. Welch and James G. Blight, "The Eleventh Hour of the Cuban Missile Crisis: An Introduction to the ExComm Transcripts," *International Security,* XII (Winter 1987–88), 27.

which provided a buffer for European and U.S. oil interests in the Persian Gulf—but in Europe as well.³

Under the Eisenhower administration, assumptions that undergirded Turkey's accession to NATO were reinforced and Turkey's role in U.S. defense policy was strengthened. In 1955 Turkey joined the Western-sponsored Baghdad Pact and, in the aftermath of the Suez crisis and the revolution in Iraq, joined the Central Treaty Organization (CENTO). High-altitude U-2s were stationed at Incirlik air base near Adana beginning in 1956, and important electronic installations for gaining information from the Soviet Union were set up along the Black Sea. In accordance with an agreement reached in 1957, the United States stationed American strike aircraft equipped with tactical nuclear weapons in Turkey. Turkey granted extensive military facilities to the United States and made it possible to extend U.S. capabilities to mount effective air strikes against the Soviet Union.⁴ Turkish bases were potentially useful for contingencies in the Middle East and were used by U.S. forces (who notified rather than consulted with Turkish authorities about their plans) as a staging area for the crisis in Lebanon in 1958.⁵

During the Eisenhower administration, U.S. military assistance to Turkey averaged approximately $200 million a year. In 1951, when he was SACEUR, General Eisenhower had underscored Turkey's strategic value and advocated giving arms to the Turks in a briefing for President Truman and his cabinet. Four years later, as president, Eisenhower pointed out to Secretary of the Treasury George Humphrey that it was still better and cheaper to assist the Turks to build up their own armed forces than to create additional U.S. divisions. Economic assistance to Turkey, he believed, was the best possible way to buttress U.S. security interests in the Near East. These thoughts were echoed by his cabinet. "When we go to the Hill on defense matters," Secretary of State Dulles told the Turkish ambassador, Feridun Erkin, in 1955, "Turkey is our No. 1 exhibit."⁶

When Sputnik dramatized the Soviet long-range missile threat to the United

---

3. See Bruce R. Kuniholm, *The Origins of the Cold War in the Near East: Great Power Conflict and Diplomacy in Iran, Turkey and Greece* (Princeton, 1980); and Bruce R. Kuniholm, *The Near East Connection: Greece and Turkey in the Reconstruction and Security of Europe, 1946–1952* (Brookline, Mass., 1984).

4. Francis Powers, *Operation Overflight* (New York, 1970), 41; George Harris, "Turkey and the United States," in *Turkey's Foreign Policy in Transition, 1950–1974*, ed. Kemal Karpat *et al.* (Leiden, 1975), 56; NSC 5708/2, 29 June 1957, in *Foreign Relations of the United States, 1955–1957*, Vol. XXIV (Washington, D.C., 1989), 720–21; and NSC 6015/1, "U.S. Policy Toward Turkey," 5 October 1960, in *Foreign Relations of the United States, 1958–60*, Vol. X, Part 2 (Washington, D.C., 1993), 888–99.

5. George Harris, *Troubled Alliance: Turkish-American Problems in Historical Perspective, 1945–1971* (Washington, D.C., 1972), 67.

6. Financial Appendix to NSC 6015/1, "U.S. Policy Toward Turkey," 5 October 1960, Department of State, S/S-NSC Files: Lot 63 D351, NSC 6015; 31 January 1951, *Foreign Relations of the United States, 1951*, Vol. III, Part 1 (Washington, D.C., 1981), p. 454; 5 January 1955, *Foreign Relations of the United States, 1955–1957*, Vol. XXIV, pp. 608, 643.

States in October 1957, the United States effected a decision at the NATO Heads of Government meeting in December (attended by the prime minister of Turkey, who participated in the decision) to deploy missiles and stocks of nuclear warheads on the Continent to respond to what the Eisenhower administration perceived as a potential loss of confidence in the U.S. commitment to Europe. General Norstad, as SACEUR, determined the siting requirements—a euphemism, apparently, for finding countries that would accept the missiles. Although most members of the alliance were reluctant to take on this additional burden, the Turks were not—in spite of strong opposition to their stand by the Soviet Union.[7]

In October 1959 the United States and Turkey reached agreement on the deployment of a squadron of Jupiter missiles, although they agreed to make no public comment. The almost two-year delay in reaching an agreement apparently was owing to the complicated details involved. By the end of 1959 the Turks had selected the fields for their deployment outside of Izmir, and Turkish foreign minister Fetin Zorlu, who in December expressed his appreciation to Eisenhower for the Jupiters, looked forward to getting them up as soon as possible. The missiles were not installed until the fall of 1961, apparently became operational in March or April 1962, and were formally handed over to the Turks only on 22 October 1962, in the midst of the Cuban Missile Crisis. The missiles, which were owned by Turkey, were under the operational control of SACEUR, who could make the decision to use them only with the agreement of the Turkish and U.S. governments—the United States retained custody of the warheads. Deployment was delayed because of the technical complexities of the problem, the specialized training that was necessary before the Turks could man the missiles, and the fact that the Jupiters were already obsolete before they were deployed; hence they were the subject of second thoughts on the part of both the Eisenhower and Kennedy administrations.[8]

John McCone, then chairman of the Atomic Energy Commission, visited the

7. Memorandum from William Brubeck (Department of State) to McGeorge Bundy (White House), "Jupiters in Italy and Turkey," 22 October 1962, in JFKL; State Department memorandum from William R. Tyler to Secretary Rusk, "Turkish and Jupiter IRBM's," 9 November 1962, and memorandum from Secretary Rusk to President Kennedy, "Political and Military Considerations Bearing on Turkish and Italian IRBM's," along with the attachment, drafted by R. L. Garthoff, 9 November 1962, in *Declassified Documents Reference System*, No. 003160 and No. 003161, respectively.

8. Department of State Telegram 1085 to American Embassy, Ankara, 7 October 1959, and Memorandum of Conference with the President, 6 December 1959, both in DDEL; sources cited in the previous note; Barton J. Bernstein, "The Cuban Missile Crisis: Trading the Jupiters in Turkey?" *Political Science Quarterly*, XCV (Spring 1980), 100. Bernstein's revision of the essay, "Reconsidering the Missile Crisis: Dealing with the Problem of American Jupiters in Turkey," in *The Cuban Missile Crisis Reconsidered*, ed. James A. Nathan (New York, 1992), 55–129, now argues for March or April 1962 instead of July 1962. Bernstein is particularly critical of the manner in which access to crucial documents has been controlled. See also Raymond L. Garthoff, *Reflections on the Cuban Missile Crisis* (Washington, D.C., 1987), 37; Harris, *Troubled Alliance*, 92.

Turkish bases in the fall of 1960 with a subcommittee of the Joint Committee on Atomic Energy and recommended to President Eisenhower that the Jupiters be removed from Turkey and be replaced with Polaris submarines, but administration officials thought that the Turks would resist. In April 1961 President Kennedy asked for a review of the Jupiter deployment to Turkey. In June, a response drafted by George McGhee, chairman of the Policy Planning Council and former U.S. ambassador to Turkey, concluded (with General Norstad's concurrence) that cancellation of the deployment might be seen as a sign of weakness in the aftermath of Khrushchev's hard-line position at Vienna. When Secretary of State Rusk had discussed the matter with the Turkish foreign minister, Selim Sarper, at a CENTO meeting in April 1961, McGhee observed, the latter reacted very negatively. McGhee saw any attempt to persuade the Turks to abandon the project as unlikely to succeed because General Norstad himself, in discussing the matter with Sarper, had emphasized their military importance.[9]

The Jupiter missiles were liquid-fueled (hence slow in their reaction time), "soft" in their configuration, and therefore vulnerable. Thus they were obsolete relative to submarine-based Polaris missiles that were solid-fueled, mobile, and therefore relatively invulnerable. But though they have been disparaged, particularly in retrospect, by former officials such as Dean Rusk who assert that Turkish motorists could strike them with a BB-gun or a .22 caliber rifle and that they were so out of date the United States could not be certain which way they would fly, they were thought by some administration officials at the time, including General Norstad and Secretary of State Rusk, to be a significant military asset. Eighty percent of the missiles were maintained in a state ready for deployment on short warning, Rusk observed in a memo to the president shortly after the Cuban Missile Crisis. This meant that tactical warning of a Soviet attack would permit the Turks to launch twelve of their fifteen 1.45-megaton warheads at targets inside a fifteen-hundred-mile radius within fifteen minutes. The three squadrons of Jupiters (two in Italy and one in Turkey), moreover, were targeted on over one-third (45 of 129) of the Soviet MRBM-IRBM sites facing Europe. Of significance to the rest of their NATO allies in Europe was the presumption that Turkey and Italy would divert Soviet missiles aimed at other targets in Western Europe.[10]

The Turkish attraction to the missiles, U.S. ambassador to NATO Thomas

9. *Executive Sessions of the Senate Foreign Relations Committee* (Historical Series), Vol. XV, 88th Cong., 1st sess., 1963, p. 104; National Security Action Memorandum No. 35, "Deployment of IRBM's to Turkey," 6 April 1961, in *Foreign Relations of the United States, 1961–63*, vol. XVI (Washington, D.C., 1994), 695; Memorandum for McGeorge Bundy from George McGhee, "The Turkish IRBM's," 22 June 1961, in JFKL. See also Raymond Hare, recorded interview, 19 September 1969, p. 22, in JFKL Oral History Program.

10. Welch and Blight, "The Eleventh Hour," 17n.36; Michael R. Beschloss, *The Crisis Years: Kennedy and Khrushchev, 1960–1963* (New York, 1991), 439. See Rusk memorandum to President Kennedy, 9 November 1962. See also the memo from Tyler to Rusk, 9 November 1962. Both are cited in n. 7. As Welch and Blight observe in "The Eleventh Hour," "It is clear that the full story of the technical status of the Jupiters has yet to surface" (18).

Finletter observed, was that, whatever the custodial arrangement, the Turks felt more assured by a weapon on their own territory and somewhat in their own hands. Even if they did not control the warheads and the missiles were subject to a dual key arrangement, it was important from their point of view that they could participate in the process and share control. The Turks saw the Jupiters as symbols of the alliance's determination to use atomic weapons against a Soviet attack on Turkey—this, Finletter asserted, was "a fixed GOT view"—and hence they saw them as symbols of the U.S. commitment to deter such an attack. As Robert Komer observed in a memo to McGeorge Bundy about their removal shortly after the crisis: "I fear that in looking at the Jupiter question we may be far too rational and logical about a problem which is really high in subjective emotional content. McNamara knows the Jupiters are of no military value. But the Turks, Italians, and others don't—and that's the whole point."[11]

Subjective factors such as confidence, or the more elusive question of national character, and their role in a country's determination to confront adversaries were not always easy to calculate. U.S. ambassador to Turkey Raymond Hare had nonetheless attempted to do so in a cable to the secretary of state during the crisis when he noted that the

> Turks are [a] proud, courageous people who do not understand [the] concept or process of compromise. It is this quality of steadfast, even stolid, courage in both spirit and policy, together with traditional Turkish military skill which is actually their greatest asset to [the] US and to [the] West generally and by the same token it is here that we would have [the] most to lose if in [the] process of [the] Jupiter removal [the] Turks should get the impression that their interests as an ally were being traded off in order to appease an enemy.[12]

Given Turkish perceptions, and in spite of the rational arguments for not deploying Jupiters in Turkey, the missiles *had* been deployed. Their removal during the Cuban Missile Crisis, were it necessary, presented the Kennedy administration with even greater problems than reversing the earlier decision because of the conclusions that the Turks, NATO allies, and adversaries might draw. It was not enough to say that such weapons invited attack and held the United States hostage in major crises; that their removal would enhance national security and strengthen deterrence; that removal had been proposed earlier and would have

11. See State Department telegrams from Secretary Rusk to Thomas Finletter in Paris (2345) and to Raymond Hare in Ankara (445), 24 October 1962, in JFKL, and from Thomas Finletter to Secretary Rusk (Polto 506), 25 October 1962, in *Foreign Relations of the United States, 1961–63*, XVI, 730–33. See memo from Robert Komer to McGeorge Bundy, 12 November 1962, in *Declassified Documents Reference System*, no. 001620.

12. See telegram 587 from Ankara (Raymond Hare) to Secretary Rusk, 26 October 1962, in Department of State Central Files, 611.3722/10-2662.

be it effected sooner or later anyway; and that it could contribute to a face-saving solution to the crisis.

As administration officials knew, the United States had sold the Turks on the military value of the missiles, and the Turkish Parliament had only recently appropriated money for their deployment. The Soviet ambassador to Turkey had told the Turks that a nuclear war was on their doorstep.[13] Under these circumstances, to withdraw the missiles under pressure risked creating the impression that the U.S. move was a sellout, a bargain at Turkey's expense, a weakening of Europe's defenses to remove a threat in the Western Hemisphere. Withdrawal could establish a precedent for other concessions and raise profound questions about the credibility of the U.S. commitment to deter Soviet adventures in Europe. At the very least, U.S. officials recognized, the Jupiters would have to be replaced by hardened land-based nuclear missiles, a seaborne nuclear force, or substantial economic and military assistance.[14]

It is not my purpose here to discuss the origins of or possible explanations for Khrushchev's Turkish missile trade proposal on 27 October 1962 or to examine the negotiating strategies involving the missiles in Turkey that the Kennedy administration considered during the Cuban Missile Crisis. These questions have been addressed in some detail by others.[15] Suffice it to observe that David Welch and James Blight are probably correct in asserting that the president was prepared to trade the missiles in Turkey for the Soviet missiles in Cuba if the alternative were military action.[16] This does not mean that he would have done so *publicly* (I will discuss the question of whether he did so *privately* in a moment), only that he was prepared to consider it if the developing situation required it and the circumstances permitted. The Executive Committee meetings of 27 October 1962, where the dominant issue discussed was the question of trading missiles in Turkey for missiles in Cuba and President Kennedy came across as the strongest advocate of the trade, suggest that he was seriously exploring this possibility. But even the so-called Cordier ploy, in which Dean Rusk asked the former UN offi-

13. Ferenc Vali, *Bridge Across the Bosporus: The Foreign Policy of Turkey* (Baltimore, 1971), 129.

14. See, for example, the memorandum from Roger Hilsman, Director of the Bureau of Intelligence and Research, to Secretary Rusk, 27 October 1962, and the memorandum from Walt Rostow to McGeorge Bundy, "Turkish IRBM's," 30 October 1962, both in JFKL.

15. See, for example, Bundy, *Danger and Survival*, 404–407, 428–39; Bruce J. Allyn, James Blight, and David Welch, "Essence of Revision: Moscow, Havana, and the Cuban Missile Crisis," *International Security*, XIV (Winter 1989–90), 157–59, 163–65. See also "Cuban Missile Crisis Meetings," 27 October 1962, *Presidential Recordings*, in JFKL. Several recent books provide further light on the Jupiter missiles in Turkey: Philip Nash, *The Other Missiles of October: Eisenhower, Kennedy, and the Jupiters, 1957–1963* (Chapel Hill, 1997); Anatoly Dobrynin, *In Confidence: Moscow's Ambassador to America's Six Cold War Presidents (1962–1968)* (New York, 1995); Alexsandr Fursenko and Timothy Naftali, *"One Hell of a Gamble": Khrushchev, Castro, and Kennedy, 1958–1964* (New York, 1997); Ernest R. May and Philip D. Zelikow, eds., *The Kennedy Tapes: Inside the White House During the Cuban Missile Crisis* (Cambridge, Mass., 1997); and, of course, the relevant volumes in the *Foreign Relations of the United States* series.

16. Welch and Blight, "The Eleventh Hour," 15, 18. Theodore Sorensen and Arthur Schlesinger share this belief. See Garthoff, *Reflections*, 59.

cial and Columbia University professor Andrew Cordier to be ready to propose that U Thant publicly suggest such a trade, did no more than keep the option open.[17]

In any event, following execution of the so-called Trollope ploy (President Kennedy's decision to respond to Nikita Khrushchev's 26 October message and ignore his message of 27 October which proposed the removal of the Jupiters in Turkey as a condition for the withdrawal of Soviet missiles from Cuba), Robert Kennedy on 27 October made a concession on the Turkish missiles to Soviet ambassador Dobrynin (the missiles would be out of Turkey in four to five months). Whether Allied interests (or at least Turkish interests) were sacrificed depends on one's interpretation of this concession on the Turkish missiles. Whether what the president's brother offered the Soviet ambassador was an assurance, a concession, or a trade, and whether it was a *private* (as opposed to a *public*) "deal" may be a question of semantics. Clearly a bargain was struck, as is indicated by Robert Kennedy's scribbled notes of the meeting: "Also if you should publish any document indicating a deal then it is off." The word "it" obviously refers to the bargain that was being struck—perhaps more usefully referred to as an understanding, an assurance that acted as a diplomatic solvent, or a face-saving "concession," since the latter terms have less sinister connotations than a "deal." Special Counsel to the President Theodore Sorensen's revelations in 1989 that the diaries on which Robert Kennedy's *Thirteen Days* were based (and which he edited after Kennedy's death) portrayed the missile trade as an explicit deal and that he revised the account because the deal was still secret suggest that an understanding was reached—or that a concession or private deal was struck. Soviet ambassador Dobrynin's recently published cable to the Soviet Foreign Ministry on 27 October 1962, Robert Kennedy's draft memorandum of the 27 October 1962 meeting, and Dobrynin's telegram to the Soviet Foreign Ministry on 30 October 1962, reporting on Kennedy's refusal to accept a letter from Khrushchev explicitly affirming the private deal further support the interpretation that an agreement was reached, however complicated the layers of intent on both sides that undergirded it.[18]

Although Kennedy's national security adviser, McGeorge Bundy, will concede that only in the narrowest sense can subsequent denials by the administration's inner circle that there had been a deal be considered true, Kennedy's secretary of defense, Robert McNamara, who was also in the room during the

17. See Allyn, Blight, and Welch, "Essence of Revision," 159; "Cuban Missile Crisis Meetings," 27 October 1962, pp. 3, 43, 50; Bundy, *Danger and Survival*, 435–36. See also Welch and Blight, "The Eleventh Hour"; and Blight and Welch, *On the Brink: Americans and Soviets Reexamine the Cuban Missile Crisis* (New York, 1989), 83–84, 103, 108–109, 113–15, 137, 151, 161–62, 184–85, 190, 330 n. 68, 333–34 nn. 4–5, 352–53 n. 68.

18. See Schlesinger, *Robert Kennedy*, 520–25; Allyn, Blight, and Welch, "Essence of Revision," 163–65; Cold War International History Project *Bulletin* V (Spring 1995), 80–81; Dobrynin, *In Confidence*, 90–91; Cold War International History Project *Bulletin*, VIII and IX (Winter 1996–97), 304, 345–47.

discussion over what Bobby Kennedy should tell Dobrynin on 27 October, insists that there was no deal—primarily because of his understanding of "what the President intended and how the deal was to have been expressed." Secretary of State Dean Rusk, who initially came up with the idea of assuring Khrushchev that the United States would withdraw the missiles from Turkey and who subsequently reminded Kennedy's brother Bobby that the United States was not making any agreement on the question of a missile trade (but who reminded Bobby of this point *after* the latter had already talked to Dobrynin), continues to see the information Bobby Kennedy passed on to the Russian ambassador as "an important piece of information" but not part of an agreement.[19]

However one chooses to interpret the understanding that was reached, it is clear that, following Khrushchev's decision on 28 October to withdraw the missiles from Cuba, the Kennedy administration began immediately to consider how to remove the Jupiters in Turkey while avoiding any appearance that Allied interests had been sacrificed.[20] Dean Rusk, in a seven-page memorandum to the president on 9 November, for many of the reasons already discussed, opposed phasing out the Jupiters in Turkey and Italy until the crisis receded and more modern and effective weapons systems came into being. "For political and psychological reasons, supported by less significant but real military reasons as well," he told the president, "it would not be in the US interest to propose the removal of Turkish and Italian IRBM's in the immediate future." General Norstad also opposed their removal. Secretary of Defense McNamara, however, appears to have been anxious to effect their removal as expeditiously as possible—a goal that elicited the concern expressed in Robert Komer's memo of 12 November 1962 (mentioned earlier) to McGeorge Bundy.[21]

McNamara, presumably, reflected the president's desire and commitment to carry out his part of the understanding that had been reached, and he carried the day. "You're seeing Ray Hare so that when he returns to painful task of unselling Turks on Jupiter, it will be with your obvious blessing," Komer noted in a memorandum to the president on 9 January 1963. When Kennedy met with Hare, he authorized the ambassador, if there were any question about the Jupiters, to tell the Turkish government on his behalf that removal of the Jupiters had not been part of any deal with the Russians. Hare was then informed of the administration's plan to remove the missiles and instructed to get them out before the end of April. Two weeks later, on 23 January, the president announced that the

19. Allyn, Blight, and Welch, "Essence of Revision," 157–59, 163–65; Bundy, *Danger and Survival*, 432–36; Blight and Welch, *On the Brink*, 174, 190–91.

20. See memorandum for McGeorge Bundy from W. W. Rostow, "Turkish IRBM's," 30 October 1962; and Department of State telegram 460 from Rusk to the American Embassy in Turkey, 29 October 1962, both in JFKL, in which Hare was authorized to convey the message, "As GOT knows, no 'deal' of any kind was made with USSR involving Turkey."

21. See the Rusk memorandum, cited in n. 7; Department of State telegram 2082 from Paris (Bohlen) to the Secretary of State, 11 November 1962, in JFKL; and memo from Komer to Bundy, 12 November 1962, cited in n. 11.

Jupiters in Italy and Turkey and the Thors in Britain would be replaced by Polaris—"a much more modern weapon . . . that provides a more adequate security." On the following day, Dean Rusk, who had opposed their immediate removal, pulled a few punches in an executive session of the Senate Foreign Relations Committee, leaving Senator Mike Mansfield with the impression that negotiations on the substitution of Polaris for Jupiters had been under way for some time and that the administration, while reacting negatively to the offer of a trade because it did not want to connect a NATO problem with the Cuban crisis, had gone ahead because it did not think the recent crisis should delay the timetable.[22]

When Hare returned to Turkey, he found the Turkish military establishment opposed to the dismantling of the missiles. If they were to lose what they regarded as a strong deterrent, they wanted compensation in the form of an aircraft modernization program, tanks, armored personnel carriers, SS-11 missiles, and naval craft. Hard bargaining ensued, and the missiles were removed just before the deadline that Hare had been given. "The last Jupiter missile in Turkey came down yesterday," Robert McNamara informed the president in a handwritten note on 25 April; the last Jupiter warhead, he also noted, would be flown out of Turkey by the end of the week (one month after the deadline struck in the understanding between Robert Kennedy and Soviet ambassador Anatoly Dobrynin).[23] The quid pro quo for Turkish acquiescence to the removal of the Jupiters, aside from the commitment of Polaris submarines, was U.S. agreement on several requests, including an aircraft modernization program.

The role of Turkey's Jupiter missiles in the Cuban Missile Crisis clearly was central, however limited our understanding of some aspects of the crisis may be. Even today, as two scholars have observed, "It is clear that the full story of the technical status of the Jupiters has yet to surface."[24] Beyond technical details, it seems clear that the Jupiters were far less important in and of themselves than that they were perceived as important by the Turks. U.S. officials were less worried about their military value than about their psychological value: how the decision to remove them would be interpreted by allies such as Turkey, the assessments that adversaries such as the Soviets would make of that decision, and the effect of the decision on our allies' belief in the U.S. commitment to deter a Soviet attack. To the extent that the Jupiters invited attack and were obsolete by the time they were installed and to the extent that assurances regarding their removal were consistent with strategic plans, strengthened deterrence, and in no

22. Memorandum from Robert Komer to the President, 9 January 1963, in JFKL; Hare interview, 19 September 1969, p. 24; Paul Hare, *Diplomatic Chronicles of the Middle East: A Biography of Ambassador Raymond A. Hare* (Lanham, Md., 1993), 130; *American Foreign Policy: Current Documents, 1963* (Washington, D.C., 1967), 380–81; *Executive Sessions of the Senate Foreign Relations Committee,* Vol. XV, pp. 103–106.

23. Hare, *Diplomatic Chronicles,* 130–31; Memorandum from McNamara to President Kennedy, 25 April 1963, in Ball Box 125, JFKL.

24. Welch and Blight, "The Eleventh Hour," 18.

way compromised Turkish trust in the United States, their removal appears to have been a wise decision. What happened—however one chooses to characterize the understanding that was reached—permitted the United States to assert that in fact there had been no deal and allowed Khrushchev not only to avoid complete humiliation but also to argue (at least within the Kremlin) that the Soviets had achieved some concrete gains. Private understandings sometimes permit such felicitous interpretations. Defusing a difficult situation was imperative, and although the Jupiters were important enough to deploy (at least at the time the decision was taken), they were not important enough to stand in the way of resolving a confrontation they were designed to deter in the first place.

Even a public trade, which would have been far more problematical than the private agreement that was reached, might not have been as disastrous as some critics claim. In spite of the enormous difficulties posed by publicly trading missiles in Turkey for missiles in Cuba, discussed earlier in this essay and echoed in the transcripts of the Executive Committee of the National Security Council during the crisis, there are reasons to believe that Kennedy, if necessary, could have survived even them. McGeorge Bundy has argued that the United States could have marshaled compelling arguments to counter the perception that it would sacrifice the interests of a small ally in response to Soviet pressures and that there would have been substantial support for the president's unwavering belief that the Turkish missiles (which were more symbol than substance) did not justify bloodshed and that our basic interests required a peaceful end to the crisis.[25]

In the aftermath of the Cuban Missile Crisis, a seed of doubt about NATO commitments was planted among the Turks, who began to appreciate the fact that possession of particular weapons systems, while providing certain assurances and addressing some of their security needs, could also make them a target and render them vulnerable to decisions that were made in Washington. From then on they would be far more sensitive to the possibility that the alliance could pull them into a crisis that was of no direct concern to them. These concerns were widely discussed in the Turkish press, and assumptions about Turkish foreign policy, more freely questioned in the aftermath of the 1960 revolution, had an impact on official attitudes. The withdrawal of the Jupiter missiles from Turkey diminished Ankara's importance in U.S. nuclear strategies and removed an impediment to Turkey's better relations with Moscow. Official visits were exchanged with the Soviet Union, and improved Turkish-USSR relations slowly followed. This does not mean that U.S.-Turkish relations immediately deteriorated. In fact, when President Kennedy was assassinated in November 1963, public places of entertainment were closed, a street was named after him, and there was an outpouring of sympathy for him in Turkey.[26] What really compli-

25. Bundy, *Danger and Survival*, 436–37.

26. Harris, *Troubled Alliance*, 93–95; Harris, "Turkey and the United States," 58–59; Hare, *Diplomatic Chronicles*, 132–33.

cated U.S.-Turkish relations in subsequent years was not the Cuban Missile Crisis but the Cyprus crisis that began in late 1963, *after* the death of President Kennedy.

In Turkish eyes, the culprit in the Cyprus crisis was President Johnson, who warned Prime Minister Ismet Inonu in a June 1964 letter that he should not use any U.S.-supplied equipment to invade Cyprus. In that letter, Johnson called into question U.S. obligations under NATO if Turkey took a step that resulted in Soviet intervention. This so-called Johnson letter, as it was being drafted by Dean Rusk (with the assistance of Harland Cleveland and Joseph Sisco), was described at the time by Under Secretary of State George Ball as "the most brutal diplomatic note I have ever seen" and produced what he subsequently characterized as "the diplomatic equivalent of a time bomb." Whether Rusk's willingness to send such a harsh letter was influenced by his earlier concern about the Turkish reaction to the withdrawal of Jupiter missiles during the Cuban Missile Crisis—a concern that, retrospectively, he may have seen as excessive—is an interesting if unanswerable historical question. It is fair to say, however, that after the Cyprus crisis, U.S.-Turkish relations were less tied to the axioms and enforced solidarity of the early postwar years. A clear example of this shift can be found in the statements of Prime Minister Inonu, who as late as August 1963 could deny that any "deals" had been made on the question of Soviet missiles in Cuba but who by January 1970 was complaining that a bargain had been made and the Turks never notified.[27]

Historical judgments are extraordinarily complicated because the past requires time to play out before one can make informed judgments. How something turns out matters. History, moreover, has no control groups, and one cannot replay it under different scenarios. It is also fair to say now that with the Cuban Missile Crisis, the Cold War reached a critical turning point. From Khrushchev's point of view, the "agreement" to remove Jupiter missiles "was primarily of moral significance. . . . Kennedy recognized that the time had passed when you could solve conflicts with the USSR by military means."[28] Kennedy could have said much the same about Khrushchev. Common interests were more easily perceived, and rapprochement between East and West became possible, although it would take almost thirty years before the Cold War would end. As the Cold War turned the corner, doubts about the U.S. commitment to Turkey, first generated by the Cuban Missile Crisis and reinforced by the Johnson letter, however problematical at the time, did not destroy the U.S.-Turkish alliance. Rather, they produced a Turkish response to the emerging international situation that was desirable if not inevitable: a more realistic assessment of Tur-

27. George W. Ball, *The Past Has Another Pattern: Memoirs* (New York, 1982), 350; Bruce R. Kuniholm, "Turkey and NATO: Past, Present, and Future," *Orbis*, XXVII (Summer 1983), 424–26; Harris, *Troubled Alliance*, 93 n. 19.

28. *Khrushchev Remembers: The Glasnost Tapes,* ed. and trans. Jerold Schecter (Boston, 1990), 179.

key's problems and a more independent, multifaceted conception of its options than had been possible in the early Cold War years. Even when Turkey invaded Cyprus in 1974—and some would argue that Turkish officials were virtually compelled to do so because of public sensitivity to the way Turkey had been treated in 1964—U.S.-Turkish relations survived and, after several rocky years, even prospered.

The bottom line in the U.S.-Turkish relationship during the Cold War was that when U.S.-Soviet relations were troubled (as they had been in the 1950s), relations between the United States and Turkey were generally good. Good relations were founded on U.S. military and economic assistance as well as a U.S. guarantee of Turkey's security—a guarantee that served as a deterrent against a Soviet attack—in exchange for the use of Turkish facilities and bases and an important Turkish role in the defense of the West. But as U.S.-Soviet relations improved, the U.S.-Turkish relationship became more troubled as first one and then another party raised questions about the relationship and challenged the other's notion of their reciprocal obligations. This development was virtually inevitable after the relationship had achieved its primary goals and the threat that bound the allies together began to recede.

The Cuban Missile Crisis, in a sense, served as a catalyst for changes already under way and signaled the beginning of the end of the Cold War. It legitimized a new generation of leaders in the United States and the Soviet Union who, learning from experience, were prepared to take steps necessary to reduce the potential for catastrophic conflict; it underscored both the challenges and the opportunities provided by a more sober assessment of the new weapons systems at their disposal—an assessment that included a greater appreciation of their vulnerabilities and limitations as well as their potential for destruction.

The U.S.-Turkish relationship was central to Western security in the early Cold War years and it was crucial to Turkey's survival. But as changes occurred, adaptive measures were necessary and even desirable. The demise of Stalin, the advent of Khrushchev and his campaign of destalinization, the gradual acquisition of new weapons systems in the Soviet Union and the United States, and the gradual evolution of the international balance of power toward a rough parity all contributed to a new climate of opinion in which thoughtful voices would articulate new points of view and help pave the way for a relaxation of tensions and the more complicated international environment of the post–Cold War era. The road would not be smooth, and one could argue about the milestones, but the direction was clear.

On 19 February 1963, Robert Komer, who would later become the U.S. ambassador to Turkey, wrote Assistant Secretary of State Phillips Talbot an insightful memo in which he noted:

> We have never really decided in our own minds whether to treat Turkey primarily as a NATO partner (whose main need was military aid for the defense of Europe) or as an underdeveloped country whose

primary need was to become a going concern. As a result we have pursued both aims—and fully succeeded at neither. My own bias is well known: i.e., that the threat to US interests from Bloc aggression involving Turkey is less urgent than that arising from Turkey's failure to become a going concern. . . .

Can we (and our European allies) afford to alter the proportions of our assistance sufficiently to get Turkey well on the road to self-sufficiency (except for the major hardware) over the next decade, without incurring unacceptable military risks? This, to me, is the nub of the problem and one on which we ought to make up our minds.[29]

This observation characterized differences in official thinking about Turkey toward the end of the Eisenhower administration, as well as in the Kennedy administration, and it would continue to characterize differences among U.S. officials who were unable to make up their minds on the question until the end of the Cold War, when Turkey could worry less about unacceptable military risks and begin to focus much more directly on the difficulties of becoming "a going concern." Following the end of the Cold War, Turkey has sought integration into the world economy and has attempted to contribute to the restructuring of a greater Europe of which it aspires to be a part.[30] If it eventually achieves this ambitious goal, it will be in no small part a tribute to the U.S.-Turkish relationship, to the leadership of President Truman, whose administration first contained the Soviets on the Turkish border, and to the leadership of President Kennedy, who made it possible, without sacrificing Turkish interests, for the United States and the Soviet Union to embark on a journey that would bring an end to the Cold War.

29. Memorandum for Phillips Talbot from Robert Komer, 19 February 1963, in *Declassified Documents Reference System*, no. 002366.

30. Bruce R. Kuniholm, "Turkey and the West," *Foreign Affairs*, LXX (Spring 1991), 34–48.

# 8

## Missiles or Socialists?
## The Italian Policy of the Kennedy Administration

### *Leopoldo Nuti*

∽

Between 1961 and 1963 Italy was hardly an issue of primary importance for the Kennedy administration, especially when compared with other—critical—problems in U.S.-European relations of the same period: the tensions provoked by Gaullist France, the recurrent crises over Berlin and the future of Germany, or even a relatively minor question such as the destiny of the Portuguese colonies in Africa.[1] Nevertheless, even if an analysis of the Italian policy of the Kennedy administration may look like a case study of only secondary importance, it can still contribute some interesting observations—not only from the viewpoint of Italian politics but also in the broader perspective of U.S. foreign policy in general.

U.S.-Italian relations in the early 1960s, in fact, feature some of the main themes of Kennedy's diplomacy. In the first section of this essay I focus on the extent to which Italy was influenced by the emphasis the Kennedy administration, and in particular many of the liberal intellectuals who worked in the White House staff, placed on the necessity for the United States to win the confrontation with the USSR not just by matching or overcoming Soviet military strength but also by winning "the hearts and minds" of the people of the Third World,

1. Abbreviations used in the notes:
   ACS       Archivio Centrale dello Stato, Rome
   ASP       Arthur Schlesinger Papers (JFKL)
   AUSSME   Assistant Under Secretary of State
   DDRS      Declassified Documents Research System
   DS        Department of State
   FO        Foreign Office (PRO)
   JFKL       John F. Kennedy Library, Boston
   NARA     National Archives and Records Administration, Washington, D.C.
   NSF       National Security Files (JFKL)
   POF       President's Office Files
   PRO       Public Record Office, London
   RG59      Record Group 59 (NARA)
   SMD      Submarine Mine Depot

where the struggle with the Soviets was perceived as most likely to intensify in years to come. This goal could be achieved only by giving U.S. foreign policy a more ideological outlook, making clear that one of its primary objectives was "to export democracy" and promote social reforms, not just to align the United States with the reactionary forces committed to a worldwide fight against communism. As is well known, such a policy was far from being consistently formulated and implemented. It provoked sharp divisions in the ruling classes of the countries to which it was addressed as well as within the U.S. forces that were called upon to accomplish it, often pitting the more liberal White House staff against the more traditional bureaucracy of the State Department and the Pentagon, with a most ambiguous president cautiously leaning toward the former. While this ideological strain and the tensions that came with it were mostly present in U.S. foreign policy toward the Third World—and the most clear-cut cases that come to mind are the Alliance for Progress in Latin America and the White Revolution in Iran—nevertheless it trickled down and percolated through U.S. policy toward Italy to an extent unknown in U.S. policy toward other Western European allies.[2]

In the second section of the essay I look at U.S.-Italian relations in the more "customary" context of Euro-Atlantic diplomacy. I describe the various degrees of cooperation between the two countries in areas such as nuclear sharing, the strategic posture of NATO and its military doctrine, and the future of European integration. This discussion is based on the assumption that reduction of the risk of nuclear war was one of the primary objectives of the Kennedy administration and that this goal was sought after as consistently as possible, even at the expense of introducing some tensions into an Atlantic Alliance lulled into what was perhaps an excessive confidence in the political power of nuclear weapons by years of massive retaliation theories. As this dimension of the foreign policy of the new administration began to emerge, Italy, which encouraged and supported the nuclearization of NATO but regarded alignment with the United States as the cornerstone of its diplomacy, gradually reacted and adjusted to it.

Finally, I attempt to assess the combined effect on Italy of both these components of U.S. foreign policy and of their interplay. I conclude that by 1963 the

2. I wish to express my gratitude to Professor Tony Smith for a long afternoon of discussions on this point and for providing me with a copy of his article on the Alliance for Progress before its publication. On the White Revolution in Iran, see James Goode, "Reforming Iran During the Kennedy Years," *Diplomatic History,* XV, (Winter 1991), 13–30; James A. Bill, *The Eagle and the Lion: The Tragedy of American-Iranian Relations* (New Haven, 1988); Barry M. Rubin, *Paved with Good Intentions: The American Experience and Iran* (New York, 1980). On the Alliance for Progress, see Richard Goodwin, *Remembering America: A Voice from the Sixties* (New York, 1988); Jerome Levinson and Juan de Onis, eds., *The Alliance That Lost Its Way* (New York, 1970); Tony Smith, "Exporting Democracy to Latin America: The Case of the Alliance for Progress," in *Exporting Democracy: The United States and Latin America,* ed. Abraham Lowenthal (Baltimore, 1991); Stephen G. Rabe, "Controlling Revolution: Latin America, the Alliance for Progress and Cold War Anti-communism," in *Kennedy's Quest for Victory: American Foreign Policy, 1961–1963,* ed. Thomas G. Paterson (New York, 1989), 195–222.

initial contradictions between the two aspects of U.S.-Italian relations had gradually begun to disappear and that a new synthesis was slowly emerging.

## *"Operation Nenni"*:
### *The Political-Ideological Dimension of U.S.-Italian Relations in the Kennedy Years*

The story of American interest in Italy goes hand in hand with that of U.S. involvement in European affairs during World War II and at the onset of the Cold War. Although it might not have been one of the main catalysts of this involvement, Italy certainly played a major role in the early years of postwar confrontation between the superpowers, culminating in the famous political elections of April 1948. After the stabilization that followed the success of the anticommunist forces at the polls, Italy turned into a partial anomaly in the otherwise successful picture of Western European reconstruction through the Marshall Plan and NATO. Italy's international alignment, in fact, lay in the hands of a flimsy majority of pro-Western parties centered around the Christian Democrats, pitted against the largest Communist party outside the Soviet bloc and a fellow-traveling Socialist party that was the third largest political force in the country. Frequent cabinet crises and perennial political instability seemed to prevent Italy from successfully completing its reconstruction. Furthermore, the coalition governments led by the Christian Democrats gradually lost much of their previous reformist approach, and to the United States and other outside observers they seemed unable to promote the social transformation that would modernize Italian society and help cut the roots of communist strength.

One way out of the predicament seemed to be in the gradual distancing of the socialists from the communists and in their eventual inclusion in the democratic camp.[3] Such a change, which might isolate the communists and promote social reforms at the same time, had long been under scrutiny in Italian politics under the name of "opening to the left." It found, however, strong opponents both in Italy and in the United States. Because of the heavy neutralist streak in the socialists' foreign policy, as well as their record of cooperation with the communists, the Eisenhower administration—in spite of some limited interest in its possible results—regarded the "opening" as a risky initiative that could easily backfire and threaten Italian alignment with the West. Even those who showed some interest in its possibilities, moreover, believed that an aggressive stance would be the best way to force the Partito Socialista Italiano (PSI) to distance itself from the communists and possibly reunite with the pro-Western Social Democratic party. In the words of U.S. ambassador Claire Booth Luce, herself

---

3. Italian historian Pietro Scoppola believes that such a development was almost a foregone conclusion after the failure of the 1953 de Gasperi attempt to modify the Italian electoral system. See his *La republica dei partiti: Profilo storico della democrazia in Italia, 1945–1990* (Bologna, 1991), 320.

never too friendly toward the Nenni socialists: "Nenni will move more to the center than [Social Democratic leader] Saragat will move to the left. . . . However, the marriage will be much more meaningful if his movement toward the center is not made too easy for him."[4]

Aggressive defense of a fragile and conservative status quo thus became the hallmark of U.S. policy toward Italy, especially during the tenure of Ambassador Luce (1953–56). Her successor, James D. Zellerbach, toned down somewhat the uncompromising nature of U.S. opposition to the PSI but did not alter the course set in the early years of the Eisenhower administration.[5] By the end of 1960, the opening to the left was no closer to its conclusion than when it had first been discussed several years before.

The standstill in Italian politics quickly came to the attention of some liberal members of the Kennedy staff. With their ideological penchant for supporting fellow reformist groups and their inclination to tackle problems in a most straightforward manner, such people as Arthur Schlesinger, Averell Harriman, and Robert Komer developed a keen interest in promoting a coalition between the Christian Democrats and the socialists that could prove the solution to Italy's social and political stagnation. They quickly turned around the approach of the Eisenhower administration and rather than putting pressure on the socialists to make them change their political stance, they instead adopted a policy of friendly encouragement to spur them toward greater cooperation with the Christian Democrats. The story has been told several times, and here it is necessary only to recap its main features before making some observations about the existing interpretations of it.[6]

As in many other instances, the élan of the "doers" in the White House staff was met with strong resistance by other sectors of the administration, in particular by the State Department midlevel bureaucracy and by the embassy staff in Rome.[7] When their designs were thwarted by what they regarded as a mixture

4. Claire Booth Luce, "Italy and the European Situation," 8 January 1957, in Minutes of Meetings, Archives of the Council for Foreign Relations, New York.

5. There were forces even in the 1950s that looked upon the "opening to the left" as a real opportunity for the United States: William Colby, *Honorable Men: My Life in the CIA* (New York, 1978), chapter 4, "Covert Politics in Italy"; Alan Arthur Platt, "U.S. Policy Toward the 'Opening to the Left' in Italy" (Ph.D. dissertation, Columbia University, 1973), 137–38.

6. Arthur M. Schlesinger, Jr., *A Thousand Days: John F. Kennedy in the White House* (New York, 1965); Platt, "U.S. Policy Toward the 'Opening to the Left' "; Roberto Faenza, *Il malaffare: Dall'America di Kennedy all'Italia, a Cuba, al Vietnam* (Milan, 1979); Spencer M. Di Scala, *Renewing Italian Socialism: Nenni to Craxi* (New York, 1988); Leo Wollemborg, *Stars, Stripes and Italian Tricolor: The United States and Italy, 1946–1989* (New York, 1990).

7. According to at least one account, the split was repeated even inside the CIA, with the "analysts" in favor of the experiment and the "operatives" against it: see Faenza, *Il malaffare,* 64. For further discussion of the CIA attitude, see also Di Scala, *Renewing Italian Socialism,* 122–23. CIA director John McCone seems to have supported the "opening," or at least this is what he said to Fiat president Vittorio Valletta during his trip to the United States in May 1962: Piero Bairati, *Valletta* (Turin, 1983), 311–12. Head of counterintelligence James J. Angleton was on the contrary quite hostile to the initiative and reportedly even suspected Arthur M. Schlesinger, Jr., of being a Soviet agent; see David C. Martin, *A Wilderness of Mirrors* (New York, 1980), 183–84.

of bureaucratic shortsightedness and sheer conservatism, the pro-opening members of the Kennedy administration turned to the highest authority in the government, the president himself. Here the story becomes blurred and difficult to unravel. According to the versions of Arthur Schlesinger, Jr., and to the later accounts of Leo Wollemborg from the *Washington Post* and Spencer M. Di Scala, Kennedy quickly sided with the pro-opening people and from his first meeting with Italian prime minister Amintore Fanfani in June 1961 made clear his sympathy for the opening to the left. Alan Platt's 1973 dissertation, however, presents Kennedy as much more cautious toward the suggestions of his liberal advisers and as basically noncommittal. Platt suggests that JFK actually let his aides continue their initiatives without his formal backing to avoid a showdown with the State Department over what was regarded as a relatively minor issue. After many frustrations and setbacks, however, the Italian experiment got started, first through a coalition with external socialist support, and then in November 1963 with full socialist participation in the cabinet, opening a new period of Italian postwar political history.[8]

The existing reconstructions of U.S. interest for the opening must be integrated by several observations. The first is that, with the exception of Schlesinger's, the accounts look at Italy as an isolated case study and therefore fail to see the cleavage in the administration's Italian policy as a reflection of the broader schism caused by the attempt to set up a "progressive" foreign policy. They fail, in other words, to see the problem in the context of the Kennedy administration's inner dynamics. This in turn leads to an interpretation of the "Italian case" as a mere bureaucratic struggle rather than one more example of the difficulties faced by the Kennedy administration in changing the course set by its predecessors and in the process resharpening the tools with which the Cold War had to be waged.

A second remark must be made about the real nature of the fight that developed between the enemies and the supporters of the opening. This regards the actual extent to which the "doers" were ready to go to see their designs implemented. After the first setbacks in their dealing with the State Department, the pro-opening members of the White House staff tried to mobilize other sources of support for their policy. The president's own brother and some liberal trade union leaders, such as Walter and Victor Reuther, joined the effort to "democratize" Italian politics. This is mentioned by all the authors quoted above, but without any concrete reference to the exact role played by these other characters.[9] A closer look at the initiatives of the Reuther brothers, however, makes

8. The climax of this United States–PSI rapprochement was probably the famous meeting of John F. Kennedy and Pietro Nenni in the Quirinale gardens during the U.S. president's short trip to Italy in June 1963. For a brilliant description of the event, as well as of its impact on the other Italian party leaders, see the recorded interview of William Fraleigh, JFKL Oral History Program; and Pietro Nenni, *Gli anni del centro-sinistra, 1957–1966: Diari* (Milan, 1982).

9. Only Leo Wollemborg briefly touches on the problem of financial assistance in the Italian edition of his book, much longer than the American one: Leo Wollemborg, *Stelle, strisce e tricolore: Trent'anni di vicende politiche tra Roma e Washington* (Milan, 1983).

clear that, other than adding their prestige to the cause, their task was to mobilize union financial support for a poverty-stricken Socialist party. Largely dependent on communist financing until the late 1950s, the PSI had been steadily losing a good deal of its funds since then. If it had to play a role in stabilizing Italian democracy, it needed a steady flow of funding somewhat comparable to the one the Christian Democrats had received via the CIA throughout the 1950s. This was all the more true since the reformist group in the PSI, Pietro Nenni's autonomists, was constantly being harassed by several other factions in the party, including a very vocal, and apparently well-financed, pro-communist one.[10]

To spell out the details of the operation is difficult. Many documents are still classified and some crucial ones, namely those of Nenni's old friend and Italo-American leader of the Amalgamated Clothing Workers, August Bellanca, have been destroyed.[11] Nevertheless, it is possible to conclude that (possibly from the end of 1961) the Socialist party began to receive financial support from some of the more progressive American unions, that at least one major initiative in the labor field was set up largely as a result of the Reuthers' initiatives,[12] and that this operation was known, and thus tacitly approved, by the White House.[13]

The extent of this support is not easy to figure out, but it was probably rather limited compared to the sums previously invested in supporting the Christian Democrats at the polls. It is the quality of the initiative, however, that must be

10. In his autobiography, Victor Reuther tells of a meeting in which he and his brother tried to persuade the NSC to support the opening to the left. The following day an anti-Reuther right-wing columnist specializing in labor matters, Victor Reisel, wrote an article in which he criticized the initiative and accused the brothers of having staged the meeting to ask the CIA for financial support to "penetrate and win over union leaders within the Communist CGIL." See Victor Reuther, *The Brothers Reuther and the Story of the UAW* (Boston, 1976), 352. When I interviewed Victor Reuther, he denied the charges made against him by Reisel but confirmed that later on some financial assistance was provided to the PSI by the UAW and some other Italo-American unions. He said, however, that this assistance was very little when compared with the amount provided to the Christian Democrats in the 1950s. The possibility of financial assistance was also confirmed in my interviews with McGeorge Bundy and Ray Cline, the latter of whom had been rather critical of the initiative in his *Secrets, Spies and Scholars: Blueprint of the Essential CIA* (Washington, D.C., 1976).

11. Interview with Richard Strassberg, Archivist, Labor-Management Documentation Center, M. P. Catherwood Library, Cornell University, Ithaca, N.Y.

12. A late 1961 memo by Fabio Luca Cavazza of *Il Mulino*'s study group for Arthur Schlesinger, Jr., states that Nenni told Cavazza that he was "in the position . . . to make public statement of the fact that the American Labor Unions have helped the Party." See undated memo for Arthur Schlesinger, Jr. [but actually sent 12 December 1961], in Subject File, Italy: 1–29 February 1964, ASP, JFKL. Between September and December 1962, the Amalgamated Clothing Workers and the UAW provided a grand total of $82,790 to the UIL and the Socialist component of the CGIL to train labor cadres and strengthen those socialists among the trade unions who supported the opening to the left. See Adolphe Graedel to W. P. Reuther, 25 May 1964, in Box 444, Folder 5, Walter Reuther Papers, Walter Reuther Library of Labor and Urban Affairs, Wayne State University, Detroit, Mich.

13. According to some sources, the British Labour party had anticipated the Americans in the task of supporting Nenni's road toward democracy: Bureau of Intelligence and Research, Intelligence Report 7870, "The Outlook for Italy," 10 December 1958, p. 12, in Institut National de la Radio files, North African Waters; and memorandum from George Lister to Mr. Velletri, "Leader Grant visit of Cesare Bensi, Italian Socialist," 14 May 1962, in Box WH-12a, ASP, JFKL.

stressed because it helped to improve relations between the Nenni Socialists and the White House. The whole operation must also be evaluated in the overall context of U.S.-Italian relations.[14] Although the liberals in the White House staff might have succeeded in mobilizing some help for their cause, the official diplomatic line remained very cautious toward the opening for some time, and some other steps taken by the administration actually pointed in other directions. It is surprising, for instance, to learn that when William Harvey of Task Force W was removed from Operation Mongoose in early 1963 because of his behavior during the Cuban Missile Crisis, he was appointed CIA chief of station in Rome, where his unruly behavior—let alone his drinking habits—hardly played a positive role in the delicate balancing act of sponsoring the opening.[15] If anything, this episode can be taken as one more example of the low priority of the Italian operation for the White House. It seems clear, however, that from a certain point the real issue at stake was no longer whether to support the opening but, in the words of Bundy himself, "how much to support the Left socialists [in the coming elections]."[16]

The socialists, however, were far from unanimous in cooperating with the Christian Democrats. Years of close cooperation with the Partito Comunista Italiano (PCI) had exacted a heavy ideological toll on the party's identity, and on many foreign policy issues the PSI was still influenced by a deep mixture of neutralism and anti-Americanism. The crucial issue on which their participation in the government rested quickly became the role the socialists envisaged for Italy in the Atlantic Alliance.[17] As a State Department paper aptly summed up the question, "Italian democracy (and American interests in Italy) may be faced with the alternative of one governing coalition which seems to present more opportunity for reducing PCI strength, and another which would be a more cooperative ally of the US in NATO and in foreign affairs in general."[18]

This leads to a final remark about yet another shortcoming in most of the existing reconstructions of the story, namely their failure to focus in depth on the

14. It would also be interesting to know whether the United States followed the suggestion given to President Kennedy and to John McCone by Fiat president Valletta, namely that the financial support for the PSI should be handled through the Christian Democrats to keep a tight rein on the socialists. See Bairati, *Valletta*.

15. On Harvey's removal, see Martin, *Wilderness of Mirrors*, 181–89; Thomas Powers, *The Man Who Kept the Secrets: Richard Helms and the CIA* (New York, 1979), 141–42; John Ranelagh, *The Agency: The Rise and Decline of the CIA* (New York, 1987), 388. Also see author's interview with Ray Cline.

16. Bundy to the President, "Weekend Reading," 12–13 January 1963, in Box 318, NSF, JFKL.

17. For a balanced assessment of PSI foreign policy, see research memorandum REU-40, "Italian Socialist Foreign Policy," 27 April 1962, in Box WH 12, ASP, JFKL. I am very grateful to John Orme for his assistance in obtaining the declassification of this document, and to Mrs. Forbes of the Kennedy Library for promptly sending me a copy a few days before the October 1992 conference "Kennedy and Europe."

18. "Italy," Department of State Guidelines for Policy and Operations, January 1962, in Box 120, NSF, JFKL.

interplay between the opening to the left and the broader international context of the time.[19] It is this intersection between the two aspects of U.S. foreign policy, sketched out in the introduction to this essay, that can throw some additional light on the issue and that will be investigated in the final section. To evaluate it properly, however, one must first assess the extent of U.S. security interests in Italy that could have been jeopardized by the opening to the left and briefly look at what was defined at the beginning of the essay as the Euro-Atlantic dimension of U.S.-Italian relations.

## The Euro-Atlantic Dimension

Since the inclusion of Italy in the Atlantic Alliance, Italian foreign policy had mostly maintained a close alignment with that of the United States, marked by only a few episodes of contrast and diffidence. This trend was strengthened after 1956, when the aftermath of the Suez crisis made Italian politicians all the more interested in reinforcing their cooperation with the United States in order to fill the gaps left by what seemed the sudden decline of French and British influence in the Mediterranean.[20] By the late 1950s such an alignment had developed much further because of the appearance of Gaullism in France: Italian exclusion from the quadripartite ambassadorial group on Berlin and the Gaullist suggestion for the creation of a Franco-Anglo-American "Directorate" had sharpened Italian sensitivities and reinforced Italy's support for NATO as the best forum for debating major international issues.[21]

Such a latent contrast with de Gaulle played an important role in shaping U.S.-Italian relations in the Kennedy years, as Italy and France eventually chose alternate approaches to the problems that bedeviled Western Europe at the time, with Italy usually taking a more pro-American line. In truth, Paris and Washington were probably the two most important reference points of Italian foreign policy, and any contrast between them was bound to provoke serious headaches in the Italian Foreign Ministry. Thus, throughout 1961 and 1962 Italian foreign policy worked hard to prevent an open split in the Western camp by displaying great interest both in the French proposals for a European political union and in the British application to join the EEC, playing an important mediating role that was "very close to [the] U.S. position" and much appreciated by the State Department. Fanfani displayed great interest in the eventual success of a political

19. Again, only Arthur M. Schlesinger, Jr., and, in more detail, Leo Wollemborg dedicate some attention to the international aspects of the opening to the left.
20. Ennio Di Nolfo, "Italia e Stati Uniti: un'alleanza disuguale," in *Storia delle Relazioni Internazionali* (1991).
21. Position paper on Atlantic Area Problems, in Box 121, NSF, JFKL. For a good example of the spirited Italian reaction to de Gaulle's tripartite proposals, see memorandum of conversation (the President, the Acting Secretary, the Italian Ambassador, Mr. Jandrey), 6 October 1958, in Box 3155, RG59, NARA.

union while also trying to steer de Gaulle's proposals into formulas (such as the one for politico-military coöperation among the "Six") that would not disrupt the existing pattern of Western European and Atlantic relations. At the same time, the Fanfani government had been quietly supportive of British efforts to bridge the gap between the "Six" and the "Seven" since the visit to Rome of the Lord Privy Seal, Edward Heath, in August 1960, and frequent contacts between the British and the Italian governments had made clear that both Macmillan and Fanfani shared the concern that the economic division of Europe might lead to a political one and that they both wanted to find a common solution to the problems that separated the United Kingdom from the EEC.[22] Most Italian political parties, moreover, were hostile to a Paris-Bonn axis within the EEC and openly favored British inclusion in the Community.

The Italian government was therefore seriously worried about the prospect of an open break in the Brussels negotiations and repeatedly expressed its reservations to Paris lest the Franco-German entente became a politico-institutional, rather than a psychological, one.[23] The Italian prime minister asked to be invited to Washington in January 1963 to discuss with President Kennedy a way of avoiding a breakdown in the negotiations, while at the same time Italian foreign minister Attilio Piccioni visited Bonn for the same purpose. In Rome there was great concern over de Gaulle's January 1963 salvo against British entry, and the government reacted to the Franco-German Treaty of Friendship and Cooperation by holding top-level discussions with Macmillan in Rome in early February. The maverick Republican party budget minister, Ugo La Malfa, even went as far as proposing a new European "political alignment of states" to encourage democratic forces in Germany to take that country out of the French embrace.[24] The general feeling in the government, however, was to keep playing a cautious and prudent mediating role so as not to "further rock the EEC boat."[25] In the Rome talks Macmillan and Fanfani agreed to avoid any "new formal engagement" while utilizing to [the] fullest the already existing multilateral and bilateral

22. Reinhardt (Rome) to State Department, 7 December 1962, in Box 120, NSF, JFKL; Gavin (Paris) to the Secretary of State, 6 April 1962, in Box 71, NSF, JFKL; "Record of Meeting at the Villa Madama," 22 August 1960, in FO371/153318, PRO.

23. Fanfani said so to Couve de Murville during their meeting on 12 October 1962, and after several warnings the French Embassy in Rome was formally informed of the Italian concern on 12 January 1963. See the remarks by Prime Minister Fanfani in Verbale del Consiglio dei Ministri (minutes of a Cabinet Meeting), 23 January 1963, in fascicolo "La grossa questione dell'Inghilterra," b. 75, Carte Ugo La Malfa, ACS. For the Italian concerns, and Fanfani's in particular, see also Wollemborg, Stars and Stripes, 78ff.

24. Reinhardt (Rome) to Secretary of State, 1 February 1963, in Box 120, NSF, JFKL. See also La Malfa's letter to Walter Lippmann, where the leader of the Republican party draws a dramatic picture of the alignment of the progressive-conservative forces in Western Europe and concludes that the victory of progressive forces in Italy was the first step toward keeping right-wing would-be followers of de Gaulle at bay: La Malfa to Lippmann, 25 January 1963, in Box 83, Folder 1271, Walter Lippmann Papers—Series III, Yale University Library.

25. Reinhardt (Rome) to Secretary of State, 6 February 1963, in Box 120, NSF, JFKL.

organizations and arrangements."[26] Along these lines, the Italian government continued to display a warm interest in bringing the United Kingdom into closer relations with the EEC, with such gestures as the Italian foreign minister's visit to London in early March 1963.[27]

The aftermath of the January crisis thus proved that Italy was not willing to follow de Gaulle's lead along Adenauer's example and that if things came to a head, Washington would remain the pivotal point of Italian diplomacy. Kennedy, in his European policy, was willing to go a great length toward finding a way to satisfy de Gaulle and keep France happily within NATO, but he gradually grew more aware of the importance of Italy in the general context of European turbulence. As he said to Ambassador Frederick Reinhardt in March 1962, "Italy would become increasingly important to us in view of the predictable difficulties with France and the fact that both Belgium and the Netherlands were deeply disturbed by our attitude on colonial questions."[28] Especially after the January 1963 crisis, therefore, the fact that Rome and Washington continued to share similar views about the future of Western Europe remained of great importance to U.S. foreign policy.

An even closer alignment between Italy and the United States can be detected in matters of security and defense policy. As atomic weapons evolved into the central instrument of Western strategy, the Italian government had tried to meet the challenge posed by access to the new status symbol by developing a strategy of cooperation with other powers. After briefly toying with the idea of a Franco-Italo-German consortium to produce nuclear weapons, Italy returned to the safer course of cooperation with the United States within a NATO framework.[29] By the late 1950s, therefore, the Italian government had become active in a range of initiatives related to military applications of nuclear power, all of which were based on close cooperation with the United States,[30] and in late 1960 had

26. Reinhardt (Rome) to the Secretary of State, 5 February 1963, in Box WH 12a, ASP, JFKL. The complete text of the Rome talks can be found in the fascicolo "La grossa questione dell'Inghilterra."

27. Reinhardt (Rome) to State Department, 19 February 1963, in Subject File, Italy: 1–28 February 1963, ASP, JFKL.

28. Memorandum of conversation (the President, Reinhardt, Bundy) 22 March 1962, in Box 120, NSF, JFKL.

29. For an analysis of the attempt at Franco-Italo-German cooperation, see the articles by Colette Barbier, Eckart Conze, and Leopoldo Nuti in *Revue d'Histoire Diplomatique*, nos. 1–2 (1990). See also " 'Me too, please': Italy and the Politics of Nuclear Weapons, 1945–1975," *Diplomacy and Statecraft*, IV (March 1993), 114–48.

30. In 1958 the Italian army had received from the United States its first tactical delivery means. See L. Nuti, "The Role Model? Italy and U.S. Armed Forces, 1945–1963," in *U.S. Forces in Europe: The Early Years*, ed. S. Duke and W. Krieger (Boulder, Colo., forthcoming). In the same year the Italian navy had also made clear to the U.S. Navy its interest in nuclear propellants either for a surface vessel or for a submarine, and shortly thereafter the U.S. Joint Chiefs of Staff gave a first positive appraisal of the Italian request: JCS—Decision on JCS 1808/52, A Report by the J-5 on Italian Navy Interest in Development of Nuclear Propulsion Systems, JCS 1808/52, 16 September 1958, in DDRS, 1981/463a; see also William Macomber, Jr., to Clinton Anderson, 23 October 1959, in Box 3622, RG59, NARA.

followed the example of other NATO countries and concluded an agreement with the United States on the uses of atomic energy for mutual defense.[31] Paramount among these Italian initiatives had been the decision in summer 1958 to accept the deployment of two squadrons of fifteen Jupiter MRBMs, leading to the 26 March 1959 agreement and the subsequent setting up of the 36th Air Brigade of the Italian Air Force which manned and operated the missiles together with special U.S. teams. The Italian military was never completely satisfied with the Jupiters, however, and was receptive to the proposals by General Norstad to come up with a second-generation weapon that would replace the Jupiters and enhance NATO's control over the MRBMs, especially if the United States would provide the funds.[32]

In short, at the time when nuclear sharing was fast becoming the central theme of Atlantic relations, the Italian government reached the conclusion that the only way to a nuclear status of some sort would be through close cooperation with NATO and the United States. This strategy was for some time specular to, and fully compatible with, the nuclear sharing schemes put forward by the Eisenhower administration, as well as with the more general U.S. interest in strengthening the Western military posture. As Marc Trachtenberg has noted, moreover, all these nuclear sharing schemes developed in the late Eisenhower years had a rather ambiguous meaning, since they could "function as a bridge to the acquisition by the Europeans of nuclear capabilities under their own control."[33] Such an ambiguity probably explains the Italian interest both in the development of the Norstad project and in a NATO solution for joint control of atomic weapons which in time might give Italy a stronger voice in the decision to use the alliance's nuclear arsenal.

It was only natural, therefore, that Italy followed with particular attention the attitude of the Kennedy administration on nuclear matters. For quite some time the presence of widely different positions on the issue of nuclear sharing within the ranks of the new administration, as well as the lack of a definite stance on this problem, made it seem likely that the policy of the Eisenhower administration might be continued. From the very beginning of the Kennedy years, however, there were signs that puzzled those Italians interested in further development of nuclear sharing, such as the emphasis placed by the new U.S.

31. The Italian Defense Staff was particularly interested in avoiding any wording in the agreement that might prevent future provision of nuclear weapons and special nuclear materials, and it tried in vain to obtain at least a new definition of the scope of the treaty which would leave the door open to the release of such materials. A final text was therefore postponed until late 1960, and the agreement was signed on 3 December 1960. For the agreement for cooperation on the uses of atomic energy for mutual defense purposes, see Turco, *Bilateral Treaties Between Italy and the U.S.,* 82. For the position of the Defense Staff, see Attività del 3° Reparto durante il mese di gennaio 1960, in AUSSME, DS SMD.

32. For the attitude of the Italian military toward the Jupiters, see L. Nuti, "L'Italie et les missiles Jupiters," in *L'Europe et la crise de Cuba,* ed. Maurice Vaisse (Paris, 1993). See also Attività del I Reparto nel mese di febbraio 1960, in AUSSME, DS SMD.

33. Marc Trachtenberg, *History and Strategy* (Princeton, 1991), 188.

administration on conventional defense and its suggestions for a revision of NATO strategy leading to the gradual dismissal of massive retaliation. Commenting on the new U.S. military thinking in June 1961, the Italian Defense Staff expressed its concern about the possible repercussions of the new course on established NATO strategy: since Italian military doctrine relied heavily on the early use of tactical nuclear weapons, the army and the Defense Staff were particularly concerned with the consequences of the "rise in the nuclear threshold" advocated by the Kennedy strategists.[34] In late 1961 and early 1962, as the United States pressured NATO to postpone the debate about the need for the deployment of new MRBMs, Italy went along with the American request, provided that this did not imply the total cancellation of the project.[35] At the same time, however, the Italian Defense Staff continued to follow with attention the NATO debate about the proper procedure for the use of the alliance's nuclear arsenal, with the firm intention of ensuring that Italy would be consulted about any decision to go nuclear.[36]

Thus, in spite of the mixed signals coming from Washington, the Italians probably expected through most of 1962 that in the future the Jupiters might be replaced with sea-based Polaris missiles under Italian control, possibly with a bilateral U.S.-Italian agreement as in the case of the first generation of MRBMs.[37] This might help to explain why throughout 1961 and 1962 the Ital-

34. Relazione sulle attività del I reparto, giugno 1961, in AUSSME, DS SMD; Memorandum of Conversation (the President, Ambassador Manlio Brosio, Mr. McBride) 11 April 1961, in Box 120, NSF, JFKL. The issue was debated during the first meetings with the new president by both the Italian ambassador in Washington, Manlio Brosio, and Prime Minister Fanfani. In both cases Kennedy tried to reassure the Italians that the emphasis on conventional defense did not imply a reduction of U.S. nuclear commitments.

35. Promemoria 110/12611 in data 4 October 1961, quoted in Attività del I Reparto, October 1961, in AUSSME DS SMD. Whenever the permanent representatives of the North Atlantic Council discussed the issue of MRBMs, however, the Italian representative made clear that according to his country the subject had to be picked up again as early as possible. After U.S. secretary of state Rusk told NATO secretary general Stikker in February 1962 that the United States was now prepared to proceed with a NATO approach to the MRBM problem, Stikker introduced the new document NDP/62/2, which raised once more the issue of control of the alliance's nuclear arsenal, to the NAC. The Italian response was similar to the one already outlined in 1961: Italy favored a delegation of power in case of an emergency and otherwise a system of weighted voting in which the country hosting the weapons would play a prominent role.

36. The Defense Staff argued that whenever possible the use of the alliance's nuclear weapons should be decided by a majority of members with a system of weighted voting, in which each country would be allowed decision-making power related to the weapons deployed in its territory; some form of physical control of the weapon systems, in other words, was regarded as the best way to make sure that the host country would be consulted about their use. Relazione sull'attività del I Reparto durante il mese di aprile 1961, in AUSSME DS SMD.

37. Already in 1960 Italian diplomats were hinting that "Italy was much in favour of mobile bases as a means of keeping bases out of Italy and out of Italian politics" and that the Italian government was "thinking in terms of regarding the Polaris programme as an alternative to the plan for having MRBMs stationed in Italy." Minute by Lord Home about a meeting with Count Zoppi, 31 October 1960, in FO371/153314, PRO; and Sir Evelyn Shuckburgh to Sir F. Hoyer Millar, 20 October 1960, *ibid.*

iafi ii ii y worked on the transformation of the cruiser *Garibaldi*, installing and testing four launching tubes with both mock and real Polaris missiles. The outcome of the Cuban Missile Crisis, however, marked a first turning point in the history of U.S.-Italian cooperation in nuclear matters. First, the Kennedy administration somehow committed itself to an anticipated withdrawal of both the Turkish and the Italian Jupiters; then, during discussions about the possible creation of "a pilot NATO Southern Command multilateral sea-based force" based on the *Garibaldi* experiment and meant to facilitate the phasing down of the Jupiters, the opponents of the idea in the administration succeeded in scuttling the initiative; finally, the decisions taken at Nassau sealed the fate of any possibility of U.S. assistance to national nuclear deterrents, removing most of the ambiguity from the nuclear sharing schemes of the late Eisenhower-Dulles years.[38] Although it might not have become immediately clear to the Italians, this turn of events basically altered the chance of a continuation of nuclear cooperation between the two countries along the previous path.

The removal of the Jupiters showed nonetheless the remarkable extent of Italian willingness to comply with U.S. requests. While expressing some concern that Italy "would lose its current 'one-up' position among non-nuclear alliance members," the top Italian politicians accepted the U.S. reasons for the withdrawal, and though some had a negative reaction at being faced with a fait accompli that ignored local political repercussions, none thought of actually opposing the removal of the missiles. The moderate left, and in particular the PSI leadership, was actually pleased with the removal, thus providing one of the first examples of a possible path of cooperation between the New Frontier and the center-left alternative to the former Cold War scenarios. The cabinet discussed the issue on 23 January 1963 and accepted the withdrawal of the MRBMs without much fuss.[39]

Important as nuclear aspirations were for the Italian government, alignment with the United States remained paramount. Thus when in late 1961 the Kennedy administration had begun to signal its preference for a quick buildup of conventional forces, the Italian government and the Defense Staff had also agreed with the new order of priorities.[40] The U.S. military continued to find the Italians inclined to acquiesce to U.S. initiatives.[41] In the fall of 1962, in par-

---

38. Giorgio Giorgerini and Augusto Nani, *Incrociatori Italiani* (Rome, 1964), 675–85; Memorandum, "Turkish IRBM's," 30 October 1962, in Box 226, NSF, JFKL; John Steinbruner, *The Cybernetic Theory of Decision Making* (Princeton, 1974), 233–34.

39. Ainsworth (Rome) to the Secretary of State, 17 January 1963, in WH12a, ASP, JFKL; Consiglio dei Ministri del 23 gennaio 1963, verbale ufficiale, in Ugo la Malfa Papers, busta 75, fascicolo "La grossa questione dell'Inghilterra," ACS.

40. For the new U.S. order of priorities, see for instance Rusk to USRO Paris, 28 July 1961, and Bowles to USRO Paris, 27 September 1961, both in DDRS, 1991/916; Rusk to Finletter, 9 March 1962, in DDRS, 1991/886.

41. When President Kennedy's personal military adviser, General Maxwell Taylor, visited Italy in March 1962, he found the Italians willing to agree with the U.S. position on NATO's immediate tasks: Reinhardt (Rome) to the State Department, 31 March 1962, in DDRS, 1989/2742. Later

ticular, Italy had met U.S. aspirations and signed an agreement for the purchase of a substantial quantity of U.S. conventional military hardware meant to offset American defense expenditures.[42]

Italian flexibility in meeting the shifting requests of U.S. policymakers is also shown by the case of the MLF. When in the spring of 1963 the Kennedy administration decided to give the project a try to counter the crisis in Atlantic relations brought about by de Gaulle's January declarations, the Italian government also began to display a greater interest in the idea, in spite of some former misgivings about the feasibility of the multinational mixed-manning approach.[43] The Italian position soon appeared to be one of "qualified endorsement," as opposed to the growing skepticism of other European partners.[44] The Italians were as reassuring as possible throughout the negotiations run by the special team of Ambassador Merchant in the spring of 1963, and Italy came to be regarded in the United States as one of the warmest supporters of the MLF concept.[45] Even though the impending political elections of June 1963 prevented the Italian government from making a further step and taking a firm stance in favor of the MLF proposal, Italian Foreign Ministry officials stressed that Italian interest in the MLF was such that Italy might even consider participating alone should other European partners refuse to join.[46] Thus Ambassador Merchant concluded that as far as Italy was concerned, "if there is no significant shift to the left in the elections any new government would insist on becoming a member of the MLF, if they believed that Germany and the US were determined to move ahead with its creation (even with such thin political cover as Greece and Turkey alone) and that, if this proved true, would then be the clincher to bring the UK into the MLF."[47]

---

that same year, in his farewell visit to Rome as SACEUR, General Norstad discussed NATO's problems with Prime Minister Fanfani, who once again expressed Italy's willingness to follow a cooperative strategy within NATO to solve the alliance's nuclear problems: American Embassy Paris (Stoessel) to Department of State, "General Norstad's Farewell Visit to Rome," 5 October 1962, in DDRS, 1989/2746.

42. In November 1962, Italy placed orders in the United States amounting to $124 million and made additional orders for $40 million in 1963.

43. Prime Minister Fanfani was reported to have stated that the United States would merely allow Italy to provide "the cooks," but that "he saw little Italy could do but try to upgrade its participation to extent feasible": Ainsworth (Rome) to the Secretary of State, 17 January 1963, in Box WH12a, ASP, JFKL.

44. "Briefing Item: Initial West European Assessment of US Multilateral Force Proposal," 7 March 1963, in Box 217, NSF, JFKL.

45. Finletter to the Secretary of State, 19 March 1963, in Box 218, NSF, JFKL. By the late spring, however, the Italian navy had reconsidered the project of the *Garibaldi* and decided to support a multilateral force based on submarines, as a consequence either of second thoughts about the ship's performance in testing the launching tubes or of the many U.S. doubts about the project.

46. Rome Embassy to Secretary of State, 4 March 1963, in Box 217, NSF, JFKL.

47. "Overall thoughts on the MLF en route from Ankara to Naples," 29 April 1963, in Merchant Papers, Box 10, Seeley G. Mudd Manuscript Library, Princeton University.

## A New Alignment of Forces?

The remark by Ambassador Merchant indicates that the intention of the more progressive-minded members of the administration to open up a new path for Italian democracy had to be reconciled with the security commitments in which Italy was involved through NATO, as well as with the broader aims of U.S. policy toward Western Europe. Would a center-left government be regarded by the USSR as a sign of appeasement and U.S. weakness, or would it strengthen Italy's pro-Western stance? Would it add more problems to an already confused European picture, or would it strengthen Italian-American relations? Especially in the very confused picture that Atlantic relations presented in 1963, with the "concealed time bomb of French instability" and "the dangers of Germany adrift", the United States could not afford to add a further element of uncertainty to the European picture.[48] And yet in the spring and summer of 1963 a stronger consensus began to emerge at different levels of the Kennedy administration about the positive role of the opening to the left in Italian politics.[49] Although the first coalition government with external socialist support had not produced all the reforms that were expected from it, and in spite of the persistence of many doubts, reinforced by the controversial electoral performances of the parties involved, the opening came more and more to be seen as the only possible approach to stabilize the Italian political system.[50]

Some members of the administration also began to stress the possible positive foreign policy repercussions of the new course in Italian politics: Arthur Schlesinger, for instance, described at some length to the president the beneficial effects of strengthening the moderate left all over Western Europe to counter the Gaullist attacks on U.S. supremacy in the Atlantic Alliance.[51] Nor was he alone in this belief, which was widely shared by other supporters of the opening such as Victor Reuther or by media pundits such as Walter Lippmann.[52] The extent to which U.S. policy was affected by this conceptual-ideological approach, how-

48. Memorandum for the President, "The Mess in Europe and the Meaning of Your Trip," 20 June 1963, in DDRS.

49. An important factor in bringing the State Department in line, as Arthur Schlesinger, Jr., points out in *A Thousand Days,* was the appointment of Averell Harriman as under secretary of state for political affairs on 14 April 1963.

50. See, for instance, the remarks about the consequences of a possible failure of the center-left in "The President's European Trip," June 1963, Part III, The Current Situation in Italy, in DDRS, 1977/276B.

51. Memorandum for the President, "How to Deal with the Popular Front Threat," by Arthur Schlesinger, Jr., 22 June 1963, in DDRS.

52. See, for instance, Victor G. Reuther to Willy Brandt, 3 April 1963, in Victor Reuther Papers, Box 27, folder 26, Walter P. Reuther Library of Labor and Urban Affairs, Wayne State University. For Lippmann's support for the center-left as an alternative to a Gaullist Europe, see Wollemborg, *Stars and Stripes,* 83; and Lippmann's column in the *New York Herald Tribune,* 28 December 1962.

ever, was probably never as clear-cut as the picture of a "progressive Europe," mirroring the New Frontier and containing the Gaullist threat, which Schlesinger would have liked to see implemented.[53] Many Italian parties, however, saw de Gaulle's policy not just in its international dimension but also as a possible source of domestic reinvigoration for the Italian right. As the Gaullist challenge grew stronger in early 1963, even the Italian socialists started advocating a firm U.S. leadership role in Atlantic matters, hoping that this might stop any further development of the Paris-Bonn axis, let alone its extension to Madrid.[54] Many socialist leaders also made clear that they were not hostile in principle to the MLF, in particular because of its nonproliferation aspect that allowed the project to nip in the bud any national German initiative.[55]

At the same time, the new atmosphere of détente in U.S.-USSR relations after the Cuban Missile Crisis had a powerful impact on the Italian domestic scene. As disarmament and arms control seemed to gain momentum with the signing of the Partial Test-Ban Treaty, the moderate Italian left seemed more inclined to share governmental responsibilities and support U.S. foreign policy. The dilemma described in 1961 by the State Department of an "Italian democracy faced with the alternative of one governing coalition which seems to present more opportunity for reducing PCI strength and another which would be a more cooperative ally of the US in NATO and in foreign affairs" was therefore gradually being modified by changes in the international picture.[56]

The turning point of this process was probably the Cuban crisis. The response of the Italian government to President Kennedy's speech declaring the quarantine was a much weaker manifestation of solidarity with the U.S. position than on previous occasions, probably because of Fanfani's need not to jeopardize the precarious balance of his government by alienating the socialists with a strong expression of support for the United States. One State Department memorandum noted that Fanfani's excessive concern with domestic priorities was a possible cause of apprehension for the United States because "in any future world crisis, Italy will be likely again to exhibit less open solidarity with us than in the past, so long as the Italian government is dependent on an alliance with the PSI, since it is doubtful that the PSI will move very rapidly toward active support of Alliance solidarity." The same document, however, concluded that "the desirability of drawing the PSI into the democratic coalition in Italy and of thereby strengthening Italy politically, socially, and economically may make some sacrifice of Italian open solidarity with us in fields of foreign policy matters a tolerable

53. Schlesinger, *A Thousand Days,* 804–11.

54. For the socialists' fears of a Spanish extension of Franco-German cooperation, see Pietro Nenni to Ugo La Malfa, 18 January 1963, in fascicolo "La grossa questione dell'Inghilterra."

55. Fraleigh (Rome) to the Secretary of State, "Recent conversations with PSI leaders," 24 June 1963, in Subject File, Italy: 1–30 June 1963, ASP, JFKL; Fraleigh (Rome) to the State Department, " 'Il Punto' Round-Table on 'Europe today and Tomorrow,' " 6 April 1963, in Subject File, Italy: 1 March–30 April 1963, *ibid.*

56. See Wollemborg, *Stelle, strisce e tricolore.*

one, so long as the ultimate reliability of Italian adherence to the alliance is not compromised."[57]

Other analysts also noted that several socialists, "although critical of the US action and skeptical about its necessity and results, reassured Embassy officers that there would be no question of where the Socialist Party would stand in the event of an East-West showdown over the Cuban controversy" and pointed out that "the Nenni socialists . . . refused to join the Communists in 'united action' in the streets and in Parliament." The CIA 1963 National Intelligence Estimate for Italy concluded that "support of the Socialists for the coalition does pose problems" and that their foreign policy views "do suggest considerably less agreement with some significant Western policy views than that demonstrated by past Italian governments." It also noted, however, that the center-left coalition had strictly adhered to the traditional cornerstones of Italian foreign policy (NATO and the EEC) and that "if there has been any change in policy since the coalition was formed, it is a matter of tone rather than substance, of emphasis rather than content."[58] In short, the crisis seemed to prove that, all things considered, the foreign policy risks involved in the opening were limited and for the time being outweighed by the prospect of further isolating the Communist party.

In 1963 the orientation of U.S. foreign policy toward détente on one side and containment of de Gaulle on the other further helped to reduce the contradiction between the two objectives of Washington's Italian policy; this, in turn, made a center-left government more palatable not only as an instrument for reducing PCI influence but also as a further guarantee of U.S.-Italian alignment in Western affairs. If foreign policy had been the most divisive issue and the most difficult obstacle to the conclusion of a compromise between the PSI and the Christian Democrats—"one of the greatest difficulties to the achievement of any agreement on a political program between the Christian Democrat Party and the Socialist Party," in the words of British ambassador Sir Ashley Clarke—it seems likely that a change in the international scenario, limited as it might have been, also eliminated some of the difficulties and thus made it easier for the two parties to find an agreement on this point as well. This opinion was shared by some U.S. observers because in late 1958 an Institut National de la Radio study had concluded that "an opening to the left would depend also on the international climate. A relaxation of international tension would very likely encourage a rapprochement between the center parties and the Nenni socialists."[59]

57. Memorandum for Arthur Schlesinger, Jr., "The Italian Center-Left Government and the Cuban Crisis: Lessons for American Foreign Policy," 30 November 1962, in Box 37, NSF, JFKL.

58. Research Memorandum REU 75, "Our Major European Allies and the Cuban Crisis," 3 November 1962, in Box 50, NSF, JFKL; National Intelligence Estimate 24-63, "Implications of the Center-Left Experiment in Italy," 3 January 1963, in Box WH12, ASP, JFKL.

59. Sir Ashley Clarke to the Earl of Home, 11 December 1962, in FO 371/160662, PRO "The Outlook for Italy," Intelligence report 7870 (originally prepared as the IRA contribution to National Intelligence Estimate 24-58), 10 December 1958, in INR reports, NARA.

This connection between domestic politics and international affairs was also clear to hard-core opponents of the opening such as Claire Luce, who in early 1963 warned President Kennedy against too harsh an anti-Gaullist policy. Such a line was fraught with dangers, warned the former U.S. ambassador to Italy, because

> the Italian government . . . cannot survive a debacle of the French center, and Italy will probably anticipate it by bringing the pro-Communist Socialists into power. In passing, Mr. President, take a very *close* look at your plans to visit Italy. In the present climate, there is a real possibility you may be very embarrassed by the enthusiastic reception you will get from the Communists! I can see the banners now: "Vivo [*sic*] Kennedy e Khrushchev! Down with de Gaulle and Mao Tse Tung."[60]

Far from being an exclusively domestic affair as Italian politicians claimed at the time and afterward, therefore, the opening to the left can also be seen as an offspring of the broader chain of events determined by the evolution of the international system in late 1962 and in 1963. The new dimensions of international relations that began to emerge in 1963, in other words, paved the way to that realignment of forces in the Italian political system that several years of transatlantic wrangling between supporters and opponents of the opening had not been able to accomplish.

This was closely related to the general atmosphere of détente and to what Marc Trachtenberg has defined as the testing and the clarification of "the basic structure of world power" through the major crises of the Kennedy years.[61] Thus the conclusion—informal, gradual, and never acknowledged as it was—of some kind of a postwar settlement and a partial improvement of the superpowers' relationship, combined with the halfhearted emphasis of the Kennedy administration on social reform and strengthening democracy, eventually helped to promote a gradual shift in the domestic Italian balance of power. At the same time, the new moderately leftist coalition that began to emerge in Italy was favorably inclined toward supporting a less confrontational attitude in the Cold War and toward various forms of disarmament and arms control, thus creating a sort of virtuous circle that could help in implementing that policy. This is still an oversimplification of the events, since nothing was as clear-cut as this formal description seems to make it.[62] U.S. policy toward Italy in the Kennedy years, in fact,

60. Claire Boothe Luce to Kennedy, 5 February 1963, in Box 31, POF, JFKL.
61. Trachtenberg, *History and Strategy,* chapter 4, "Making Sense of the Nuclear Age."
62. The best example of how uncertain the new course was (and how curious) is certainly the multilateral force: halfheartedly sponsored by the United States to meet the European quest for access to nuclear hardware, it was consistently used by right-wing forces in Italy as an acid test of socialist allegiance to the West, even if many of the U.S. proponents of the MLF themselves had doubts about its validity.

can best be described as a delicate balancing act between old and new approaches, since between 1961 and 1963 U.S.-Italian relations followed a stop-and-go course, with several setbacks and contradictions, which makes it hard to identify any clear-cut direction. And yet, out of this apparent labyrinth, a slow, gradual process of change and the early signs of a realignment of forces can be detected with a certain consistency.

# 9

# Kennedy, Portugal, and the Azores Base, 1961

*José Freire Antunes*

~

One of Europe's smallest countries (eighty-nine thousand square kilometers, or about the size of the state of Maine), consisting of the mainland territory and the archipelagoes of Madeira and the Azores, Portugal accumulated over the centuries a vast empire.[1] Its possessions spanned the globe: Angola, Mozambique, Guinea, Cape Verde, São Tomé e Principe, and the Fort of São João Baptista de Ajudá in Africa; Macau, Goa, Daman, and Diu in Asia; and Timor in Oceania. These territories amounted to twenty-five times the landmass of mainland Portugal, and together they constituted a unit of such iconographic greatness as to lead General Óscar Fragoso Carmona, president of the republic from 1926 to 1951, to state that Portugal was "not merely a European, but a world power."[2] Fear of external threats was fundamental to the formulation of Portugal's African policy, and the ideological consensus of the educated elites centered on the preservation of the empire.

The Azores, nine volcanic islands almost in the middle of the North Atlantic, became in the early 1940s the key to relations between the United States and Portugal. Situated 660 maritime miles from Lisbon and 2,100 miles from New York, the Azores were crucial for the dominance of the Atlantic. Adolf Hitler, who several times considered invading the Azores, saw the archipelago as "the only facility for attacking America, if she should enter the war."[3] From 1941 on, given the possibility of Nazi occupation, the Azores were considered a U.S. outpost by the Department of Defense, and the U.S. armed forces unilaterally as-

1. Abbreviations used in the notes:
   DDEL    Dwight D. Eisenhower Library, Abilene
   FDRL    Franklin D. Roosevelt Library, New York
   JFKL    John F. Kennedy Library, Boston
   HSTL    Harry S. Truman Library, Independence
   LBJL    Lyndon B. Johnson Library, Austin
   NARA    National Archives and Records Administration, Washington, D.C.
2. "Portugal," 13 October 1949, Copy no. 1 for the President of the United States, Central Intelligence Agency SR-31, in HSTL.
3. William L. Langer and S. Everett Gleason, *The Undeclared War, 1940–1941* (New York, 1953), 80.

sumed the military oversight of the Azores within the defense system for the Western Hemisphere.

António de Oliveira Salazar, absolute master of Portugal between 1932 and 1968, never truly overcame his visceral dislike for America and American democracy. In 1945, the OSS men reported from Lisbon that "the United States, in Salazar's thinking, appears to represent the chief exponent of the 'nineteenth century democracy and liberalism' of which he has tried so hard to rid Portugal."[4] Like other European statesmen of his generation, Salazar was upset by the United States' rise as the new leading power of the West. He abhorred the American world vision and perceived the United States as subverting traditional European life. He feared the ambition for dominance implicit in U.S. economic and military might, as well as its capacity to erode the vulnerable Portuguese empire.

In October 1943, when negotiations for the use of an air base in the Azores were causing great unrest in Lisbon, the American chargé d'affairs, George F. Kennan, explained in a message to Washington that "Salazar . . . fears association with us only slightly less than with the Russians." Two weeks later, in an attempt to allay those fears, Franklin Roosevelt assured Salazar in writing that "I do not need to tell you that the United States has no designs on the territory of Portugal and its possessions."[5] Despite this formal guarantee, it was only at the end of 1944, when the military decline of Germany and Japan became clear and Salazar's own political survival was at stake, that he pragmatically accommodated himself to the supremacy of the United States in both the Atlantic and the Pacific Oceans.

Salazar was willing to accept U.S. supremacy because he understood that a weakened Britain would no longer be able to protect Portugal and its multicontinental empire and that the old Anglo-Portuguese alliance would be invalidated by the newly forged American links. As in other periods of its history, Portugal now opted to ally itself with an established maritime power (formerly Britain, now the United States) against a threatening continental power (in the past Spain, now the Soviet Union). In 1944, the year of the Normandy invasion, at the end of dramatic negotiations, the United States gained access to one air base on the Azores. The initial Portuguese-American agreement was restricted to the runway on Santa Maria Island, and the United States promised, in exchange, to support Portugal in recovering its Oceanic territory of Timor, which had been occupied by Japan.

After World War II, Portugal became part of the strategic web of U.S. protectorates and had a useful role in the success of the containment strategy. In February 1949, Secretary of State Dean Acheson, announcing to the Senate that Por-

4. "Anti-American Sentiment and Propaganda in Portugal," 23 March 1945, in Office of Strategic Services Research and Analysis Branch No. 2951, NARA.
5. Lisbon 2469 (Section 1), "Department's 1816," 20 October 1943; White House Letter from the President to the Prime Minister of Portugal (António Oliveira Salazar), 4 November 1963, both in FDRL.

tugal had been invited to join NATO, spelled out American interests: "Portugal is of vital importance because of the Azores."[6] The Azores base and NATO membership represented a safety net for Salazar's dictatorship in the context of the Cold War, for they assured American protection. The United States proposed that Portugal be admitted to the United Nations (a proposal vetoed until 1955 by the Soviet Union), supported Portugal in its legal dispute with India regarding the territory of Goa, and abstained until March 1961 from the UN votes on resolutions condemning Portuguese policies in Africa.

The basic modus operandi for Portuguese-American cooperation was determined by the manner in which Salazar administered Portugal's overseas territories, as well as by the extreme sense of nationalism he promoted—a refusal to sacrifice Portugal's domestic priorities to those of the alliance. Secretary of State John Foster Dulles stressed to Eisenhower the need to overturn "the Portuguese feeling of reluctance to follow too closely our lead in the international field." While Salazar confined Portugal in the bounds of xenophobia, Acheson, Eisenhower, and Dulles shared the same pragmatic attitude toward a stable and convenient regime that was long outdated according to Anglo-Saxon criteria of political organization. On 9 November 1960, one day after Kennedy's election, speaking of Salazar and his regime in the Oval Office, outgoing president Eisenhower told the American ambassador in Lisbon, C. Burke Elbrick, that "dictatorships of this type are sometimes necessary in countries whose political institutions are not so far advanced as ours."[7] The relationship between the two countries during the 1945–61 period, although to some extent determined by the distance inherent to differing political philosophies, was nonetheless crisisfree.

The Lajes Base Agreement of 6 September 1951, which was renewed in 1957 and was due to expire on 31 December 1962, applied to both peace and war situations. In the case of the former, the United States would remain for a period of five years; in the latter, it would use the Azores for the duration of NATO's existence, so long as both countries were involved in the same conflict. Instead of paying rent, as it did for comparable facilities in countries such as Spain, Morocco, and Libya, the United States would grant military aid to Portugal so the country could participate effectively in NATO.

Salazar pressed, to no avail, for the integration of Portuguese Africa into NATO's scheme of geostrategic protection, which was limited to the region north of the Tropic of Cancer. In the meantime, through the Lajes Base Agreement, Salazar was able to achieve partially, via bilateral relations, that which he

---

6. U.S. Senate, *Hearings Held in Executive Session Before the Committee on Foreign Relations, Eightieth Congress, Second Session on S. Res. 329 and Eighty-First Congress, First Session on Executive L (The North Atlantic Treaty), the Vandenberg Resolution and the North Atlantic Treaty, Made Public August 1973* (Washington, D.C., 1973), 89.

7. Department of State Memorandum for the President, "Proposed State Visit of President Lopes of Portugal," 29 October 1954; White House memorandum of conversation with the President, "Portugal," 8 November 1960, both in DDEL.

had not succeeded in doing through NATO. In fact, the United States secretly promised, in notes exchanged between the two governments, that NATO's military equipment could be used in African "Although the consent of the American government would in principle be necessary for any transfer of armament supplied for the defense of Portuguese metropolitan territory, there is no doubt that this consent would be promptly forthcoming for a transfer of armaments, which perchance may be necessary, from metropolitan Portuguese territory to any Portuguese colonial territory."[8] The implications of this secret codicil were particularly important after the outbreak of war in Angola on 15 March 1961.

The Lajes base, considered indispensable by the Pentagon, was a center of communications between the United States and Europe, an air, sea, and submarine vigilance post, as well as a vital air bridge in times of crisis. It was used in 1958, for example, in the airlift of U.S. marines to Lebanon and in 1960 by UN Blue Berets en route to the Congo. In 1960 more than 70 percent of all American military air traffic to Europe and the Middle East was flowing through the Lajes base.

Kennedy brought to American foreign policy a new activist perspective on the nationalist uprisings throughout the Third World. He rehabilitated the internationalist tradition of Woodrow Wilson and Franklin Roosevelt by emphasizing the anticolonial heritage of the United States. In 1956, when he was thinking of running for the vice-presidency, Kennedy guaranteed that under Democratic leadership the United States would not abstain from UN votes on "colonial issues." His bold speech regarding Algeria, delivered on 2 July 1957, gave Kennedy national fame as an independent voice of American foreign policy. He attacked Eisenhower's position of noninvolvement in the conflict which since 1954 had placed the French army in opposition to the guerrillas of the National Liberation Front, criticized the use of American arms in the conflict, and defended a negotiated political settlement.[9] Kennedy had caused embarrassment in Washington, irritation in Paris, disorder in Algeria, and surprise all over the world.

Africa remained one of Kennedy's fundamental concerns. He believed that communism could be eradicated on the continent only through the imposition of nationalist, pro-Western alternatives. He opposed the prevalent Eurocentrism in Washington, maintaining that "we can no longer think of Africa in terms of Europe." As chair of the African Subcommittee of the Senate Foreign Relations Committee, Kennedy became the American on whom African nationalist leaders

8. Lisbon A-524, "Basis for US Presence in the Azores," 15 April 1963, in JFKL.
9. John F. Kennedy, "Colonialism and American Foreign Policy," Remarks by Senator John Kennedy, Town Hall Luncheon, Los Angeles, California, 1 April 1956, quoted by Richard D. Mahoney, *JFK: Ordeal in Africa* (New York, 1983), 187; John F. Kennedy, *The Strategy of Peace* (New York, 1960), 67–69.

would assume power in Lisbon. Delgado had acquired the reputation of "being strongly pro-American."[15] The hijacking of the ship captured public attention worldwide for the next two weeks.

Contrary to Salazar's wishes, the United States did not consider the capturing of the *Santa Maria* an act of piracy. In the United Kingdom, Labour party leader Hugh Gaitskell expressed his solidarity with the captors of the ship, describing them as freedom fighters. Washington declined to intercept the ship by force. Kennedy's cautious attitude amounted to a political rebuff for Salazar. As Pedro Theotónio Pereira, the Portuguese ambassador in the United States, would later note, Kennedy's reaction indicated the "new ways of the American Administration." Enormous pressure was placed on the U.S. embassy in Lisbon, and during the crisis of the *Santa Maria* anti-American sentiment emerged in embryonic form. Denial of access to the Lajes base was for the first time suggested by the Portuguese.[16] For the Kennedy administration, the incident was useful in two ways. First, it proved to the world the existence of anti-Salazar forces that were democratically aligned; it also prepared the international community for the new U.S. policy regarding Portuguese Africa.

At sunrise on 4 February 1961, hundreds of blacks attacked the Casa de Reclusão Militar de Luanda (a military prison) to liberate political prisoners. Forty of the assailants and seven policemen were killed in the attack. As had occurred in Algeria during the first attacks against the French government, retaliation by the white population was brutal. An explosion of violence and panic fell upon Angola. The mythical harmonious racial and social coexistence—the key to Portuguese policies in Africa—suffered a severe blow to its credibility. Angola, the pearl of the Portuguese empire, became a salient issue on the international scene.

Meanwhile, in Lisbon, a group of pro-American generals, led by the minister of defense, General Botelho Moniz, defended the view that the black-initiated violence in Angola and the foreseeable eruptions in Mozambique and Guinea demanded urgent state reforms. Under Kennedy's influence, and already set in the laissez-faire attitude that he adopted with regard to the *Santa Maria* crisis, the minister initiated an approach to the United States. On 17 February, Botelho Moniz told the American ambassador, C. Burke Elbrick, and the CIA chief of station, Fred Hubbard, that "the military would not hesitate to act." CIA officers in Lisbon were considering the possible scenarios for a change of regime and encouraging some of their Portuguese connections; the time had come for "Salazar's substitution."[17] The American objective was to secure a pro-Western succession for the regime.

15. *Keesing's Contemporary Archives 1961*, p. 17,951; Department of State Memorandum to Brig. Gen. A. J. Goodpaster (the White House), "Personalities Involved in the 'Santa Maria' Case," 27 January 1961, in JFKL.

16. Benjamin Welles, "U.S. Retreat on Piracy Stand Worries Officials in Portugal," *New York Times*, 27 January 1961; Pedro Theotónio Pereira, recorded interview by Joseph E. O'Connor, 18 December 1966, pp. 6–7 in JFKL Oral History Program; Lisbon 272, 3 February 1961, in NARA.

17. Lisbon 290, "Conversation with Minister of Defense Botelho Moniz on Situation in Conti-

Besides clandestine action, the Kennedy administration had opted for a direct confrontation, with continued diplomatic pressure on Portugal. On 7 March, following Dean Rusk's instructions, Elbrick told Salazar that the United States felt it was increasingly difficult and disadvantageous to the interests of the West to support Portuguese policy in Africa or to keep silent about it: "The United States feels that it would be remiss in its duties as a fellow NATO member of Portugal if it did not point out its conviction that step by step actions are now imperative for the political, economic and social advancement for all the inhabitants of Portuguese African territories towards full self-determination within a realistic timetable." Rusk concluded his message by stating that Portuguese inaction seemed likely to lead "to catastrophic upheavals of Congo type or worse."[18] Under Rusk's instruction, Elbrick had previously informed General Botelho Moniz of this position.

Salazar told the American ambassador that he was profoundly worried about Washington's failure to recognize the danger in which its policies for Africa placed the Western world at large: "Russians are clearly attacking Portugal via Africa and it would appear that Americans are ingenuously playing their game. It is manifestly impossible to be an ally of Portugal in Europe and an enemy in Africa." He rejected the idea of self-determination and spoke of the sentiments attached to the African issue. It was not just he who fought for maintaining the Portuguese territories; it was also the majority of the population who had strong ties with the African provinces after five centuries of involvement there. Moreover, he said, any government that should come into power, with the exception of the communists, would also feel obliged to take whatever measures were necessary for maintaining the territories. He commented on the black inability to govern: "Without white men Africa would be nothing and would rapidly return to tribalism."[19] Salazar noted that the transition had been calm only in former British colonies where there were few whites; and that was not Angola's case. In short, he refused the U.S. proposal.

On 15 March, the American delegation to the United Nations joined the Soviet Union and the Afro-Asian bloc to condemn Portuguese policy in Africa. The United States had made a historic rupture with Eisenhower's policies and the Eurocentrism of the postwar period. Many of the Third World countries, Arthur Schlesinger notes, viewed Kennedy as "a friend of oppressed people." Conservative circles in Washington, headed by Dean Acheson, saw the vote on Angola as a catastrophic initiative. Arguing against the U.S. mission to the UN, headed by Adlai Stevenson, and the African Bureau of the State Department,

---

nental and Overseas Portugal," 17 February 1961, in JFKL; Carlos Viana de Lemos, interview with the author in Lisbon, 22 August 1987. Colonel Lemos was assistant to the cabinet of the minister of national defense from 1959 to 13 April 1961 and was under secretary of state of the army at the time of the 25 April 1974 Portuguese revolution.

18. Department of State outgoing telegram 471, "For Ambassadors Elbrick and Barbour from Secretary," 2 March 1961, in JFKL.

19. Lisbon 572, "Meeting with Salazar," 7 March 1961, in JFKL.

to impede at all costs Washington's attaining solidarity in its plan to exert pressure on Portugal. General de Gaulle told the new Portuguese ambassador in Paris, Marcello Mathias: "Don't count on a change in the US's attitude. Look for new support. Resist. France will help you." On the very day of the de Gaulle-Kennedy meeting in Paris, on 31 May, the *New York Times* ran an interview with Salazar. Aside from his usual arguments of rejecting self-determination in Portuguese Africa and stressing the importance of the military pacification, Salazar promised reforms: "Populations will be brought more and more into local political and administrative life."[25] As Elbrick stressed to Rusk, U.S. pressure was beginning to work: Salazar was actually speaking about reforms.

De Gaulle and Kennedy discussed the Angolan issue on 1 June. The French president agreed that the Portuguese attitude was inflexible, but he also thought that putting too much pressure on Salazar could cause a revolution in Portugal, as well as open the way for the possibility of a communist regime in the Iberian Peninsula. Kennedy answered that the changes in Africa were inexorable, thereby justifying the U.S. position in the UN, and claimed that blocking those changes would only help the communists. De Gaulle said he would seek to persuade Salazar to adopt more constructive policies and that although he could not uphold the United States' views, he would not contradict them. Kennedy and Khrushchev also discussed Angola on 3 June in Vienna. The Soviet leader defined the nationalist struggle for independence as a "sacred war."[26]

Kennedy's trip to Europe had not helped Salazar's international standing in the least. The Soviet Union competed with the United States for Angolan independence, and France and Britain would not intervene in favor of Salazar's policy, as Portugal had hoped. Khrushchev's vehemence regarding the Angolan issue at the same time prompted a greater mobilization and clearer positions on the part of the United States. Assistant Secretary of State for African Affairs G. Mennen Williams observed to Kennedy on 4 July that "Angola has become for much of the world, as Berlin is for Europe, the center of the great battle between freedom and oppression. . . . The United States can take only one position in this struggle. We support freedom." The most Salazar managed to achieve, in his diplomatic appeals, was the abstention of Paris. Mathias remembers the feeling of abandonment: "We only had France on our side. De Gaulle, that is."[27] Even this support was not especially comfortable, keeping in mind de Gaulle's great difficulties in Algeria.

On 9 June, the United States, the Soviet Union, and seven other members of the Security Council voted in favor of a UN resolution calling for a special com-

25. Mathias, interview with the author, 15 December 1983; Lisbon 953, "Benjamin Welles interview with Doctor Salazar," 30 May 1961, in JFKL.

26. Schlesinger, *A Thousand Days,* 235; Presidential Task Force on the Portuguese Territories in Africa, "Recommendations for Action," 12 July 1961, in JFKL.

27. Report of the Chairman of the Task Force on the Portuguese Territories in Africa, "Recommendations for Action," 4 July 1961, in JFKL; Mathias, interview with the author, 15 December 1983.

mittee of the UN to investigate the situation in Angola and calling on Portugal to stop "all repressive measures." France and Britain abstained. The Portuguese foreign minister, Franco Nogueira, called the resolution the "green light for terrorism in Angola." Salazar's government refused to cooperate with the UN, not recognizing its competence to investigate the situation in Angola, which it considered a purely internal problem. On 19 June, the government of Norway announced that it had decided to stop selling arms to Portugal. Britain also changed its position. Harold Macmillan announced that London would also set up an arms embargo against Angola.[28] The siege on Portugal within NATO was tightening.

Salazar called an extra session of the National Assembly for 30 June. He launched a formal attack on Kennedy's policy. He accused the United States of sponsoring the subversion of Africa and favoring the communist strategy: "The United States, although it has different intentions, is carrying out in Africa a policy parallel to that of Russia." He once again rejected the possibility of applying the theory of self-determination to Portuguese Africa. Kennedy's reaction was blunt. Under his orders, Rusk instructed Elbrick to transmit Washington's deep disappointment to Salazar and to remind him that "we believe that the long-run interest of all of us will be adversely affected if political and economic measures are not soon indicated that would respond to this situation."[29] A spokesperson for the State Department regretted the criticisms of the United States made by the Portuguese leader.

Both positions became more radical. On 10 July, an emotional and aggressive Franco Nogueira told Elbrick, among other things, that the United States was the chief architect of Portugal's difficulties in Africa. He increased the semantic stakes: "Nogueira made it clear that Portugal would go to the bitter end in maintaining its overseas territories and said that a world war might result. To my question whether Portugal would attempt to drag the whole world down because of Angola, he replied in the affirmative, saying that as far as Portugal is concerned Angola is much more important than Berlin." On 15 July, Salazar told Elbrick that nationalism did not exist in Angola or Mozambique but that the Americans had invented it; Portugal would continue its four-hundred-year effort to construct a multiracial society in Angola, and "US policy in the UN has only served to encourage terrorists in Angola." At the end of the meeting, Elbrick, who was not the most convincing transmitter of Kennedy's political energy, revealed the American offer: economic aid would be given to Portugal in exchange for reforms in Portuguese Africa. Salazar appeared to be vaguely curious about the idea, or rather, basically disinterested. The ambassador conceded to Rusk: "I cannot report success."[30] There was no room for negotiation.

28. Lisbon 428, 9 June 1961, in NARA; *Daily Observer* (London), 7 July 1961.

29. "Salazar Attacks U.S. on Angola. Likens Policy to Stand by Soviets," *New York Times,* 1 July 1961; DEPTEL 17, 6 July 1961, in JFKL.

30. Lisbon 51, 11 July 1961, and Lisbon 73, 15 July 1961, both in JFKL.

The Angola/Azores dilemma stirred up problems in the Kennedy administration between the Africanists and Europeanists and caused "continuous wrangling." Underlying the heated discussions in Washington was the possibility of Portugal's unilateral rupturing of the Azores agreement, which would expire on 31 December 1962. Dean Acheson, who constantly intervened in favor of Salazar, irritated the liberals. From New Delhi, Ambassador Galbraith wrote to Kennedy on 1 July: "I have difficulty in appreciating your use of Dean Acheson. . . . He will be a source of trouble for he wants the policy that serves his ego, not your needs." Galbraith, for his part, irritated the Europeanists by accusing them of trading basic political principles for "a few acres of asphalt in the Atlantic."[31] Kennedy considered Angola a priority of foreign policy and put Mennen Williams in charge of a presidential task force on Portuguese Africa.

The task force debates became very complex. The Pentagon was not ready to sacrifice access to the Azores base. The Joint Chiefs of Staff, presided over by General Maxwell Taylor, declared that "we have no fully satisfactory alternative to the Azores for tactical and troop movements in limited or general war in Europe, the Middle East or Africa; and for certain significant communications or intelligence requirements." Mennen Williams argued that Salazar would not take so radical a decision against the United States as to eliminate the American base on the Azores because "the self-interest of the other NATO partners will restrain Portugal from making so rash a move." The CIA, however, concluded that the possibility of the United States renewing the Azores agreement for more than five years, under Salazar's regime, would be "scarce." Two basic possibilities emerged from the debates, reflecting the opposing views of the African Bureau and the Pentagon. Kennedy's position was both pragmatic and ambivalent. He remained unmoved by Acheson's warning that continued U.S. pressure on the Angola issue would jeopardize the Lajes base. On 14 July he wrote to Acheson: "It would be easy to serve one of these interests by neglecting the other. Our purpose must be to serve them both."[32]

Kennedy's decisions, contained in a National Security Action Memorandum (NSAM), the highest form of presidential authorization for foreign policy, were the following: send a special envoy to Lisbon to tell Salazar that, in the United States' opinion, Portugal should immediately enact "basic and far-reaching reforms in her African territories" and inform France and Great Britain of this ahead of time, and, when action was taken, Spain; consult with France and Brit-

31. Schlesinger, *A Thousand Days,* 562; Galbraith to Kennedy, 11 July 1961, quoted in Mahoney, *JFK,* 211.
32. Department of State (George Ball) memorandum for the President, "U.S. Strategy in the UN Security Council to Portuguese Territories," 13 July 1963, in JFKL; Report of Chairman of the Task Force on the Portuguese Territories in Africa, 4 July 1961; National Security Council memorandum from Samuel Belk to McGeorge Bundy and Walt Rostow, 21 June 1961, in JFKL; Draft letter from John F. Kennedy to Dean Acheson, 14 July 1961, in JFKL.

ain to coordinate "pressure on Salazar"; explore with the Vatican, Spain, and Brazil the possibility of "interceding with the Portuguese"; formulate an agenda of American activities in the UN; should the previous initiatives fail, raise the problem in NATO with the purpose of "impressing upon Portugal" the U.S position; make every effort to assure that Military Aid to Portugal (MAP) military equipment would not be "diverted to Africa"; deny authorization of licenses for exporting arms to both sides in the conflict in Angola; increase aid to war refugees; increase educational assistance to Africans of Portuguese Africa; offer economic aid, especially in the training of the work force, to the Africans; if Salazar liberalized his policies for Africa, allow him "reasonable request for economic assistance"; and act discreetly in all matters to bring about reforms in Portuguese colonial policy and "minimize the possibility of losing the Azores."[33] The diplomatic offensive and the practical initiatives outlined in this memorandum were systematically carried out in the following months by the Kennedy administration.

The secret codicil of the Azores agreement of 1951, stipulating U.S. military aid to Portugal in case of an emergency in the overseas possessions, introduced a legal dilemma for the Kennedy administration. As McNamara reminded Kennedy on 25 August, the use of MAP equipment by the Portuguese in Angola was illegitimate without prior U.S. consent; he continued, however, that "by a secret exchange of notes in 1951 the US stated there is 'no doubt' that such consent would be forthcoming in an emergency." From Lisbon, Elbrick reminded Rusk that Salazar could publicly mention the secret clause of 1951—and make the United States out to be a hypocritical arms dealer.[34] Kennedy was not impressed by this suggestion.

In the second week of August, under the president's orders, Rusk told Elbrick to inform Salazar that, without exception, U.S. "actions amount to a complete arms embargo against arms and munitions control items intended for use in Portugal's overseas territories." The secretary of state outlined the method for implementing the embargo: the United States considered the diversion of equipment supplied under MAP to be in contradiction to the bilateral agreement on assistance; equipment already diverted to Africa should be returned; and the United States would continue to supply Portugal with whatever military equipment it could demonstrate was necessary for its European NATO troops. Franco Nogueira had a "bitter reaction" and answered peremptorily that regarding the

---

33. National Security Action Memorandum 60, from McGeorge Bundy (Special Assistant to the President for National Security Affairs) to Secretary of State, Secretary of Defense, Secretary of the Treasury, Director of Central Intelligence, Director of the Bureau of the Budget, Director of the United States Information Agency, Director of International Cooperation Administration, "U.S. Actions in Relation to Portuguese Territories in Africa," 17 July 1961 (revised 18 July 1961), in JFKL.

34. Memorandum for the President from Secretary of Defense (Robert McNamara), "Portuguese Use of Military Equipment in Angola," 25 August 1961, and Lisbon 184, 3 August 1961, "Re DEPTEL 125," SECRET, 16 August 1961, all in JFKL.

second point of Elbrick's memorandum, concerning the return of equipment already in use, "this would not be done while Portugal was fighting in Angola." After consulting with Rusk and McNamara, Kennedy decided that the United States would not make public the arms embargo.[35] Many licenses for the selling of arms to Portugal that had been authorized to private firms by the Department of Defense were revoked under NSAM 60.

~

Meanwhile, military pacification made its way through the vast regions of Angola. The 10 August recapture of Nambuangongo, seat of the UPA's provisional government, was a turning point in the war. On 28 August, Salazar's government made public a series of reforms whose main objective was to abolish the existence of the native, established in 1954 in the Statute of the Native. The Portuguese people, according to the government, would now be endowed with a law that was equal for all, with no distinction of race, religion, or culture. Elbrick stressed from Lisbon that though the Portuguese claimed that the reforms had long been planned, "their adoption at this time is doubtlessly a result of pressures in the UN and the events in Angola." Kennedy and others in Washington reacted to the announcement with a famous joke: "The Portuguese, having given three Angolans a University education were now about to embark on their second five-hundred-year plan."[36] Through timid reforms of the political administration, however, the Portuguese government sought to decrease the nationalists' base of social support.

Anti-Americanism had become a virtual psychosis in Portugal. Elbrick commented that "the US has been identified as public enemy no. 1." Anti-Americanism was manifested through selective attacks on members of the Kennedy administration—Mennen Williams and Adlai Stevenson were the favorite targets—and political maneuvers that primarily affected the missionaries working for the Angolan nationalist cause. Of the 300 American missionaries who were in Angola on 15 March, only a few dozen remained by the fall. In the meantime, Kennedy approved a plan for emergency food and medical aid for the Angolan refugees, 125,000 of whom were in the Congo by midsummer 1961. The United States started another humanitarian initiative with regard to Angola: to give university education to Angolan students.[37] Salazar did not react favorably to this help, and his foreign minister cited the "bad example" of Kwame Nkrumah, who had studied in the United States.

35. National Security Action memorandum 77, from the President to Secretary of State and Secretary of Defense, 20 August 1961; memorandum for the President from Robert McNamara, 25 August 1961; memorandum for the President from Dean Rusk, 29 August 1961, all in JFKL.

36. Lisbon, 56, and Lisbon 85, JFKL; both in Roger Hilsman, *To Move a Nation: The Politics of Foreign Policy in the Administration of John F. Kennedy* (New York, 1967), 249.

37. Lisbon 38, and Department of State Operations Center, "Report of Actions Taken Portuguese Territories in Africa," 5 September 1961, both in JFKL.

The CIA kept up-to-date on the situation in Portugal and planned scenarios for Salazar's downfall while trying to make connections and promote signs of internal dissatisfaction. Although activities for CIA officers in Portugal had become much more difficult since Botelho Moniz's coup attempt, hopes remained high in June 1961: "Although the Salazar regime appears in no serious danger at the moment and the dictator to be in good health, it is possible that he will be replaced in office before negotiation of the Azores agreement."[38] In Washington, Europeanists and Africanists continued to bicker about the Angola/Azores dilemma.

Would it be possible to support self-determination for Angola, which ran contrary to Salazar's policies, and maintain use of the Lajes base? Would it be politically legitimate to abandon the position on Angola just to maintain the use of the base? Could the Pentagon find an effective alternative to the Lajes base? Would Salazar's overthrow be the only solution to the problem? How could diplomatic pressure from the State Department be efficiently articulated with the CIA's covert actions in Portugal? These were the pressing questions carried over into 1962.

Kennedy found himself arbitrating between the Africanists and the Europeanists in his administration and tried to preserve a balance that would serve the policy regarding Angola while allowing for the maintenance of the Azores base. From New Delhi, Ambassador Galbraith tried to convince Kennedy that Portugal, "as the last colonial power," was for the United States "an increasingly prickly companion." Acheson, in McNamara's presence, told Kennedy that a strong position on Angola would prevent the United States from getting the Azores agreement extended.[39] The result of Kennedy's dual policy was that the liberals became impatient with the moderation that sometimes caused them to remain silent, while the conservatives became angry with the radical possibility that they might alienate their NATO ally.

By the end of 1961, after the invasion of Goa by the Indian army, Salazar was balancing between his combative desire to defend overseas Portugal and the tragic feeling that the empire was in inevitable collapse. He did not easily recover from the blows he had been dealt: "They want to set me on fire. That's OK. But let me first explain things as they really happened. Then they can destroy me." Salazar saw hypocrisy of Machiavellian dimensions in Kennedy's attitude toward the fall of Goa, and he was preparing to use his trump card, the Lajes base. On 28 December, the CIA's Lisbon station reported that "the office of the Prime Minister gave instructions to the International Police (PIDE) to obtain the names and addresses and control the movements of all American nationals living off the limits of the Lajes Base in the Azores." The CIA obtained the information through a high-level Portuguese informer and interpreted this gesture of Sala-

38. CIA Special National Intelligence Estimate 27.2-61, "The Outlook for Retention of U.S. Azores Base Rights in the Event of Certain Courses of U.S. Action," 27 June 1961, in JFKL.
39. New Delhi 1611 (Section 2 of 2), 6 December 1961; Acheson interview, 27 April 1964.

zar's as "a possible initial step in revoking the Azores Base agreement."[40] The conflict between the two related but differing national policies increased, leaving no middle ground for compromise.

~

This extraordinary year, 1961, was the most difficult in contemporary Portuguese-American relations. Kennedy's election was an important catalyst for the Angolan nationalists and circles of the Portuguese opposition. The worldwide scandal over the hijacking of the *Santa Maria* and the internationalization of the war in Angola brought a sense of urgency to the Portuguese question and to the need for a clear American stand.

The intensely mutable world of Kennedy and the perennially static world of Salazar shared nothing in common. Salazar rejected democracy and did not believe that black populations had the capacity for self-rule. He saw Angolan nationalism as a mere disguise for communism and thought that the end of Portuguese rule in Africa also signified the end of Portuguese influence in the Continent. Kennedy believed that Angola and the other Portuguese colonies would not ultimately be condemned simply to choose between colonialism and communism and that, with time, Africans would also uphold the superiority of democratic values.

Salazar's regime had begun in a centuries-old imperial structure and the tradition of indisputable Portuguese presence in Africa. Therefore, he used all his resources to preserve that overseas patriarchy. For him, self-determination and independence were synonymous, and any flexibility on the regime's part would open the way for the loss of the territories as well as the automatic communization of Portugal. Moreover, Salazar saw no difference between Moscow's anticolonialism and Washington's anticolonialism in the Kennedy version: "If things continue in this direction, within 20 or 30 years the whole world will be communist."[41] His prophesy was not fulfilled.

Kennedy had chosen open political confrontation and pressure, combined with covert interventions. He voted in the UN against a NATO ally, he supported reformers in Lisbon and a military coup attempt, he financed nationalists in Angola, and he imposed on Portugal an arms embargo that would last until 1974. His policy also expressed a conflict between security needs and basic political principles, between continued American influence in Africa and continued access to the vital Azores air base. But Kennedy was not counting on Salazar's capacity for standing alone against the world and surviving both domestic challenges and diplomatic isolation.

Yet Angola's self-determination was not the easy affair that in 1961 some

40. "Diários pessoais de Franco Nogueira," 18–20 December 1961; CIA TDCS OB-3/648 988, "Portuguese Intentions Regarding U.S. Base in Azores," 28 December 1961, in JFKL.
41. "Diários pessoais de Franco Nogueira," September 1961.

American policymakers had thought it would be. The pro-Western UPA did not have a national strategy for the Angolan rebellion and had little support outside the Bakongo area. The communist MPLA was restricted to some urban areas. Thus the Portuguese government was able to bring about military pacification with the support of the white community. Of course, the guerrilla war did not end in 1961, as Salazar had expected. But the pattern set in the Congo did not apply to Angola. The Portuguese colonial presence in Africa was not to be compared to the Belgian or the British. Salazar had been sure of this and had warned Kennedy.

Reforms in Portuguese Africa in 1961 were partially a result of American political pressure. They were one of the consequences of the unfinished struggle between Kennedy's commitment to self-determination and Salazar's political fundamentalism.

# Part Three
*Trade and Finance*

# 10

## Plugging the Dike:
## The Kennedy Administration Confronts the
## Balance-of-Payments Crisis with Europe

### *Thomas Zoumaras*

The six-year interval between January 1958 and the end of 1963, in the words of a Treasury Department history commissioned in 1968 by President Lyndon B. Johnson, "brought to a close a long postwar period in which the underlying strength of the U.S. balance of payments position had been taken for granted." American foreign policy had resulted in building up foreign exchange reserves in the rest of the world from almost zero in 1945 to $17 billion in 1958.[1] At the end of World War II the United States held $22.9 billion of the $38.8 billion in gold supplies. But for six years beginning in 1958 liquidity deficits averaged $3.1 billion per year for a total of $18.4 billion, as compared to an average of $1.1 billion per year between 1952 and 1958. The deficits caused the drawing down of U.S. gold reserves to $15.6 billion by the end of 1963. The "rather striking change . . . taking place in the international position of the United States and of the dollar" precipitated grave concern among U.S. policymakers.[2]

When President John F. Kennedy took office in January 1961, he and his chief economic advisers, Treasury Secretary C. Douglas Dillon and Walter W. Heller, chairman of the Council of Economic Advisors (CEA), were aware of the dangers inherent in the balance-of-payments deficit—the likelihood, if the dollar weakened, that foreign holders of dollars might turn nearly all of the assets in for gold held by the United States. Such action would send shock waves

---

1. Main abbreviations used in the notes:
   DDEL    Dwight D. Eisenhower Library, Abilene, Kansas
   HHFP    Henry H. Fowler Papers, Roanoke College Library, Roanoke, Virginia
   JFKL    John F. Kennedy Library, Boston
   NSF    National Security Files, JFKL
   TCSP    Theodore C. Sorensen Papers
   WWHP    Walter W. Heller Papers, JFKL
   2. See page 1 of chapter 12 of the "Administrative History of the Department of the Treasury," Box 1, Vol. I, Part II, in Lyndon B. Johnson Papers, Lyndon B. Johnson Library, Austin, Texas (hereinafter cited as "Treasury History").

through the U.S. and international economies as well as make it difficult, maybe impossible, to continue collective security programs in conjunction with diplomatic initiatives to end the imbalance of payments. Kennedy's efforts succeeded in "shoring up the system" without fundamentally addressing the structural causes of the crisis, that is, the growing costs of fighting the Cold War and the declining competitive position of the United States relative to its key trading partners in Europe and Japan. As an official report admitted, "It was only in the fall of 1963 that it seemed safe to undertake a longer-range study of international liquidity without disturbing confidence in the dollar." Thus the Kennedy administration did not correct the problem it inherited, but its efforts created sufficient confidence in the dollar to avoid a collapse of the Bretton Woods system. This bought the United States time to develop cooperative mechanisms that would lead to the development of the exchange system established in 1973.[3]

The resumption of currency convertibility in 1958 by ten European countries testified to the success of U.S. foreign policy after 1945. The administrations of Harry S. Truman and Dwight D. Eisenhower had employed their nation's strong currency and gold position as well as its industrial might to help Japan and the noncommunist European nations to emerge from the devastation caused by six years of war. U.S. currency filled the dollar gap for the cash-starved world while manufacturing products and military equipment helped rebuild and defend free world countries. As the European and Japanese economies revived, the United States purchased durable goods and military equipment from them to stimulate further their economies. In effect, the Bretton Woods Agreement, the Marshall Plan, other economic and military programs, U.S. investment overseas, and pursuit of liberal trade brought an end to the dollar gap in 1958 that as recently as 1953 some economists considered a permanent fixture.[4]

The resumption of convertible currencies also highlighted the growing vulnerability of the U.S. economic position. As the economic and military pillar of the Western nations, the United States had been depleting and neglecting its resources and productive base and seemed unable to afford to underwrite the bulk of the costs associated with the Cold War and stimulate vigorous economic growth at home at the same time. The balance-of-payments problem began to unfold in 1955 as a result of three recessions during Eisenhower's presidency, mounting national security costs, and the growth of U.S. investments in reconstructed countries rather than at home. At first, only a few officials, such as Treasury Secretary George M. Humphrey, expressed concern when gold reserves

3. Quoted *ibid.* For background on the Bretton Woods system, see Alfred E. Eckes, Jr., *A Search for Solvency: Bretton Woods and the International Money System, 1941–1971* (Austin, 1975). For information on the payments crisis, see Robert V. Roosa, *The Dollar and World Liquidity* (New York, 1967); Seymour E. Harris, *Economics of the Kennedy Years* (New York, 1964); David Calleo, *The Imperious Economy* (Cambridge, Mass., 1982); David Calleo and Benjamin Rowland, *America and the World Political Economy: Atlantic Dreams and National Realities* (Bloomington, Ind., 1973); Fred Block, *The Origins of International Economic Disorder* (Berkeley, 1977); and Robert Triffin, *The World Money Maze* (New Haven, 1966).

4. Charles P. Kindleberger, *Europe's Postwar Growth* (Cambridge, Mass., 1967).

dropped from $24.77 billion in 1949 to $21.79 billion in 1954 with $13 billion in potential claims held by other countries. Most officials, including Eisenhower, saw little danger. They did not notice a negative trend. "A lot of bad things," Eisenhower lectured Humphrey, "would have to happen in a hurry to get in real trouble."[5]

The attitude of members of the Eisenhower administration changed when the trade surplus plunged from $6.1 billion in 1957 to only $1 billion in 1959. European competitiveness had begun to threaten the U.S. ability to fund the export of dollars relied on by its allies and trading partners. Eisenhower and Under Secretary of State C. Douglas Dillon, the president's chief foreign economic policy adviser, unsuccessfully tried to reduce the costs of the Cold War and prodded members of the Organization of European Economic Cooperation (OEEC) to boost aid to developing countries during meetings in Paris in December 1959. Led by Germany, France, and Britain, the Europeans agreed in principle but refused to commit funds because they doubted that the boom enjoyed by the European economies would last. More perturbing to Eisenhower and Dillon, each country's representatives felt that its neighbors should take the lead and bear a greater portion of the costs associated with any multilateral European foreign aid program.[6]

A frustrated but undaunted Dillon believed OEEC members could and should do more to ease the pressure on the U.S. economy. To this end, in January 1960 the United States offered to join the eighteen OEEC members in a new body, the Organization for Economic Cooperation and Development (OECD). Dillon wanted the OECD to promote international economic cooperation, but domestic and overseas complications limited it to exchanging information and engaging in discussions on matters of mutual concern.[7]

More drastic action became necessary in October 1960. The balance-of-payments situation embarrassed Vice-President Richard Nixon during his campaign for the presidency. Kennedy had already chastised the Republican administra-

5. Letter from Eisenhower to Humphrey, 26 April 1955, in Box 22, Administration Series, Ann Whitman File, Presidential Papers of Dwight D. Eisenhower, 1953–1961, DDEL; hereinafter cited as AWF. This essay benefited from three fine overviews. For the period between 1958 and January 1961, see Burton Kaufman, *Trade and Aid: Eisenhower's Foreign Economic Policy, 1953–61* (Baltimore, 1982), particularly 176–96. For the Kennedy years, see the essays by Frank Costigliola, "The Pursuit of Atlantic Community: Nuclear Arms, Dollars, and Berlin," and William S. Borden, "Defending Hegemony: American Foreign Economic Policy," both in *Kennedy's Quest for Victory: American Foreign Policy, 1961–1963*, ed. Thomas G. Paterson (New York, 1989).

6. Telegram, Douglas Dillon for the President, 16 December 1959, Box 12, Administrative Series; and A. J. Goodpaster, memorandum of Conference with the President on 19 December 1959, Paris, France, 1615 Hours, Box 46, DDE Diary Series (hereinafter cited as DDED), both in AWF, DDEL.

7. Kaufman, *Trade and Aid*, 186–88. The OEEC had been established to coordinate economic recovery activities under the Marshall Plan. The OECD established operational policies that required unanimous consent of all but the abstaining voting members. Dillon's role in forming the OECD is discussed in an unedited transcript of an interview of Douglas Dillon by the author, 26 October 1988.

tion for foreign policy setbacks in Cuba, Berlin, and Asia, as well as for allowing a supposed missile gap. In December 1959 Kennedy gave an address in which he called for the transformation of NATO into "an alliance among equals" that would "lead the way in a new program of common action on the major issues which confront the Alliance." Kennedy's call for sharing the burden implied that the Eisenhower administration had missed the opportunity to consider "in common a method for economizing international reserves which would exploit the new strength of the pound and the Continental currencies."[8]

Gold reserves stood at $18 billion when the election took place, but statutes obligated sterilizing $12 billion to cover domestic reserves. Europeans held sufficient dollars, meanwhile, to lay claim to $9.5 billion of the gold stocks. Gold prices reached $40 an ounce in London, $5 above the Bretton Woods rate. Nixon tried to blame Kennedy during the campaign for the declining confidence in the dollar, which had caused the surge in gold prices. He alleged that the Democrat would pursue fiscal irresponsibility at home to assuage labor and other interest groups. Kennedy responded in a widely publicized address he and his staff worked on at great length. On October 31 in Philadelphia he promised, if elected, to maintain the collective security system without devaluing the dollar or restricting liquidity needed to assure growing international trade.[9]

Political necessity put a premium on dealing with the payments crisis. Eisenhower, like his youthful Democratic critic, insisted on maintaining the political and economic credibility of the United States at home and abroad; therefore, he too pledged not to rectify the imbalance either with trade restrictions or by devaluing the dollar to raise the value of U.S. gold holdings. Having limited his options, Eisenhower reluctantly accepted the entreaties of Treasury Secretary Robert B. Anderson to cut security expenditures overseas. Anderson envisaged a two-pronged attack. First, he wanted to bring home 15,000 military dependents each month until 284,000 of the 484,000 had returned. Second, Anderson insisted that Germany in particular had a strong enough economy to pay for NATO-related U.S. expenses there. Dillon disagreed. He argued that the real problem was not security expenditures but high short-term interest rates in Europe which attracted U.S. investors. He added that anything intimating a reduction of U.S. commitments to NATO might drive U.S. allies toward neutrality or unilateral agreements with the Soviet Union.[10]

Eisenhower acknowledged the dangers inherent in Anderson's plan, but he

8. Arthur M. Schlesinger, Jr., *A Thousand Days: John F. Kennedy in the White House* (Boston, 1965), 65–72; W. W. Rostow, *The Diffusion of Power: An Essay in Recent History* (New York, 1972), 118–25; John F. Kennedy, *The Strategy of Peace,* ed. Allan Nevins (New York, 1960), 99–101.

9. Theodore C. Sorensen, *Kennedy* (New York, 1965), 406; Roosa, *The Dollar,* 265–70.

10. Dwight D. Eisenhower, *The White House Years: Waging Peace, 1956–1961* (Garden City, N.Y., 1965), 604–606; Wilton B. Persons, memorandum for the Record, 4 October 1960 in Christian A. Herter Papers, 1953–1961, Box 6, DDEL; and John S. D. Eisenhower, memorandum of conference with the President, 15 November 1960, in Box 35, DDED, AWF, DDEL. Dillon's opposition to Anderson's offset plan is covered in an interview of Douglas Dillon by the author, 19 June 1991.

decided to remove the dependents and to ask Chancellor Konrad Adenauer to cover the $600 million it cost the United States yearly to maintain troops in Germany. He told his advisers that the time had come to end the "too easy" treatment of Europe in carrying the burden created by the Soviet threat. Eisenhower insisted that he had compelling reasons to take a tougher line with the European governments. The balance-of-payments deficit had risen from $3.5 billion in 1958 to $3.7 billion in 1959 and was projected to hit $4 billion in 1960. The deficits facing Washington did not cause the German head of state to see matters from Eisenhower's point of view. The meeting between Adenauer, Anderson, and a loyal but disagreeing Dillon largely proved disappointing to all concerned. Adenauer, as Dillon had warned, feared the United States would remove some of its forces. He agreed to begin a $1 billion aid program in the coming year but refused to cover troop costs on the grounds that his electorate would not stand for it and that the American forces served U.S. as well as German interests. Anderson returned in a fury. He wanted drastic cuts to U.S. force levels overseas.[11] Eisenhower and Dillon, both dedicated internationalists with a resolute commitment to contain communism, endured the setback rather than jeopardize the collective security system.[12]

Kennedy, then, entered office in the midst of an international economic crisis. The Europeans' ire over Anderson's threats had not abated. They wanted explicit indications that such heavy-handed tactics would not have a place in the new administration. Adenauer and Charles de Gaulle, the French president, sought reassurance that Kennedy's address of 31 October was more than campaign bombast. European central bankers wanted action, not oratory, from the U.S. government. They demanded that Kennedy balance the fiscal budget and tighten credit. Walter H. Heller and John Kenneth Galbraith, meanwhile, stressed the need for growth-oriented Keynesian policies, such as job programs, that would pull the economy out of recession. Dillon, the new treasury secretary, agreed that the 5 percent unemployment rate was unacceptably high, but he wanted a 7 percent investment credit, which he asserted would lead to more jobs as well as improve the productivity of manufacturing in the United States. He informed Kennedy that this would improve the faltering balance of trade by making U.S. goods more competitive with those produced overseas. The result, he believed, would be the collection of more foreign exchange, which would offset the balance-of-payments deficit and reduce the pressure from abroad to cut overall expenditures.[13]

11. Martin Mayer, *The Fate of the Dollar* (New York, 1980); and Eisenhower, *White House Years,* 604, 607.

12. For a discussion of the national security system created by Harry S. Truman and adopted by Dwight Eisenhower, see Melvyn P. Leffler, *A Preponderance of Power: National Security, the Truman Administration, and the Cold War* (Stanford, 1992); and Michael J. Hogan, *The Marshall Plan: America, Britain, and the Reconstruction of Postwar Europe, 1947–1952* (New York, 1987).

13. Drawn from unedited transcripts of four interviews with Douglas Dillon conducted by the author, in the author's possession. Also see James N. Giglio, *The Presidency and John F. Kennedy* (Lawrence, Kans., 1991), 126–27.

Few topics concerned Kennedy during his presidency more than the balance-of-payments crisis. He equated its solution with his ability to confront communist challenges wherever they arose, which he knew required a healthy domestic economy. The president understood that annual economic growth of 5 percent required confidence in his administration's policies among business and finance sectors, both at home and abroad. To that end, he appointed Douglas Dillon to serve as treasury secretary. Dillon had credibility on Wall Street and in the capitals of Washington's important allies. His father, Clarence, had turned Dillon, Read and Company into an important investment banking house in the 1920s. The younger Dillon's tenure in the Eisenhower administration as ambassador to France followed by his role as deputy under secretary and then under secretary of state for economic affairs gave him knowledge about international relations and earned him the respect of foreign leaders. Equally important, Dillon and Kennedy agreed that the government could stimulate economic growth and reduce the fiscal budget deficit at the same time.[14]

Kennedy frequently articulated his concern about the payments crisis both for the public and in private meetings with his senior advisers. He highlighted the issue in his second speech before Congress on 2 February 1961. Privately he lamented how the payments deficit undercut relations with NATO allies and held the United States up to ridicule. Kennedy told the National Security Council on 22 January 1961 that the time had come to do less for Europe and more for the United States. He wanted to make sure that the nation's trading position returned the surplus necessary to maintain national security commitments. It especially irritated him that the recipients of U.S. military protection would use the payments deficit, incurred largely through defense obligations in Europe, as a "stick with which to beat" his administration.[15]

His advisers reinforced his predisposition to link the effectiveness of Cold War policies with an end to the imbalance of payments. Walt Rostow apocalyptically told Kennedy before the inauguration: "We will not be able to sustain in the 1960's a world position without solving the balance of payments problem." Rostow, Dillon, Heller, and others found that Kennedy quickly and eagerly grasped the complexities and the importance of international economics.[16] The dilemma for Kennedy and his team was to find a way to maintain economic growth at home while regenerating confidence in the dollar abroad. They

14. Dillon interview by the author, 3 March 1990. Also see Carl Bauer, *Presidential Transitions: Eisenhower Through Reagan* (New York, 1986), 73; Giglio, *Kennedy,* 20; and Schlesinger, *A Thousand Days,* 133–36.

15. For an example of Kennedy's interest in this issue and his eagerness to undertake corrective action, see Kennedy to Secretary of the Treasury, National Security Action memorandum 81, "U.S. Gold Position," in Meetings and Memoranda Series, NSF, Box 31, JFKL. For his address, see "Special Message to Congress: Program for Economic Recovery and Growth," 2 February 1961, in *Public Papers of the Presidents of the United States: John F. Kennedy, 1961* (Washington, D.C., 1962), 41–53. Quoted in Costiglia, "Atlantic Community," 30, from Sorensen Oral History, JFKL.

16. Interview of Walt W. Rostow, 2 June 1992, JFKL Oral History Program. Also see Rostow, *Diffusion of Power,* 123, 136–37.

patched together a combination of tax cuts, innovative monetary controls, and pathbreaking formal and informal international agreements on currency and gold transactions in a desperate effort to maintain the stability and viability of the dollar while transferring some of the burden for the Bretton Woods system to Japan and the stronger European countries. In this endeavor the Kennedy administration stabilized and then reduced the deficit, but it never could eliminate the outflow of dollars and gold. The efforts produced friction within the administration, ridicule among U.S. businessmen and bankers, and a mixture of grudging admiration and contempt from foreign bankers and political leaders.

Every one of Kennedy's important advisers placed a high premium on solving the balance-of-payments problem. Nevertheless, building a consensus behind a program or a series of initiatives did not come easily. Heller and his Council of Economic Advisors initially emphasized promotion of economic growth at home over balancing payments overseas. He tended to believe that a stronger, more productive economy would automatically solve the existing imbalances. The State and Treasury Departments agreed that domestic economic and political considerations mandated an expanding GNP; however, Dillon and Under Secretary of the Treasury for International Monetary Affairs Robert V. Roosa countered arguments made by the CEA staff with the warning that the international monetary system could collapse if the government did not act promptly and vigorously to rebuild confidence in the dollar.[17]

While, in Heller's words, a "tug-of-war" continued over whether to emphasize noninflationary growth over international economic stability, it quickly became apparent that addressing either problem depended on addressing both. Heller made this clear before the Société d'Economie Politique in Paris on 7 November 1963: "Existence, side-by-side, of a stubborn balance of payments deficit abroad, and stubborn unemployment, excess capacity, and price stability at home has confronted policy-makers with a set of conditions hitherto unknown. . . . We have moved from a situation in which we could act as if we were in a closed economy to one in which we must act . . . in an open one." Heller added that the "search for economic policies that could serve both masters simultaneously" resulted in "a little-realized but significant shift in economic philosophy, policy, and practice."[18]

The somewhat awkward cooperative spirit took root because Treasury and CEA officials agreed that "the dollar is not just another currency, but that it is a key reserve currency." Only the United States maintained complete convertibil-

17. Roosa, *The Dollar,* 7–18; Memorandum from Heller to Kennedy, 15 September 1961, in Walter W. Heller Papers, Box 16, JFKL; Seymour E. Harris to Henry H. Fowler, letter and attachment, "Comments on the Council's Economic Report—First Three Chapters," 29 December 1961, in Box 3, HHFP. Harris served as an adviser to the Treasury Department.

18. See Harold B. Dorsey, "Investment View," *Washington Post,* 9 December 1963. Dillon and Roosa agreed that the Treasury and CEA learned to work well together on behalf of both goals; Douglas Dillon, interview by the author, 2 March 1990, and Robert V. Roosa, interview by the author, 28 June 1990.

ity between gold and its currency at a fixed price, something American officials thought the Europeans did not appreciate. The president felt obligated to reiterate repeatedly the immutability of this policy in order to bolster confidence in the dollar among holders of large surpluses. He also faced calls from legislators to change the price of gold, which one adviser likened not only to "burning down the house to roast the pig but also one of using a sledge hammer to force through a thumb tack." The administration accepted the primary responsibility for devising internal solutions to the payments crisis, but Dillon and others impressed on the leaders of European countries holding surpluses that they had a stake in helping the United States. Before 1963 Roosa and Dillon believed that the problem required fine-tuning of monetary and fiscal policies rather than structural changes. Kennedy, who was not interested in running the risks that could develop from "radical new departures in policy," eagerly implemented a variety of devices to staunch the outflow of dollars while he expanded military expenditures.[19]

The Berlin Crisis of 1961 disposed Kennedy, Dillon, and Roosa to agree with Heller's stand for "steady and rapid economic growth with price stability and full employment," in part because they did not want a weak economy to impair their "capacity to cope effectively with other Berlins." Kennedy realized that each confrontation with the Soviets strained U.S. resources and that anything other than maximum productivity jeopardized the pledge in his inaugural address to "pay any price, bear any burden, meet any hardship, support any friend, oppose any foe to assure the survival and success of liberty." Fighting communism and advancing liberty required economic strength at home and the confidence this would create overseas.[20]

Kennedy was the first president to face the fact that the United States needed its allies to share the load because fifteen years of Cold War policies meant that the nation could no longer afford to "bear any burden." Europeans and Japanese did agree to carry more of the burden of foreign aid, international banking, and collective security expenditures, but each advance was limited and came only after tedious, sometimes acrimonious, negotiations. At the meeting of American Bankers Association in Rome in 1962, Dillon implored European bankers to improve their banking operations. Dillon revealed that poor capital market mechanisms in the European capitals drove European and U.S. investors on the

19. Memorandum from Seymour E. Harris to Robert Roosa, "Reduction in the Price of Gold," 12 March 1962, in Box 18, HHFP; Robert V. Roosa, Remarks at the Monetary Conference of the American Bankers Association, Rome, Italy, 17 May 1962, and Douglas Dillon, Remarks at the Ninth Annual Monetary Conference of the American Bankers Association, Rome, Italy, 18 May 1962, both *ibid.*

20. Quoted from Douglas Dillon, Address Before the Commonwealth Club of California, San Francisco, "Our Inseparable Domestic and Foreign Economic Policies," 8 September 1961, in Box 19, HHFP; *Public Papers of . . . Kennedy, 1961,* p. 1. For the president's concern about the economic costs associated with larger military commitments to Europe, see memorandum from Kennedy to Secretary of State and Secretary of Defense, 8 September 1961, in Meetings and Memoranda Series, NSF, Box 331, JFKL.

Continued to seek long-term capital in New York City. The annual transfer of up to $2.5 billion more than counteracted efforts to reduce the short-term flow and to reduce national security transfers. Within a year, Europe, particularly Italy, had complied willingly, largely because it cost nothing and promised mobilization of savings and higher profits on loans.[21]

Other programs under the category of burden sharing progressed less readily. The French, for example, regularly strained the dollar by converting their surplus holdings into gold. They accounted for 21.6 percent of all transfers with the Continent. French policy favored holding gold over dollars because they believed large dollar accounts would fuel inflation. Other reasons existed for the accretions. To Dillon's horror, while in Rome in 1962, American bankers chastised the president's Keynesian policies. The normally cordial treasury secretary struggled to maintain decorum as he lectured his fellow Americans on the damage they did to European confidence in the dollar at a time when the government had made considerable headway in the battle to end the outflow of gold for dollars.[22]

Internationalizing development banking proved no easier. In 1961, the United States provided 44 percent of the $6 billion in foreign aid to developing nations. Some progress had been made in reducing the U.S. burden, such as the formation in 1960 of the soft-loan International Development Association (IDA). The OECD countries provided $900 million worth of hard currency. Commitments required another $250 million per year by 1962. The United States put up $321 million, or carried 43 percent of the burden, but in 1962 the Kennedy administration asked Britain, France, and Germany each to share 15 percent of the burden so that the U.S. portion could be reduced to one-third. The European governments hesitated. Chancellor of the Exchequer Reginald Maudling informed Dillon that economic necessity mandated that Great Britain reduce its share of the burden too, but he agreed to support a new allocation if Germany and France matched Britain's. The French refused to increase their portion by more than $1 million, and the Germans balked at adding $10 million to their quota until the French agreed to equal the German share. It infuriated Kennedy that the British, French, and Germans rebutted his burden-sharing efforts over such small amounts. He worried that the American people and Congress might sour on aid and other security expenditures in the face of such parsimony. The seven major European countries, Canada, and Japan reminded Kennedy that their aid burden had risen from $1 billion in 1956 to $3.4 billion

21. Douglas Dillon, Remarks at the Tenth Annual Monetary Conference of the American Bankers Association, Princeton, N.J., "Our Unfinished Task of Improving the U.S. Balance of Payments," 7 March 1963, in Box 22, HHFP. For a report on the meeting in Rome see memorandum from George H. Willis to Dixon Donnelley, 24 May 1962, in Box 15, HHFP.

22. See memorandum from McGeorge Bundy to the President, "The U.S. and de Gaulle—The Past and the Future," 30 January 1963, in President's Office Files, Box 116A, JFKL.; "Treasury History," 2; and Dillon interviews, 20 January 1990, 1 March 1990 (on dollars and inflation in France), and 2 March 1990 (on meeting with bankers in Rome).

in 1961. The French added that they had special obligations to their former African colonies. Maudling pointed to Britain's heavy defense burden and the shakiness of the pound. Finally, a breakthrough occurred in 1963, when Dillon offered to increase the U.S. obligation to 38 percent.[23]

Policymakers in Washington chafed at their allies' reticence to take on more of the burden in international banking. Heller lamented having to "muddle through" internationalizing the banking system. Efforts to reduce other defense and aid outflows annually averaging $2.6 billion faced difficulties with analogous results. Herculean efforts saved $700 million in 1962, thanks largely to a cooperative logistics agreement with Germany wherein Bonn purchased U.S. military equipment and services roughly offsetting the $675 million it cost to maintain American forces in Germany. Italy signed a similar agreement. Dillon hailed the arrangements before the annual meeting of the International Monetary Fund (IMF) as proof "that a more equitable sharing of these defense burdens can and must be reached." He was too optimistic. Europeans feared Kennedy might reduce U.S. forces stationed in their countries. This concern was a legacy of Anderson's mission to Germany during the waning days of Eisenhower's presidency. Kennedy dispatched former secretary of state Dean Acheson to Paris to dispel this notion. He cleared the air enough to allow more relaxed negotiations for offsets to resume. Germany and Italy cooperated out of an interest in an integrated defense and because their central banks held more dollars than they could trade without jeopardizing the price ratio between the dollar and gold. Generally governments in Europe doubted that their recent prosperity would last. De Gaulle refused to sign a countervailing agreement for two reasons—he did not want an integrated multinational force, and he decided to punish Kennedy for not helping France to develop its own nuclear weapons system.[24]

Kennedy's advisers saw burden sharing as a necessary but insufficient treatment in the battle to cure the balance-of-payments hemorrhage. They concluded

---

23. See Philip Geyelin, "U.S. Ready to Funnel More Aid Funds into World Lending Unit," *Wall Street Journal,* 19 September 1962. For more on the controversy, see Dillon letters to Maudling, 1 November and 20 December 1962, 10 January and 9 April 1963, and Dillon letter to Ludwig Erhard (German minister of economics), 20 December 1962, all in Box 37, HHFP.

24. Heller is quoted in his memorandum for the president, "Gold and Domestic Policy," 5 May 1962, in TCSP, Subject Files 1961–1964, Box 29, JFKL. Dillon is quoted in Harold B. Dorsey, "Economic View," *Washington Post,* 24 September 1962. See memorandum from Acheson to the President and Secretary of State, March 1961, in NSF, Box 70, JFKL; and Paul Nitze, memorandum of Conversation with General Lavaund, in NSF, Box 71, JFKL; Costiglia, "Atlantic Community," 30–31; and Borden, "Defending Hegemony," 81–82. Mounting troop levels in Vietnam led the Defense Department to consider reducing the number of units in Germany. This led to an end of the German agreement in 1966. Dillon approved of the offsets negotiated by the Kennedy administration. In the period following the Anderson fiasco he had reached three conclusions: the balance-of-payments problem was larger than he had anticipated and more difficult to bring under control; the European economies had become even stronger; and Kennedy had increased force levels because of the Berlin Crisis. Thus offsets were necessary to reduce the deficit. See Dillon interview 1 March 1990.

that increasing the favorable trade balance by about $3 billion annually would end the strain on the Bretton Woods system. Kennedy actively tried to reduce trade barriers, but, in spite of effective lobbying in Congress for the Trade Expansion Act and accomplished negotiations for the Kennedy Round of the General Agreement for Trade and Tariffs, passage for the first did not occur until September 1963 and rancor prevented conclusion of talks for the latter before 1967.[25] Annual trade levels rose $3 billion during Kennedy's presidency, but dollar outflows negated the effect.

These delays elevated the importance of a concurrent tactic to promote economic growth at home and to erase the payments problem, that is, a combination of tax incentives and boosterism to encourage new investments and anti-inflation measures to solve what Roosa termed the "environmental" sources of the deficit. According to Under Secretary of the Treasury Henry H. Fowler, the Treasury, the Federal Reserve Bank, and the CEA agreed that new business investment would do more than anything to reduce unemployment and end the balance-of-payments problem. But he added, "Until we make investment in the United States more attractive for both foreign and domestic capital we cannot find a lasting solution to our balance of payments problem."[26]

The administration placed its hopes on a 7 percent investment tax credit, the heart of the Revenue Act of 1962. Monetary incentives had been rejected by late 1961. High short-term interest rates in Europe made it impossible to maintain lower rates in the United States—this would drive more dollars overseas. The credit reduced business taxes by $2 billion a year. It fueled economic growth and certainly made at least some businesses more competitive against foreign concerns, but it is impossible to quantify what impact the act had on the trade balance.[27]

In any case, Dillon, who guided the administration's campaign for the investment credit, faced an uphill battle on two fronts. Senator Albert Gore (D.-Ark.) led antibusiness populist legislators who believed Dillon, the Wall Street banker, had manipulated Kennedy into supporting a sweetheart deal for businessmen who refused to reinvest their profits at a rate commensurate with those of their counterparts abroad. Dillon publicly ignored references to his background. He acknowledged the veracity of Gore's assertions regarding reinvestment, but he and Heller countered that this was beside the point. It was important, they stated, to prod the business sector to invest more so that U.S. firms reattained

25. See Borden, "Defending Hegemony," 69–78; and John W. Evans, *The Kennedy Round in American Trade Policy: The Twilight of the GATT?* (Cambridge, Mass., 1971).

26. Robert Roosa, Remarks at the Joint Luncheon of the American Economic Association and the American Finance Association, "Reconciling Internal and External Financial Policies," New York City, 28 December 1961, in Box 23, HHFP; Fowler, Speech Before the National Industrial Conference Board, Atlanta, 21 November 1963, in Box 22, HHFP.

27. Douglas Dillon, Remarks Before the White House Labor-Management Conference on Fiscal and Monetary Policy, Washington, D.C., 15 November 1962, in TCSP, Subject Files, Box 40, JFKL.

their competitive position with the Japanese and European plants that had been constructed after World War II. They added that investment offered the quickest path toward lower unemployment levels, which, if left to hover around 5 percent, would weaken confidence in the dollar and assure the continued loss of gold reserves. On the second front, Treasury Department spokesmen had to counter the attitude among businessmen that, with about 15 percent of plant capacity lying idle, excess capacity devalued the worth of investment credits. Dillon and others countered by mobilizing the Treasury Department's advisorial Business Council and by arguing that excess capacity would disappear when plants became productive enough to compete overseas.[28]

The CEA and Treasury thought all their efforts to promote a larger trade surplus as well as full employment would be worthless unless they avoided a wage-price spiral and maintained low short-term interest rates. Kennedy thoroughly agreed. This helps to explain why he insisted that U.S. Steel roll back the $6 per ton price increase its president, Roger Blough, announced after Kennedy had written an open letter asking his corporation and the other eleven largest firms to help him with the balance-of-payments struggle by holding their prices at their current levels. Kennedy noted that labor rates per ton of steel were at 1958 levels and that the industry's profits were already strong. Blough's announcement particularly incensed President Kennedy because the administration had just prevailed upon the Steelworkers Union to accept a new contract that lacked a wage increase and included only fringe benefit increases of ten cents an hour.[29]

Kennedy faced a considerable challenge in rebuilding his already tattered bridges to the business community after the steel price dispute; however, his single-minded commitment to hold firm against inflationary wages and prices earned high praise in European capitals among bankers who worried about the value of the dollar. In the face of such pressures, Kennedy's cabinet officers admitted that there were "no easy solutions" to "the art of maintaining steady growth at full capacity." On the eve of Kennedy's assassination, they could take solace that wage costs had not risen since 1961 and that wholesale prices had not changed significantly in five years. Indeed, U.S. officials referred to this accomplishment when Europeans repeated their frequent refrain that the United States was primarily responsible for getting its house in order if it wanted to solve the

28. *Ibid.*; memorandum, Henry H. Fowler for the President, "Business Council Meeting," 15 May 1962, in Box 23, HHFP; and Douglas Dillon, interviews by the author, 19 and 20 January 1990. For background on Gore, see "Quiet Senate Firebrand: Albert Arnold Gore," *New York Times,* 12 November 1963; and author's notes of a conversation with Dillon, 19 January 1990.

29. For a discussion of the 1962 steel price dispute, see Sorensen, *Kennedy,* 443–59; Schlesinger, *A Thousand Days,* 634–40; Giglio, *Kennedy,* 129–33; Thomas C. Reeves, *A Question of Character: A Life of John F. Kennedy* (New York, 1991), 330–33; Wallace Carroll, "Steel: A 72-Hour Drama with an All-Star Cast," *New York Times,* 23 April 1962; and Douglas Dillon, interviews by the author, 1 March 1990 and 14 June 1990. For President Kennedy's comments on the issue, see telephone messages to Labor and Management leaders following the Steel Settlement, 31 March 1962, News Conferences of 11 and 18 April 1962, all in *Public Papers of the Presidents of the United States: John F. Kennedy, 1962* (Washington, D.C., 1963), 284, 315–22, 331–39.

balance-of-payments crisis. In this respect, the Kennedy administration did better than the European Economic Community. As the economist Paul A. Samuelson observed in 1963, devaluation was unlikely because "the wage inflation . . . in Europe is doing more to correct our international balance of payments than anything we have yet contrived."[30]

U.S. officials also pointed to their manipulation of the monetary system whenever Europeans claimed they need not do more to help ease the payments crisis until the administration undertook serious efforts to check the outflow of dollars. "Operation Twist," or "Operation Nudge," as it was known, was almost entirely the brainchild of the "brilliant" though "politically inexperienced" Roosa, who had been with the Federal Reserve Bank in New York before joining the Treasury. Roosa's advice represented the first overt use of monetary policy for international reasons since the Depression. Kennedy and Dillon deferred to his judgment on the innovative Operation Twist because they considered him one of the two or three most knowledgeable Americans in the abstruse field of international monetary affairs. After a series of meetings fully supported by Dillon, Roosa convinced the Fed chairman William McChesney Martin, Jr., in October 1961 to end the eight-year-old policy of stimulating economic growth through the lowest possible short-term interest rates.[31]

Fed policy had become a liability in mid-1960 when the recession in the United States drove investors to shift their dollars into higher-interest-bearing accounts overseas. Weekly meetings between Roosa, Dillon, and other Treasury officials maintained the Fed's independence but assured that short-term rates rose by half to three-quarters of a percent while long-term rates held steady or declined. The latter was essential to assure continued investment by the business sector and to keep mortgage rates within reach of potential home buyers. The Twist worked surprisingly well until mid-1963, when the balance-of-payments deficit jumped to a yearly rate of $3.3 billion, up from $2.5 billion in 1962. On 16 July, after Dillon called for higher short-term rates before the Joint Economic Committee of the Congress, the Fed launched "Super Twist"—it raised the discount rate half a point to 3.5 percent.[32]

Nothing caused more consternation among Heller and his associates on the CEA than the Twist. Heller initially feared Roosa's innovation would blow the

30. See Dillon's remarks before the National Press Club, 20 June 1961; Dillon's remarks at the Tenth Annual Monetary Conference of the American Bankers Association, 7 March 1963; and Dillon interview, 1 March 1990. Samuelson is quoted in "Tax Investment Plan Branded 'Giveaway' by M.I.T. Professor," *American Banker,* 26 February 1963. For efforts to improve relations with the business sector, see memorandum, Henry Fowler to the President, "Business Council Meeting," 15 May 1962.

31. Roosa interview, 28 June 28 1990; Dillon interviews by the author, 19 June 1991 (for the quote by Roosa) and 1 March 1990; and Roosa, *The Dollar,* 19–22, 54–55.

32. Joseph R. Slevin, "Treasury Trying Varied Tonics to Build Up Dollar," *New York Herald Tribune,* 6 November 1961; Slevin, "U.S. Action to Defend Dollar: Higher Discount Rate," *ibid.,* 17 July 1963; and Dillon's statements before the Joint Economic Committee, 7 March 1961, in Box 3, and 8 July 1963, in Box 15, both in HHFP.

top off long-term rates. He argued passionately in meetings with Kennedy, Dillon, Roosa, Martin, and Budget Director David Bell that combating the balance-of-payments crisis this way would trigger a recession. When Super Twist was under consideration, Heller wrote Kennedy a private cover note stating: "This memo spells out the basis for my queasiness about a rediscount boost. I am not sending a carbon to Doug Dillon!" Kennedy, as was his style, listened carefully to each of his advisers, but following agonizing consideration, he sided with Dillon, who counseled that inaction doomed any hope of saving the Bretton Woods system. Dillon added that close monitoring would give the president the opportunity to alter monetary policy. Heller ultimately recognized that monetary manipulations worked as advertised. He also accepted Operation Twist because he agreed with Dillon that fiscal stimulus could trigger growth if Congress enacted a series of tax cuts.[33]

The CEA chairman preferred an across-the-board tax cut, especially after the Twist raised the short-term interest rates that had been relied on to stimulate the economy.[34] Dillon and Stanley S. Surrey, his chief tax adviser, countered that they wanted time to construct a complex and politically risky package of cuts and reforms. In the interim they offered a series of alternative tax initiatives, including the investment credit, that they hoped would quickly stimulate the economy and reduce the payments deficit. Surrey, an ardent but politically impractical proponent of a more equitable tax system, proposed elimination of tax incentives for dividends earned by Americans who invested in developed countries as opposed to developing countries in Latin America, Africa, and Asia. The State Department and key legislators objected that this would harm U.S. businesses operating overseas and that it would undermine the trade surplus.[35]

Surrey rebutted that every dollar invested in Europe generated only eight cents in exports whereas every dollar invested in Latin America led to U.S. exports worth forty cents. He added that reinvested earnings would not face taxation; moreover, he argued, given the dollar's exposure, it was illogical to maintain tax havens for investors who chose to move their capital from the United

33. Quoted from cover letter accompanying memorandum, from Heller to the President, "Proposed Discount Rate Boost," both 7 July 1963, in Box 6, WWHP. Also see memorandum from Heller for the President, "Monetary Policy Today—The Uneasy Truce Between Domestic and Balance-of-Payments Consideration," 6 April 1963, *ibid.* On Heller's coming to terms with Operation Twist, see Heller, memorandum for the Files, "Notes on Quadriad Meeting with the President, September 12, 1963," 18 September 1963, in TCSP, Subject Files, Box 51, JFKL.

34. For examples of the Heller-CEA position, see memorandum, Heller to Whom It May Concern [CEA Members], "Activities from March 17 through March 24, 1961," 27 March 1961, in Box 6, WWHP; memorandum, Council of Economic Advisors for the President, "The Strategy of Tax Reduction and Tax Reform," 16 June 1962, and memorandum from Heller for the President, "The Range of Tax-Cut Choices Before Us," 8 August 1962, both in TCSP, Subject Files, Box 40, JFKL.

35. Dillon interview, 2 March 1990. For Under Secretary of State for Economic Affairs George W. Ball's general dissatisfaction with the Treasury's balance-of-payments program, see his *The Past Has Another Pattern: Memoirs* (New York, 1982), 203–207.

States to Switzerland, Germany, Britain, and France, countries that transferred dollars for U.S. gold rather than hold onto the currency. Kennedy and Dillon supported Surrey's position for they saw ending tax havens in developed countries as a way to transfer some of the burden to nations with stronger economies while continuing Cold War programs designed to strengthen weaker economies.[36]

Many European economic specialists such as the Gaullist economic adviser Jacques Rueff took issue with this brand of American self-help. He lectured U.S. officials that they should raise taxes to balance the budget and tighten credit as the IMF required of all other countries with deficit fiscal policies.[37] OECD delegates, Dillon called them representatives of "responsible financial opinion abroad," endorsed tax cuts, and opposed contraction in the United States once it became clear that the Twist reduced the outflow of dollars by at least $300 million. Early in 1963 the IMF's managing director, Per Jacobsson, forecast a payments surplus if the U.S. Congress reduced taxes across the board and closed tax loopholes as Kennedy had requested in January.[38]

Although the CEA disagreed with Surrey's insistence that reform provisions accompany the president's tax proposal, the CEA and Treasury agreed that the tax cut would, as Dillon declared, "do more for our economy and more for curing the balance of payments than any step." In private, Kennedy too was effusive about what he called "the most important action" Congress could take. He chose, however, not to emphasize the tax bill's importance to solving the balance-of-payments problem in his address at the meeting of the IMF less than two months before his murder. Kennedy knew he faced a long legislative battle.

36. See Stanley S. Surrey to Carl Kaysen (deputy special assistant for national security affairs), Letter and Attachment, "Report: The Revenue Act of 1962 and the Alliance for Progress," 4 April 1962, in NSF, Box 290, JFKL; memorandum from Teodoro Moscoso for Kaysen, "Comment on the Report of the Department of the Treasury Entitled 'The Revenue Act of 1962 and the Alliance for Progress,'" 9 April 1962, Surrey for Kaysen, Letter and Attachment, "Re Memorandum of Mr. Teodoro Moscoso, dated April 9, 1962, Relating to the Revenue Act of 1962," 16 April 1962, and Surrey to Theodore C. Sorensen, Letter and Attachment, "Balance of Payments and Taxation of Foreign Income," 14 May 1962, all in TCSP, Subject Files, Box 29, JFKL.

37. Jacques Rueff, "The Gold Standard" in American Foreign Economic Policy, ed. Benjamin Cohen (New York, 1968), 155–59; Jacques Rueff, The Balance of Payments: Proposals for Resolving the Critical World Economic Problem of Our Time (New York, 1968). For an example of a country-by-country discussion, see memorandum, Nathan N. Gordon for Secretary Dillon, "Report on Tax Discussion in Paris and Zurich," 17 October 1961, in Box 37, HHFP.

38. See Dillon, Remarks Before the White House Labor-Management Conference, 15 November 1962; Raoul D. Edwards, "Dillon Calls Tax Plan Major Aid to Payments Deficit," American Banker, 1 February 1963; Henry C. Wallich, "Budget, Payment Balance Deficit Problems Linked," Journal of Commerce, 27 February 1963; and Special Message to the Congress on Tax Reduction and Reform, 24 January 1963, Public Papers of the Presidents of the United States: John F. Kennedy, 1963 (Washington, D.C., 1964), 73–92. Otmar Emminger, a member of the Board of Directors of the Deutsche Bundesbank, provides an example of so-called responsible financial opinion in "The Dollar: Speculation and Reality," n.d. [but transmitted to Fowler on 16 August 1962], in Box 18, HHFP.

Apparently he did not want to heighten anxiety that might weaken the position of the dollar if the legislation seemed to stall.[39]

Reducing apprehension by improving lines of communication preoccupied officials from the Treasury and State Departments. They relied on the OECD, Dillon's creation near the end of the Eisenhower administration, in this quest. In the estimation of John Leddy, the U.S. ambassador to the OECD, it lacked the mechanisms to develop a real consensus and enforce the will of the majority. He applauded it and its subcommittees, however, for holding meetings with a manageable number of attendees. This resulted in discussions that corrected misperceptions by offering a quiet setting in which Leddy could explain the nuances of a given program undertaken or planned to reduce the balance-of-payments deficit. Leddy credited the OECD meetings for the coordination of short-term interest rates once the Twist had begun. Explaining how the Twist would work resulted in European banks stabilizing their rates, which reduced the flow of dollars from the United States.[40] The Germans and the French acted vigorously and publicly to hold their rates steady. Dillon saw this as a significant breakthrough for both countries had a history of maintaining high interest rates and trading dollars for gold. The German and French finance ministers, Ludwig Erhard and Valery Giscard d'Estaing, led European central bankers to do the same during their regular meetings in Basel, Switzerland. Giscard d'Estaing took this position after his country purchased $112.5 million in gold from the United States early in July 1963. The French expressed surprise when the transactions caused alarm about the dollar's stability. He announced that France would follow Germany's path and use dollar surpluses to fund early debt repayments to the United States worth $970 million after making the first installment of $293.4 million in July.[41]

Frequent conversations with representatives to the OECD led to the estab-

39. Dillon is quoted from "Slower Spending Rate Claimed for Kennedy: Dillon Explains," *Evening Star* (Washington, D.C.), 9 September 1963. For Kennedy's speech and an analysis, see Address at the Meeting of the International Monetary Fund, 30 September 1963, *Public Papers of . . . Kennedy, 1963,* pp. 749–52; and "Kennedy Plugs Anew for Tax Cut; Says It Is Not Main Way to Combat Payments Gap," *Wall Street Journal,* 1 October 1963. For agreement on tax reduction by Heller and Dillon after Kennedy's death, see memorandums, Heller for the President, 29 December 1963, and Dillon for the President, "The Tax Bill," 25 November 1963, in TCSP, Subject Files, Box 28, JFKL.

40. Memorandum, John C. Bullitt to Secretary Dillon, "OECD Review," 3 July 1963, and the attached memorandum from John Leddy, "Appraisal of OECD and Suggestions for Further Action," 18 June 1963, both in Box 37, HHFP; John Leddy, interview by the author, 4 August 1990; Douglas Dillon, interview by the author, 26 October 1988. Leddy and Henry Fowler, Dillon's under secretary of the treasury and his successor at Treasury, believe that a permanent full-time secretariat at the OECD would have improved communication and cooperation; author's notes from a three-hour meeting with Henry H. Fowler, 21 March 1992.

41. Letter from Dillon to William Proxmire, 23 July 1963, in Box 36, HHFP; memorandum, Roosa to Dillon, "French Discount Rate Increase and Related Matters," 14 November 1963, *ibid.*; and "France to Curtail Buying U.S. Gold; Will Repay Debts," *Wall Street Journal,* 23 July 1962. In addition to Germany, Sweden and Italy had already begun debt repayment as an alternative to gold transactions.

lishment of "swap" agreements devised by Roosa. First the Fed and then the Treasury borrowed exchange currency from countries holding surplus dollars. The United States sold the "Roosa bonds" in an effort to avoid exchanging dollars for gold. Swaps worth over $2 billion had been negotiated by the close of 1963. Prior consultation made it possible for this to occur without central bankers jumping to the conclusion that the United States would destabilize their respective countries' currency. This simple innovation resulted in central bankers and finance ministers telling each other exactly what they were doing and why. Not only did misunderstanding diminish, but their efforts cut down on policies that unwittingly undermined each other's actions.[42]

Robert Roosa deserves most of the credit for seeing the potential in cooperative consultation, but this did not eliminate apprehension. The prospect that the United States would succeed in its crusade to eliminate its balance-of-payments deficit prompted calls for a new international reserve medium to finance ever-growing trade. Rueff raised the issue in October 1961. He wanted an end to the rigid connection between the dollar and gold because he contended that the United States used the exchange standard to control the European economies. U.S. economist Robert Triffin had already advocated the establishment of an international central bank with a new reserve currency. And at the November 1962 meeting of the IMF, the British advanced the "Maudling Plan," which called for reserve holdings of surplus sterling and dollars to be deposited in a special IMF account for use by Britain and the United States whenever their currencies faced heavy demand.[43] Dillon, Roosa, Per Jacobsson, and Max W. Holtrop, head of the Netherlands Central Bank, led the opposition to this chorus. They argued that no rigid correlation existed between the ratio of reserve currency and the volume or value of trade. Dillon wanted to strengthen the dollar before entering into international monetary negotiations. Roosa added that consultation with the OECD could identify potential shortages and arrange corrective swaps. Holtrop pointedly objected to any institution and new currency that reduced his country's sovereignty.[44]

In essence, Roosa and his allies believed that the balance-of-payments crisis was not structural and that adjustments would enable continuation of the Bretton Woods system. Roosa considered a super bank unworkable, moreover, he wrote, "Our financial institutions and our markets were well equipped to service the payments requirements of the world." He added, "It is a role which naturally accompanies our leading economic and political position."[45]

42. "France to Curtail Buying U.S. Gold"; Roosa, *The Dollar,* 3 33; and Christina Kirk, "More Trade, Sound Dollar," *New York Herald Tribune,* 23 September 1962.

43. "Treasury History." Also see Jacques Rueff, Address before the International Monetary Fund, "The Money Problem of the West," 16 October 1961, in the author's possession.

44. A good discussion is found in "Does the IMF Have the Muscles?" *Business Week,* 10 November 1962. Also see Schlesinger, *A Thousand Days,* 645–55; and Roosa, "Comments on: 'Proposal for the Solution of the Gold Problem,' " 2 July 1962, in TCSP, Subject Files, Box 29, JFKL.

45. Roosa, "International Liquidity," Draft no. 2, 19 July 1962, in TCSP, Subject Files, Box 29, JFKL.

Dillon and Roosa nevertheless recognized the need for medium-term international credit arrangements to "forestall or cope with an impairment of the international monetary system." They negotiated the General Arrangement to Borrow with nine nations in 1961 and 1962, which established standby credit facilities of up to $6 billion in the IMF as an alternative to a new reserve currency. The participants soon were known as the Group of Ten.[46] The Ten met on a regular basis to discuss the monetary system. The standby agreement retarded but did not halt the British, French, German, and Japanese representatives' calls for a study to explore liquidity needs and the adequacy of the dollar if the payments crisis continued or if a solution to the crisis attenuated its reserve function to other countries. With this as the backdrop, on 27 February 1963 President Kennedy instructed the secretary of state to undertake negotiations that would "make sure that financial elements in our relations with other countries are given proper weight." He added that any agreements "with other countries [should] tie in with our broader foreign policy needs."[47]

Dillon had begun to reconsider his conviction that the balance-of-payments dilemma reflected the need for modifications to the Bretton Woods system rather than its radical revamping, admitting as much before the Joint Economic Committee early in 1963, when he stated that two years of fine-tuning had stopped the dollar's hemorrhaging. It had built a foundation for open and frank exchanges between finance ministers. But he surprised his audience when he commented that "the improvement in our balance of payments thus far is simply not good enough if we are to maintain a strong dollar and fulfill our basic commitments for aid and defense."[48] Thus Dillon and the president had concluded that they might have to risk sharing control of the international monetary system with other industrial nations in the free world if they were to continue to contain communism.

The administration signaled its new approach at the IMF meeting in early October. Dillon opened the conference with the announcement that, in light of the conceivable end of the U.S. payments deficit, which might reduce liquidity, the Group of Ten would study future changes in the global monetary system. He promised that the Ten would not change the price of gold. Group of Ten members had made it clear that they would demand a study at the IMF meeting. They publicly called for explorations to see if improvements were possible, while taking care to express their confidence in existing arrangements. In private, the British, French, German, and Japanese representatives indicated that they wanted to free themselves from the inflexible dollar system. They had a new ally, who probably made delay impossible even if that had been the route preferred by the Ken-

46. "Treasury History." The members were Belgium, Canada, France, Germany, Great Britain, Italy, Japan, the Netherlands, Sweden, and the United States.

47. Kennedy, National Security Memorandum 225, 27 February 1963, in NSF, Meetings and Memoranda, Box 340, JFKL.

48. See Dillon's statement on 31 January 1963, in Box 22, HHFP.

nedy administration. M. Pierre-Paul Schweitzer, the new managing director of the IMF, favored constant review of monetary reserve problems, unlike Jacobsson, his predecessor, who had always expressed confidence in the dollar and rejected the likelihood of a liquidity crisis.[49]

Kennedy delayed U.S. involvement in any review and tried to set the parameters for the Group of Ten's study by announcing on 2 October 1963 that he had appointed a thirteen-man task force to look into ways to promote increased foreign investment in the securities of U.S. private companies overseas and in America. Headed by former treasury under secretary Fowler, the task force actually would end up exploring all facets of the payments issue.[50]

Kennedy did not live to see results from the Group of Ten. It took two years to produce two progress reports, which laid the foundation for the 1965–68 negotiations that resulted in the IMF establishing Special Drawing Rights to supplement international reserves.[51]

The Kennedy administration had temporarily plugged the dike that held the Bretton Woods system in place. It had established an international network for consultation and cooperation. It obtained tax legislation and set the stage for President Lyndon B. Johnson to sign the broadest and largest tax cut to that point in the nation's history. It improved the current account thanks to an annual trade increase worth $3 billion. Currency swaps and higher short-term interest rates reduced short-term transfers from $2.4 billion in 1960 to less than $1.5 billion in 1963. Most impressive of all, Kennedy's policies accounted in part for an average annual real rise in economic activity of 5.7 percent for the period 1961–63. This set the stage for comparable economic growth through 1968.[52]

These successes, significant as they were, disappointed Dillon, Roosa, Heller, and the president. They had been overly optimistic about the nation's ability to fight the Cold War, deal with the payments deficit, and promote economic growth at the same time. This can-do mind-set pervaded the Kennedy team from the outset. John Kenneth Galbraith recognized this trend by late 1961. He took Dillon, Heller, and the president to task for their overconfidence, saying that they "insisted in a kind of masochistic fashion in setting standards which

49. Dillon, Remarks Before the Annual Meeting of the International Monetary Fund, 1 October 1963, in Box 38, HHFP. On the IMF meeting, see "Study of World Monetary System to Mull Possible Changes Is Planned by 10 Nations," *Wall Street Journal*, 3 October 1963; and letter from Edward M. Bernstein to Henry H. Fowler, 11 October 1963, in Box 38, HHFP. For an excellent overview of the problems confronting the dollar, see Bernstein's "Understanding the U.S. Payments Problem," paper presented at a meeting of the U.S. Council of the International Chamber of Commerce in New York, 9 December 1963, in Box 38, HHFP.

50. Memorandum, Dillon for the President, "Continuation of Task Force Appointed by President Kennedy to Study Ways of Promoting Increased Foreign Investment in the Securities of U.S. Private Companies, etc.," 9 December 1963; and notes of meeting with Fowler, 21 March 1992.

51. "Treasury History"; and notes of meeting with Fowler, 21 March 1992.

52. Memorandum, Seymour E. Harris to Secretary Dillon, "Monetary Policy," 20 February 1964; Bernstein, "Understanding the U.S. Payments Problem."

you could not possibly meet." CEA member Richard Cooper tried to exonerate Heller and Kennedy. On two occasions he accused Dillon of presenting the president with overly optimistic appraisals of the balance-of-payments position and of preventing debate of his analysis.[53]

In spite of the Kennedy team's frenetic efforts, large balance-of-payments deficits persisted. Overseas military costs had risen from $5.5 billion in 1955 to a conservative $7.2 billion in 1962. Investment flow to developed countries continued at an annual rate of $1.5 billion. Short-term transfers remained troubling and required constant attention. Private capital transfers seemed immune to all treatments—they were still at $4.5 billion in 1963, down only $500 million from their high in 1961.[54] Ironically, in his less than satisfactory effort to end the payments deficit, Kennedy found that he had to violate IMF rules for deficit countries; he restricted the free flow of capital, a linchpin of U.S. economic policy after World War II. In short, because the Kennedy administration refused to come to terms with the limits of the nation's power, it planted the seeds for the demise of the Bretton Woods system in 1973 and for overwhelming the economic resources of the United States in order to maintain its security commitments overseas. In fairness to the hardworking and innovative men who made up Kennedy's team, few in the early 1960s foresaw the quagmire Vietnam would become for the United States, or the phenomenal rise in defense costs when the Soviets spared no expense to reach military parity, or that the manufacturing sector would fall so far behind its competitors in Asia and Europe. The "best and brightest" in the administration were too much the products of the postwar world—they had been intoxicated by the heady wine of hegemony. Criticism of their myopia is reasonable, but it is not equitable unless later generations remember both the milieu from whence Kennedy and his advisers came and that they operated in a new and largely unanticipated international economic environment.

53. Memorandum, Galbraith to Dillon and Heller, "Reflections on Economic Policy, Public Posture and the Will to Put the Worst Foot Forward," 5 November 1961, Box 19, HHFP. Galbraith wrote in a cover note that he had sent the original to the president, "whom I deem to have a collateral responsibility." Cooper's allegations are from an interview of Dillon by the author, 2 March 1990. The classic treatment of the Kennedy team's can-do attitude is David Halberstam's *The Best and the Brightest* (New York, 1972).
54. Bernstein, "Understanding the U.S. Payments Problem."

# 11

## "Two Souls, One Thought"? The EEC, the United States, and the Management of the International Monetary System

### Richard T. Griffiths

In February 1961, Kennedy's new treasury secretary, Douglas Dillon, tried to calm the fears of the European Economic Community over the American balance of payments.[1] His memorable suggestion was that Europe and the United States represented "two souls, one thought."[2] The significance of this encounter lies less in the nature of the reassurance than in the fact that the exchange took place at all. Three or four years previously, it would have been unthinkable that the fledgling Community, so carefully nurtured by U.S. policy, would have lectured its patron in this way. The facade of American preeminence in trade, payments, and military security would have precluded such presumption. Even though, with hindsight, the weakness in the dollar's position should have been apparent, its slide took most observers by surprise. Having labored for a decade and a half under the cloud of a "dollar shortage," the European economies were

1. On the European side this essay is based on the official reports of the EC finance ministers meetings, the discussion papers, and the somewhat less full Dutch delegation reports; the Dutch delegation reports of the EC monetary committee, the discussion papers, and the (more often than not useless) official reports; the Dutch delegation reports of meetings of the Group of Ten deputies and the less informative official reports; and the Dutch delegation reports of OECD Working Paper 3. American material was obtained from the John F. Kennedy Library. Unfortunately, the Dillon and Roosa papers were inaccessible because they are still awaiting classification. The following abbreviations are used in the notes:

CEE     Communauté Economique Européene
DGES    Directoraat-generaal voor Economische Samenwerking (MBZ)
GT BBV  Generale Thesaurie, Buitenlandse Betalingsverkeer (MF)
JFKL    John F. Kennedy Library, Boston
POF/DA  President's Office Files, Departments and Agencies (JFKL)
MBZ     Ministerie van Buitenlandse Zaken, The Hague
MF      Ministerie van Financieen, The Hague
NSF     National Security Files (JFKL)

2. Code telegram from van Roijen to MBZ, 10 March 1961, GT BBV 215, MF.

confronted, in a surprisingly short period after the restoration of convertibility in December 1958, with the phenomenon of a "dollar glut."

The hemorrhaging of dollars from the United States had started in 1958 with a sharp deterioration in the current account surplus, which had worsened the following year and had not been offset by any corresponding contraction on the capital account. In the last year of the Eisenhower administration, however, a considerable improvement had occurred, and the Kennedy administration inherited a current account balance as healthy as that in any of the post–Korean War years (with the exception of the peak of 1957). The problem now was a renewed surge in capital outlays. Although government expenditures had continued to expand (a reduction in net military expenditures being more than offset by increased outlays in civilian programs), the cause of the problem became private capital expenditures, both short and long term. This expenditure had already reached $3.5 billion in 1960. It rose further to $3.8 billion in 1961 and fell back to $3.2 billion the following year before surging to $4.2 billion in 1963. The deficits on regular transactions, the key variable in all subsequent discussions in the three years of the Kennedy administration, were $3.4 billion, $3.6 billion, and $3.4 billion respectively.[3] This fact alone, however, cannot explain the intense cooperation with continental Europe in these years.

Continental Europe was seen as an increasingly important component in the deficit. Again the problem lay not in the current account balance, which actually improved modestly over these years, but in the growth of private capital movements. These movements increased annually from $305 million in 1960 to $748 million, $906 million, and $2 billion in the years 1961 to 1963. As a result, whereas in 1960, Europe had contributed 29 percent to the overall deficit on regular transactions, by 1963 the figure had grown to 86 percent. Europe, however, was more than part of the problem. The last three years of the Eisenhower administration had seen U.S. gold reserves fall by slightly over $5 billion. The Kennedy administration was determined not to tolerate gold outflows on such a scale, but, unless it succeeded in cutting the deficit, it had to persuade its commercial partners to accept some other means of payment. Europe, therefore, was also an increasingly important part of the solution.

The EEC coordinated its policy in a Monetary Committee (EC-MC) of high officials that met on almost a monthly basis. At a higher level, every three months, the finance ministers of the EEC and the central bank presidents met to coordinate their responses to international developments. In March 1961 the Organization for Economic Cooperation and Development decided to constitute Working Party 3 (WP3) to examine monetary policy. Its membership included representatives of the EEC as well as Canada, Sweden, Switzerland, the United Kingdom, and the United States. Its chairman, Emile van Lennep, also

---

3. Figures taken from *Survey of Current Business, 1968* (Washington, D.C., 1969) and converted into the earlier system of categorization used until 1965. The American practice of including short-term capital is not common in Europe.

chaired the EC-MC, and many of the EEC delegates to WP3 sat on the EC-MC. A final forum within which EEC views could be represented was the Group of Ten (G10) countries that in December 1961 signed the General Agreement to Borrow. They included the EEC countries (minus Luxembourg), Canada, Japan, Sweden, the United Kingdom, and the United States. Once again, the EEC delegation was drawn from the same tight circle of high officials from finance ministries and central banks.

~

The presidential election and the early months of the Kennedy administration were a time of extremely unsettled international money markets. This situation prompted the EC-MC to discuss the dollar's problems and to come up with three immediate options for restoring confidence: the United States could draw on its IMF holdings to the full 75 percent permitted, implying a loan of $600 million; it could raise U.S. interest rates or, in coordination, reduce those in Europe; or it could give a gold guarantee on European central banks' holdings of dollars (an option favored by the French).

In the longer term, none of the Europeans expected the United States to eliminate the current account deficit fully because the political fabric could not withstand the ferocious deflationary policy such action implied. So attention turned to curbing the outflow of U.S. private foreign investment (for example, by phasing out the fiscal incentives dating from the Marshall Plan) and by restricting foreign access to the New York money markets. Europe could also help, although the EC-MC ruled out any inflationary impulse to demand, and thus also to U.S. imports, for the reverse of the reasons that it had rejected U.S. deflation. Instead, European states could recycle some of the dollars gained from American capital export for early debt repayment rather than converting them into gold. Another variant lay in increased development aid, although the Dutch objected to using aid to compensate incidental changes in the balance of payments. Finally, the EEC could help reduce the outflow of foreign investment by lowering the common external tariff, since the prospect of the Common Market had been a factor in accelerating the flow in the first place.[4]

The administration had its first chance to explain its policy to the Europeans at a meeting of the Bank of International Settlements in January 1961. It expected to inherit a deficit substantially less than that of 1959. The balance of payments in 1960 (excluding military expenditure) would show a turnaround of $3.5 billion, and the Federal Reserve wanted a further improvement of $2 billion in 1961. Partly because of this change, its analysis differed from that of the EEC: it foresaw considerable problems in drawing on the IMF; it considered

4. "Verslag van de vierentwintigste zitting van het Monetair Comite van de EEG te Brussel op 13 en 14 november 1960," DGES 996.27, MBZ; "Verslag van de vijfentwintigste zitting van het Monetair Comite van de EEG te Brussel op 13 en 14 december 1960," *ibid.*

that the anticipated improvements in the balance of payments rendered any change in domestic monetary policy unnecessary; and it made clear that any European request for gold guarantees would be refused. Moreover, the administration was wary of restrictions on capital movements because, in contrast to European opinion, it feared that this would further undermine confidence in the currency. Still, any early repayment of debts would be welcome.[5]

This news was not well received by the EEC finance ministers and bank presidents. The French Central Bank president, Wilfrid Baumgartner, saw little evidence that the administration was prepared to enact the change of course necessary to correct matters. Nonetheless, it was in nobody's interest to alter the price of gold. Although Baumgartner considered it the debtor's task to solve its problems, the United States was entitled to a degree of international solidarity. France had done its bit by early debt repayment, estimated at $1.6 billion, by an accelerated removal of quota discrimination, and by its support for an early unilateral tariff reduction. Similar measures were announced by the other ministers present, but none thought them sufficient to resolve the problem.[6] Thus, although few were as strident as the French, all agreed that, in the absence of appropriate policies in the United States itself, further European credits (in the IMF or elsewhere) should be under revised terms and conditions. Despite the informal, nonbinding character of the meeting, the representatives decided to inform the new administration of the consensus achieved, underlining the necessity for a rise in U.S. interest rates, the need to restrict capital exports, and the EEC countries' support for a U.S. drawing on the IMF. The task of drafting the letter was left to the Dutch finance minister and host of the meeting, Jelle Zijlstra.[7]

The turmoil of foreign exchange markets, with flows of currency out of both the dollar and sterling and into the stronger continental European currencies, continued through the early months of 1961. The year also witnessed a spate of confidence-building measures, including the adoption of Article VIII of the IMF (February 1961); the revaluation of the Deutschmark (DM) and Dutch guilder and the conclusion of the swap agreements (March 1961); and the conclusion of the General Agreement to Borrow (December 1961).

In February 1961 the EEC countries accepted their full obligations in the IMF. Although a degree of convertibility had been restored in December 1958,

---

5. Germany was contemplating an early repayment of $500 million, possibly in return for deblocking $200 million of "enemy assets." The EC-MC deplored the idea that such conditions might become general. See "Verslag van de zesentwintigste zitting van het Monetair Comite van de EEG te Brussel op 10 januari 1961," *ibid.*

6. Germany announced that it was removing some quota restrictions and making a $600–700 million early repayment of U.S. debt. Negotiations were also in progress on sharing local defense costs, but these were not expected to yield much of a dollar saving. Guido Carli, the Italian Central Bank president, observed that although conditions in Italy led many to consider capital exports "comme une crime," these had nonetheless increased so that in 1960 they had totaled $492 million.

7. "Projet de proces-verbal de la sixième reunion des ministres des finances de la C.E.E. tenue à la Haye les 13 et 14 janvier 1961," II/507/61-F, GT BBV 215, MF.

the Europeans still were sheltered under the transitional regime of Article XIV of the IMF charter. This had permitted earlier discrimination and would allow the reimposition of similar measures in the future. By moving to Article VIII, they would accept more restrictions on interference with trade and payments. Moreover, the step was irreversible: the only remaining recourse to discrimination lay in Article VII (the Scarce Currency clause) that has still to be invoked. The implications of the switch for confidence in the system, and therefore in the dollar, were unmistakable. Ironically, the move could have been made much earlier, but it was delayed by an EEC decision to take action jointly, a decision that tied progress to that of the slowest member. First, it was delayed by the French, who required extra time to prepare their overseas territories for the move. Then, when the French wanted to accelerate, more cautious ministers preferred to defer any decision until the outcome of the elections was known. Only a German threat to make a unilateral announcement propelled the ministers toward a decision and an offer to the British to make the announcement jointly.[8] In February 1961, almost a year after the IMF had first suggested the step to the German government, the move to Article VIII was made. In one step, the Kennedy administration received a guarantee that no new lopsided currency discrimination would be aimed against the United States. The adoption of Article VIII also served as notification that, in the eyes of the IMF, they were now all equals.

A mirror of the flight from the dollar was the accumulation of short-term funds in the Deutschmark. Since the end of 1959, the German authorities had been trying to quash domestic inflationary pressures by a tight monetary policy but had seen this effort undermined by the expansion of the monetary base caused by the inflow of foreign credit. A currency realignment had been a topic of debate for several months, and the announcement on 5 March of a 5 percent revaluation of the DM (and the guilder) was not unexpected. The surprise lay in the timidity of the move. The EC MC had few illusions that the modest revaluation would eliminate the structural imbalance between Germany and the rest of the world. At the most, the payments surplus might fall from 5 billion DM in 1960 to 3.5 billion DM in 1961. By revaluing, however, the Germans appeared to believe that they had done their bit—it was up to the deficit countries to do the rest.[9] The modesty of the revaluation, and the expectation that the further

8. "Verslag van de twintigste zitting van het Monetair Comite van de E.E.G. te Brussel op 21 juni 1960. Projet de Compte Rendu de la Vingtième session du Comité Monetaire (tenue le 21 juin 1960)," 4 July 1960, II/3817/60-F, GT BBV 147, MF; CEE, "Projet de proces-verbal de la cinquième reunion des ministres des finances de la C.E.E. tenue à Luxembourg les 24 et 25 octobre 1960," II/6297/60-F, GT BBV 215, MF; "Verslag van de vijfentwintigste zitting van het Monetair Comite van de EEG te Brussel op 13 en 14 december 1960," DGES 996.27, MBZ; CEE, "Projet de proces-verbal de la sixième reunion des ministres des finances de la C.E.E. tenue à la Haye les 13 et 14 janvier 1961," II/507/61-F. The United Kingdom replied affirmatively three days after receiving the letter. See Zijlstra to Selwyn Lloyd, 17 January 1961, and Selwyn Lloyd to Zijlstra, 21 January 1961, GT BBV 215, MF.
9. "Verslag van de negenentwintigste zitting van het Monetair Comite van de EEG te Brussel op 14 en 15 april 1961," DGES 996.27, MBZ. Emminger explained that a 7 percent revaluation

adjustment might follow, led to the most chaotic week in the currency market since convertibility as foreign funds poured into Germany and Switzerland. Since the revaluation, 700–800 million DM had been added to German reserves. The German finance minister laid part of the blame on the U.S. authorities who had welcomed the revaluation as a "first step" toward redressing international imbalances. Both the Dutch and the Germans were insistent that no more realignment was to follow. The EEC finance ministers agreed on a joint statement reaffirming their commitment to fixed exchange rates.[10]

The Council of Economic Advisors suggested to Kennedy that there was now general agreement that the currency speculation was less a reflection on the American economy than an inherent weakness in the international system. It wanted a mechanism that, "in a regular and predictable way," compensated for outflows of short-term private capital by reverse flows of official capital: "There is no reason to permit every whim of private speculators to move gold from country to country."[11] This is exactly what Europe's central bankers accomplished, in Basel in mid-March, when they negotiated the first swap agreement whereby they would hold each others' currencies (in this case, mainly sterling) for three months (renewable) on condition that it then be replaced "at the same exchange rate as the original transfer." They also agreed to "recycle" inflows of "hot money" by depositing a corresponding sum in the account of the central bank from which it had fled.[12]

The increasing movement of hot money which had characterized the early 1960s and the fact that it could be directed against "key currencies" in the international monetary system had raised two related points—whether the Fund's resources *in total* were sufficient to allow it to help countries in balance-of-payments problems as a result of such currency shifts and whether it was not in need specifically of currencies *other than* dollars and sterling. The IMF's solution, first raised in February 1961, was the possibility of itself issuing medium-term, interest-bearing debentures. The initial European reaction to this idea was frosty. The EC-MC thought that if the IMF needed scarce currency, it would do better to sell some of its gold rather than to resort to the expensive and cumbersome recourse of borrowing. But if it had to borrow, the loans would obviously need to

---

had been considered; but the acceleration in wages, which at 9.5 percent in 1960 had outstripped productivity, had made that impossible.

10. CEE, "Document de travail établi en vue de la session de Mars de la Conference des Ministers des Finances," 10 March 1961, II-6/FBGms/10.III, BBV GT 215, MF.

11. Memorandum for the President, "International Monetary Reform and Related Problems" (Heller) 18 March 1961, in White House Central Subject File, 242/FO4, also POF/DA, 73 (CEA), JFKL.

12. Susan Strange, *International Monetary Relations* (London, 1976), 84–85. The operation to prop up sterling continued to the end of the year. The most outstanding had been £325 million, but during the crisis the United Kingdom had also borrowed £536 million from the IMF and arranged a standby credit of £179 million. The swap arrangements were not used again until February and March 1963. Again the United Kingdom was the beneficiary. See Brian Tew, *The Evolution of the International Monetary System, 1945–1977* (London, 1977), 136.

come from the surplus countries, and, in that case, the EC-MC felt that the countries involved should at least be consulted. The French were particularly reluctant to lend directly to the IMF, while the Bundesbank, by contrast, considered such (guaranteed and interest-bearing) investment an attractive proposition. The Germans nevertheless supported the general position that any new borrowing facilities should be accompanied by a new mechanism for consulting the creditor countries in their use.[13]

Privately, the French foreign minister, Maurice Couve de Murville, told Walter Heller, the head of the CEA, that he could not see why he should bail out the United Kingdom, especially since it had not resolved the structural maladjustments of its economy. He also suggested that although de Gaulle was not much interested in economic problems, he considered the IMF "an alien and objectionable organization." Baumgartner later told Dillon that France feared that if the IMF received additional resources, it would lose its will or ability to impose restraints on the policy of debtor countries. Moreover, the disposition of additional resources would be decided by a weighted vote of the entire IMF membership, which was often compliant to U.S. influence.[14] Dillon disregarded these signals and instructed the U.S. director at the IMF to push "energetically" for $3 billion in convertible currencies other than the dollar and sterling. The United States would then put in $2 billion and the United Kingdom $1 billion. It was recognized that since there was no visible shortage of dollars or sterling, these last amounts would be "nominal," but they were seen as essential to maintain U.S. leadership in the IMF.[15]

By the time the EEC ministers next met in July 1961, the positions of the Benelux states and the French were extremely close. They questioned whether the IMF's reserves were indeed inadequate, given the relatively limited use made of them. If, however, resources were to be increased, they favored loans to an increase in quotas because a general quota increase would automatically increase the size of debtors' drawing rights. Therefore, they preferred arrangements whereby IMF resources were supplemented for specific ends and approval was specifically obtained from the lenders in each case. The Italian finance minister, Paolo Taviani, was slightly less dogmatic, but he did want the IMF's use of its new resources to be subject to review by the creditors. The German Central Bank president, Otmar Emminger, on the other hand, recognized a need to

---

13. Strange, *International Monetary Relations,* 107–109; "Verslag van de achtentwintigste zitting van het Monetair Comite van de EEG te Brussel op 1 maart 1961," DGES 996.27, MBZ; CEE, "Proces-verbal de la septième reunion des ministres des finances de la C.E.E. tenue à Dusseldorf les 20 et 21 mars 1961," II/2487/61-F, GT BBV 215, MF.

14. Memorandum for the President, "Paris Report No. 3: International Monetary Developments and French Recalcitrance (Heller), 16 May 1961, POF/DA 73 (CEA), JFKL; Strange, *International Monetary Relations,* 108–109.

15. Memorandum, Dillon for the President, 5 July 1916, in POF/DA 89 (Treasury), JFKL. The $2 billion was to be borrowed (on the basis of Article VII of its statutes) for three to five years and was to be denominated in creditor currency. It would be repaid either in gold or in the creditor's currency, thus guaranteeing the loans against the effects of any devaluation.

strengthen IMF reserves, and he questioned the structural uncertainty built into the French and Benelux arrangements. He was anxious that when a crisis arose, the IMF would be in a position to react quickly. Although he shared the idea that creditors had rights to be consulted, he suggested that this need could be satisfied by giving the Europeans a majority voice in advising on the use of the credits without right of veto. Baumgartner, however, wanted to know who would judge whether conditions justified the use of the credits. As Max Holtrop, the Dutch Central Bank president, pointed out, it was impossible to cover all future eventualities in a satisfactory formula. The question was referred back to the EC-MC for further discussion.[16]

After being informed of these discussions, Dillon, in a note to individual ministers, applauded the fact that "agreement" had been reached to increase the IMF's resources, thereby ignoring the evident reluctance and mistrust inherent in the discussion over how to achieve this goal. He suggested that matters be concluded by further negotiations in the IMF Executive Board. He did, however, express doubts whether a borrowing agreement that left the decision to lend in the hands of the creditors would do much to increase confidence in the Fund. Instead, he offered an arrangement whereby there were "firm commitments by each participating country to lend to the Fund up to a stated amount of its own currency" on the basis of "operating safeguards" on their use.[17]

Despite its other disagreements, the EC-MC united in opposition to certain positions adopted by Dillon. It rejected the notion that there was any general shortage of IMF resources. At the most, it recognized the need for supplementary funds for special circumstances such as runs on the key currencies. Nor did it want the negotiations to go to the Executive Board, where countries that were not likely to be called on to do any extra lending would participate in the decision. Moreover, the presence on the board of underdeveloped countries might result in an overall increase in quotas (which would extend their own borrowing rights, however modestly).

The main sticking point remained the nature of controls over the additional resources, which, it was now agreed, would be only for special cases and would take the form of a general loan agreement among the most important industrial countries. Germany and Italy were prepared to accept an *a priori* commitment to partake in any loan operation, albeit to a maximum sum and under certain safeguards, because a simple statement of goodwill would not be sufficient to restore confidence in the Fund. Besides, they doubted whether the United States would participate without a definite European commitment. Among the condi-

16. "Proces-verbal de la huitième reunion des ministres des financies des pays de la C.E.E. tenue à Ostende les 17 et 18 juillet 1961," 12 September 1961, II/5409/61-F, in GT BBV 215, MF. "Verslag van de achtse Conferentie van de Ministers van Financien van de landen van de Europese Economische Gemeenschap gehouden op 17 en 18 juli 1961 te Ostende."

17. Dillon to Zijlstra 22 August 1961, GT BBV 216, MF.

tions to be fulfilled were that the IMF would concentrate its borrowing on "real" surplus countries and that the additional resources would not be used for inflationary financing. The creditors expected to be consulted on the question of whether the "exceptional circumstances" truly justified the loan. France and Belgium were less willing to accept commitments. They did not want the Fund itself to decide when a loan was needed or the amount in question. The most they would accept was a declaration of intent that, should conditions warrant it, they would be willing to sign a credit agreement. The Dutch took a middle course, namely, that accepting a commitment did not mean that no conditions could be attached. Thus the group could itself decide if circumstances justified a loan, where the sums were to be raised, how much was to be borrowed, and for how long.[18]

All of this had been vehemently opposed by Per Jacobsson, president of the IMF, because it threatened irreparably to undermine the Fund's authority. He had insisted that the borrowing authority had to lie with the Fund, though he was willing to leave some control over the decision whether to lend to the lenders themselves. He had originally wanted each country to commit itself to lend to the IMF sums within a predetermined range. The distribution of the currency basket would be determined by as yet unspecified rules of the IMF. His fears of the creation of a special group within the IMF were substantially dissipated when the less developed countries made no objection to this procedure. Moreover, he was convinced of the firmness of the European position.[19]

This agreement left the sums involved as the only unsettled question. Thus in December the EEC finance ministers found themselves examining a possible commitment of $6–$6.5 billion. The United States favored the upper limit, distributed as listed in column 1 of Table 1. The final outcome (in column 2 of the table) suggests that, after the total had been pruned back, the EEC countries had acquiesced fairly painlessly. Italy had judged its original assessment too high because of its international debts, but, as the Belgians pointed out, if IMF quotas had first been recalculated to reflect the shifts in world trade it would have been higher still. The Dutch objected to their assessment because they feared the prospects of seeing no less than 40 percent of their reserves being tied up in the IMF (when they covered only five months' imports), and this probably contributed to the reduction made in their case. All countries, however, agreed on these sums

18. "Proces-verbal de la neuvième reunion des ministres des financies des pays de la C.E.E. tenue à Bad Godesberg le 5 septembre 1961," 28 November 1961, II/6130/61-F, *ibid.* "Verslag van de negende Conferentie van de Ministers van Financien van de landen van de Europese Economische Gemeenschap gehouden op 5 septembre 1961 te Bad-Godesberg."

19. "Statement Relating to Creation of Special Resources for Use by Participating Countries Through the International Monetary Fund, Draft Decision of Executive Directors on General Arrangements to Borrow," n.d. [end of November 1961], *ibid.* See also J. K. Horsefield, *The International Monetary Fund, 1945–1965,* I (Washington, D.C., 1969), 510–11. Memorandum, Dillon for the President, 25 September 1961, NSF/DA 289, JFKL.

## Table 1

Distribution of New Borrowing Facilities Extended to the IMF
(millions of dollars)

| Country | 1 | 2 |
| --- | --- | --- |
| United States | $2,000 | $2,000 |
| Germany | $1,100 | $1,000 |
| United Kingdom | $1,000 | $1,000 |
| France | $500 | $550 |
| Italy | $500 | $550 |
| Benelux | $400 | $350 |
| Canada, Japan, Sweden | $1,000 | $550 |
| Total | $6,500 | $6,000 |

Source: *Memorandum for the President, "Paris Report No. 3: International Monetary Developments and French Recalcitrance" (Heller), 16 May 1961, in PDF/DA 73 (CEA), JFKL.*

only after insisting on the right to revoke the loans in the event that they should find themselves under speculative pressure.[20]

The decision on the General Agreement to Borrow was announced at a NATO finance ministers meeting on 13 December. In March 1963, Switzerland, not a member of the IMF, joined the General Agreement to Borrow with a contribution of $200 million. The agreement's role in this period was more symbolic than real. It was not until the end of 1964 that it was first used, and then to support sterling.[21]

Treasury under secretary Robert Roosa described the piecemeal reforms as part of an integrated, coherent plan, which could be realized only through confidence and through confidential negotiations. Thus it has been made public in snippets, creating the impression that it represented only "a patchwork improvisation of minor devices." Nonetheless, he commented later, "These are an impressive array of innovations; the intricate details of what has been arranged in each of these areas would already make a record of formidable size."[22]

⁓

20. "Projet de Proces-verbal de la dixième reunion des ministres des financies des pays de la C.E.E. tenue à Paris le 1ᵉʳ decembre 1961," 6 January 1962, II/8910/61-F, GT BBV 216, MF. "Verslag van de tiende Conferentie van de Ministers van Financien van de landen van de Europese Economische Gemeenschap gehouden op 1 december 1961 te Parijs."

21. Strange, *International Monetary Relations,* 112–13; Tew, *Evolution of the International System,* 129–30.

22. Memorandum, Dillon for the President, 20 July 1962, and enclosure, "International Liquidity" (Roosa), n.d.; Memorandum, Dillon for the President, and enclosure "The New Convertible Gold-Dollar System" (Roosa), 9 August 1962, both in POF/DA 89a (Treasury), JFKL.

The U.S. balance of payments had meanwhile been discussed in OECD WP3. In October 1961, before the meeting, Roosa had written to the chairman, van Lennep, to obtain his cooperation in steering the discussion in a direction that would reinforce certain U.S. policy imperatives. He did not want the United States to abandon its growth policies for the balance of payments; indeed, growth was a prerequisite for attaining long-term payments equilibrium. He wanted support for the government's work in discouraging excessive price increases and in keeping wage increases in line with productivity; if the Europeans could specifically mention the need for restraint in the steel sector, so much the better. WP3 could stress the need to increase manufacturing investment and to reform the tax structure to facilitate that goal. There should be a mention of the link between the U.S. deficit, its military expenditure (inter alia for defending Western Europe and the European surpluses. Finally, any help in gaining access to foreign markets would be welcome because it would contribute to relieving protectionist pressures at home. Nevertheless, the United States would oppose any suggestions for restrictions on capital flows, any proposals for untying development aid, and any advice to increase long-term interest rates because that would repress economic growth.[23]

Regarding the balance of payments, WP3 recommended that further reductions in protection be investigated, while the United States continued to encourage an export drive and to provide the necessary credit facilities. Van Lennep argued also for the importance of the competitive position and (surprise, surprise) received a description of the lengths the government was willing to go to limit cost increases. Not everyone, however, was willing to endorse the symmetry between the U.S. deficit, military expenditure, and the European surplus although all welcomed attempts to reduce the foreign exchange cost of military outlays. Questions were also raised about the fact that almost two-thirds of $3.5 billion in development aid was tied to purchases in the United States. Roosa replied that the choice had been between tying aid or drastically reducing it. When the balance of payments improved, some untying could take place. As for direct investment, the government was determined to remove the fiscal stimulus to foreign investment.

Even if the balance of payments recovered by 1963, considerable deficits would have to be tolerated in the coming two years, especially with the economy now recovering. The Swiss, French, and Italians all questioned the impact of such deficits on confidence in the dollar and asked how they would be funded. Certainly it was feared that renewed gold sales would lead to renewed speculation. Some also mentioned that the problems would be eased if there was a change in the relative interest rates between the United States and Europe. Roosa replied that interest rate policy could not be solely dependent on external considerations and that any tightening of monetary policy could choke off

23. Van Roijen to MBZ, 20 October 1961, conveying text of letter from Roosa to van Lennep, DGES 996.231.1, MBZ.

The question then arose of how the total deficit, estimated for 1963 at between $1.25 billion and $1.75 million even after discounting an early debt repayment of $500 million ($660 million in 1962), would be funded. The Americans expected gold sales of $900 million (the same as in 1961 and 1962) and hoped to borrow the rest. Individual European countries would be approached to test their readiness to accept Roosa (medium-term, exchange rate guaranteed) bonds. Both van Lennep and Emminger, supported by the Swiss, were forceful in condemning this strategy as a way of shirking responsibility for taking adequate corrective measures to restore equilibrium. If the budget deficit were financed on the capital market, it would mop up excess liquidity and have a salutary impact on capital export.[31]

Nonetheless, working on the assumption that uncovered deficit for 1963 and 1964 would be $2 billion each year, the EC-MC considered that half could be funded by gold sales. But that was about the limit without coming dangerously close to the ceiling of reserves dictated by the necessity to cover the domestic note issue. The remainder could be covered by prepayment of debt and by loans. Already the United States had placed Roosa bonds worth $129 million with Switzerland and $200 million each with Germany and Italy. On top of this, it had negotiated $1.1 billion in swap arrangements. The French representative, however, still considered that the United States should use the normal IMF channels and thus submit to IMF discipline.[32]

In April 1963, Roosa returned to WP3 with a less optimistic prognosis. The U.S. deficit was estimated at $3.5 billion in 1962 and $3 billion in 1963. He blamed the lack of improvement on the fact that U.S. recovery was sucking in imports but quoted wage restraint policies, an active export policy, and a reduction in the foreign exchange costs of official overseas expenditure as evidence of the administration's determination to rectify matters. None of this, however, did much to increase the confidence of the Europeans: the failure of earlier promises to materialize muted any natural tendency toward optimism that may have existed. Roosa suggested that the deficit could be covered by $750 million early debt repayment, $1 billion gold sales, $500 million accumulated foreign exchange by Canada and Japan, and $750 million in Roosa bonds. Van Lennep's position that there had to be some control over U.S. policy now received more support than it had previously. Yet, when asked about this and about a possible role for WP3, Roosa replied that the U.S. position had almost become a fixed agenda point for WP3 already.[33]

The patience of Valéry Giscard d'Estaing, France's finance minister, was al-

31. "Verslag van de Zestiende Zitting van Werkgroep 3 van de OESO (Werkgroep Van Lennep) op 25 en 26 februari 1963," DGES 996.231.1, MBZ.

32. "Verslag van de negenenveertigste zitting van het Monetair Comite van de E.E.G. te Brussel op 5 April, Projet de Compte Rendu de la Quarante-neuvieme session du Comite Monetaire (5 avril 1963)," 9 April 1963, 3969/II/63-F, GT BBV 146, MF.

33. "Verslag van de Zeventiende Zitting van Werkgroep 3 van de OESO (Werkgroep Van Lennep) op 29 en 30 april 1963," DGES 996.231.1, MBZ.

most exhausted. The U.S. deficit was increasing with no end in sight. Some means had to be found to make American policy more sensitive to external factors. As long Roosa bonds were being used to fund the deficits, central banks were ill-placed to demand conditions. The other ministers of the Six concurred. They had participated in the Roosa bond operation to tide the United States over an immediate "gold crisis," and none entertained any illusion that they were helping to effect even a medium-term solution. Yet, in July 1963, Roosa told WP3 that in addition to $536 million already funded in this way, he hoped to place a further $350 million by the end of the year: $150 million more than the prognosis three months earlier.[34]

All the time, U.S. options for funding the deficit were becoming more circumscribed. In addition to the Roosa bond operation, the IMF had been buying up dollars. In 1962 alone, it had augmented its stock by $1.2 billion. Further operations in 1963 had taken it to the level of 75 percent of the U.S. quota. Thus in September 1963, the United States was forced to request a "standby" credit of $500 million: still within its gold tranche and still a long way from the day when the full rigor of IMF controls might come into force, but slowly moving toward that moment. All this, however, still begged the question what would happen when, and if, the world's major reserve currency was forced to the status previously reserved for a handful of developing countries. It was to postpone, or preferably to avoid, this moment that the U.S. authorities pressed for review of the international monetary system. Equally, the European anxiety about the U.S. deficit and the feeling of impotence in their ability to influence, however slightly, the direction of U.S. monetary policy spilled over into this debate.

Before this point of joint talks on the future of the international monetary system had been reached, since the middle of 1961 a debate on institutional reform had been gathering momentum within the Kennedy administration. Advocates for the primacy of economic growth in administration policy such as John Kenneth Galbraith, recently appointed as ambassador to India, and Heller had never been convinced that manipulation of short- and long-term interest rates would not retard economic growth. Early on, Galbraith decried such an approach as "mystic claptrap." Heller was nervous that the drain of dollars would turn into a speculative run and derail policies for domestic expansion. In September 1961 he began to advocate measures to boost confidence in the dollar, the cornerstone of which would be to give a gold guarantee on dollars held in official reserves, "a guarantee by the United States that our official creditors will not lose by a possi-

34. "Projet de Proces-verbal de la quinzième reunion des ministres des financies des pays de la C.E.E. tenue à Spa le 10 et le 11 juin 1963," 1 August 1963, 7754/II/63-F, GT BBV 217, MF. "Verslag van de vijftiende conferentie van de Ministers van Financien van de landen van de E.E.G. op 10 en 11 juni 1963 te Spa"; "Verslag van de 19e Zitting van Werkgroep 3 van de OESO (Werkgroep Van Lennep) op 12 juli 1963," DGES 996.231.1, MBZ.

ble devaluation." Three months later, he returned to the same theme. Although economic growth would ultimately solve the problem, for the intervening eighteen to twenty-four months the United States would have to bridge the deficit. He urged that this could be done only in collaboration with Europe through negotiating a prepayment of the $7.5 billion long-term debt owed by European countries, through coordinating policies with Europe to reduce the impact of short-term capital movement, through borrowing from the IMF, and through a gold guarantee. He informed the president, "Many people will be ready to tell you the disadvantages of these techniques, but the techniques will work, and their disadvantages are as nothing compared to the costs of alternative measures which would hold down the domestic economy."[35] In May 1962 he returned to this theme. The dollar overhang would continue to plague the U.S. economy long after the basic balance was achieved. He was skeptical whether balance could be attained without, in the interval, a run on gold or the adoption of measures that would seriously damage the economy. The core of the problem, in his analysis, lay in the United States' international banking function, and it was time to spread the burden: "It is both technically feasible and politically possible to reform the international monetary system so the US can escape from the trap we are now in, while at the same time our creditors receive assets they will be happier to hold than unguaranteed dollars."[36] By this stage, Carl Kaysen, a member of the White House staff, and Kermit Gordon, the budget director, had added their voices to the chorus. Although "few would advocate gold guarantee as a complete solution to the gold problem; many would argue it forms an important part of the solution."[37]

By August 1962 an overall package of measures, in the form of an "interim international monetary arrangement" to be agreed by G10 (plus Switzerland) had been completed. All members of the club would agree to freeze any conversion of official dollar reserves for two years. To fund the U.S. deficit in the intervening period, the administration would negotiate a drawing right of $5 billion with the IMF (for two years instead of the usual one year); acquire a further

35. Memorandum, Galbraith for the President, "Interest Rates and Your Meeting Tomorrow with the Banking Svengalis," 16 February 1961, in White House Files, JK Galbraith 77, JFKL; Memorandum, Heller for the President, "The Future of the Dollar," 15 September 1961, POF/DA 73 (CEA), JFKL; Memorandum, Heller for the President, "The Balance of Payments Dilemma," 22 November 1961, *ibid.*

36. Official foreign holdings of dollars amounted to $10.3 billion and private holdings to a further $10.8 billion. Against this the United States held $16.8 billion in reserves, of which $11.4 billion was frozen to provide cover for domestic currency. Its free reserves, therefore, were $5.4 billion. Ten years previously they had been $11.7 billion as opposed to total foreign dollar holdings of $9.1 billion. Memorandum, Tobin for the President, "Gold and Domestic Policy," 5 May 1962, in POF/DA 74 (CEA), JFKL. In a similar vein, see also Memorandum, Heller, Gordon, and Tobin for the President, "Government Overseas Programs and the Balance of Payments," 27 June 1962, and Memorandum, Heller for the President, "Visit of Giscard d'Estaing," 16 July 1962, *ibid.*

37. Memorandum, Kaysen and Gordon for the President, "Gold Guarantees," 18 July 1962, POF/DA 89a (Treasury), JFKL.

$1.7 billion (in addition to existing holdings of $800 million) through swap arrangements; engage in substantial forward arrangements, possibly saving up to $1.5 billion; and conduct gold sales up to $1 billion (possibly in such a way as to produce a convergence in dollar-to-gold ratios in official reserves). During the two years in which the arrangements were in place, negotiations on longer-term reform could take place. The goal would be to get more credit from Western Europe than might otherwise be the case (and far in excess of probable requirements) and, by mobilizing such defenses, deter speculative attacks. At the same time, the United States would get a breathing space to put its external accounts in order. Heller considered that international monetary reform should seek to defend all currencies against speculative attacks, to internationalize the burden of being a reserve currency, and to provide for a means of orderly increments of world liquidity.[38]

Roosa wasted little time in dismissing these proposals. He pointed out that the administration had already been engaged in constructing an impressive array of multilateral defense measures that were proving their worth in coping with the existing situation and that were at least as capable as any of the panaceas on offer of meeting the future requirements of the world economy. He considered the interim arrangements politically naive in assuming that any country would sign away automatic credits on the scale envisaged without demanding conditions in advance. And if, as one would expect, those conditions would seek to place limits on domestic monetary and fiscal policy, the whole exercise would be self-defeating. Moreover, he saw no role for any "synthetic currency device" that could not be better fulfilled by "a single national currency, supported by the economic resources of the world's most powerful economy." Dillon fully concurred with this assessment, adding for good measure that the abandonment of free convertibility would shake the system to its core in the same way as the German standstill announcement of 1931 or the dollar devaluation of 1933 had done. He agreed that the existing arrangements left plenty of still untapped potential for raising support for the dollar without recourse to the alternatives offered by the interim arrangements. Martin was equally aghast: "The proposed plan for a standstill monetary agreement, if accepted, would hit world financial markets as a declaration of US insolvency and a submission to receivers to salvage the most they could out of the mess to which past US policies had led. It is incredulous to expect from it any resurgence of confidence in the present international monetary arrangements. Quite the contrary!"[39]

38. "An Interim International Monetary Agreement" (Leddy) 9 August 1962, *ibid.;* Memorandum, Heller for the President, "Why We Need an Interim International Monetary Agreement," 9 August 1962, in POF/DA 75 (CEA), JFKL.

39. Memorandum, Dillon for the President, 20 July 1962 and enclosure, "International Liquidity" (Roosa) nd.; Memorandum, Dillon for the President, and enclosure, "The New Convertible Gold-Dollar System" (Roosa) 9 August 1962; Memorandum, Dillon for the President, and enclosure, "Appraisal of Problems in the Proposal for an 'Interim International Monetary Arrangement,' " 16 August 1962, and "Treasury Program for Further International Monetary Action," 16 August 1962; "Commentary on 'An Interim International Monetary Agreement' " (Martin), 20 August 1962, all in POF/DA 89a (Treasury), JFKL.

The Treasury and the Fed opinions carried the day, and the interim arrangements were never endorsed by the administration. Instead, it was agreed to make confidential approaches to European governments to encourage more compliant and responsible behavior on their parts. But there was to be no hint of reciprocal concessions and certainly no hint of a gold guarantee. Unfortunately, these efforts required the active cooperation of the French, and the climate in which this was possible was destroyed by the refusal later in the year to sell nuclear and missile technology to France. Already in October 1962 negotiations on offsetting military expenditures in France had ground to a halt, and three months later Dillon was preparing a balance of the potential mutual damage should the tension with France spill over into an assault on the dollar.[40]

As the dollar's position again deteriorated through the early months of 1963, the discussion within the administration flared up once more. Walt Rostow of the White House staff came out in favor of a twin strategy of repealing the requirement that domestic currency be backed by gold, thereby releasing billions for the defense of the dollar, and of negotiating substantial ten-year borrowings from the Europeans to mop up the outstanding dollar overhang. Tobin (now a former member of the CEA but obviously still in the policymaking circuit) also wanted a campaign of regular long-term borrowing, possibly at the rate of $1 billion a year from the Europeans over a period of five to ten years. Not surprisingly, Dillon's reaction was distinctly cool. He did not think that there would be a congressional majority for removing gold backing, and the very fact that the issue was under discussion would undermine confidence. He also was unimpressed with the idea that the United States could consolidate "our present liquid liability into ten year loans and then promptly create new short term liabilities to take their place." Not only would Europeans never accept it, but the dollar could never, after such arrangements, regain its position as a world currency. Clearly irritated by the continual sniping at his policies, he offered the following criticism of the "philosophy" behind the proposal:

> This philosophy is the natural reaction of those who find their preferred policies threatened by balance of payments difficulties. It is only natural that they search for ways to make this very real problem go away without interfering with their own projects be they extra low interest rates in the US or the maintenance of large US forces in Europe. However, such individuals are asking the impossible. The sine qua non of all international monetary dealings, under whatever system may be imagined, is that no country can consistently run a large balance of payments deficit.[41]

40. Memorandum, Kennedy for the Secretary of the Treasury, etc., 24 August 1962, *ibid.*; Memorandum, Dillon for the President, "Report on Measures to Improve the Balance of Payments," 9 October 1962; Memorandum, Dillon for the President, "The Mutual Financial and Economic Potential to Exert Pressures—U.S. and France," 24 January 1963, both in POF/DA 90 (Treasury), JFKL.

41. Memorandum, Dillon for the President, 11 February 1963, in POF/DA 90 (Treasury), JFKL. Tobin to Acheson, 20 February 1963, and enclosure, in POF/DA 75a (CEA), JFKL.

Tobin also suggested that the administration should reconsider its attachment to the dollar's gold parity of $35 an ounce. It was not worth defending the parity if the price were draconian domestic deflation. In the event of an agreement that the payments problem had become intractable, and before a run on gold forced the issue, the administration should devalue the dollar: "Neither God nor the Constitution set the value of the dollar in gold or other currencies, and the world would not end if it were changed." The attack on the devaluation option came ironically from within the "economic growth" camp in no less a person than Galbraith. He too was utterly fed up with the drift in policy occasioned by a combination of inadequate measures and overoptimistic forecasts. His solution lay in slashing troop levels in Europe, suspending long-term capital outflows to Europe, breaking off the Kennedy Round (whose results would probably not favor the United States anyway) and raising tariffs against European goods, and implementing a much tighter policy of tied aid: "Strong surgical action may do less damage to military, trade, aid, and other important things, including our domestic political situation, than the continuing erosion of half-hearted measures that are not really corrective." But he ruled out a devaluation because he felt that any U.S. action would immediately be nullified by similar moves by the major trading partners.[42]

Tobin reacted violently to Galbraith's suggestions. He was not advocating immediate devaluation, although its threat might make the Europeans more willing to consider the type of long-term loan scheme he favored. But if devaluation were necessary, it would be preferable to recreating "the world of Hjalmar Schact just to maintain the shadow of convertibility without substance." The devaluation issue was discussed in the cabinet in September 1963, and the issue was shelved. Reflecting on that meeting afterward, Tobin commented, "The unspoken premise, or perhaps the spoken but unargued premise . . . is that such suspension would be a catastrophe of the first order—like the end of the world or a nuclear attack." He condemned Dillon and Rossa's concern with the dollar's value without counting the cost: "Their standing with their constituents and their place in financial history depend on getting through this difficult period without devaluation and without suspension of gold sales. . . . The priorities of financiers are understandable. Why Ken Galbraith should share them is puzzling." He still felt that if the time ever came to implement the Galbraith proposals, it would be preferable to sever the gold-dollar link instead.[43]

⁓

The path favored by Dillon and Roosa had, from the beginning, been to construct and strengthen multilateral arrangements to support the international

42. Tobin to Acheson, 20 February 1963, and enclosure, in POF/DA 75a (CEA), JFKL; "The Balance of Payments," 28 August 1963, in POF/DA 90 (Treasury), JFKL.

43. "The Galbraith Proposals" (Tobin), 11 September 1963, in POF/DA 90 (Treasury), JFKL; Memorandum, Tobin for the President, "The Balance of Payments," 11 October 1963, in POF/DA 76 (CEA), JFKL.

to lend assistance in times of crisis. The debate on the liquidity problem was eventually resolved by the creation of Special Drawing Rights within the framework of the IMF. Although erring on the side of caution, the reform did provide a means of augmenting international liquidity. Unfortunately, by the time it was agreed on, few would argue that scarce liquidity was even a remote problem. Because of the failure to construct a system to discipline American policy and because of the continuous American deficit, the world economy was awash with liquidity. Meanwhile, the French-led attempts to replace the dollar with a new European reserve asset had been abandoned in 1965, once it was realized that it would be impossible to negotiate. Instead, France embarked on a campaign to displace dollars from its own international transactions and reserves by immediately changing any dollars reaching the central bank into gold. This lasted until the strikes and inflationary pay settlements that accompanied the "events" of 1968 provoked a wave of speculation against the franc and eventually forced its devaluation.

The period spanned by the Kennedy administration marked a watershed in European-American relations as the dollar outflow outran the absorption capacity and turned into the "dollar glut." It was in these years that the U.S. payments position first became a problem for the rest of the international system, and, indeed, it has remained so ever since. The debate, then, over the blame retains a certain awesome familiarity with that today. Real factors, linked to competitiveness, protectionism, and growth, vied with monetary variables, dependent on fiscal policy and real interest rates. Policy errors were attributed variously to the surplus or to the deficit economy, depending on the perspective of the commentator. Thus, more than disagreements over security policy that hinged primarily and exclusively on relations with France, the U.S. payments position drove the first major wedge between the EEC and North America. These three years, therefore, are worthy of closer scrutiny because they straddle a turning point in American international relations.

They also mark an interesting transformation in the quality and the context of the debate on the problem. The period opened with concern over how to manage and ameliorate the U.S. payments position, how to fund the deficit until it could be brought under control. There was a definite willingness to pull together to resolve the problem: "two souls, one thought." But the priorities were different. The U.S. authorities were anxious to fund their deficit in ways that would absolve their policies from outside controls, even or especially those of their own creation, the IMF. So recourse was made increasingly to Roosa bonds that guaranteed *incremental* borrowing against devaluation as a means of finance. In this period, when the United States was squirming with a seemingly intractable problem, the authorities also encouraged institutional experiment. The General Agreement to Borrow was part of this solution (although even that contained too many constraints), and so was the initiation of the liquidity debate. Ironically, as the financing problem diminished toward the end of 1963 and into 1964, the U.S. authorities shrank from radical solutions and reverted to more conservative, and now less threatening, ways of obtaining credit within the IMF. In Europe, however, the opposite development was taking place. If the United States had sought institutional reform as a means to avoid discipline, so the surplus EEC states saw therein increasingly the means to impose constraints. U.S. economic power and temporary external economic improvement enabled it to duck the issue. Yet the essential problem remained unresolved: how to create a system in which the supply and distribution of international liquidity did not depend on the vagaries of the domestic economic policy of the major world economy. It is still with us today.

# 12

## European-American Trade Policies, 1961–1963

### *Ynze Alkema*

∽

Studies of European-American trade relations during the presidency of John F. Kennedy are usually written against the background of the Trade Expansion Act of 1962.[1] This legislation gave Kennedy the possibility to enter trade negotiations with the European Economic Community on very liberal terms. Since Kennedy himself never negotiated on the basis of the Trade Expansion Act, he is never associated with the somewhat disappointing progress of the Kennedy Round of the General Agreement on Tariffs and Trade (GATT). Kennedy is therefore remembered as the American president who established the most liberal trade legislation of the twentieth century and not as the president who failed to influence the trade policy of the EEC at a time when that policy was still open for interpretation. In fact, the Kennedy administration may have lost too much time by focusing on legislation and the preparation of a new round of trade negotiations in the GATT. Its actual achievements in the field of European-American trade relations were rather poor, and American policy could not convince the EEC and its member states to adopt a more outward-looking policy. The trade disputes described in this essay reveal that the trade policy of the Kennedy administration was mainly a reaction to problems in the United States. The policy did not lack consistency, but its implementation was too fragmented. Therefore, the years of the Kennedy administration might well be considered an interlude between the period in which the Eisenhower administration successfully guided the establishment of the European Economic Community and the main attempt of the Johnson administration to limit the negative effects of the creation of the EEC on European-American commercial relations in the Kennedy Round negotiations. The period of the Kennedy administration, therefore, remains one of trade disputes such as the "Chicken War." These disputes, the negotiations in the GATT on the compensatory adjustment the United States wanted from the EEC member states, and the trade negotiations in the Dillon

1. Abbreviations used in the notes:
   GT   Generale Thesaurie (MF)
   MF   Ministerie van Financieen, The Hague

212

Round are the subject of this essay. Less emphasis is placed on the liberal attitude of the administration, as shown by the Trade Expansion Act, and more attention is given to the solution of conflicts. The essay is largely based on European sources, describing the EEC's attitude toward American policy, and is limited to developments in the GATT.

## Negotiations in the GATT

When John F. Kennedy took over the United States presidency, a tariff negotiation round in the GATT had been going on in Geneva for almost a year. According to the initial schedule, the first phase of these negotiations, the so-called Article XXIV:6 negotiations, should have been completed by the time Kennedy swore his oath and the second phase, a round of talks on tariff reductions, the Dillon Round, already begun. But the negotiations were behind schedule, and the new president therefore had to take a position on the Article XXIV:6 negotiations.

Negotiations under Article XXIV:6 of the GATT had become necessary because the member states of the European Economic Community wanted to begin adapting their tariffs to their common external tariff on 1 January 1962.[2] Since the member states were all contracting parties to the GATT they had to respect the rules of the General Agreement. The GATT does not object to contracting parties creating a customs union, as long as the external tariff of the group is not higher or more restrictive than the general incidence of the duties and regulations of commerce applied by the group's members before the formation of the union. This implies that the common tariff should be a sort of average of the preexisting duties, the higher ones being reduced and the lower ones raised. If in the process of establishing the common external tariff a contracting party proposes to increase the rate of duty inconsistently with the provisions of Article III (the binding of schedules), compensatory adjustment should be provided. In providing this adjustment, due account should be taken of the compensation already afforded by the reductions brought about in the corresponding duty of other members of the customs union.

The negotiations opened in May 1960, after the EEC had supplied a list of items bound by member states under the GATT. The list specified to which country the member states were bound and how the Community intended to accomplish compensation. Although the Community claimed that the list, excepting agricultural products and the products on List G, balanced, none of the other contracting parties was willing to accept the proposal.[3] One reason was

2. The common external tariff of the EEC was the arithmetical average of the former external tariffs of France, Germany, Italy, and the Benelux.
3. List G included those tariff items for which the EEC member states failed to reach agreement before the signing of the Treaty of Rome in 1957 and for which they still had to decide the level of the common external tariff.

that the others did not agree with the exceptions made, another that for these parties it was not the global internal balance between tariff increases and decreases that was relevant but the situation of each supplying country before and after the establishment of the common external tariff. The Article XXIV:6 negotiations therefore became prolonged and difficult.

Both the European Commission and the EEC member states wanted to conclude the Article XXIV:6 negotiations before the suggested negotiations on tariff reductions began. To negotiate tariff reductions, the EEC had to have an established common external tariff (CET). Once the CET was accepted by the contracting parties, the EEC could participate in tariff negotiations. During the Council of Ministers meeting of 10 to 12 May 1960 a scheme for tariff negotiations had been outlined, including a 20 percent reduction of the CET for industrial goods, if adequate reciprocity was obtained. There were, however, some exceptions to this rule: first, the products on List G could, on the request of a member state, be exempted; second, rates could not be reduced below the agreed-upon common external tariff (which was the agreed CET minus 20 percent). The latter exception resulted from a compromise between the low-tariff and the high-tariff countries in the Community. The former wanted to reduce the CET even without reciprocity, the latter did not want to reduce it at all.

As the results of the Article XXIV:6 negotiations remained meager in January 1961, the outlook for the talks on tariff reductions appeared gloomy. The United States increased pressure on the EEC to compromise because it wanted the Dillon negotiations to start as soon as possible. The opening of the Dillon negotiations depended, according to the American spokesman in the Trade Negotiations Committee (TNC), Carl Corse, on the commission's answers to the questions concerning the reduction of duties and the problems in the agricultural sector. Most other delegations in the TNC expressed similar opinions: they wanted the EEC to make concessions, thus opening the door for the Dillon negotiations.[4]

In late April 1961, according to the EEC negotiators, an agreement between the EEC and the United States seemed within reach. They were therefore surprised, twenty-four hours before what they thought to be one of the final meetings with the American delegation, to receive a memorandum from Washington containing further requests. The memorandum demanded European concessions on agricultural products and included terms for a wheat agreement. The demands went "much further than the plans which had been discussed on various levels with the Americans so far." For that reason it was concluded "that the American proposal almost [seemed] to have the intention of torpedoing the ongoing and all but completed negotiations."[5] A failure of the negotiations be-

4. "Bijeenkomst van de Tariff Negotiations Committee (TNC) op 9 januari 1961," GT/1.88/141, in MF.
5. "Comité 111 (Tariefconferentie Genève); vergadering van 25 april 1961," GT/1.88/177, in MF.

tween the EEC and the United States would almost certainly lead to a total fail-ure of the Article XXIV:6 negotiations because several countries had made the signing of their agreement with the EEC dependent on an agreement between it and the United States. Both the commission and the EEC member states therefore decided to disregard the memorandum and ignore these "clumsy" American tactics.

The reaction of the EEC suggests that the American memorandum came out of the blue. Taking into account the progress of the negotiations, the message of the document was more or less an ultimatum to the Community. Either it had to accept the American proposal and reopen negotiations on agriculture or risk the possibility of a failure of the negotiations, thus leaving the EEC without an accepted common external tariff. As the acceptance of the CET was a *conditio sine qua non* for the EEC to begin the Dillon negotiations, the memorandum might have led to a deadlock in the talks. Washington must have been aware of the impact of the memorandum but nevertheless decided to send it. Was this a sign that the new American administration had established its course in the tariff negotiations? Or had the administration become aware that the Geneva talks were heading in the wrong direction and therefore decided to overrule the deci-sions taken by the American delegation? Had the administration become aware of the possible consequences of the common agricultural policy (CAP), toward which the EEC had taken its first steps?[6] In that case, however, a memorandum might have been expected not from the United States but from Canada, which was the spokesman for the United States, Australia, and New Zealand in the ne-gotiations with the EEC on wheat. (Canada had almost reached an agreement with the EEC, both on wheat and on industrial products.) There might be some of all this in the answer to the question why, but the solution to the problem probably lies in the visit of the British prime minister, Harold Macmillan, to Washington in the middle of April. During this visit, Macmillan informed Presi-dent Kennedy that Britain had resolved to apply for membership in the EEC. Therefore, the American memorandum to the EEC might very well have been a

6. It was clear from the beginning of the GATT negotiations that the Community was not will-ing to make any lasting agreement on agriculture as long as no definitive decisions had been taken on the nature of its common agricultural policy. Initial steps toward a CAP were made early in 1961. On 30 and 31 January 1961, the Council of Ministers decided to introduce a system of levies and a series of transitional measures for wheat, i.e., regulations for moving from national wheat tariffs to a common tariff. (Although the measures related to wheat, it was clear that equivalent measures could also be applied to other grains, pig meat, butter, and eggs in the near future.) The ministers decided that during the transitional period the percentages of the national tariffs would be deconsoli-dated but that the percentage of the common tariff would not be consolidated. The EEC was willing to start negotiations with interested exporting countries concerning the repercussions on exports to the EEC member states of applying the system. If, as a result of the measures taken, a marked overall decline ("*fléchissement marqué*") of EEC imports of high-quality wheat from exporting countries manifested itself, then the member states would take transitional measures. The fulfillment of these obligations, however, implied the simultaneous activation of sections of the common agricultural policy assuring, in accordance with the Treaty of Rome, the sale of wheat by member states.

last-minute attempt to improve the position of American agricultural producers in the EEC market. If Britain became a member of the EEC, then the EEC would have to find an arrangement for the preferential treatment of the Commonwealth countries on the British market. The United States "could hardly accept a system which would give Commonwealth farm products a permanent position in the Common Market more favorable than that enjoyed by competing products from the United States."[7] The United States had to improve its bargaining position before the negotiations between the EEC and Great Britain began, and therefore it needed better results from the Article XXIV:6 negotiations than it would have accepted without the information from Macmillan. That it drafted the memorandum without the help of Canada and the other Commonwealth countries was, under the circumstances, not surprising.

Immediately after the receipt of the American memorandum, the commission proposed to Committee 111 that the EEC take no notice of the demands it contained.[8] Furthermore, the Community should try to isolate the United States by granting concessions on aluminum and canned salmon to Canada, provided that Canada thereupon initialed the agreement with the Community. The German, Italian, and Dutch delegations supported the commission. The French and Belgians opposed granting any further concessions. They wanted the Community to make clear that it considered the Article XXIV:6 negotiations closed. This suggestion led to a dilemma. If the Community considered the first phase of the negotiations to be closed, could it then start the Dillon negotiations with those countries with which it had not reached an agreement?[9] Committee 111 suggested agreeing to negotiate with these countries. The Community should facilitate such negotiations by proposing package deals of concessions. The commission disliked the idea of mixing the Article XXIV:6 and Dillon negotiations in this way. Within a few days, however, it had to accept this solution because another memorandum was received from the American administration. In the new memorandum, dated 30 April 1961, the United States made clear that it no longer made sense for the Community to hold on to the idea of concluding the Article XXIV:6 negotiations before opening the Dillon Round. If the EEC in-

7. Arthur M. Schlesinger, Jr., *A Thousand Days: John F. Kennedy in the White House* (Boston, 1965), 845–46.

8. Committee 111, which assisted the commission in conducting negotiations on the basis of the common customs tariff, was named after Article 111(2) of the Treaty of Rome, which stated that "the Commission presents to the Council recommendations with a view to tariff negotiations with third countries on the common customs tariff. The Council authorizes the Commission to open the negotiations. The Commission conducts these negotiations in consultation with a special Committee appointed by the Council to assist it in this task, and in the framework of the directives which the Council may address to it."

9. At the end of April 1962 the EEC had reached no agreement with Brazil, Canada, Czechoslovakia, Denmark, Norway, Switzerland, the United States, and Uruguay. An agreement had not been signed, but was within reach, with Australia, Austria, Ceylon, Chile, India, Indonesia, Japan, New Zealand, Pakistan, Peru, Sweden, and the United Kingdom.

sisted on doing so, it would be solely responsible for any failure of the negotiations.

The Council of Ministers thereupon decided, in early May, to confirm the decision of 20 March 1961 that no new concessions would be given in the Article XXIV:6 negotiations.[10] The Community considered the first phase of the negotiations to be ended, and proposed 10 May 1961 as the official closing date. The Dillon Round could then start on 15 May 1961. The Community reaffirmed its offer of a 20 percent reduction of tariffs. It suggested that the contracting parties, who were planning to withdraw concessions from the EEC in retaliation, wait until after the Dillon negotiations before effecting such measures.

The American administration probably had not foreseen the direct implications of its first memo, particularly the refusal of the EEC to cooperate and the resulting risk that the negotiations might fail, but it quickly corrected this omission with the second memorandum. The EEC, of course, was not in an enviable position (but neither was the United States in the long run). After the first memorandum it could bravely claim that it would take no notice of the American demands. But it would not have gotten much support from third parties in a conflict with the United States because most of the contracting parties in the GATT were unhappy with the results reached in the long negotiations with the EEC. It would not have been too difficult for the American administration to force its will on the Community. Yet even if the American administration had improved its position, could it expect to get much better results from mixing the two sets of negotiations given its limited negotiating power?

Since the EEC had already formulated its negotiating aims as early as May 1960, the Dillon negotiations did not cause the Community many internal problems. For its negotiating partners the position of the Community was also clear. The EEC was willing to discuss a linear reduction of its external tariff of 20 percent for industrial products, excluding those on List G. It was not willing to negotiate on agricultural products, which would shortly be covered by a "market organization" under the common agricultural policy.[11] It was only in the au-

10. During the meeting of the council, Sicco Mansholt, the commissioner for agriculture, opposed closing the Article XXIV:6 negotiations. He wanted to find a compromise with the United States and the other food-exporting countries. The Community should make a last effort to find a solution for those tariff problems arising from the direction taken by the common agricultural policy. It would not be expedient to start negotiations in the Dillon Round without closing the Article XXIV:6 negotiations because this would simply delay the solution of these problems. See "Projet de proces-verbal de la réunion restreinte tenu à l'occasion de la 45ème session du Conseil de la Communauté Economique Européenne (Bruxelles, mardi 2 et mercredi 3 mai 1961)," GT/1.88/269, in MF.

11. In fact, agriculture played a minor role in the GATT before the Kennedy Round. Originally GATT regulations on agriculture were limited. It was only in the second half of the 1950s that restrictions in trade in agricultural products became an issue in the GATT. In 1958, as a result of the Haberler Report, the so-called Committee II, as part of an overall examination of the international trade situation, began studying the problems arising from the widespread use of nontariff measures for the protection of agriculture. Until that time, the United States in particular had tried to limit as far as possible the influence of GATT regulations on agriculture. The change in the attitude of the United States had everything to do with the balance-of-payments problems that emerged in the late 1950s; agriculture was the country's biggest single exporting sector.

tumn of 1961 that some problems arose involving the Community's attitude toward the United States. The Council of Ministers was unable to resolve these problems completely, and one of them, the disparity issue, that is, the difference in the tariff structures of the EEC and the United States, could thus resurface during the Kennedy Round.

In October 1961 the Council of Ministers discussed the position the EEC would have to adopt during the rest of the Dillon negotiations with the United States. The chairman of Committee 111, George Frederick Reinhardt, complained during this meeting that so far the United States had not been very generous. The Americans were hiding behind the GATT rules, which they interpreted so strictly that "one could not expect that they would permit reaching an *équilibre parfait*."[12] Some of the delegations in the committee warned, however, that the United States would move toward a largely protectionist tariff policy should the Community not show a willingness to compromise. Therefore, five delegations continued to support the 20 percent reduction of the external tariff on industrial goods offered by the EEC at the start of the negotiations. Only the Italian delegation refused to go further than a 15 percent reduction, recommending, moreover, important exceptions to this limited reduction regarding the tariffs of certain "critical" products on which the EEC should make no concessions at all. The Italian minister, Emilio Colombo, explained that the negotiations with the United States caused the Italian government great difficulties for which it had yet to find a solution. He therefore requested postponing the assessment of a common standpoint until the next meeting of the council, on 6 November 1961. Commissioner Jean Rey replied that although the American offer was modest, the EEC's offer did not involve products of much interest to economic milieux in the United States. During its next meeting, therefore, the council would have to produce an initiative capable of saving the Dillon Round.

In the Council of Ministers meeting of 6 November, Reinhardt once more explained that, with the exception of the Italian delegation, all members of Committee 111 considered, *en principe*, that the conditions for the consolidation of a 20 percent linear reduction of the common external tariff were complied with. The Italian delegation had thereupon formulated a compromise: the EEC should limit its offer of a linear tariff reduction of 20 percent on industrial products to products for which the United States was the Community's principal supplier; it should retract its offer for all the other partners at the negotiations. With the other nations the EEC would negotiate according to the classical method, position by position. Furthermore, the Italian delegation asked for exceptions to these rules for automobile parts, aluminum, and domestic sewing machines. The Italian proposal was acceptable neither to the commission nor to the other delegations. They preferred to see it as a last-ditch possibility, depend-

12. "Projet de proces-verbal de la réunion restreinte tenue à l'occasion de la 53ème session du Conseil de la Communauté Economique Européenne (Bruxelles, lundi 23, mardi 24, et mercredi 25 octobre 1961)," GT/1.88/272, in MF.

ing on the offers received from counterparts. For the agricultural sector, the committee found it extremely difficult to determine concessions to the United States, particularly compensation for the deconsolidation of the wheat tariff during the Article XXIV:6 negotiations. The delegations would like to see arrangements on ordinary wheat, maize, sorghum, and poultry and also a reduction of the tariff on tobacco. The Italian delegation opposed any reduction of the tobacco tariff.

Rey asked the council to consider the consequences a failure of the negotiations might have for the EEC's future relations with third countries. He drew attention to a recent speech of the American under secretary of state for economic affairs, George Ball, placing the efforts of the American administration in the context of the reinvigorated protectionist mood developing in the United States. Colombo explained that Italian reservations resulted from the unsatisfactory nature of the offers thus far made by third countries and emphasized the importance of reaching an agreement with the United States. He thought that the proposal made by the Italian delegation in Committee 111 could, with some modifications, produce a positive result for the EEC in the negotiations. The German and Dutch ministers and the representatives of the commission stressed their desire to maintain the 20 percent reduction for all countries, but because of the importance of reaching an agreement with the United States, they were willing to accept the Italian proposal. The French permanent representative, Jean-Marc Boegner, claimed that it was in the Community's interests to obtain a reduction on the tariff level of products for which the United States had "excessive" protection. He suggested that the 20 percent reduction not be applied to products the United States protected with extremely high tariffs. The council decided to assign Committee 111 to examine a formula combining the Italian and French proposals. The committee, reporting to the ministers later in the council meeting, recognized that the French suggestion took into account the *"intérêts légitimes"* of European industries. But four delegations considered that combining the Italian and French proposals would weaken the negotiating position of the commission. Should the council nevertheless decide to combine them, it would have to find a solution for the unresolved problems concerning the duties on automobiles, automobile parts, aluminum, and tobacco.[13]

Discussion in the council became increasingly intricate. The Belgian state secretary, Henri Fayat, announced that the Benelux countries could support the

13. Although the United States was not the EEC's main aluminum supplier, the aluminum problem was related to the negotiations with the United States. Canada, the main supplier, was not willing to accept the solution for wheat proposed by the EEC. The refusal of Canada to agree on an arrangement also meant that the EEC could not reach an agreement with the United States because a solution had to be found simultaneously with Canada and the United States. To overcome the deadlock, Germany and the Benelux countries were willing to reduce the tariff on aluminum from 9 to 8 percent. Italy did not want to go any lower than 8.5 percent. France stated it did not see why aluminum, on which it did not want to reduce the duty, had to be discussed during the current meeting of the council.

Italian proposal only if a solution could be found for all the remaining difficulties. So the ministers combined the duty on cars with that on tobacco. Belgium wanted a difference of at least nine points between the duties on automobiles and on parts of automobiles to protect its auto assembly industry. Italy was willing only to agree on a reduction of the maximum levy on tobacco from 42 to 40 Units of Account per 100 kilograms and a reduction of the ad valorem duty of one point. The Benelux countries could accept the combination on the condition that the commission was allowed to reopen the discussion in a future meeting of the council should problems arise with third countries in the GATT. Boegner, however, was not willing to link the duty on tobacco with the reduction of rights on automobiles and on automobile parts.[14] He claimed that the anticipated right of 15 percent on automobile parts meant a reduction of 20 percent of the initial common external tariff on this item. France was not willing to accept a larger reduction than this. Colombo suggested that the Community should consolidate a duty of 23 percent for automobiles and of 15 percent for automobile parts in the Dillon negotiations. If the Belgian assembly industry could not maintain its output at the present level, the duty on parts would be automatically reduced to 14 percent. Rey believed that if the reductions did not contain a gesture to the United States they would be unacceptable to the American administration. Belgium did not want to accept the compromise, suggesting a reduction of the duty on automobile parts to 14.5 percent. A further compromise was necessary because France refused to accept the Belgian demand. The French delegation was asked if it would accept a duty of 14.5 percent were the council to agree on the French suggestion of withdrawing from its offer of linear reductions those products for which the United States had particularly high tariffs.

The council did not arrive at a consensus during the meeting. Germany was against withdrawing certain positions, as suggested by France, if France maintained its reservations on automobile parts. France declared that as the link between the Italian proposal for linear reductions of 20 percent and the French suggestion of exceptions had not become clear during the meeting, it could no longer support the Italian proposal. Italy thought that it had already made enough concessions.

The remaining differences of opinion did not prevent the Community from reaching an agreement with the United States. On 7 March 1962 the EEC and the United States signed an agreement concluding their tariff negotiations. According to the commission, the agreement marked an important stage in global commercial relations because it not only meant acceptance of the EEC's common external tariff but also demonstrated the willingness of the EEC and the United States to contribute to the expansion of trade through a liberal tariff pol-

14. The reduction of the tariff on automobiles had not, in fact, given much trouble. It was only in connection with the reduction of the tariff on automobile parts that problems arose. Italy, in first instance, did not want the tariff below 17 percent, France 16 percent.

icy.[15] In the first phase of the negotiations, the Article XXIV:6 negotiations, the EEC and the United States had reached an agreement on concessions covering approximately the same value as had been covered in the former agreements of the six member states. On the basis of imports from the United States in 1958, the concessions amounted to about $1,500 million.[16] The mutual concessions made in the Dillon Round amounted to $1,600 million. The reductions in the duties of the common external tariff for industrial products were, with a few exceptions, around 20 percent, as initially offered by the Community. Among the exceptions were certain products in the chemical sector, withdrawn from the initial offer because the United States could not make sufficient concessions as a result of limitations in its trade legislation. The EEC made some 560 concessions to the United States, the United States about 575 to the EEC. The issue of agriculture was not solved in the agreement. The United States and the EEC formally agreed that the Americans had unsatisfied negotiating claims. These were identified in "standstill agreements" for hard and soft wheat, corn, sorghum, rice, and poultry. The claims were identified as being those held by the United States on 1 September 1960. As T. K. Warley notes, "By settling for this understanding the United States had permitted the CAP and its levy system to exist."[17]

The results of the Dillon negotiations between the EEC and the United States were neither better nor worse than might have been expected at the beginning of the talks. The foundations for the Dillon Round were laid in the Article XXIV:6 negotiations. These could have been disappointing given the attitude of the EEC, but as the common external tariff was at stake a cautious attitude on the Community's part was predictable. The EEC member states had put a lot of time and effort into negotiating their common external tariff, and therefore it could not have been seriously expected that they would be willing to alter the basis of the CET during the GATT negotiations. The serious difficulties in the negotiations were produced by a factor that was beyond the CET, the Community's agricultural policy in the making. The EEC did not want to commit itself

15. *Cinquième Rapport Général sur l'activité de la Communauté (du 1er mai 1961 au 30 avril 1962)*, 247.

16. Gerard and Victoria Curzon write of these concessions that "characteristically the Community did not admit to having made any unrequited concessions to the United States in the XXIV:6 negotiations. The United States, to the contrary, announced with some pride that 'as a result of the negotiations with the EEC under Article XXIV:6 [it] obtained concessions on trade of $1,677 million, of which $1,583 million under the form of direct bindings to the United States.' What actually happened was that when the Community bound its tariff during the XXIV:6 negotiations, it had to identify a 'principal supplier' with whom to bind it. Since the United States was the Community's principal supplier on a wide range of goods, the U.S. delegation could claim to have chalked up a huge victory—which it did." See Gerard Curzon and Victoria Curzon, "The Management of Trade Relations in the GATT," in *International Economic Relations of the Western World, 1959–1971*, ed. Andrew Shonfield (London, 1976), 171.

17. *Cinquième Rapport Général sur l'activité de la Communauté (du 1er mai 1961 au 30 avril 1962)*, 246–47; T. K. Warley, "Western Trade in Agricultural Products," in *International Economic Relations of the Western World*, ed. Shonfield, 379.

to any long-term agreement before it had worked out a common agricultural policy. The United States wanted to secure its agricultural exports, not only before the EEC produced the CAP but also before Britain entered the EEC. As the GATT had only limited competence in the agricultural field, the EEC could not be forced to compensate contracting parties for changes in the agricultural policy of EEC member states. The Article XXIV:6 negotiations were therefore disappointing to many foodstuff-exporting countries, including the United States. These countries could only hope that in a future round of negotiations the GATT would have broader powers to regulate agricultural disputes. So, taking the background of the Dillon negotiations into account, the talks between the EEC and the United States produced results that could have been predicted in advance.

It became clear from the Dillon negotiations that the way the talks were pursued was outdated. Or, as Gerard Curzon writes, "The actual negotiation of the 'Dillon Round,' at a time when most interested countries with the exception of the United States were lowering tariffs automatically and globally by prearranged percentage and timetable, showed the absurdity of the time-honored practice of the item-by-item type of negotiation."[18] The negotiating space of the United States was too limited to react to offers such as the 20 percent linear reduction proposed by the EEC. The American administration, therefore, at the same time as the Dillon negotiations were concluded, presented to Congress a new trade bill with far broader powers: the Trade Expansion Act. This bill would make possible linear tariff reductions of up to 50 percent. It also foresaw the possibility of negotiating on agricultural products in the same way as on industrial products.

## The Dispute About Glass and Carpets

Within two weeks of the signing of the agreement between the EEC and the United States a new trade conflict was born between the two when, on 19 March 1962, President Kennedy raised emergency import duties on carpets and glass.[19] Since it was public knowledge at the time that the reports of the U.S. Tariff Commission had been in Kennedy's hands for months, the timing of the announcement seemed, according to Gerard and Victoria Curzon, "clearly designed to demonstrate, at a strategic moment, the President's sympathy with domestic producers who had suffered from measures of trade liberalization, and to underline his commitment to the 'no-injury' criterion, with which Congress had always attempted to restrain the Administration's tariff-cutting zeal."[20]

18. Gerard Curzon, *Multilateral Commercial Diplomacy: The General Agreement on Tariffs and Trade and Its Impact on National Commercial Policies and Techniques* (London, 1965), 100.
19. The duties on sheet glass were raised from 4.8–20.0 percent to 6.8–46.7 percent, the duties on carpets from 21 percent to 40 percent.
20. Curzon and Curzon, "Management of Trade Relations in the GATT," 178.

The commission was highly indignant about the American measures because they were damaging for Belgian, French, and German industries. During its meeting with the Thah Experts on 20 March, the commission announced that it would protest strongly and take appropriate countermeasures.[21] Not to sign the textile agreement, as had been suggested by the Belgian delegation, however, would be improper because the United States would not be the first country hit. The commission itself considered withdrawing some major concessions from the recently signed agreement. The representative of the commission at the GATT was ordered to ask for consultations with the United States. To be able to negotiate successfully, the commission asked the member states not only to take a firm stand during the negotiations but also to prepare countermeasures should it prove impossible to conclude them successfully. This latter demand turned out to be a problem. All the member states were prepared to follow the commission in a justified reaction, but all had doubts about at least one of the products on which the commission wanted to raise the duty in retaliation.

The EEC had reason to be indignant, of course. Raising duties within two weeks of signing an agreement on tariff reductions shows neither good manners nor evidence of trustworthiness. Moreover, the United States had not been extremely generous during the negotiations. The Kennedy administration could claim that it had inherited only limited negotiating powers from the former administration and was not therefore in a position to make generous offers. President Kennedy, however, in making his decision, could not hide behind decisions made by others because he was free to ignore the advice of the Tariff Commission. Internal American interests, the protection of an American industry and employment, prevailed in the president's decision. The Kennedy administration claimed that the Trade Expansion Act was a break with past trade legislation. The new trade legislation removed from the Tariff Commission the power to set peril points. But the new legislation allowed American industries to ask the Tariff Commission to investigate whether tariff concessions made by the United States were harmful to them.[22] Besides, the president himself also remained vulnerable to arguments from national industries. In that sense, the Trade Expansion Act could not prevent disputes such as that over glass and carpets. Even with the

21. One year earlier, in July 1961, when President Kennedy first received advice from the Tariff Commission to raise the duties on sheet glass, the Community had threatened to withdraw cooperation from the American effort to solve the problem of textile imports from the low-wage countries. The president had then asked the Tariff Commission for a more detailed study.

22. The Trade Expansion Act of 1962, as sent to the House of Representatives, stated: "In addition to articles covered by outstanding proclamations under the national security or escape clause provisions of existing law, or the bill, the President would be required, in certain circumstances, to reserve from negotiation any article with respect to which the Tariff Commission found that imports of such article were seriously injuring or threatening such injury to the domestic industry concerned. . . . the President includes any such articles on a proposed negotiation list and the Tariff Commission finds and advises him, upon application of the interested industry, that the economic conditions in such industry have not substantially improved since the date of the last Tariff Commission escape-clause investigation."

Trade Expansion Act the point of departure in trade policy remained the national interest. The last point was also true, of course, for the EEC member states.

On 14 and 15 May 1962, the Council of Ministers discussed the demands of the commission and a list of items that could be used for retaliation.[23] Germany wanted the Community to avoid any suggestion of the possibility of a trade war between the EEC and the United States because it was greatly concerned about its internal price level (which was under strong pressure). It did not agree with the proposed increase in the duties on poultry, canned fruit, and fruit juices because the import of these products from the United States had a "beneficial effect" on the German price level. State Secretary Alfred Müller-Armack instead suggested raising duties on some of those industrial products for which European industry could use extra protection. The Dutch delegation asked whether it would not be a better idea to use quantitative restrictions. Such restrictions had more effect than increasing duties, particularly because they could be applied to agricultural products. Jan Willem De Pous, Dutch minister of Economic Affairs, opposed the inclusion of tobacco on the retaliation list because the Netherlands already had made numerous concessions on tobacco during the preceding tariff negotiations.[24] Luxembourg supported the Dutch view on tobacco, raising similar objections against using tobacco for retaliating purposes. Italy first suggested that European countermeasures should include only exceptionally sensitive American products. Colombo urged the council to reach agreement; a threat made sense only if it could be carried out.

The position of the EEC in the world would be weakened if no decision could be reached. Indecisiveness would be taken as an indication by other countries, especially the United States, that there was no real cohesion between the Six in the field of trade. Couve de Murville asked whether it made any sense for the Six to talk about political cooperation if the council could not even reach agreement on a point of minor importance such as retaliation measures. The Belgian delegation was indignant about the German attitude, Maurice Paul Brasseur accusing Germany of blocking an effective reprisal by the EEC "simply because, evidently, political relations between the Federal Republic and America were strained." According to the Belgian minister, "the solution of these problems [did not depend] on the import duty on fruit juices."[25] Belgian indignation was fed in part by a declaration of Müller-Armack earlier in the meeting. When discussing the trade negotiations with Sweden and the French refusal to lower the

23. "Projet de proces-verbal de la réunion restreinte tenue à l'occasion de la 67ème session du Conseil de la Communauté Economique Européenne (Bruxelles, lundi 14 et mardi 15 mai 1962)," GT/1.88/274, in MF.

24. Minister de Pous also opposed inclusion of automobiles on the list because the American car industry, a "liberal" industry, should not be punished for the protectionism of other industries: "Bijeenkomst van de Raden van Ministers (67e E.E.G. en 50e Euratom) op maandag 14 en dinsdag 15 mei 1962," BBV/782, in MF.

25. *Ibid.*

EEC duty on paper, Müller-Armack had stated that the trade relations of the Community should not take into account only the interests of one country or those of the least interested country. A collective assessment of the situation should take place, considering both the protection of the competing EEC industries and the export interests of the different member states. This was the heart of the integration problem: whether the member states were willing to set aside their own interests for the greater interest of their partners or of the Community as a whole.[26]

During the subsequent meeting of the council, early in June, the ministers had to make a final decision on retaliatory measures. Committee 111, therefore, had drafted two lists of products eligible for use in countermeasures against the American tariff increases. The first list included agricultural and industrial products, the second only industrial products. All member states accepted the second list as a possibility for reprisal. The first list was accepted by all except Germany. Müller-Armack repeated that the German government could not accept the measures on agricultural products, which would have "very grave repercussions" on the German price level. Rey thought it regrettable that Germany would not accept the first list. The increase of duties on agricultural products (soya oils and cotton oils) was at a very reasonable level: 50 and not 100 percent. He judged that, if this list were adopted, the Community would be in a better position to demonstrate its will to defend itself. Brasseur claimed that strong measures against the United States were necessary because the American government had effectuated its measures in view of the lack of a common attitude among the member states and as a punishment for the negative opinion of the American delegation during the consultations in the GATT. He therefore once again asked the German delegation to agree to the fuller list, including soya and cotton oils, because it would have a much stronger impact on the American administration. The German delegation, however, was unwilling to sacrifice the maintenance of the federal price level. Müller-Armack added that during the last meeting of the council it had been Minister Couve de Murville who stressed that, since the American measures all fell within the industrial sector, it would be normal for the reaction of the Community also to be limited to this sector. In the end, the council decided to suspend five tariff concessions previously agreed with the United States and to increase duties for the United States on four positions.[27]

The retaliatory measures were reported to the GATT on 18 June 1962. According to the rules of the General Agreement, the countermeasures would become effective thirty days after notification. For the American government, the

26. "Projet de proces-verbal de la réunion restreinte tenue à l'occasion de la 67ème session du Conseil de la Communauté Economique Européenne (Bruxelles, lundi 14 et mardi 15 mai 1962)."

27. The tariff concessions on polythene, polystyrene, synthetic fiber material, artificial material, and varnish and paint were suspended; the duties on polythene, polystyrene, synthetic fiber material, and artificial material were raised by 100 percent.

retaliatory measures of the EEC made revising its decision impossible, as the American ambassador to the EEC wrote to Boegner.[28] According to the United States, further negotiations in the GATT would make no sense.

## The Trade Expansion Act

The Trade Expansion Act of 1962 was the Kennedy administration's solution to many problems the United States faced during the early 1960s. Free trade, meaning expansion of American exports through the reduction of barriers abroad, would strengthen the economies of the free world, making the capitalist system more attractive for less developed countries and blocking communist expansion. The Trade Expansion Act, however, was not chiefly developed as an answer to global problems but to those the American economy itself was facing. The most important goal for the United States was to gain access to the rapidly growing market of the EEC. The American economy, it was said, needed to expand and could do so only by increasing exports. The White House wrote to Congress: "Our efforts to expand our economy will be importantly affected by our ability to expand our exports, and particularly upon the ability of our farmers and business men to sell to the Common Market."[29]

Kennedy had become president promising annual economic growth of 5 percent, far higher than the United States had achieved for some time as a result of the repeated recessions of the 1950s. Economic growth had been slow, and at the time Kennedy took over the presidency both unemployment and the balance-of-payments deficit had reached levels unknown in the postwar years. The latter problem occupied Kennedy the most because it was decisive for the success of his policy for stimulating the American economy.[30] The deficit was the result of American overspending abroad, both private and governmental. Not enough dollars were earned abroad to balance this overseas spending. Finding a solution for the problem within the framework of Bretton Woods was not easy.

The solution seemed to be to cut down government overseas spending, but this was not the easy solution it seemed because most of the aid given was then spent in the United States. Cutting down aid, therefore, meant a decrease in

28. "218e bijeenkomst van het Comité van Permanente Vertegenwoordigers bij EEG en Euratom op dinsdag 12 en woedensdag 13 juni 1962," GT/1.88/60, in MF.

29. "Message from the President of the United States Relative to the Reciprocal Trade Agreements Program," in House of Representatives, 87th Cong., 2d Sess., on H.R. 9900, p. 2.

30. Susan Strange writes: "Though U.S. policies were in some measure responsive to the pressure from the balance of payments, it must be stressed that this was not yet by any means the prime objective of the new Administration's economic policies. The President's special balance-of-payments message to Congress on 6 February 1961 set out four economic objections—all domestic. Only a few days later, as a kind of afterthought, did the President add his fifth objective: to restore confidence in the dollar and to cut the US payments deficit." See Strange, "International Monetary Relations," in *International Economic Relations of the Western World*, ed. Schonfield, 82.

American exports and a slump in American economic activity.[31] Even the complete linking of aid to purchasing American goods would not improve this situation as long as it was thought that all dollars sent abroad would one day return to the United States to be spent there. As H. G. Aubrey noted, "If we 'tie' our foreign aid to American purchases, we may gain in the short-run, but some countries would lose; if they in turn were to cut their purchases of American goods our dollar savings would be reduced."[32] So, since for economic and political reasons it was thought impossible to economize on aid and military assistance, the only solution was for the European allies to take over part of the burden.[33] Furthermore, the allies were persuaded to buy more of their military equipment in the United States and the American army abroad was ordered to use more American materials.[34] It was clear, however, that without structural economic change the United States could not continue to act as the leader of the free world in the way it had done in the 1940s and 1950s.

Devaluation of the dollar might provide the necessary structural change. The position of the dollar as the key currency in the Bretton Woods agreement, however, ruled out a devaluation of the currency, without the agreement of the United States' partners, as a solution for the American balance-of-payments disequilibrium. A unilateral American devaluation would be followed by the devaluation of other currencies, nullifying any advantages for the United States. It is doubtful whether Kennedy ever took seriously the possibility of devaluation; he was opposed to any change in the Bretton Woods agreement and the position of the dollar.

If spending could not be cut back and devaluation was not possible, reducing imports might be considered. But a major part of American imports was raw materials and products that could not be produced in the United States. It would not have been easy to reduce these imports. Besides, if restrictions were placed on imports, exports would be reduced by countries whose ability to buy American exports was diminished as a result. The only remaining solution, therefore,

31. Apart from this economic motivation, the increasing amount of aid provided by communist countries also made it difficult to cut down American aid for political reasons

32. H. G. Aubrey, "Financial Policy and American Purpose," *Foreign Affairs XXXIX* (1961), 476.

33. As J. D. Montgomery notes, however, Western Europe was not inactive in the field of aid: "Between 1956 and 1964 the European nations had offered about the same amount of aid to the underdeveloped world that the United States had invested in European recovery under the Marshall Plan in 1948–1952. . . . In 1962, 44 percent of the noncommunist aid was provided by other than United States bilateral programs." See Montgomery, *Foreign Aid in International Politics* (Englewood Cliffs, N.J., 1967), 94.

34. H. Schelbert-Syfrig concludes that between January 1961 and July 1965 the Department of Defense reduced its purchases of commodities and services abroad by $232.8 million. Yet the net exchange savings that could be obtained by a depreciation of the "defense dollars" of 27.4 percent on average did not exceed $81 million. The additional cost for the department amounted to at least $63.8 million. In all probability the costs were even higher and the savings lower. See Schelbert-Syfrig, *Das "Buy American" Prinzip und die amerikanische Zahlungsbilanz* (Zürich, 1968), 56.

was to create an outflow of government dollars and increase the flow of commercial dollars moving in the opposite direction.

It was thus mainly internal economic conditions that shaped the external economic policy of the United States. The Trade Expansion Act was only part of a series of measures the Kennedy administration took in 1962 to protect the dollar and to fight the deficit. Arrangements were made on a series of reciprocal credit lines with other Western countries, the so-called dollar swaps. The United States obtained additional foreign exchange by occasional direct issues of foreign currency securities in the German Federal Republic, Italy, and Switzerland. Furthermore, higher short-term interest rates and new tax incentives were announced to keep short-term capital at home.

During its campaign to get the Trade Expansion Act accepted, the Kennedy administration stuck to a relatively simple story: European economic growth was made possible by American policies. The United States had invested large sums of money in the Western European countries in the postwar years, and it had accepted the disadvantages caused by trade restrictions and a balance-of-payments deficit resulting from the European dollar shortage. American troops were stationed in Western Europe to protect the allies from a Soviet attack, and the United States, as the leader of the free world, was spending large sums of money on aid to newly independent countries. Now that European economic recovery and integration were well under way it was time for the Europeans to show that they were open to the world and to justified American claims.

The Kennedy administration judged the EEC a challenge and a threat to the United States. If the United States wanted to profit from the opportunities provided by the Common Market, negotiations had to be started soon, before the countries of the Community had completed their new tariff structure. There would be no second chance: "If . . . the common external tariff can be brought down so as to narrow or eliminate the competitive disadvantage which internal tariff eliminations will bring, we stand to share in the trading benefits promised by the economic growth of the EEC."[35]

The administration claimed that because American industry had never been as dependent on foreign markets as industry in other countries it had never taken full advantage of "expanding by exports." The only possibility to expand for many sectors of American industry lay abroad because the domestic market was growing less rapidly than in previous decades. Now that the Europeans were moving toward an American standard of living, the possibilities this new prosperity created for American economic growth had to be grasped: "As its consumer incomes grow, its consumer demands are also growing, particularly for the type of goods that we produce best, which are only now beginning to be widely sold or known in the markets of Europe or in the houses of its middle-income families."[36]

35. Trade Expansion Act of 1962, Report of the Committee on Ways and Means, House of Representatives to accompany H.R. 11970, p. 8.
36. "Message from the President of the United States Relative to the Reciprocal Trade Agreements Program," in House of Representatives, 87th Cong., 2d Sess. on H.R. 9900, p. 3.

It was certainly not with the same enthusiasm that the Trade Expansion Act had been discussed in the United States that the American proposal for a new round of GATT trade negotiations was discussed in the EEC. During the meeting of the Council of Ministers on 1 and 2 April 1963 all the ministers accepted a new negotiating round, emphasizing that this would give the EEC the opportunity to demonstrate its "liberal" and "open" character and the possibility to quiet the "anxieties of third countries." The council, however, made acceptance dependent on two conditions: it did not want discussion of tariff reductions on agricultural products in the form proposed by the Trade Expansion Act, and it wanted a solution of the "disparity issue" before the negotiations started.

The EEC was prepared to begin negotiations on agriculture but did not want to discuss the reduction of protection on agricultural products in the same way as the reduction of protection on industrial products. According to the council, this made no sense because agriculture was protected not only by tariffs but in varying ways by different countries. Therefore, none of the various means should be excluded from the negotiations at the outset. Discussion within the EEC focused on the question of how the common agricultural policy should be brought into the negotiations. France wanted the internal agricultural regulations accepted first. Only after these regulations were applied could negotiations with third countries in the GATT begin. The other member states agreed with France in principle but were willing for the regulations not to be applied immediately after acceptance.[37]

At the meeting of the council on 8 and 9 May 1963, France accepted that the whole CAP need not be worked out before the GATT negotiations on agriculture commenced. But it was against negotiating on those agricultural products for which a regulation was in preparation or for which a market regulation was foreseen. The meeting concluded with the statement that the EEC was prepared to take part in the GATT negotiations on agricultural products. Opinion was divided on how the statement should be interpreted. What had been agreed on was not clear to all member states. There was confusion over which products were included in the common position. At the permanent representatives meeting the week following the council it was agreed that *"la détermination d'une position commune aura lieu au sens de l'article 10 du Traité du Rome seulement pour les produits qui font l'objet des négociations Kennedy et pour lesquels, au sein de la Communauté Economique Européenne, une organisation de marchés existe ou a été prévue"* (only for the products that would be part of the Kennedy negotiations and for the products for which there was a market organization or for which such an organization was foreseen, a common position would be determined).[38]

37. The American delegation at the GATT had for some time tried to convince the EEC member states that they should accept the agricultural regulations without actually applying them. Memorandum 1001'63, 29 April 1963, "Te nemen beslissingen Ministersconferentie GATT, 16–21 mei 1963," GT/1.88/142, in MF.

38. "Projet de Compte Rendu Sommaire de la réunion restreinte tenue à l'occasion de la 257ème réunion du Comité des Représentants Permanents (Bruxelles, mardi 14, mercredi 15, et jeudi 16 mai 1963)," GT/1.88/301, in MF.

During the GATT Ministers Conference in Geneva in May 1963 little attention was paid to agricultural products. All parties agreed that *all* forms of protection, not simply tariffs, should be part of the forthcoming negotiations. As no concrete proposal existed for discussing these forms of protection, the Trade Negotiations Committee was instructed to define the rules and methods for creating acceptable conditions for admitting agricultural products to world markets.[39] Real decisions, and the problems involved in reaching them, were postponed.

"The disparity issue," according to John W. Evans, United States economics minister in Geneva until 1965, "probably contributed much more than any other to the pollution of the atmosphere of the Kennedy Round."[40] Looking at the positions adopted, it is clear that the whole issue resulted from the different approaches taken to the negotiations by the United States and the EEC. The United States wanted to change the rules for international trade so as to expand its trade, whereas the EEC wanted to change the rules to make possible an expansion of world trade.

The disparity problem resulted from the different tariff structures of the United States and the EEC. Whereas the American external tariff was the result of decades of building and demolishing trade barriers, protectionism and negotiations, "escape clauses," "peril points," and compromises, the EEC external tariff was the arithmetical mean of four tariff structures. As a result, the common external tariff had a fairly even structure, with only a few tariffs over 20 percent. The American external tariff was on average lower, including many zero duties on raw materials, but with some very sharp peaks. The EEC countries feared that by reducing industrial tariffs by half, as proposed in the Trade Expansion Act, the EEC would be left totally unprotected: about 90 percent of the EEC tariffs would have been below 10 percent, and tariffs below 10 percent were considered to give no real protection. Perhaps the EEC would have been willing to accept such a reduction in any case, were it not that the United States would still have had about 20 percent of its tariffs between 15 and 30 percent and some even higher. It was feared that if tariffs were cut according to the American proposals the EEC would have no cards to play in future negotiations and would therefore be unable to bargain down the remaining high American tariffs in a future round. Consequently, the EEC needed to find an alternative to the proposed method of reduction. The solution was an earlier scheme for the structure of the CET, proposed but not finally adopted during the negotiations on the

39. The ministers agreed that the Trade Negotiations Committee, in elaborating the trade negotiating plan, should deal *inter alia* with "the rules to govern, and the methods to be employed in, the creation of acceptable conditions of access to world markets for agricultural products in furtherance of a significant development and expansion of world trade in such products. Since cereals and meats are amongst the commodities for which general arrangements may be required, the Special Groups on Cereals and Meats shall convene at an early date to negotiate appropriate arrangements. For similar reasons a special group on dairy products shall also be established." Memorandum 1233'63, "GATT-bijeenkomst ministeriëel niveau 16–21 mei 1963," GT/448, in MF.

40. John W. Evans, *U.S. Trade Policy: New Legislation for the Next Round* (New York, 1967), 24.

Treaty of Rome. The idea, suggested by the German delegation in Committee 111, implied the subdivision of industrial tariffs into three categories: raw materials, semimanufactured goods, and end products. The three categories would have different tariff structures.

The discussions on the disparity issue between the EEC and the United States in the GATT were not simply about a technical issue but also involved a different approach to world trade. During the first round of discussions, in the GATT Ministers Conference, the United States was in a stronger position because it was able to influence European decision making.[41] Opinion within the EEC was split over American objections to its proposal. At the meeting of the Council of Ministers on 8 and 9 May, Committee 111, composed—according to Rey—*"de fonctionnaires les plus qualifiés pour examiner les problèmes commerciaux"* (of officials most qualified to examine trade problems), advised in favor of the proposal; the Committee of Permanent Representatives, which, once more according to Rey, *"s'est préoccupé en premier lieu des aspects politiques de la question"* (were preoccupied first of all with the political aspects of the problem), advised against.[42] The commission supported the proposal, but most of the member states had yet to reach a final decision. The council decided to hold on to the proposal as long as possible. As a result, the GATT Ministers Conference decided to form a working group to find a solution for the disparity problem. As working groups tend to be slow in finding a solution, when they find one at all, the disparity issue remained to pollute the atmosphere of the Kennedy Round.

## The Chicken War

In the first week of June 1963, some two weeks after the GATT Ministers Conference, the commission received a letter from the American representative at

41. The handling of the proposal in the Netherlands can be seen as an illustration of the working of American influence. The director general for foreign economic relations, van Oorschot, explained the German proposal in a memorandum to the minister of economic affairs. The advantages of the plan, he wrote, were great. It remained within the structure of the Trade Expansion Act; therefore, the United States could make no objections. If the Americans rejected the plan and if the EEC stuck to it, the negotiations would fail. In that case the responsibility, given the reasonableness of the proposal, could be put on American shoulders. From a European perspective, therefore, there was no reason not to stick to the proposal. Nevertheless, van Oorschot advised the minister to reject the plan. He stated that there was ample reason to believe that the United States would take a negative attitude toward it. In Geneva, so far the Americans had not shown any willingness to take the tariff disparities into account. Moreover, it was the high tariffs in the American system, the really protectionist tariffs, on which major concessions had to be won. Therefore, he concluded, the danger of negotiations failing embodied in the plan made a certain reserve justified. It was better to keep the door open for more pragmatic solutions, based on linear reductions. Memorandum to the Minister, "Tariefonderhandelingen GATT," 29 April 1963, GT/1.88/142, in MF.

42. "Projet de proces-verbal de la réunion restreinte tenue à l'occasion de la 101ème session du Conseil de la Communauté Economique Européenne (Bruxelles, mercredi 8, jeudi 9, et vendredi 10 mai 1963)," GT/1.88/279, in MF.

the EEC, John Willis Tuthill, communicating the American administration's decision to invoke the rights arising from the commitment made by the EEC in concluding the Article XXIV:6 negotiations on agricultural products. The Community had committed itself, among other things, to begin negotiations with the United States on the export of American poultry to the EEC as soon as the Community had agreed on a common policy. The EEC system of a variable levy on poultry, which had been introduced on 30 July 1962, threatened the American export of broilers to EEC member states because it doubled the previous GATT-bound duty of roughly 15 percent. Poultry had become a growing American export industry in the second half of the 1950s, and its main overseas market was the German Federal Republic. Exports to Germany had risen from 3.5 million pounds in 1956 to 122 million pounds in the year ending June 1962, 56 percent of total American poultry exports at the latter date.[43]

The commission's answer declared that the Community would fulfill its obligations and was prepared to start talks. The talks focused on two points. First, was the United States really the "principal supplier" in the period of reference? Second, what negotiation rights had been reserved to the United States in the agreement with the EEC of 7 March 1962? For the commission, Denmark, and not the United States, had been the principal supplier to the EEC, and it contested American calculations of exports to the EEC. The United States used actual imports by the EEC in 1960, which were then doubled to compensate for the quantitative restrictions operating at the time. The commission claimed that 1958 imports rather than those for 1960 should be used, as had been done with all other products during the Article XXIV:6 negotiations. Furthermore, it believed that the doubling of the figures was totally unfounded.

In the meeting of the council on 10 and 11 July 1963, Rey told the ministers that the United States had calculated its negotiation rights at a volume of trade equivalent to $46 million. The United States asked the Community to meet its obligations either by guaranteeing that the maximum protection on poultry in the CAP would be no more than the equivalent of an ad valorem duty of 25 percent or by offering a tariff contingent at a reduced level. Rey thought neither suggestion was favorable to the Community. He asked the ministers for instructions for the negotiations permitting that a solution to the dispute be proposed through lowering the conversion coefficient (the amount of feed grain required for the production of one kilogram of chicken) and consequently the sluice price. He urged that the council not leave the decision to ministers of agriculture, who were not responsible for trade policy and who would have an understandable tendency to see the problem primarily from an agricultural point of view. Sicco

43. E. H. Preeg, *Traders and Diplomats: An Analysis of the Kennedy Round of Negotiations Under the General Agreement of Tariffs and Trade* (Washington, D.C., 1970), 74–75. In the Council of Ministers meeting of 12–14 November 1963, Mansholt claimed that in 1961 and 1962 large-scale speculative imports had taken place, thus falsifying the figures. "Bijeenkomst Raad van Ministers (115e EEG) op dinsdag 12, woensdag 13, donderdag 14 november 1963," GT/782/206, in MF.

Mansholt suggested to the council that the Community make some concessions because the Community's poultry market was too strongly protected. The existing level of protection would lead to overproduction in the internal market. The commission, therefore, advised member states to make some alterations to the common policy on poultry. In this way overproduction could be avoided and, at the same time, the Community would be in a position to lessen American anxieties. The council decided that the Community should demonstrate its willingness to find a solution that met the United States' concerns respecting the export of poultry to the Common Market while taking into account the legitimate interests of EEC producers.[44]

Germany did not want to accept a reduction of the sluice price, however, so no real solution could be found before the summer recess. It was decided that the commission would reopen negotiations with the American delegation to explore possibilities for a solution but could not make decisions binding on the member states. After the summer, the German permanent representative announced the Federal Republic's agreement to the commission proposal of reducing the levy on poultry by eleven pfennig, with no conditions attached. The council could formulate its negotiating position during its next meeting. The EEC offered a reduction of the levy on poultry at the frontier of eleven pfennig per kilogram. The reduction resulted from a modification of the conversion coefficient used in the calculation of the sluice price and of the (external) levy. In return, the EEC asked the United States to relinquish the negotiation rights on poultry assigned under the agreement of 7 March 1962.[45]

The United States rejected the EEC proposal and suggested asking for GATT consultation. The commission had its doubts about a consultation because the EEC and the United States could not agree on an interpretation of such concepts as "arbitration" and "panel." Consequently, it thought that the best way to approach the Americans was by stating that the Community would examine the American proposal with interest but that it would like clarification in advance on the question to be posed to the GATT and on the procedure.[46] Later, in October, the Council of Ministers formulated directives for the consultation. The council wanted the GATT panel to establish the value of American exports of poultry to the German Federal Republic on 1 September 1960, on the basis of the rules and practices of the GATT, to make it possible to judge the implications of the deconsolidation measures. The question at issue, according to the Curzons, was

44. "Projet de proces-verbal de la réunion restreinte tenu à l'occasion de la 107ème session du Conseil de la Communauté Economique Européenne (Bruxelles, les mercredi 10 et jeudi 11 juillet 1963)," GT/1.88/280, in MF.

45. "Projet de proces-verbal de la réunion restreinte tenue à l'occasion de la 110ème session du Conseil de la Communauté Economique Européenne (Bruxelles, les lundi 23 et mardi 24 septembre 1963)," GT/1.88/280, in MF.

46. "271e bijeenkomst van het Comité van Permanente Vertegenwoordigers bij de EEG en Euratom op woensdag 2 en donderdag 3 oktober 1963," GT/1.88/61, in MF.

whether the "value" of a concession could be expressed in terms of dollars on the basis of actual trade in any one year or whether, if that trade was growing rapidly, the "value" of a concession on such trade was not, in fact, considerably greater than just a recorded trade flow which did not take the growth factor into account. In terms of conciliation procedures, however, it may indeed be psychologically very helpful to be able to reduce a major issue of principle to a pseudo-academic discussion of this type.[47]

When the panel decided that the value of the American exports was $26 million, Rey declared in the Council of Ministers meeting of 2 and 3 December 1963 that the Community could be reasonably satisfied with the decision. The council agreed with Rey's suggestion that negotiations be continued with the United States on the basis of the proposed eleven-pfennig reduction of the levy.

## Some Conclusions

For the politics of European-American trade, the years 1961–63 were an interlude in which the results of the policies of preceding years set the agenda. It became clear that two items would determine future trade relations between the EEC and the United States: the extension of the EEC and the development of the EEC's common agricultural policy. Another theme coming to prominence was the problem of the American balance-of-payments deficit. All these themes found their way into the Trade Expansion Act, leading to the Kennedy Round.

The agricultural policy of the EEC had been a cause for concern for nonmember states ever since the signing of the Treaty of Rome. American concern about the common agricultural policy grew when Great Britain announced its application to join the Community. The United States wanted to reach an agreement with the Community on agriculture during the Article XXIV:6/Dillon negotiations but, as a result of the EEC's unwillingness to make a final settlement, it got only standstill agreements. The Kennedy administration used the standstill agreement on poultry to fight the CAP during the "Chicken War." By taking the dispute to the GATT, the United States probably hoped to get an unbiased judgment on the legitimacy of the CAP. Its unwillingness to discuss an arrangement based on altering the calculations, leaving the policy itself unchanged (as suggested by the EEC), also indicates that for the United States poultry was a test case.

The application of Great Britain for membership in the EEC was partly connected with the American concern about agriculture. If the Commonwealth countries got access to the EEC market through British entry, the position of American foodstuff exporters would greatly deteriorate. Furthermore, the overall position of the United States vis-à-vis the enlarged Community would also worsen.

47. Curzon and Curzon, "Management of Trade Relations in the GATT," 212.

# 13

## A Watershed with Some Dry Sides: The Trade Expansion Act of 1962

### *William Diebold, Jr.*

The Trade Agreements Act . . . must be replaced by a wholly new instrument. . . . Fundamentally new and sweeping developments have made obsolete our traditional trade policy. . . . As NATO was unprecedented in military history, this measure is unprecedented in economic history.

*—John F. Kennedy, 1962*

We regard this legislation as of major importance. Not only should it prove an effective tool for advancing and protecting the interests of U.S. trade—and thus providing new business opportunities and job opportunities for Americans—but it should also constitute a necessary instrument for strengthening the bonds between the two sides of the Atlantic.

*—George Ball, 1962*

The United States has allowed its own policies to grow blunted and distorted. . . . An unending series of little concessions to domestic pressures has turned our trade legislation into a group of ambivalent statutes which hamstring the President in any effort to reduce the trade barriers of the United States and which constantly force him to increase the existing restrictions on imports.

*—Raymond Vernon, 1961*

President Kennedy took the plunge when treading water would have been understandable, and he got the greatest advance in trade legislation since 1934.

*—William Diebold, Jr., 1967*

One could expand this small anthology of quotations to the length of the whole essay without finding any serious dissent. If it were in vogue to write histories of American tariff policy, the current edition would undoubtedly still say that the Trade Expansion Act of 1962 (TEA) is a landmark in American foreign trade policy. The basis for this conventional wisdom is that the TEA introduced a set of clearly identifiable innovations and greatly enlarged the president's powers to reduce trade barriers.

This essay is mostly about those changes, where they came from, why they were adopted, and, more briefly, how they were used. To see these matters in the proper perspective one must look at some other innovations in trade policy that were not part of the TEA and also call attention to some potential innovations in trade policy that were not introduced. There are connections with perennial questions about the relation of trade policy to foreign policy; these connections were thought to be stronger than usual in the TEA. Finally, it would be irresponsible for an author who has the presumed benefit of several decades of hindsight not to try to reassess the place of the TEA in three perspectives: the record of the Kennedy administration, the evolution of American relations with Europe, and the history of American foreign trade policy.

To follow these meandering but eventually always interconnecting strands over so much territory while respecting some limits of time and space requires generalization and condensation on a scale that frequently conceals fairly complex analysis. I have sometimes relied on memory rather than documentation and sometimes drawn on my own experience (more as an observer than a participant).[1] When I came by them easily, I have used quotations from the past, sometimes less to prove a point than in the hope that with luck they will sound a bit livelier than latter-day summaries and paraphrases or at least give some flavor of the time, especially when they come from fugitive or unpublished writings. There are a few traces of my original plan to examine the intellectual history of some of these ideas, but lack of space made me give up that attempt. It is likely that I have made some mistakes, but I have not hesitated to note what I do not know and pose questions in the hope that others will answer them. The unanswered questions in the text are left more or less as they were in the original version because they were not answered during the conference. That answers can be found seems obvious, and I even know who to ask about some of them, but I leave the further pursuit of these matters to others. I have borrowed from my own past writings and even quoted from them, perhaps too freely. In this kind of work there is no room for false modesty, or perhaps any modesty at all, and this will not be the first essay about the history of our times that occasionally has an overtone—or more than that—of "I told you so."

## The Start

When John F. Kennedy took office, the state of the American economy was clear. Out of that clarity came uncertainty, not least about foreign trade policy.

1. As always when I want to recall any period since 1945, I refreshed my memory by looking through the relevant volumes of *The United States in World Affairs,* an annual formerly published by the Council on Foreign Relations. For this essay I used the volumes for 1961, 1962, and 1963 by Richard P. Stebbins.

There was a recession, with growing unemployment. Worry about the deficit in the balance of payments was spreading, and the president put the need to do something about it near the top of his list of priorities. The Common Market seemed finally to be taking shape; as a result, it looked as if discrimination against American exports would increase in a major segment of the world economy in which growth, current and prospective, seemed to be a good deal healthier than in the United States. The fag end of the Dillon Round of tariff negotiations showed how little could be accomplished through what was left of the president's powers to strike bargains to reduce trade barriers, and even these powers expired in June 1962. That was also a year of congressional elections; Democratic strength was not to be taken for granted. A renewal of trade legislation that might lead to increased foreign competition did not seem the way to increased popularity.

What foreign trade policy would suit these circumstances? How important was it to do something in that field compared to all the other things the new administration wanted to do? Every course had its serious advocates whose arguments were met by the honest doubts of others. People with ulterior motives had at hand a larger than usual tray of arguments and rationalizations. In a background paper for the first meeting of a discussion group at the Council on Foreign Relations in November 1961, Helena Stalson and I put the case for a strong and innovative step:

> For some years now there has been a widespread, and probably growing, feeling among people concerned with trade policy that this country has about reached the end of the road marked by repeated renewals of the Act first passed in 1934. In part this is a feeling that the policy embodied in the Act has, at best, virtually come to a standstill or else, as is often said, that there has been so much erosion—of the policy, the will behind it, and the law and procedures—that the position is not only defensive but crumbling. . . . Another part of this feeling is the view that while an unprecedented quarter-century of tariff reduction is nothing to be underestimated, something new in trade policy is called for by changes in the rest of the world, the needs of American foreign policy and, perhaps, the requirements of the American economy. While those who hold these views have been for the most part proponents of a liberal trade policy and, to a considerable extent, people who have worked closely on these matters, in and out of the Government, the feeling that something new is needed is shared by others as well. One hears repeatedly of Senators and Representatives who have said that it will no longer be possible to get Congress to put forth the energy needed to pass another renewal bill that involves heavy fighting to secure very minor changes or to defend provisions that seem more symbolic than practical.

We also showed why such arguments might not carry much weight with other people:

> War and reconstruction sheltered American producers from the effects of foreign competition while major reductions were made in the United States tariff. Inflation and relatively easy markets at home and abroad provided a cushion until, during the 1950s, the revival of European and Japanese production began to have a perceptible effect. To a degree, this was a cumulative impact of some years of tariff reduction. Of course, there were many other forces at work as well, but the visibility of the tariff and the foreignness of the competition provided a sharper focus than other factors. During the 1950s American imports of manufactured goods increased greatly and many American producers met much stronger foreign competition at home and abroad. A new concern arose about the competitiveness of American industry. Apparent cost advantages of foreign producers, especially in wages, increased the pressure for protection. Recession inevitably strengthened the feeling that something should be done about imports, and the persistence of unemployment helps keep the feeling alive. The discovery that the United States, too, could have balance of payments difficulties lent support, however vaguely, to the sentiment for limiting imports and complicated the argument of those advocating further tariff cuts.[2]

Two other authors of rather greater prominence put their emphasis on a broad political argument that seemed to some people more aspiration than actuality. Writing before the TEA had been introduced, Christian Herter and William Clayton said:

> The nations of the free world must work together as the Common Market "six" are doing already. . . .

2. Both quotations are from William Diebold, Jr., and Helena L. Stalson, "The Background of the Decisions to Be Made," Background Paper Number 1, for meeting of 20 November 1961, Council on Foreign Relations, Discussion Group on United States Foreign Trade Policy (mimeographed), 2, 5, 6. Later references to the materials of this group will be abridged. The documents include additional background papers and also "Digests of Discussion" of the group's four meetings. All this material is to be found in Council on Foreign Relations *Archives*, Records of Groups, Vol. LXXXVII, 1960/61/62.

The chairman of this splendid group was Willard Thorp. Among its members were people with a close knowledge of trade policy and economics such as Percy Bidwell, Richard Gardner, Ben T. Moore, Alfred Neal, Gardner Patterson, Leroy Stinebower, Raymond Vernon, and Henry Wallich. There were businessmen from six or seven industries; Stanley Ruttenberg and Solomon Barkin came from the AFL-CIO; and government officials who took part included Jack Behrman, Emerson Brown, William Dale, Peter Jones, and Robert Schaetzel. The discussion leaders at the four meetings were Myer Rashish, Stanley Ruttenberg, Howard Petersen, and W. M. Blumenthal. Helena Stalson and I wrote papers for each meeting. Although I have limited citations to quotations, I have drawn on these records throughout this essay.

> We believe that the United States must form a trade partnership with the European Common Market and take the leadership in further expanding a free world economic community.[3]

All this was no news to the people forming the Kennedy administration. The task force on trade policy set up before the new president took office had recommended a series of steps to enlarge the president's powers to negotiate with other countries so as to further a "prime objective . . . to dispel the aura of fear which surrounds most of our moves in the field of trade policy."[4] The task force favored proposing such a revision when the existing legislation expired in the summer of 1962, but some people—including George Ball for a while—thought it would be best to wait until after the elections or until the negotiations about British entry into the Common Market had taken a decisive turn. That delay seemed dangerous to many veteran advocates of a liberal trade policy, but quite a few of them believed that a modest prolongation of existing authority was as much as it would be prudent to try to get at a time when a further increase of imports, especially from Europe, could be depicted as a threat to employment, the balance of payments, and even American competitiveness.

There was nothing crystal-clear in President Kennedy's record on trade policy. New England was not a natural home for trade liberalization, and his congressional record on these matters had been a bit spotty.[5] As chief executive, his first major action on trade had been to force the negotiation of an international agreement that restricted trade in cotton textiles and apparel. The traditional Democratic endorsement of low tariffs no longer carried much weight. There was a good bit of support for the idea of doing something to respond to the "challenge of the Common Market," but many people who used that cliché were

3. *A New Look at Foreign Economic Policy,* originally prepared for the Subcommittee on Foreign Economic Policy of the Joint Economic Committee, 87th Cong., 1st Sess., reprinted in *House Hearings,* 1485ff., with quotations from 1489, 1494.

4. At least, I think they thus concluded; I was on the task force and do not remember much opposition to those views, but the quotation is from what appears to be a penultimate draft on which members of the task force were asked to comment. George Ball's thank-you letter of 3 February 1961 said, "Distribution of copies . . . has been restricted by the President to a limited number of people within the Government"; both documents are in my files. At one point in his memoirs *The Past Has Another Pattern: Memoirs* (New York, 1982; hereinafter cited as *Memoirs*), 197, George Ball says, "I had already expounded my own approach toward trade liberalization in the task force report on foreign economic policy"; so the final version may have included some different views of his own. In this essay, later references to the task force pertain to the copy just described. Copies of the final text may now be found, but I elected not to search for them for this essay.

5. For example, Ball notes in his memoirs that in 1949 Kennedy had voted to recommit the extension of the Trade Agreements Act to the committee from which the bill had come (which might well have broken the continuity of American trade policy at a crucial time); see his *Memoirs,* 166. Representatives and senators often hedged on trade policy by the way they voted on various measures at different stages of a renewal, sometimes in the expectation that the measure they were nominally supporting would not pass and they could then rationalize what amounted to an opposite vote at the next stage.

thinking not of the incentives the United States could offer by opening its markets wider but of ways of pressing, or even threatening, the Europeans to get them to reduce their discrimination against American trade.

The story of how the choice between action and delay was made has been told by George Ball—the principal advocate and architect of the policy finally adopted—and by others. I have no reason to question this standard version. No doubt others who dig into the documents—or in some cases their memories—can give us a fuller account of who said what and why one adviser or politician carried the day on such and such a point rather than someone else. That will be interesting; but even if a story emerges that is different from the one we now accept, it can hardly eliminate the picture of the TEA as a watershed, which is our present subject. Perhaps the most interesting line of inquiry would be how it was that so major and potentially troublesome a piece of legislation should in the end have faced only modest opposition in the business and agricultural communities and passed through Congress with such substantial majorities. How much was persuasion, how much negotiation, and how much logrolling?[6]

In the face of uncertainty about the economy, conflicting advice on trade policy, and the wish to find good ways of dealing with the changing realities in Western Europe, President Kennedy finally decided on what Ernest Preeg, a Foreign Service officer deeply involved in the later tariff negotiations, called "the Ball approach for a bold new program."[7] More rhetoric went into the exposition of the TEA and more claims were made for it than had been heard for many years in the periodic renewal of the Trade Agreements Act of 1934, the basis of it all. The justification for the language and the claims, as for the place the TEA has taken in the conventional wisdom as a landmark, lies largely in some fairly specific innovations in the law and some less precise views of its potential as a tool of foreign policy.

### The Innovations and Where They Came From

The innovations were interconnected; each strengthened the case for the others; one led to another. Naturally, the decision to take a major step forward in trade policy instead of simply prolonging the status quo meant that something had to be done to expand the president's bargaining power, which meant, in turn, that he had to be given greater authority than before to reduce the tariff. The bill provided several different ways of doing these things; some expanded familiar

6. One interpretation worth examining was put forward by some specialists in communications soon after the event: "The strategy of Administration supporters . . . was one of quiet approaches to special interests, deals offered to split the opposition, and work with businessmen rather than the general public. Thus, in 1962 (in contrast to 1955) a rather more drastic reform got, if anything, rather less public attention." See Raymond A. Bauer, Ithiel de Sola Pool, and Lewis Anthony Dexter, *American Business and Public Policy: The Politics of Foreign Trade* (New York: 1963), 83.

7. Ernest Preeg, *Traders and Diplomats* (Washington, D.C., 1970), 45.

powers, but others were unprecedented. More was proposed than simply undoing the erosion of recent years. In explaining the situation to a largely German audience, a colleague of mine and I at the time were expressing a common view when we said, "If Congress gives the President the essentials of the powers he has asked for, the United States will be in the position of being able to take greater steps to improve trade relations than ever before."[8] Because of their scope it is reasonable to look at these measures collectively as innovative, although one has to remember that individually they simply modified existing powers.

For the next five years, the president was to have the power to cut tariffs to half their current levels, a great improvement over the limits that had been in effect for some years. Duties that were already 5 percent or below could be removed entirely; this was the first time the creation of a zero tariff by presidential action was made possible. A more important step was the elimination of "peril points." These were advance judgments made by the Tariff Commission of levels below which it would be dangerous to reduce duties; they had often been a serious check on bargaining. To increase the president's discretion in the use of the escape clause to increase duties or otherwise limit imports, new criteria were laid down for determining when domestic producers had suffered "injury"—a term of art—as the result of past tariff reductions.

All these measures liberalized established practices. The act also broke new ground in giving the president some powers that he could use only when making agreements with the European Community. Duties on farm products could be completely removed if the result was to maintain or expand the market for American agriculture in the Community. Tariffs or other restrictions could be taken off tropical agricultural or forestry products "not produced in significant quantities in the United States" if the Community made "comparable reductions." The most striking step was that "in carrying out any trade agreements" with the Community the president could eliminate duties on a very significant range of products: those in which the combined exports of the United States and the Community amounted to 80 percent of world exports, not counting exports of communist countries or trade within the Community. The Department of Commerce estimated that twenty-five groups of products met this test, including such important categories as vehicles, most kinds of machinery, and most chemical products.[9]

Taken together these changes seemed to make possible another major innovation in American trade policy—tariff cuts across the board. This was not spelled out in the law, but the administration had made clear its intention to move in

8. William Diebold and Helena Stalson, "Die Handelsvorschläge der Amerikanischen Regierung," *Europa Archiv,* Folge 10, 1962, p. 351 (retranslated).

9. The list appears as Annex A of the testimony of Secretary of Commerce Hodges, *House Hearings,* 97. Although many comments emphasize high technology, the list includes coal, furs, glass, paint, leather products, rubber goods, confectionery, and tobacco products.

that direction. The task force had recommended the same course. Cutting tariffs across the board was generally thought of as meaning that instead of negotiating specific reductions on each item, a country would undertake to reduce all its tariffs (probably with some exceptions) by a certain percentage. Although some people used different formulas, there was a good bit of support—in Europe and the United States—for the view put forward by Miriam Camps as early as 1957 that if the United States was going to undertake major negotiations with the Common Market the ability to cut tariffs across the board provided "the best hope of achieving meaningful reciprocity in tariff concessions."[10] In the Dillon Round the Community negotiators had made a proposal for an across-the-board cut of 20 percent which they must have known could not be carried out by the Americans. Camps told me that when she first made these arguments she was told by her friends in the government who had handled trade matters for years that she was "living in a dream world." That judgment was not unreasonable at the time and was in line with the opinion that only a modest renewal should be attempted. Perhaps the fact that the TEA was so much of a breakthrough supports the view of those who felt that dreams were coming true in the Kennedy years.

No doubt the form that each of these proposals for change took can be explained by a close look at its history, but the sources of the view that the president's powers should be substantially expanded are hardly obscure. They had been the stock-in-trade of advocates of trade liberalization for many years, and from time to time significant increases had been granted. There was, however, little if any history of proposed links between the president's powers to eliminate certain American tariffs and related action by the European Community. The purpose of the limited agricultural possibility is clear enough, and the proposal on tropical products was thought of as a kind of burden sharing. But the major measure—the potential of removing all tariffs on products of which the United States and the Community were the world's dominant suppliers—is another matter. I do not know where this idea came from. Was it part of Ball's original recommendation "for much broader legislation" after the president overruled his

10. Miriam Camps, "Trade Policy and American Leadership," Center of International Studies, Princeton University, 26 March 1957, Memorandum 12 (mimeographed), 22; more generally, 19–24 and the Appendix. There is a good review of the European experience with some comments on different uses of the term and an argument in favor of adopting the approach in the United States in Miriam Camps, "Implications for United States Trade Policy of the European Common Market and Free Trade Area," in *Foreign Trade Policy: Compendium of Papers on United States Foreign Trade Policy, Subcommittee on Foreign Trade Policy, Committee on Ways and Means* (Washington, D.C., 1957), 443–55. At about the same time, Raymond Vernon suggested that countries might agree to reduce the average of their tariffs by a uniform percentage but be left free to decide what cuts to make on individual rates in arriving at the average. Like Camps, Vernon referred to European experience and American negotiations with the Community, but his emphasis was on getting away from the restrictions imposed by peril points and the escape clause. See *Trade Policy in Crisis, Essays in International Finance*, No. 29 (Princeton, March 1958), 14–16.

idea of "postponing the legislation for a year until Britain had gained access"—or did it have a different source?[11]

What economic results were expected is not all clear. Tariff cuts could be less than 100 percent. The statistical groupings that were used to measure 80 percent included any number of tariff classifications so there was room to choose what would be cut. The United States and the Community had to agree on the powers to be used, but there was no suggestion that both parties had to take exactly the same measures. The old and open-ended question of what is reciprocity could not be avoided. Elimination of anything like all the tariffs that were eligible would create something of a free trade area for a major part of transatlantic trade, but under normal GATT rules and American policy its benefits would be extended to every country that received most-favored-nation treatment (as would not be the case if it were formally a free trade area).

It was clear that the people in the Kennedy administration saw the TEA as part of their foreign policy. One view was that putting the matter in these terms increased the chances of getting through Congress a measure that would otherwise be judged as just another renewal of the Trade Agreements Act and probably be cut down to the size of past renewals. Others saw the matter more broadly, as Raymond Vernon did when he wrote, "There is not much doubt that the principal contribution which an appropriate trade policy for the United States has to make in the 1960s is political rather than economic." Herter and Clayton said, "We assume that there will be no hot war. We are thinking in terms of winning the cold one."[12]

But just how were these gears to mesh? "Partnership" was the password, but what that meant was at least as vague as the text of the trade law.[13] To be sure, the trade bargains the law would make possible and the expansion of economic relations to which they would lead were likely to tighten the ties between the United States and the Community. That somewhat vague process, occasionally labeled as increasing "solidarity," was what some people had in mind, probably including Herter and Clayton, who preceded the sentence just quoted with the explanation, "In our experience we have found no international issue more divisive than economic issues." If the United States were powerless to carry on major negotiations, the piling up of problems would make matters worse. Any extensive use of the power provided by the TEA could give the Atlantic relation a major boost that was symbolic and material at the same time. Perhaps the chances of either side moving very far toward the elimination of tariffs was remote, but the simple drafting of the formula drew several geographical lines that expressed some of the foreign policy views of the Kennedy administration.

11. Ball, *Memoirs*, 197, 198.

12. Raymond Vernon, "A Trade Policy for the 1960s," *Foreign Affairs* (April 1961), 460; *House Hearings*, 1489.

13. There is an interesting account of the vagueness of the public discussion of these matters during the passage of the bill in John W. Evans, *The Kennedy Round in American Trade Policy* (Cambridge, Mass., 1971), 147–48, 158–59, and passim.

One line was inside Europe. Britain was not yet a member of the Community, but unless British exports were counted the total trade in most of the products would not reach the 80 percent mark. (Paul Douglas said only aircraft would be eligible.)[14] Was this just looking ahead or was it American pressure on the Community and the British to reach agreement? Suspecting that the latter was George Ball's purpose, Senator Paul Douglas and Representative Henry Reuss proposed counting Britain's exports even if it was outside the Community. Ball argued that this would encourage the view that the British could get access to Community markets (and the United States) without joining. The proposal passed the Senate but was dropped in conference.

Another question of foreign policy was whether eliminating tariffs on important segments of trade with the United States was compatible with further movement toward European integration. Over and over some people had said that the common tariff was a major ingredient of the cement that held the Community together. If discrimination against the United States was wiped out across a wide range of major products, would the Community be weakened? No one could seriously suspect that the Kennedy administration had any such aim, but the line between weakening the internal ties of the Community and making it "outward-looking" has often been blurred and rarely agreed on between insiders and outsiders, so American rationalizations might not sit well with Europeans. But some reduction in the degree of discrimination was a major American objective. No doubt the elimination of large parts of the American tariff was an attractive thought for Europeans, but I cannot recall that anyone really believed that the Community and the United States would actually free that much trade. After a visit to Europe to explain the TEA, Robert Schaetzel reported to the Council on Foreign Relations group that the Europeans had reacted with "awe and delight" to a move that they saw as "extraordinarily constructive" although they were not "starry-eyed about the prospects of such a program in Congress." There was some feeling that in the long run an Atlantic free trade area might undermine European integration, but for the time being most Europeans were more concerned with their own problems than with American trade policy. They did not, however, like the idea of simultaneous negotiations on these matters.[15]

Another geographical line in the TEA separated the countries that fell into the group making up the 80 percent level and all other countries. The bill provided for most-favored-nation treatment of all but communist countries, and there was no indication that the Kennedy administration had any intention of departing from what had been a basic element of American policy for decades. But would the Americans and the Europeans really be happy to apply zero rates to the products of countries that did not reciprocate? Like the other rich coun-

14. *Ibid.,* 155.
15. The quotations from Schaetzel are in the report of the second meeting of Council on Foreign Relations discussion group, 2 January 1962, p. 15.

tries, the United States had agreed that developing countries did not have to offer real reciprocity, but in practice that limited the concessions made to them. Committed to supporting growth, the Kennedy administration put its main emphasis on foreign aid and a new approach to international commodity agreements (one of the innovations outside the TEA that I shall look at later). How much was expected of the possible elimination of duties on noncompetitive tropical products is not clear; many were already on the free list. We can only wonder whether the treatment of competitive manufactured goods from the Third World—when they emerged—might or might not have been foreshadowed in the textile agreement, yet another innovation outside the TEA that was certainly not unconnected with it.

Different questions arose concerning two industrial nations in the free world omitted from the 80 percent formula: Japan and Canada. Japan was not yet as formidable an exporter of manufactured goods of high quality as it became, but it was on its way. Some of its exports to the United States were held down at one time or another by "voluntary" restraints.[16] In the early 1960s many Japanese thought they still lived in a developing country. Few Americans or Europeans would go that far, but they were also not ready to treat Japan as an equal (and not only because it had been an enemy). The United States had become Japan's supporter, and goad, in moving into the machinery of international cooperation, first GATT and, early in the Kennedy administration, the OECD. Europe had dragged its feet. The prospect of zero tariffs on a wide range of Japanese exports would almost certainly have been a guarantee that the arrangements made possible by the TEA would not come into effect unless other forms of trade restraint were put in place. As a measure of foreign policy, a distinction between relations with the European Community and Japan came naturally to Washington, but it is questionable how far ahead anyone had worked out the consequences of current practices—or had tried to.

Canada was another matter. It would be nice to know to what extent the omission of Canada from the formula was deliberate or an oversight. It was presumably too early to reflect the friction that was developing between the Kennedy and Diefenbaker governments, but it might have been a deliberate decision to avoid the trouble of having to pay attention to the concerns of a relatively small neighbor who was always worried about a wide range of issues (and often with reason). Or Washington's concentration on Europe might have led to an oversight of the sort Canadians have often come to expect—but resent. I was involved at the time, and later, in a series of discussions about the place of the two countries in the world economy and can report that well-informed and

16. These bilateral arrangements had no basis in American trade law, and the task force was reflecting a view widely held among liberal traders when it said that they should be ended and a multilateral agreement worked out in GATT to ease the frictions that had frequently accompanied the rapid expansion of Japanese exports. This was before the United States initiated the drive for a multilateral textile agreement.

thoughtful Canadian officials, former officials, academics, and businessmen were much more disturbed by the omission than was ever publicly apparent, so far as I am aware. I think the worry came mainly from a feeling that there had been a change of attitude in Washington, where informing and consulting Ottawa on trade matters had been almost second nature since the war. There was also some concern about the zero list, which omitted Canada's main exports but would have included them if Canadian exports to the United States had been counted. In the judgment of very well-informed Canadians, an exchange of cuts of 50 percent with the United States would create difficulties for their country whereas reciprocal cuts to zero on a number of products would be helpful although they would force some changes in the structure of Canadian production.[17] Although the TEA remained unchanged, within a few years an impending trade dispute led the two countries to establish relatively free trade between themselves in automobiles and parts.

The sharp geographical focus introduced by the TEA, naming names of partners whose assent was required before presidential powers could be used, was something new. But the substance of the matter—that reductions of American tariffs depended on comparable action by certain other countries—was old. Under the original Trade Agreements Act of 1934 the use of the powers Congress delegated to the president depended on the negotiation of satisfactory bilateral agreements; the size of the tariff cuts and the products affected by these agreements depended on the importance, interests, and willingness of each partner. The American proposal to create organizations for the multilateral reduction of trade barriers after the war—the International Trade Organization (ITO) and GATT—was worked out in conjunction with the British, who were then seen as the essential partner if there was to be effective cooperation. The subsequent reduction of tariffs in the series of GATT rounds again depended on who took part: what was agreed to multilaterally was largely the result of bilateral bargaining. The expected performance of the European Community as a single trading unit would have made it—even without the TEA's special provisions—the key partner with whom an agreement was essential if there were to be extensive reductions of American barriers. But at no time before 1962 were these partners named in the trade law, and somehow doing that underlined the link the TEA was said to make between trade policy and foreign policy in a new way.[18]

17. A rationale for this view—a forerunner of one of the sophisticated lines of thought that led to the Canadian-American Free Trade Area Agreement—is explained, along with other issues, in *North American Trade Policy for the Nineteen Sixties: Report on a Two-Year Study Sponsored by the Canadian Institute of International Affairs and the World Peace Foundation* (Boston and Toronto, May 1962). In a shorter mimeographed statement, the unofficial participants of both nationalities recommended that the United States "give serious consideration to broadening the range of commodities which are eligible for tariff elimination and to raising with Canada the question of participation in the dominant supplier category."

18. The link had of course existed before. In the 1930s the United States made no trade agreements with Germany or Japan. The postwar agreement on trade principles at the time of the British

Any vigorous use of the president's new powers could substantially reduce the remaining elements of protection in American tariffs and other trade barriers. It would be increasingly difficult to defend the old claim that big tariff reductions could be made without injuring domestic producers. The administration faced this issue by including in the new legislation an innovation that in the past had been found politically unacceptable by most people. This was to make possible "adjustment assistance" from the federal government for workers who lost their jobs, companies that might otherwise go out of business, and communities that lost production and income because of increased imports resulting from reductions in tariffs or other trade barriers.

The idea was not new. This rather dramatic step had an intellectual as well as a political history. The earliest proposals I know of were made by Eugene Staley in 1944 and 1945 in papers of the Economic and Financial Group of the War and Peace Studies of the Council on Foreign Relations and for the International Labor Organization (ILO). After the war the idea found supporters in the United States (I was one), but there were other trade liberalizers—including Clair Wilcox—who did not see much merit in it. In practice, American tariffs came down, imports increased, and great adjustments took place in an expanding economy with little clamor for public support (except for tariffs).

Occasional public suggestions for adopting adjustment assistance came to nothing until 1954, when David McDonald, the president of the United Steel Workers, attached a fairly concrete proposal to the report of the Randall Commission, appointed by President Eisenhower to review foreign economic policy. It was not endorsed by the other members of the commission, but from then on Congress was never without one or more bills on the subject. One of the first was introduced by Senator John F. Kennedy. None passed.

Naturally enough, labor interest in the idea continued and economists for the AFL-CIO worked out plans in some detail. Sometimes they went so far as to present adjustment assistance as an alternative to the use of the escape clause. Support grew among independent economists and endorsement—at least in principle—became a standard feature of proposals for strengthening and reforming trade policy. The attractions of the idea lay in facilitating change, spreading its burdens, and gaining support for trade liberalization (though not from people who wanted protection). Businessmen mostly resisted the proposal, partly for the reasons they usually object to government intervention and partly because they thought that in the end the government would be providing subsidies to prop up inefficient businesses. Many supporters of adjustment assistance

---

loan was part of a larger pattern of American-British cooperation. After 1948 the denial of MFN to the USSR and other communist countries—and at certain times not to Poland and Yugoslavia—was a political matter. Presumably the interest of other countries in signing up with the Americans was often a reflection of foreign policy; that seems to be generally accepted with regard to the British when they made a bilateral trade agreement with the United States in 1938. In contrast, the difficulties the British put up in drafting Article VII of the lend-lease agreement reflected a dispute within the Conservative party about how the dominions should be treated in trade matters.

wanted it limited to workers. Almost everyone agreed that great care must be taken about eligibility and administration.[19]

Conventional wisdom, which so often oversimplifies the past, characterizes the inclusion of adjustment assistance in the TEA as a concession (or even a "bribe") to organized labor. No doubt the politics of getting labor support for the bill played an important part, and it would be helpful if someone would spell out this process in some detail, and frankly. But that was not the whole story. For the reasons already touched on, the idea had wider support, and if the president's new powers were used to make deep tariff cuts, especially if they were across the board, it would be logical to have means of helping workers prepare themselves for new jobs and, if possible, firms to become more competitive. Most people who supported the idea were aware of the difficulties of carrying it out well, and there was a good bit of skepticism as to how effective it would be. Businessmen continued to be opposed but not enough to withdraw their support for the TEA. Members of Congress worried about wasteful spending. The combination of these doubts and worries led to the conditions for eligibility for aid and the safeguards in the procedures being so tightly drawn that the provisions proved unusable until sometime in the Nixon administration when looser interpretations took over.

The last of the major innovations was initiated by Congress instead of the executive: the creation of the special representative for trade negotiations (now U.S. trade representative) to head the work flowing from the new law. Although he would not have proposed it himself, the president agreed that the change was "an acceptable price to pay for the broad new negotiating authority he was seeking."[20] There were explanations of the need to coordinate the work of different parts of the government which were valid enough, but the main motive was plain: to remove the State Department from the leading position it had had in trade policy in the past. Having delegated a lot of power, Congress wanted to assure itself that in future negotiations American economic interests were truly represented and that bargaining was tough and not diluted by consideration for the interests of other countries that might be of concern to the State Department. It was an old suspicion, and a fairly recent expression of it was undoubtedly in people's minds. In 1948, when Congress agreed to support the Marshall Plan, it made sure that the State Department did not control the administration of the funds by creating the Economic Cooperation Administration. That body, it made clear, was to be headed by a person of the type called "hardheaded,"

19. To save space I have written this account of adjustment assistance without references or details. Fuller versions, with references, can be found in Background Paper no. 2 that Helena Stalson and I wrote for the Council on Foreign Relations group, the digest of the discussion at that and other meetings of the group, and my later book *The United States and the Industrial World* (New York, 1972), 149–66.

20. I. M. Destler, *American Trade Politics,* 2d ed. (Washington, D.C., 1992), 19. Destler tells about the role of key individuals in this process. In other parts of his valuable book he also gives detailed accounts of matters dealt with more generally in this essay.

preferably a businessman. The description nicely fitted Paul Hoffman. In a related move, the TEA also provided for the inclusion of senators and representatives in delegations to international trade negotiations.

These innovations justified the claim that the TEA equipped the government with the means of carrying out a trade policy of much greater scope than any in the past. Instead of the near exhaustion of the president's power to cut duties and rather tight restrictions on the use of that power if it threatened to "injure" even rather small segments of the American economy, the executive now had the power to make deep and wide reductions in American tariffs, to acknowledge that some injury to some companies, workers, and localities might result, and to give assistance to people who needed it to adjust to the new circumstances. It was no longer necessary to say that gains to the whole economy (or measures that were useful in foreign policy) must be forgone to try to protect the status quo in certain parts of the country (often unsuccessfully). The same set of measures announced the intention—and ability—of the United States to try to strike bargains with the European Community that would not only reduce barriers to American exports but substantially extend the liberalization of trade in the world economy.

The new powers were given to the president by healthy majorities of both houses of Congress, in an election year, after hearings that filled forty-two hundred pages in which an impressive array of spokespersons from business, labor, and farming had endorsed the effort. It certainly looked as if the Kennedy administration had been right to choose the bold course. Even the title of the law was an innovation. You did not have to be Pollyanna to think that it meant something that what used to be a simple "extension" of the Trade Agreements Act of 1934, itself merely a two- or three-page amendment of the generally excoriated Hawley-Smoot Act of 1931, was now called the Trade Expansion Act.

## Other Innovations

The Kennedy administration made some other innovations in trade policy that were not in the TEA but were related to it, in some cases in very important ways.

One of these was the new approach to commodity agreements. Its "first objective," according to the task force on trade, was for the new administration "to get itself dissociated from the past Administration's position of doctrinaire resistance to such arrangements." But the limits, risks, and complexities of achieving very much through agreements about specific commodities or more general provisions for financial compensation to raw-material-producing countries when their exports fell were widely recognized. They open so many questions that the subject has to be set aside here except to note that the agreement on cotton textiles and apparel was also, in its way, a commodity agreement but not what either the developing countries or the Kennedy administration had in mind when they used the term.

249

We cannot, however, set that agreement aside. Without it there might not have been a TEA—or at best a much more limited one or even one that imposed restrictions. At least, that was generally believed at the time. It was not, however, the first reason for negotiating the textile agreement, a process that was started before the decision was made to go for a large rather than small trade bill. The president felt he had to carry out a campaign pledge, and the question in the new executive branch was how far did he have to go? For several reasons—not least to avoid violating GATT—the case was strong for seeking an international agreement instead of acting unilaterally. Nevertheless, the possibility of acting unilaterally on security grounds was kept alive and exercised some pressure on other countries.

The animus was protectionist, but there was some hope of reaching a textile agreement that would permit the growth of production and exports in developing countries without letting the world move farther into the maelstrom where the choice for the old producing centers was always between trying to restrict imports or letting segments of industry succumb to competition attended by a good bit of unemployment. Traces of this approach can be found in the agreement, notably the required annual percentage increases in trade and the supposed limited duration of the agreement. After accompanying George Ball on his first exploratory trip to Europe on the textile matter, I was asked to appraise the results and what might be done next and also to look back over the conversations. I could say with all honesty:

> Our statements there were consistent and clear-cut. They called for an agreement that would provide some regulation and restraint of trade over a transitional period during which increasing quantities of cheap cotton goods would be taken by the advanced countries so that at the end of the period trade in cotton textiles would be freer than it is now and than it would probably have been in the absence of this kind of agreement.[21]

Nevertheless, a preamble that would have made adjustment one of the main purposes of the agreement (drafted, I believe, by Raymond Vernon) was left in the files.

On his trip, Ball asked some of the European countries to increase their imports of cotton textiles. (The French and Italians were very restrictive; the British and Germans were undertaking more adaptation.) He also wanted them to come to an international conference to formulate an agreement. That is about all they were willing to do. With his usual energy and acumen, Eric Wyndham

21. William Diebold, Jr., "Memorandum on a Multilateral Textile Agreement," 6 June 1961, typescript, 3. This is under cover of a letter of the same date to J. Robert Schaetzel in my files. When Ball asked me to accompany him as a consultant, I reminded him that I knew next to nothing about the textile industry. "But you know about trade policy and you know how to say no," he replied. Perhaps I said no too often, but there was never any question but that my stay was to be short.

White, the secretary-general of GATT, had put his staff to work on a number of problems and had thought a good bit about the diplomacy of the issue. Ball agreed that it would be best to lodge the agreement in GATT and have the text negotiated with the exporting countries instead of working it out among the Atlantic countries—perhaps in the OECD—and presenting it to the producers as more or less a fait accompli. So perhaps one can say that an initial effort to conduct a broad-gauged Atlantic economic diplomacy gave way to the recognition of the global economy.

In the end, this more "cooperative" approach did not help much. Ball recalled in his memoirs, "I felt chagrined that I had persuaded the developing countries to go along on the promise of orderly growth." The whole episode of the textile agreement "caused me more personal anguish than any other task I undertook during my total of twelve years in different branches of the Government."[22] He did succeed in limiting the agreement to cotton textiles in spite of the cogent arguments for including artificial fibers as was done some years later in the Nixon administration when a more sweeping campaign promise led to a clumsier diplomacy that took longer and did more damage to American relations (especially with Japan) than the Kennedy effort. More important to our present concerns, the widespread textile industry and its many friends in Congress were kept from opposing the TEA—how explicitly and by what means I do not know.[23]

### Might-Have-Beens

As rich in innovations as its approach to trade policy was, the Kennedy administration did not do all it might have done. The most obvious gap was the area where the inadequacy of American trade policy had long been most clearly recognized—agriculture. The incompatibility of American farm policy and American trade policy had been recognized and explained with great clarity right after the end of the war.[24] Although frequent skirmishing and occasional pitched battles with the Department of Agriculture were the order of the day, no one in the State Department had any great hopes of altering either the emphasis on price supports—which caused the most trouble—or the priority given to domestic

22. Ball, *Memoirs*, 193, 188.

23. A brief but circumstantial account of the part played in this process by the American Cotton Manufacturers Institute is given in Bauer, Pool, and Dexter, *American Business*, 359–62. It would be interesting to know more about this and how much of the whole story it is.

24. Two books that came out almost simultaneously told the story very well: D. Gale Johnson, *Trade and Agriculture: A Study of Inconsistent Policies* (New York, 1950), and C. Addison Hickman, *Our Farm Program and Foreign Trade: A Conflict of National Policies* (New York, 1949). Johnson's book had its origins in a report he wrote several years before as a consultant to the State Department. Hickman's was backed up by discussions and critical readings by the committee of the Council on Foreign Relations Des Moines and benefited from the general guidance of Percy W. Bidwell, the council's director of studies in New York.

policy when there was a clash.[25] GATT had a loophole on the subject which was enlarged and made more explicit by a waiver granted to the United States. Most other industrial countries had the same contradictions in their policies, but for most European countries imports could be restricted under the balance-of-payments exceptions. Britain had an income support system that presented fewer difficulties but was almost certainly going to be abandoned as a condition of British entry into the Common Market. The Community's efforts to formulate a common agricultural policy would clearly perpetuate the contradiction. Sometime along the line I said to Robert Schaetzel: "It is clear that they will only be able to agree on something that will do some damage to American interests. Even if you accept the idea that a CAP is essential can we not find a way to keep the results from being as bad as they might be?" I have no doubt there was much sweet reason in what American officials said to their European colleagues, but the situation was thought to be delicate and there were bounds to what the Americans were willing to do as they accepted the argument that a common agricultural policy was essential to the integration of the Community. (It was also said that a CAP would bring about monetary unification as the only way of dealing with price discrepancies among countries.)

If one assumed that the general farm policy maintained by the United States and most other industrial countries could not be radically altered, it made little sense to keep on negotiating only about the trade barriers imposed at the borders. They were only epiphenomena, the shadows on the wall cast by the internal policies. They were logically inescapable. What one had to negotiate about were the elements of farm policy itself—support prices, production controls, or their absence—and at least some of the many farm subsidies would have to become the objects of international discussions. Students of the issues had realized this for some time, but the obstacles in the way of such a change were obvious. I do not know whether there was any serious discussion of this possibility in the drafting of the TEA, but if the idea was raised, it is very likely it was quickly dismissed as politically impossible, and that was probably correct.

Nothing more was done when in a few years' time the Kennedy administration adopted some changes in farm policy that at least reduced the conflicts with trade policy while an increase in the importance of exports gave the American farm economy a larger stake in international arrangements. Meanwhile, the CAP showed itself to be substantially more protective than the national policies that had preceded it and bound to stimulate production in the Community.

During the Kennedy Round, agriculture was, as could be expected, a source

25. I once made a try in an experimental and lighthearted vein when I was in the Commercial Policy Division of the State Department—the summer of 1946, I think. For some reason, section 22 of the Agricultural Adjustment Act was quoted in a memorandum on which I had to work. As all of us knew only too well, it said that when a domestic farm program was incompatible with a foreign trade measure, the latter had to be changed. It was easy to reverse the wording. As I expected, the reform did not get very far above my level and was certainly never near getting out of the department.

of great difficulty. Partly that was because the United States for the most part kept to the traditional position of asking for the same reductions of tariffs and other trade barriers that were negotiated for other products. Partly it was because the Community saw almost every American demand as an effort to undermine the CAP. The main novel element in the negotiations was a Community proposal to reach an agreement limiting the total amount of subsidies given to agriculture and, less clearly, to set a ceiling on the degree of self-sufficiency that would be sought. American officials had made some statements suggesting that they were willing to "deal with the implications of domestic policies."[26] But they rejected the Community's initiative, probably because as put forward it would have set levels of prices and domestic production not yet achieved and so would have made the CAP more protectionist than it already seemed to be (but not more than it became, I think).

Another possible innovation, but one even less likely to have been considered in drafting the TEA, concerned nontariff barriers (NTB). Some were covered by existing agreements such as quotas and exchange controls that governments were committed to drop once their balances of payments were in order. Others were more obscure and often complex but had long been recognized by people conversant with trade issues.[27] Some were largely matters of customs administration, but others were created by a wide variety of domestic measures. Some were designed primarily to limit imports while others restricted trade almost accidentally, or at least as a by-product of the pursuit of some reasonable domestic objective. Negotiations about these matters were bound to be more difficult and complex than the traditional ones that concerned only the reduction of barriers imposed at borders, such as tariffs. For the United States there was a special problem: Congress's delegation to the president of powers to negotiate trade agreements did not extend to most NTBs, nor was it likely that any politically acceptable formula could be found that would cover all NTBs and permit negotiations with foreign countries to alter so many laws and administrative practices without further attention from Congress.

In 1962 the full scale of the NTB problem was not widely appreciated so it is hardly surprising that no special arrangements seemed necessary when drafting the TEA. Even so, when he looked back, John Evans, a veteran American negotiator, thought "it might even then have been apparent that the legislation was wanting."[28] In any case, the problem came up. One of the bitterest disputes in the Kennedy Round concerned the use of the American selling price as the basis

---

26. W. M. Blumenthal, "The Kennedy Round," *Department of State Bulletin*, 26 April 1965, p. 634. The whole subject is dealt with more fully in William Diebold, *The United States and the Industrial World* (New York, 1972), 276–300.

27. A pioneering study had appeared before the war: Percy W. Bidwell, *The Invisible Tariff* (New York, 1939).

28. John W. Evans, *U.S. Trade Policy: New Legislation of the Next Round* (New York, 1967), 9. The task force had proposed getting rid of the American Selling Price as part of reclassification of the tariff but said it could be postponed until after the passage of the main trade legislation.

for levying duties on a number of products, mostly chemicals. When the American negotiators finally agreed it should be eliminated, they had no power to do so and had to go to Congress for special action. It was denied, so some European tariff reductions were withheld from the United States. Congress also would not approve American adherence to the antidumping code negotiated in Geneva. These difficulties helped raise awareness of the NTB problem for the future, but they also showed that although the TEA might be "wholly new" it was not new enough.

### What the Innovations Led To

One can speculate about what might have been done if some innovations that might have been thought of had been adopted. But there are actual consequences to be looked at in the effects of the innovations that were adopted and made the TEA a watershed in American trade policy.

The place to look for evidence is in the Kennedy Round, which lasted from January 1963 to June 1967 and might well have gone on much longer if the president's powers to negotiate had not been about to expire. The negotiations were difficult and often very slow. In the end, the result was in most respects a great success that looks more remarkable—and more exceptional—in hindsight and as the years pass. Tariffs were reduced to lower levels than they had been in living memory. Some other useful arrangements were made. The United States played a major part in this reduction, both in its bargaining and in what it did with its own barriers. The enlarged powers that the TEA gave the president made this possible.

It was not, however, the new kinds of powers that contributed most to this result. De Gaulle's veto of British entry to the Community had in effect nullified the 80 percent provision. Agriculture was too troublesome in various ways for the United States and the Community to think seriously of removing their tariffs in special bargains. I am not aware of any concerted action by the United States and the Community to remove duties on tropical products. If the power to move goods with low tariffs to the free list was used at all, it was used very sparingly.

One of the longest, hardest pieces of the negotiation came early. It concerned the rules to govern the bargaining, which was to an important degree a matter of what could be done across the board. The results were not at all what American advocates of that course had expected. The trouble lay in part with the exceptions everyone wanted to make. (All agricultural tariffs were exempted, each country had some special cases, and withholding by one led others to take matching action.) Another problem lay in the difficulty of getting any agreement on what constituted reciprocity. Closely connected was the contention of the Community and some others that equal percentage cuts were not equal in their effect if one country had many higher tariff rates than another. When bargaining concentrated on specific industries, it was sometimes more successful. Although cutting across the board in the Kennedy Round did not have the sweeping effect many Americans had been led to expect, Ernest Preeg's efforts to measure the results led him to conclude that "linear tariff cuts . . . did, in fact, constitute the bulk of the final agreement." But John Evans commented afterward that although the Kennedy Round "is still referred to, with some reason, as 'linear' . . . the truth is that traditional techniques have returned to dominate major areas of what had been conceived as a virtually automatic operation." In a similar vein, but emphasizing a different aspect, a later study concludes that "what was a multilateral negotiation in name became a large, complicated series of bilateral (or plurilateral) negotiations in fact."[29]

Because the main tariff cuts made in the Kennedy Round applied to manufactured products, their immediate value for the developing countries was limited. There was no emphasis on products of special interest to them. Stressing its new approach to commodity agreements—its innovation outside the TEA—the Kennedy administration worked out a coffee agreement and explored possibilities in cocoa, tin, and some other products. Nothing of great importance followed. All these measures came nowhere near satisfying the demands of the less developed countries (LDCs). By then the United Nations Conference in Trade and Development had come into existence and the LDCs were calling for preferential treatment, not simply the reduction of duties (a strategic mistake, as some of us pointed out at the time). Disappointment caused them to undervalue the concessions they actually received and helped fuel a period of dissatisfaction with GATT that led them to emphasize other forums that mostly proved unfruitful.

No doubt the elimination of peril points enhanced the flexibility of American bargaining in the Kennedy Round. In the years that followed, the stricter tests of "injury" helped reduce use of the escape clause. But the creation of adjustment assistance was no help in these matters. It was soon easy for its supporters to see that "that attractive piece of social engineering has had its wheels gummed up so that we do not really know what can be accomplished by it—and the record of the Kennedy Round shows that the prospect was not good enough to encourage" serious efforts to deal with hard cases.[30] In the Canadian-American Automotive Agreement of 1965 adjustment assistance was provided on somewhat easier terms, but there was not much call for it. The U.S. trade law was somewhat liberalized in 1974. The sensible suggestion that adjustment assistance might be given no matter what the source of disturbance instead of limiting it

29. The three quotations come, in order, from Preeg, *Traders and Diplomats,* 266; Evans, *U.S. Trade Policy,* 22; and Gilbert R. Winham, *International Trade and the Tokyo Round Negotiations* (Princeton, 1986), 65. A play-by-play account of the way the original idea of across-the-board negotiations was eroded is in Evans, *Kennedy Round,* 184–202.

30. William Diebold, Jr., statement, in *A Foreign Economic Policy for the 1970's: Hearings Before the Subcommittee on Foreign Economic Policy of the Joint Economic Committee,* Part 2, *Trade Policy Toward Developed Countries,* 91st Cong., 2d Sess., 17 March 1970 (Washington, D.C., 1970), 234–45.

to imports never made much headway. In the 1980s the rather stupid and futile national debate about "industrial policy" confused the issue. Now adjustment assistance has taken on what seems to be greater political importance than ever before in connection with the free trade area with Mexico. How much disappointment about adjustment assistance—which I have occasionally heard labor people call a "betrayal"—actually contributed to the shift in the center of gravity of the labor movement from support for a liberal trade policy to opposition is hard to say.

The idea of a special trade representative worked and has, indeed, remained alive to this day. One hears no more of the argument that it was created only for the Kennedy Round and should have been dissolved afterward. About once in each administration there has been a proposal for a new trade department or a new coordinating mechanism in the White House, either of which was planned to absorb the trade representative, but it survives. (The latest is a call for a broader NSC.) By now the trade representative shares with the State Department the accusation of being too soft on foreigners. Whether it played the part originally intended of making the results of the Kennedy Round more acceptable because the bargaining was tougher is hard to say. More than once Michael Blumenthal was accused by people in Congress or industry of being a softie while at the same time Europeans expressed shock and surprise at what they said was not the kind of behavior they expected from an American negotiator. Certainly Christian Herter's presence in the top job helped preserve some of the broadness of support that had gone into the passage of the TEA in the first place.

The textile agreement lasted and grew. Its multilateral character and its lodgment in GATT did not keep its main activities from being bilateral and accompanied by some harsh treatment by rich buyers of poorer producers. It was sometimes leaky and did not prevent a substantial flow of trade or big shifts in the structure of production. (It even stimulated some.) One would not describe the changes as particularly orderly. Whatever legitimation the GATT connection provided did not keep the United States and other governments from placing their later restrictive arrangements in other industries—such as steel, automobiles, and for a while petrochemicals—completely outside the law. Even if the textile agreement should be brought to an end in the Uruguay Round, it stands as a forerunner of the ventures in mismanaged trade that have followed. These are part of a more extensive deterioration of the liberal multilateral trading system that has been going on more markedly since sometime in the 1970s.[31]

To sum up, it appears that the TEA made it possible for the president to bargain more effectively than, probably, at any time since the beginning of the process in 1934. Its tightening of the trade laws also provided some check to protectionist moves. These gains came largely from the measures that improved

31. The scope and character of this deterioration, to which many factors and practices have contributed, are explained in Miriam Camps and William Diebold, *The New Multilateralism: Can the World Trading System be Saved?* (1983; rev. ed. New York, 1986).

existing provisions in the law. The two most striking innovations in the law—adjustment assistance and the zero power linked to agreements with the Community—had little or no effect. Of the two outside innovations, the "fresh approach" to commodity agreements intended to help LDCs turned out to be a step along the wrong road. The other, the textile agreement, continued to have a marked effect on international trade and undoubtedly contributed to the erosion of liberalism in the system—but if it was the sine qua non of the TEA, how could one strike a balance?

## Judgments in Three Perspectives

So far as American relations with Europe are concerned, a few things about the TEA are clear. It made it possible for the United States to negotiate seriously with the Community in economic matters, which it had lost the power to do. That, in turn, made possible the Kennedy Round in which the crucial bargains were between the United States and the Community.[32] The TEA helped strengthen transatlantic economic links, though the American direct investment stimulated by the formation of the Common Market probably did more. The TEA did not change the character of European-American trade as it would have done if it had created tariff-free trade in major products. But it did not keep the CAP from heavily influencing some changes in that trade, or, needless to say, did it improve the ability of the United States and the Community to deal with their problems in agricultural trade. Kennedy and Adenauer had to argue about chickens. For George Bush and Helmut Kohl, corn gluten rose to a high level.

The Kennedy Round also demonstrated that the Community could engage in extensive multilateral trade negotiations that reduced barriers without damaging its essence and probably with considerable economic benefit. It also showed that on at least some issues the Community could deal with the rest of the world as a unit—though not without strenuous efforts on its part and considerable trouble for foreigners. It does not, however, appear that the experience of the Kennedy Round stimulated the European interest in multilateral trade negotiations—judging by the steps leading up to the Tokyo and especially the Uruguay Rounds.

Can one go beyond these simple observations to say that the TEA and the Kennedy Round led to improved American relations with Europe? Ernest Preeg, who was a participant in the Kennedy Round, argues for a positive answer: "The Kennedy Round negotiation, held during a period of strain within the Atlantic community, was for much of this time the only active undertaking

---

32. This remained true of the Tokyo Round, according to its closest student: "Much of the Tokyo Round consisted of an interaction between the two preponderant parties at the negotiation: the European Community and the United States" (Winham, *International Trade*, 386). This is largely, I think, because each of them handled its relations with Japan in a mostly bilateral fashion.

to strengthen ties among these nations. . . . Successful negotiation in the trade sector, though only one of the ties among members of the Atlantic community, played a vital role in relieving the general tension and misgivings of that period."[33] This conclusion seems debatable to me, but even if it is true, it is hard to discern the "partnership" that Kennedy, Ball, Clayton, and Herter were talking about. Obviously a failure of the Kennedy Round—or the lack of an American ability to negotiate at all—would have been worse. But I must leave it to others to say if there is anything to be added on the credit side. Was it a great success for American foreign policy?

In the second perspective, I am inclined to give the TEA a fairly high place in a list of accomplishments of the Kennedy administration. It is hard to think of the TEA as "the unifying intellectual principle of the New Frontier," as Joseph Kraft seems to have called it. But was Arthur Schlesinger right to call it, at the time, "a misdirection of the Administration's limited political resources" because more could be done about "getting America moving again" by domestic measures?[34] It is not the only case, in the Kennedy administration and some others, in which the language outran the accomplishment, but the accomplishment was substantial and much of it lasted a reasonably long time. It was an example of the bold choice paying off in the face of uncertainty and doubt, at least so far as trade policy was concerned.

To be sure, the textile agreement was a pretty high price to pay for liberalization in other fields—and especially for the example and argument it gave to other countries. The price is still being paid, but if something like it was inescapable, fairly good use was made of it in clearing the way for the passage of the TEA. It is attractive to speculate about what might have been accomplished if the idea of a different kind of arrangement had won the day, but there is no escaping the fact that what was actually done put no feather in the Kennedy cap, as George Bell has shown.

The place of the TEA in the history of American trade policy is significant, but in a rather different way from what its authors expected. One can say it is a landmark, provided one remembers that landmarks come in different shapes and sizes. By permitting the reduction of American tariffs to very low levels and making possible the Kennedy Round, it marked a major turn away from a course that was otherwise coming close to stopping the process of American trade liberalization altogether. And that would have been tantamount to setting back the liberalization of the global trading system as well. Instead, the Kennedy Round was an important step in the building of a multilateral trading system that brought about the reduction of tariffs and other trade barriers. The TEA was also significant because it embodied the principle that import barriers could be cut even if the result was "injury" to some domestic producers—but whether the

---

33. Preeg, *Traders and Diplomats*, 261.
34. Arthur M. Schlesinger, Jr., *A Thousand Days: John F. Kennedy in the White House* (Boston, 1965), 847. The words I have taken to be Kraft's are on the same page.

acceptance of that idea has lasted, or was ever very deep, is not so clear. Along the same line, the TEA must surely be given landmark status for introducing the principle of adjustment assistance even though not so much has come of it.

If, however, one chooses to call the TEA a watershed, the picture is different. Adjustment assistance, zero tariffs, and close cooperation with the European Community in other drastic reductions of trade barriers and, to a considerable degree, the idea of across-the-board cuts are the dry sides referred to in the title of this essay. The stream that flowed down the far side of the watershed went in a different direction from the old one and with refreshed force. It was, however, mainly the same kind of watercourse as the old one, the selective reduction of American trade barriers by fairly familiar means. The results of the TEA were substantial—for a while—but so were those of the initial effort of 1934 and the turn from bilateral to multilateral methods in 1945.[35] But it was a familiar kind of watercourse and as time passed the flow has not continued to increase in force, depth, or breadth. The stream has not run dry, but it has become narrower, stonier, and twistier. Its present direction is far from clear.

As we look back, the international trade relations of the last twenty years give the TEA a still different shape (another characteristic of mountainous terrain). We have to admire and applaud the spirit and effort that went into it, which had not been seen except in 1934 and 1945 and have been lacking ever since the 1960s. The Tokyo Round had some good points and some weaknesses; governments have added to the latter by not making good use of the machinery they created for dealing with nontariff barriers. The method adopted by the United States to modernize some of its conduct of trade policy and overcome some of its political and constitutional problems—the fast-track procedure and congressional consultation—works reasonably well in the right hands and favorable circumstances but is, in a larger sense, part of the process by which Congress has been limiting the authority and flexibility of the executive in a variety of ways and taking back the negotiating power it once gave the president. That and a privatization of trade policy in the ways the fair trade laws can be used have done much to heighten the restrictive and troublemaking elements in American trade policy. Real economic difficulties and a failure to find constructive ways of bringing about structural adjustments have played their part as well. Few other countries have done better; they simply have different methods and different starting places. Collectively the major trading countries—and weaker ones as well—have done much to undermine the system of multilateral trade cooperation they built up in the first twenty-five years after the war.[36] In this perspective the TEA may come to mark the end of an era.

35. These things are hard to measure, and the measurements can be hard to evaluate, but I have been struck by John Evans's calculation that the bilateral agreements negotiated between 1934 and 1945, "measured solely by the statistical results . . . [,] went further toward correcting the excesses of the Smoot-Hawley Tariff than did even the most far-reaching of the subsequent multilateral negotiations until the Kennedy Round" (*Kennedy Round*, 7).

36. The developments in American trade policy that are so loosely sketched here are excellently

Metaphors may not be the best way to analyze trade policy, but they help provide beginnings and ends to essays. Whatever else may be said about the TEA, it put a stop to the nearly fatal decline of American trade policy and prolonged and to some degree enhanced a course of action unprecedented in the history of the republic which had linked one of the responses to the Depression with American international leadership in the postwar period and played a substantial part in building a new world economy. The TEA was made possible by a measure that moved in the opposite direction—the textile agreement—and after ten years or so its accomplishments began to be undermined by contradictory measures in other parts of the field. Once again it may be possible to catch the main point by looking back as well as forward. Different as 1992 is from 1962, some needs persist that do not look very different from the way they did in 1967. As I wrote at that time: "The Trade Expansion Act made major innovations in United States foreign trade policy. The Kennedy Round introduced some unprecedented features into international negotiations. Neither worked quite as it was expected to but both achieved important successes. Neither can be adopted unchanged as a model for dealing with the next set of problems we face."[37]

---

described and analyzed by Destler, *American Trade Politics.* So far as the international trading system is concerned, I have no reason to think that the directions traced in Camps and Diebold, *New Multi-lateralism,* have been greatly altered. It is hard to believe that the end of the Uruguay Round will bring more than a modest degree of correction.

37. William Diebold, Jr., "Trade Negotiating Issues and Policies in Foreign Trade," in *Compendium of Statements Submitted to the Subcommittee on Foreign Economic Policy of the Joint Economic Committee* (Washington, D.C., 1967), 3.

# Part Four

*Kennedy and the European Community*

# 14

## George Ball and the Europeanists in the State Department, 1961–1963

### David L. DiLeo

~

In one of his first official acts as under secretary of state for economic affairs, George W. Ball cautioned the new Kennedy administration about what he considered to be a subject of paramount importance. In what proved in time to be an exceedingly influential memorandum, Ball asked that "urgent priority" be given to his assertion that without a thorough rethinking of foreign economic policy the promise of the New Frontier could not be realized. "I am convinced," he cautioned Secretary of State Dean Rusk, "that unless we attempt some such *grand design* as I have outlined below we may be defeated in fulfilling those promises of growth which the American people have been given, and in conducting an effective foreign policy in the present age of change and uncertainty." Conceding that the United States was "no longer a towering, dominant economic power," Ball announced that the country needed "a comprehensive economic policy bill." The memo stressed that, in no small way, domestic prosperity depended on a successful approach to Europe. "We shall be able to keep our promise of internal growth and our hopes for a prosperous and secure Free World *only* if we swiftly move to develop a new set of economic policies in common with our allies."[1] As they so often would, events corroborated Ball's views.

The general European economic recovery of the 1950s presented the American government with startling new realities. Europe was on the move. The major economies of the Continent were growing twice as fast as that of the United States. The security equation of 1960 was also radically different from what it had been a decade earlier. Few Europeans in 1961 believed a Soviet invasion was imminent and, as Arthur Schlesinger, Jr., reminds us, "the conditions which had given rise to the Marshall Plan and NATO were substantially gone." America was caught in the throes of both a "gold hemorrhage" and a "dollar glut," and the new administration was grievously concerned—perhaps "obsessed"—with an insidious balance-of-payments deficit. Even before they came

---

1. George W. Ball to Dean Rusk, 1 January 1961, Box 12, General Correspondence Folder, 48-164, B General, 1 January to 3 March 1961, in John F. Kennedy Library (JFKL); emphasis added.

aboard, it was clear to the Kennedy team that the 1960s would be a time of consolidation and adjustment for America. Notwithstanding the grand agenda called for in the rhetoric of the New Frontier, the United States began to confront limitations on its economic and political influence after twenty years of virtually unchallenged preeminence. As Richard Barnet has argued, John F. Kennedy was "the first President who had to design policies for an America on the decline."[2]

In this disquieting atmosphere, there was considerable excitement in the summer of 1962 when Kennedy first publicly articulated the diplomatic initiatives that would soon become known as the "Grand Design."[3] Breathing new life into an idea originally put forth in Eisenhower's "Guild Hall Speech" a decade earlier, Kennedy's "concrete Atlantic partnership" proposal, announced in Philadelphia on 4 July, raised expectations (and apprehensions) both in Europe and in the United States.[4] In Washington that month, inquiries about who was doing what

2. Arthur M. Schlesinger, Jr., *A Thousand Days: John F. Kennedy in the White House* (New York, 1965), 771; George W. Ball, *The Past Has Another Pattern: Memoirs* (New York, 1982), 205; Richard J. Barnet, *The Alliance: America, Europe, Japan, Makers of the Postwar World* (New York: 1983), 199–200.

3. This tortured term has inspired books and conference papers. Ball admits to being a bit baffled by what the appellation has come to mean in certain quarters: "The phrase 'European political unity' has always meant different things to different men. Like other abstract and spacious terms that cloud our political discourse . . . it often suggests a swampland of semantic confusion." Ball's conception of Europe and the Atlantic partnership has been, not surprisingly, consistently analogous to Monnet's: formal arrangements for "consultations"—as the British preferred in the days of the OEEC—would simply not be satisfactory. Sharing Monnet's pronounced abhorrence for "intergovernmental debating societies," throughout the 1960s and 1970s Ball boldly echoed Monnet's call for the creation of a common Atlantic parliament, believing that it would, "over the years, build up a body of European statesmen by inducing politicians to seek careers for themselves in a larger political arena." *See* George B. Ball, *The Discipline of Power: Essentials of a Modern World Structure* (Boston, 1968), 57–58.

4. George W. Ball, *Diplomacy for a Crowded World: An American Foreign Policy* (Boston, 1976), 157. In describing the evolution of the concept in the Kennedy administration, Alfred Grosser notes: "The idea of a 'partnership' between the United States and a powerful Europe as presupposition for the best possible future of the Atlantic community had already been publicly expressed in December [1961] by McGeorge Bundy, one of the President's closest advisers. And in a speech entitled 'Toward an Atlantic Partnership,' another adviser, George Ball, had pointed out in February 1962 how closely this idea corresponded to the aim of the builders of Europe, among whom he had good reason to count himself. He stated: 'As long as Europe remained fragmented, as long as it consisted merely of nations small by modern standards, the potentials for true partnership were always limited. It was in recognition of this fact that since the war we have consistently encouraged the powerful drive toward European integration. We have wanted a Europe united and strong that could serve as an equal partner in the achievement of our common endeavors as an equal partner committed to the same basic values and objectives as all Americans.' The Action Committee for the United States of Europe had expressed the same idea in a statement which had been published on June 26, eight days before Kennedy's Philadelphia speech: 'The Action Committee which comprises the vast majority of the political parties of our six countries as well as the free and Christian trade unions representing ten million workers is of the opinion that only through the economic and political unification of Europe, including the United Kingdom, and the establishment of a partnership of equals between Europe and the United States can the West be strengthened and the conditions cre-

with regard to the "new European agenda" dominated government press briefings; reports indicated that a new division in the State Department was being created to manage consultations with European leaders and was to be directed by J. Robert Schaetzel (Ball's State Department staff chief and later American ambassador to the European Community). Henry Owen was given specific responsibility to study the Atlantic partnership problem; John Wills Tuthill, from various bases of operation in Europe, would serve as State Department liaison; Arthur Hartman, a young Foreign Service officer, was drawn into the European group as Schaetzel's deputy on a variety of problems; National Security Adviser McGeorge Bundy would serve as White House intermediary to the Atlanticists in the State Department.[5]

"But the mastermind behind the Atlantic partnership concept," as the administration conveyed the project to the press, "[was] Under Secretary of State George Ball, an old friend and associate of 'Mr. Europe,' France's Jean Monnet."[6] Although he might resist the appellation "mastermind," Ball became one of the primary (and certainly one of the most eloquent) spokesmen on European affairs in the Kennedy administration. And though Ball might discount his personal relationship with Monnet as a factor in his ability to advance the Atlantic partnership concept within the American government, Alfred Grosser is accurate in alleging that "the history of American policy toward the process of European unification cannot be explained without recognition of Monnet's influence."[7]

---

ated for peace between East and West' " (Alfred Grosser, *The Western Alliance: European-American Relations Since 1945* [New York, 1982], 201).

5. Although Assistant Secretary of State for European Affairs William Tyler was nominally among the group, he was not, as Robert Schaetzel and others have pointed out, "part of the fraternity." Tyler was "reliable, intelligent, and exceedingly able" but "never part of the gang"; J. Robert Schaetzel, interview with the author, 17 July 1992. Ball demurs slightly from this characterization: "He [Tyler] had lived in France, and spoke five languages. He was thoughtful, useful and reliable. He was very valuable at the Nassau meeting. He felt the dangers of incurring de Gaulle's wrath, and felt it important that we make him some offer"; George W. Ball, interview with the author, 21 July 1992.

6. *Washington Daily News*, 10 July 1962.

7. The quotation is from Grosser, *Western Alliance*, 102. Ball expresses unqualified admiration and affection for Monnet, but he has sometimes been uneasy with the implication that he was merely a Monnet protégé or Monnet's agent in the American government. In describing their relationship, a Kennedy assistant wrote: "Soon Ball became Under Secretary of State for Economic Affairs; on entering his impressive new office in the State Department, he is said to have gaily remarked, 'Monnet isn't everything.' But Monnet remained a great deal" (Schlesinger, *A Thousand Days*, 772). Ball also once remarked to the author: "Unlike your friend [Ambassador J. Robert] Schaetzel, I never became a Monnet cultist" (Ball interview, 2 March 1990). But in thanking Jean and Sylvia Monnet for a visit to France in the mid-1970s, Ball sensitively confessed: "I was grateful, as always, for your sound advice and the wisdom that informed your conversation. Although I have not always been an apt pupil, Jean has been a magnificent teacher, and I think I have learned more from you, Jean, than from anyone else" (George W. Ball to Jean and Sylvia Monnet, 14 December 1976, in Papers of George W. Ball, Lyndon B. Johnson Library, Austin, Texas). Also, Ball's wife of fifty-two years, Ruth Murdoch Ball, unhesitatingly expresses the private conviction that her husband respected and admired Monnet above anyone (Ruth M. Ball, interview with the author, 6 April 1985).

Under Secretary Ball's preoccupation with Europe served as a bridge in postwar Democratic administrations between the Atlantic orientation of the Truman years and the new exuberance for developing nations exhibited by Kennedy's New Frontiersmen. As more of the creativity and energy of the State Department was devoted to the Third World than ever before—under the rubric of "nation building"—a group of dedicated Atlanticists in and around Ball's office maintained a commitment to the Atlantic Alliance as the critical cornerstone of American foreign policy.[8] While the president and the State Department Policy Planning Office were conceiving agendas for new diplomatic arenas, Ball wielded a surprisingly free hand in European affairs.

Three factors prompted Kennedy to give greater weight to the State Department's voice on Europe than he might otherwise have done (considering his well-known misgivings about the institution).[9] The first was that Kennedy, at least until he became president, had been an "agnostic" on European integration. After his election, he remained open-minded but was not immediately convinced that European integration was inevitable or even desirable, and he was not at all sure what the policy of the United States ought to be in any event. The concept of supranational institutions was oblique to his experience and assumptions about the world. Indeed, he was initially suspicious of an economic "Fortress Europe" and harbored the conventional fear that the Common Market would trade unfavorably with the United States. Further, the consolidation of the industrial democracies of Western Europe could only diminish American prestige.[10]

When Kennedy became president, however, he was willing to be persuaded. He came to admire Jean Monnet and was deeply impressed with the French-

8. Under Secretary of State Chester Bowles and Assistant Secretary for African Affairs G. Mennen Williams were principals in the so-called Africa Group and typified the "nation-builder" mentality. There was a natural rub between those who identified with the aspirations of the African people and those whose job it was to maintain relations with former European empires in an age of rapid decolonization. This created an understandable tension in the State Department epitomized by the discordant views of Ball and Walt W. Rostow. In "New Dealer in the Cold War: The Role of Chester Bowles in American Foreign Policy" (unpublished manuscript in possession of author), Howard B. Schaffer writes: "The Africanists were opposed by the so-called 'Europeanists' who were concerned about the impact Administration positions on African issues could have on U.S. ties with its European allies. In the Europeanist view, relations with Western Europe had an importance which overshadowed the benefit of closer ties with emerging African nations or the alleged moral or domestic political advantages of helping bring about an end to colonial or minority rule" (212).

9. Kennedy did not conceal his legion of misgivings with the performance of the Foreign Service. He once complained to McGeorge Bundy: "I get more done in one day in the White House than they do in six months in the State Department." (Schlesinger, *A Thousand Days*, 377).

10. In 1975, after serving as American ambassador to the European Communities, J. Robert Schaetzel insightfully noted: "There were both Americans and Europeans whose reservations about a united Europe sprang from a conviction that an integrated Europe would inevitably become a third force. The skeptics anticipated that, instead of cooperating with the United States in a true Atlantic partnership, a united Europe would become increasingly independent, with opposition to the United States deemed essential to a separate European identity" (J. Robert Schaetzel, *The Unhinged Alliance: America and the European Community* [New York, 1975], 46).

man's resolve and passion for a "United States of Europe." He was also compelled by the close relationships Monnet maintained with members of the American foreign policy establishment (those Monnet would himself call his "well-informed friends"). But if Monnet's disciples in the American establishment were dogmatic on European integration, Kennedy remained pragmatic. Despite the continuous strengthening of his ties with European statesmen, "he had no absolute doctrines about it." Though given to fits of rhetorical flourish, he left open a wide array of options as to how integration might be achieved and how the United States might advance the process.[11] Kennedy's ambivalence induced those stalwarts of European unity in the State Department to forge a political strategy to realize the vision of an Atlantic community and, in the process, to bring their president along.

The second factor that contributed to the influence enjoyed by Ball and the Atlanticists is the deference shown them by the secretary of state. With regard to Europe, Dean Rusk contented himself with looking after political affairs and maintaining relationships with foreign ministries and with NATO. He had neither a natural nor a studied interest in European economic, social, or cultural matters and relied almost entirely on Ball for policy advice. Rusk acquiesced almost completely to Ball on economic and trade matters bearing on Europe and was persuaded to go along with proposals on other subjects (as mentioned below) that ran against the grain of his own predispositions. The economist Carl Kaysen, McGeorge Bundy's deputy in the National Security Council, is struck by the simplicity of the arrangement: "Rusk simply said economics is for George." The Atlantic world was, in Rusk's mind, Ball's great strength, and he greatly respected what he once referred to as his under secretary's "long exposure to Europe." Rusk seemed content that Ball's immersion in Europe balanced his own interest and absorption in Asia.[12]

The third factor that added gravity to the counsel of Ball and the State Department Atlanticists was their individual reputations. They were men of ability, creativity, and dedication. Ball, originally appointed under secretary for economic affairs, was elevated to under secretary in less than a year, and throughout the remainder of the Kennedy administration his political stature continued to increase.[13] Schaetzel, also a protégé of Jean Monnet, was a staunch and creative proponent of the Atlantic partnership whose bureaucratic signatures were cre-

11. Monnet quoted in Barnet, *The Alliance*, 98; Schlesinger, *A Thousand Days*, 781.

12. Carl Kaysen, interview with the author, 23 July 1992; Dean Rusk, interview with the author, 27 March 1985.

13. By November 1961 it was generally recognized that Ball had become "the No. 2 policy maker in the day-to-day political operations [of the State Department]." Indeed, there was "a general understanding" that even during the first months of the administration, "all immediate political matters be checked with either Ball or Secretary Rusk" (*Evening Star*, 25 October 1961). "By common consent," *Time* magazine reported on 17 May 1965, "the most forceful, imaginative, and hard-driving of Rusk's aides is Under Secretary of State George Ball. Ball's critics protest for instance, that 'George doesn't feel that there is anybody in Government as good as he is'—and some of them admit a bit ruefully that he is probably right."

ative energy and common sense. He had studied the Common Market and Eura-tom as a Rockerfeller Public Service Award recipient (and had also worked on organizing the State Department for the incoming Kennedy administration). Referring to Schaetzel as "an exceedingly bright fellow," Ball concedes that "Bob carried the idea of European integration even further than I did." Henry Owen, thoughtful and productive on strategic matters, was seen as "a crucial figure [in the State Department European group]," "a real engine of European integra-tion," and the "most important single individual" on European security matters at State."[14]

Perhaps most important, the Europeanists were, to a man, independent thinkers. While it was once quipped that a Foreign Service officer is a man for whom the risks always outweigh the opportunities, the Europeanists at the State Department were imaginative and took courageous positions, even to the extent of having their patriotism occasionally impugned.[15] From Kaysen's vantage point, it was clear that "this group certainly pushed more strongly on the admin-istration than the professional bureaucracy would have done." They were tied together, as Schaetzel describes, by a curious combination of experience and sen-timent. The Europeanists at the State Department "included career officers and transients in government from private life [like Ball]." Although it was "a loosely knit group," it was firmly "allied in its support of European union, sensitive to Europe's objectives and problems, and tied by close friendship to the Europeans involved." There was, as Schaetzel nostalgically wrote from the perspective of the late 1970s, "a general atmosphere of intimate cooperation," in an age when "personal relationships lubricated Atlantic relations."[16]

A discussion of Kennedy and Europe inevitably becomes, in part, a discussion of what George Ball and the Europeanists at the State Department—who mock-ingly came to be known throughout the administration as the "theologians"—thought and did. If they were indeed "theologians," Ball was the high priest of the European idea in the American government, Kennedy's most ardent and able "Grand Designer."[17] Considered by his allies and antagonists alike to be one

---

14. Ball interview 21 July 1992; McGeorge Bundy, interview with the author, 16 April 1992.

15. Schlesinger, *A Thousand Days*, 384; Alfred Grosser recollects: "An English journalist, com-menting on his influence on Kennedy, had this to say: 'Ball was a much travelled American lawyer who had known Jean Monnet for many years. He had been employed as Monnet's legal representa-tive in Washington when Monnet was running the Coal and Steel Pool. On Capitol Hill, Ball's for-eign ties were not forgotten, and at a secret joint committee meeting, when he seemed to be stating a pro-European case, an intemperate Senator sharply asked him to remember he was in the pay, not of M. Monnet, but of the American Governments' " (Grosser, *Western Alliance*, 103–104). On an-other occasion, a friend of President Kennedy asked Ball: "When are you going to take out your American citizenship papers?" See *New Haven Register*, 6 November 1962.

16. Carl Kaysen, interview with the author, 23 July 1992; Schaetzel, *Unhinged Alliance*, 45–46.

17. Schlesinger, *A Thousand Days*, 800. Ball is curiously discomforted by the characterization: "I must say I am not very happy with being characterized a 'Europeanist.' " He maintains that be-cause his responsibilities were comprehensive—paralleling the secretary's—he could not be focused on one area. He grants that his experience and interests were in Europe but dissents from being la-beled a man exclusively of one region (Ball interview, 21 July 1992).

of the most gifted public servants of his generation, Ball will be known in the annals of diplomatic history on both sides of the Atlantic as a man who spoke his mind and who habitually challenged conventional wisdom.[10] By 1961 he had developed a compelling résumé of professional experiences that included work in the Farm Credit Administration, the Treasury Department, the Lend-Lease Administration, and, in the waning stages of the war, the United States Strategic Bombing Survey.

Ball's conceptualizations of the Atlantic community and his professional and, indeed, his personal life were distinctively molded by the thirty-five-year friendship he began with Jean Monnet during the war. In 1945, he advised Monnet on his Plan for Modernization and Investment. In 1946, he made substantive recommendations as the Committee for European Economic Cooperation was taking shape. Throughout 1947, Ball apprised Monnet on developments in the European Recovery Program, and later, while he was not commiserating with his French client about the dark mood hanging over Europe, he counseled Monnet on the administration of the Marshall Plan. During the 1950s Ball advised an industrial trade association called the French Patronat, he edited a journal published to promote transatlantic investment titled *France Actuelle*, and he wrote long papers for the advancement of Franco-American investment enterprises.[19] In 1953 he was seduced into supporting the ill-fated proposal for a European Defense Community. By the end of the 1950s he was retained by all the communities Monnet helped create, including Euratom and the European Coal and Steel Community. Indeed, Ball is a citizen of Europe. He is an officer in the French Legion of Honor and a recipient of the Belgian Grand Cross of the Order of the Crown.

Ball embraced Monnet's central thesis: European integration was an inexorable process. The United States could prepare for it or be overrun by it. Kennedy, Ball believed, should act boldly to influence its evolution. Americans should not sit back, he warned the president, and be passive witnesses to the development of a "closed, autarchic, incestuous 'continental' system."[20] From the under secretary's perspective, the Atlantic partnership idea—including economic, political, and military cooperation—was an essential complement to the progressively more cohesive European Economic Community. As he had told Rusk in his Jan-

---

18. Ball was constantly frustrated by what he saw as the destructive nationalism of President de Gaulle and often said so. At a dinner honoring Jean Monnet in New York on 23 January 1963, he remarked that his friend Monnet "has never been tempted into the unhappy error—induced by a nostalgic longing for a world that never was—of seeking to recapture the past." This not-so-veiled reference to what Ball considered de Gaulle's menacing patriotism prompted one congressman to call for the under secretary's censure "for his lack of manners" (*Congressional Record,* 24 January 1963, p. 981).

19. U.S. Department of Justice, Federal Bureau of Investigation, "Special Inquiry into George Wildman Ball, Results of Investigation," Freedom of Information Act Case no. 8600931, in Papers of George W. Ball.

20. George W. Ball, Memorandum for the President, 20 June 1963, p. 15, in Papers of Dean Acheson, Harry S. Truman Library.

uary 1961 memo, if Kennedy was going to "get the country moving again," he would do so only in concert with Europe.

There is an ironic twist to the story of Ball's emerging influence with Kennedy. Although the president greatly respected his under secretary's gifts of "speed and decision," the two never developed a close personal or political relationship. Indeed, as Arthur Schlesinger, Jr., wrote, "John Kennedy and George Ball never hit it off quite as they should have done."[21] Though he was not a political insider with Kennedy, Ball's ascent at State was propelled by his ability. The president saw him as polished, informed, talented, and experienced, and as a man who got things done.[22] Still, Ball remained an outlander at Camelot. He was born, raised, and schooled in the Middle West and, as he once wrote of his disconnects with the Kennedy team, "never taught or studied on the Charles River." A consummate Europeanist, Ball often felt "surrounded" by younger men in the administration who saw Africa, Asia, and Latin America as new priorities on America's global agenda. "The young movers and shakers of the Kennedy Administration," he once mused, "thought of themselves as pragmatists, well equipped to resolve America's emergent international problems with flair and imagination," and they generated a "surfeit of theories regarding the economic development of the Third World." They had, he ruefully adds, "fewer settled views on the structure of relations among the Western industrialized democracies." Kennedy's developmental economists were, Ball believed, annoyingly predisposed to flamboyant neologisms with a "quaintly Madison Avenue ring" such as "take-off," "the big push," and "the great ascent."[23] Derogating the era's fashionable political and economic theories, then collectively known as "nation building," as "a most presumptuous undertaking," Ball openly questioned whether it was ever realistic to expect that "American professors could make bricks without the straw of experience and with indifferent and infinitely various kinds of clay."[24] Ball admits that he never fully harmonized with the intellectual

21. For remarks on Kennedy's relationship with Ball, see David L. DiLeo, *George Ball, Vietnam, and the Rethinking of Containment* (Chapel Hill, 1991), xii. In an interview with the author, Roswell Gilpatric observed that "[Ball] didn't have anywhere near the relationship with Kennedy that he enjoyed with Johnson. [Ball] didn't seem to have that many intimate associations [on the Kennedy team]. He was certainly not an intimate of Kennedy's. His Stevenson identification may have started Kennedy off more guardedly" (Roswell Gilpatric, interview with the authors 1 April 1987). But Kennedy greatly appreciated Ball's elegance of expression in an institution otherwise given to graceless rhetoric and bureaucratic patois. See Schlesinger, *A Thousand Days*, 387–88.

22. Schlesinger, *A Thousand Days*, 387–95. State Department counsel Thomas Ehrlich, who had to endure Ball's penchant for multiple redrafting of documents, once noted that "he single-handedly worked a revolution in the use of the English language within the State Department. He was fond of saying that the simple declarative sentence is man's noblest architectural achievement." See his "Introduction of George W. Ball," 31 March 1971 at Stanford University, in Papers of George W. Ball.

23. Ball, *The Past Has Another Pattern*, 164, 208; Ball, *Discipline of Power*, 224.

24. Ball's disdain for diversions from the project he had inherited from Jean Monnet—the "building of Europe"—only ripened with age. After his retirement from government for the fifth and (possibly) final time, Ball continued sardonically to deflate Kennedy's academics and, in the

style of the Kennedy team. "It's a miracle," Schaetzel once said of the inner circle of the Kennedy administration, "that Ball was able to elbow his way in there."[25]

If Ball was able to "elbow his way in," he had help. Shortly after Kennedy was nominated, the future under secretary suggested to Adlai Stevenson that the would-be secretary of state offer to develop foreign policy proposals that could be used during the campaign (and that he "clarify his position" with Kennedy respecting the possible appointment). When Kennedy acceded to Stevenson's offer, a foreign policy committee was assembled. Stevenson's idiosyncratic inattention to detail meant that the bulk of the work was delegated to Ball and a gang of the governor's political lieutenants. While they were nominally Stevenson's task force, the lion's share of the labor—including the organizing, conceptualizing, and drafting—was done by Ball. As he is temperamentally (and perhaps compulsively) prone to do, Ball took the bull by the horns that summer and autumn. Schaetzel worked closely with him on the reports, applying his special aptitude for conjoining information with insight, feverishly chasing around Washington, and working long nights and weekends on what he remembers as "a sort of clandestine operation."[26] While the Democratic party's nominee was ambling about the country blowing political wind into the sails of his campaign (not in a bus), Ball and a small group of Stevenson men were writing a foreign policy agenda for the 1960s. The resultant Foreign Policy Task Force report was, in no small way, a prelude to Kennedy's Atlantic partnership proposal.

The report declared that "America must develop and apply new policies" and warned candidate Kennedy that he would need to ask the American people for "commitments and sacrifices." "The catalytic element that can bring into play the latent resources of the Western World," the drafters advised, "requires a strong new lead from America." Ball's Eurocentric conceptions of American foreign policy are conspicuous in the report. But perhaps the most significant testimony to Ball's personal contribution to what would, in large measure, become President Kennedy's initiatives in foreign economic policy is his "Open Door" ideology, distinctively underscored throughout the entire document. In a section titled "A Comprehensive Program for the Economic Progress of the Free World," the report lamented the "parochial attitude of the Treasury Department" under Eisenhower. Ball faulted the previous administration for failing to

---

process, an integral element in the 'New Frontier mentality' by impugning what he called the "theological aspect" of foreign assistance: to wit, brimming with an "overblown nomenclature," all manner of experts during the Kennedy years, including economists, sociologists, psychologists, city planners, political scientists, "and experts in chicken diseases," embarked for the distant corners of the globe to construct all manner "new Jerusalems." With little meaningful impact on the developing nations, Ball concluded that so many Harvard and MIT economists "only succeeded in straining America's primary diplomatic relationships by their constant din of requests for more aid from European Governments for America's daring projects in the emerging nations" (*The Past Has Another Pattern*, 183).

25. J. Robert Schaetzel, interview with the author, 2 August 1992.

26. Ball, *The Past Has Another Pattern*, 159; J. Robert Schaetzel, interview with the author, 29 March 1985.

extend adequate credits and markets to developing nations (particularly in Latin America), called for the executive branch to be endowed with new and greater power to effect trade policy, and proposed a 50 percent across-the-board tariff reduction within five years. This last proposal would, two years hence, prove to be a most fertile recommendation and the core material of the grand design anticipated by Ball in his initial memorandum to Rusk.[27]

Ball's law career, his long association with Monnet, his numerous writings, and his testimony to congressional committees leave little doubt about the passion and consistency of his free trade liberalism. Ball has long held the view that a liberal trading world is a prosperous and secure world. He has (sometimes derisively) been considered a "one worlder," a "businessman's Hegelian," and a "champion for the multinational corporation." Though he lacks formal training in economics (for which he has sometimes been needled by his well-lettered economist friends), Ball is a powerful economic conceptualizer, and for three years references to the virtues of free trade were unfailingly prominent in his advice to the president.[28]

On the strategic side, the Task Force report made "particularly urgent" proposals for a coordinated NATO nuclear force, and it delivered a dire warning about the "the dangerous trend on the part of the NATO Allies toward the development of independent national nuclear deterrents." Not one given to glittering generality, Ball included a twenty-page support paper developing a plan for what he called a "partnership Between a United Europe and America within a Strong Atlantic Community." The partnership plan, not surprisingly, paralleled the integrationist principles espoused by Jean Monnet's Action Committee for a United States of Europe. Ball believed, in 1960, that NATO was in crisis. The report forewarned that "the failure to develop within NATO an integration of decision-making and command is leading today toward a breakdown of the internal machinery of NATO that has been so laboriously constructed."[29] In short order, Ball would be drawn to a creative (and controversial) scheme to concoct a coordinated nuclear deterrent.

On the diplomatic front, the Task Force report specifically recommended to Kennedy that a "high level approach to de Gaulle [be initiated immediately] to indicate the importance which the new Administration attaches to an early settlement of the Algerian conflict."[30] Also predictably, given Ball's unique taxon-

27. "Report to the Honorable John F. Kennedy from Adlai E. Stevenson, November, 1960," pp. 24, 11, in Personal Papers of J. Robert Schaetzel, Bethesda, Maryland.

28. Donald R. Katz, "The Grand Designer," *New Republic,* 13 January 1979, pp. 21–25; John Kenneth Galbraith, interview with the author, 4 April 1984.

29. Stevenson report, 5–7, and PA 1–20.

30. *Ibid.,* 12. On a point of noticeable departure with his Atlantic mentor Dean Acheson, Ball was in no way a defender of European colonialism as other State Department Europeanists were. In a letter to the author (29 July 1992), Arthur M. Schlesinger, Jr., recalls that "there was tension when concern for European Governments and their colonies conflicted with the Administration's support for national independence in the Third World."

omy of world problems, much smaller support papers on China, Sub-Saharan Africa, and Latin America were relegated to appendixes. (In a particularly elucidating passage from a section titled "The World in Revolution," directly bearing on Ball's iconoclastic views on Southeast Asia that would emerge within the year, the report declared that "it is important that we not try to impose our own political or economic ideas" on Third World nations receiving American assistance.)[31]

Upon receiving the report, Kennedy acknowledged his satisfaction: "Very Good. Terrific. This is excellent. Just what I needed."[32] He had received a foreign policy call to arms, the principal draftsman of which was largely unknown to him. In the months ahead, as Kennedy learned more about the breadth and depth of Ball's personal involvement in the Task Force enterprise, his stock in the new administration began to appreciate. Also in the months ahead, one Task Force proposal would be legislated, while one other remained a political and strategic abstraction. Both contributed to what Ball once called "the mystique of the Grand Design" and provide a measuring stick by which the efficacy and legacy of the Europeanists at the State Department might be assessed.[33]

The most constructive enterprise in pursuit of the Atlantic partnership—and the most discernible link between the Task Force report and Kennedy's legislative successes—was the rethinking of American trade policy and the passage of the Trade Expansion Act of 1962. With the Reciprocal Trade Agreements Act of the New Deal era due to expire in the summer of 1962, with a greater threat posed to the American economy by the common tariff of the Common Market, and with Britain's announced intention in the summer of 1961 to "join Europe," trade quickly became a priority for Kennedy.

Reminiscent of the manner in which Monnet viewed obstacles, Ball thought the advance of European integration and the looming threat of higher duties constituted both a danger and an opportunity for the United States. As a Washington lawyer in the 1950s he had been active in the Committee for a National Trade Policy and had closely studied the problem during the election campaign. Indeed, the Task Force report had given a great amount of attention to the balance-of-payments issue, a problem, the Task Force members conceded, that "[took] precedence over all [their] other proposals." They boldly asserted that "the authority of the President to change tariff rates must be substantially en-

<hr>

31. Stevenson report, 12, and Part II, 2, appendixes. Ball's writings on Third World assistance tend to be unemotional. As a member of the European entourage at the State Department observed, "On subjects that he was vitally interested in—primarily European—he was always perhaps the best informed of anyone on the specifics of the issues. Regarding the developing world he knew in his heart that the northern democratic countries should do much more in both trade and aid, but he really didn't wish to become involved in the details." The developing world was a subject with which he was "totally bored" (John Wills Tuthill, letter to the author, 21 July 1992).

32. Schlesinger, *A Thousand Days,* 157. Schlesinger also editorializes: "The report in the main revolved around Europe and reflected to a considerable degree Ball's preoccupations with NATO and Atlantic trading policies."

33. Ball, *The Past Has Another Pattern,* 208.

larged in order to give him the powers which may be essential to help him maintain the unity of the Atlantic Community concept." Indeed, without a trade agreement, there was no Atlantic partnership. Perhaps Ball emboldened Kennedy. As part of his New Frontier economic rhetoric, the president came more forcefully to attack what the Task Force report had denigrated as the "old isolationism" and "economic nationalism" of the past and sought to liberalize global commerce.[34]

Despite a nascent conservatism about the balance-of-payments issue that was traceable to his father, Kennedy was slowly becoming a free trader. The administration would go forward, and the under secretary of state would be midwife to the legislative initiative. It seems clear from the record that, save for the president himself, George Ball was more responsible for the 1962 trade bill than any other single individual. As he had with the Task Force report, Ball assumed theoretical and political responsibility.[35] But he was not merely the principal author of the legislation. For twenty months, between January 1961 and September 1962, he advanced the view throughout the government—often in acrimonious exchanges with congressional committees—that short-term disadvantages incurred by American exports would be offset by the escalating volume of trade with a revitalized Europe.

The "politics of economics" quickly surfaced. Special interest groups, industrial alliances, and various associations of manufacturers fought the bill. Perhaps ironically, it was Ball who was commissioned to make the administration's case on Capitol Hill and in the press against the textile lobbies. The under secretary's presentation was often unvarnished. From time to time, after he had pontificated eloquently on the values of free trade, others in the administration were called upon to repair the damage he visited on anxious legislators or industrial lobbies.[36] At one point, during a particularly nasty episode in the textile skirmish, ninety congressmen petitioned the president to fire the under secretary of state. "The President, I must say, stood up very well," Ball recalled three years later in a conversation with Joseph Kraft while he was still occupying his office on the seventh floor of the State Department.[37]

Indeed, the trade negotiations moved more swiftly and much farther than Ball anticipated they would at the outset. His original strategy had been to delay

34. Stevenson report, FEP-4, FEP-8.

35. "One Sunday," as Ball recollected, "by myself, I sat down . . . I was trying to fit in to the entry of Britain into the Common Market . . . and I blocked out the whole Trade Bill and brought it in one Monday morning after working over the weekend on it. It was substantially the bill in the form in which it was finally passed." (George W. Ball, interview with Joseph Kraft, 12 April 1965, pp. 31–32, in John F. Kennedy Library Oral History Program).

36. On one occasion a fire that Ball ignited in the textile industry had to be extinguished by the White House. "I do not believe," White House Special Counsel Meyer Feldman wrote to the general president of the Amalgamated Clothing Workers of America, "that [Under] Secretary Ball intended his speech to be construed as an acceptance of the expendability of any industry" (TAG, 105, 27 November 1961, in General Correspondence File, John F. Kennedy Library).

37. Ball interview by Kraft, 12 April 1965, pp. 16–17.

acting on trade until after the 1962 off-year elections (when congressmen would feel less heat from trade lobbies). He was surprised and delighted when Kennedy went ahead with what in administration circles came to be known as the "Ball Plan," which included a call for the comprehensive reduction of tariffs, licenses and restrictions, a lobbying effort on behalf of British entry into the Common Market, and, in the spirit of compromise, a constructive political engagement with the special interests.[38] Kennedy sent the bill to Congress on 25 January 1962 and mapped out the legislative strategy. Because the president was cognizant of Ball's liabilities as a witness in this issue, it was decided that the under secretary would follow a long list of administration voices (one hundred in all), beginning with Commerce Secretary Luther Hodges, a man well connected both on Capitol Hill and in the textile industry. After four weeks of hearings (and the compilation of two thousand pages of testimony), the House of Representatives passed H.R. 9900, the Trade Expansion Act of 1962, by 298 votes to 125; the Senate followed on 19 September by 78 to 8. In a White House ceremony, Kennedy signed the bill, calling it "the most important piece of international legislation affecting economics since the Marshall Plan."[39]

Editorials in the American press quickly touted the legislation as "the crowning achievement of the Kennedy Presidency in domestic legislation" and an enterprise "that ranks with the Marshall Plan in its constructive impact." House Majority Whip Hale Boggs of Louisiana called it "one of the significant events of this century." Initially, Boggs had been skeptical about the proposal and held the conventional view that immediate trading advantages for the Common Market outweighed potential advantages for the United States. But after Boggs visited Europe in the summer of 1961 and met with Jean Monnet, he came away impressed both with the trade proposal and with the Frenchman's ultimate vision. Like Kennedy before him, he became a convert to the long-term benefits of the plan. Instead of the item-by-item approach originally called for, Boggs

---

38. Katz, "Grand Designer," 21. Kennedy's lobbying effort on behalf of the TEA, one observer has concluded, was "brilliantly orchestrated." It is no small irony that the president commissioned Ball, perhaps the most ardent free trader in the entourage, to strike a bargain with the textile industry. The Long Term Textile Agreement, completed in September 1962, gave domestic producers needed assurances. Although it was "bitter tea" for Ball (as he has written in his memoirs) and the compromise with textiles seriously undermined the spirit of the free trade agreement with the Common Market, it was a necessary political compromise. As William S. Borden has noted, "Ball made no effort to conceal his utter disgust for the greedy textile magnates who were protecting their profit margins and inefficiency against the virtuous evolution of the world system." See William S. Borden, "Defending Hegemony: American Foreign Economic Policy," in *Kennedy's Quest for Victory: American Foreign Policy, 1961–1963,* ed. Thomas G. Paterson (New York, 1989), 71–72. Ball himself writes in *The Past Has Another Pattern* that he was determined "at all costs" to block any and all quotas. As he engaged the individual textile groups, he found himself "enjoying the confrontation." "For my private and secret gratification," Ball recounts, "I appeared before each textile group dressed in a British-made suit, a British-made shirt, shoes made for me in Hong Kong, and a French necktie" (190–91).

39. Ryan J. Barilleaux, "The President, 'Intermestic' Issues, and the Risks of Policy Leadership," *Presidential Studies Quarterly,* Center for the Presidency, XV (Fall 1985), 758.

helped to sponsor a bill that called for sweeping across-the-board powers to reduce all tariffs and trade barriers, which would solidify the Common Market and
encourage British entry. In the wake of the floor votes in the House and Senate,
as the administration and congressional leaders were basking in their striking political success, Kennedy implored Boggs, "Tell me Hale, who is the Jean Monnet
of this country?" Boggs replied, "We don't have a Jean Monnet, but there's one
man in your Administration who is closest in approach: George Ball."[40] Boggs's
salutary comment speaks volumes about Ball. It also serves as a reminder of the
extent to which Ball had internalized Monnet's methods and objectives: global
change is incremental and comes on the back of political institutions.

As consequential as the bill was for commerce, over the years Ball has maintained that the TEA had as much political as economic significance. In revisionist
quarters, the TEA is seen "as a tool to shape European development" and an
effort to "guarantee [America's] economic future and generate resources for the
West's military and foreign aid burdens." Some Europeans saw it as an effort
to advance American hegemony and undermine the Common Market.[41] Ball's
principal motivation seems to have been to strengthen rather than weaken the
Common Market and to create conditions within which Europe could shoulder
more of the cost of its defense. Engaging an economically united Europe as a
new entity conferred a new legitimacy upon the Common Market. Despite a
chorus of strident criticism on the domestic political front, Ball was asserting
what he concluded to be the national interest.[42] From the perspective of 1998,
perhaps events of the past decade reflect favorably on the decisions to promote
this vision taken in the past thirty years.

Like the Trade Expansion Act, the multilateral force was envisaged (though
not originally conceived) in the Task Force report and then hatched in the State
Department. But to the degree that they were successful in the trade negotiations, George Ball and the Europeanists at the State Department failed to advance the integration of Europe on the back of a multinational missile force.
From the outset, the MLF may have been impossibly complex.[43] Ball himself
even once inferred that it was "grotesque."[44]

40. "Historic Victory for Freer Trade," Newsweek, 1 October 1962, pp. 17–18.

41. Frank Costigliola, " 'The Failed Design': Kennedy, de Gaulle, and the Struggle for Europe,"
*Diplomatic History,* VIII (Summer 1984), 229–30.

42. With respect to the TEA, something must also be said about Eastern Europe. In the wake
of the negotiations for the bill, and while Cold War politics rendered it unfashionable to do so, Ball
consistently argued that Yugoslavia and Poland ought to be extended—to the degree possible under
the political climate of the Cold War—aid, credits, and markets then being opened to Western countries. See Paul Kubricht, "Politics and Foreign Policy: A Brief Look at the Kennedy Administration's
Eastern European Diplomacy," *Diplomatic History,* XI (Winter 1987), 58.

43. If Ball and the Europeanists at the State Department did not conceive the MLF, they most
certainly adopted it as a way of promoting European unity. It quickly became an object of derision.
There were many signals that the plan was in trouble, not the least of which was when Hyman Rickover purportedly told Kennedy that he would not allow Frenchmen on *his* submarines. See Gregg
Herken, *Counsels of War* (New York, 1987), 61.

44. Ball, *The Past Has Another Pattern,* 274.

The idea had been incubating since the mid-1950s, when the European De-
tente Community was being contemplated. By the time Kennedy was inaugu-
rated the concept had no shortage of enemies in the Defense Department, in the
White House, and, indeed, in the State Department as well.[45] National Security
Adviser McGeorge Bundy, representative of the informed opposition, advised
two presidents against the MLF, concluding that it was both technically unfeasi-
ble and politically undesirable.[46] To Ball and the dogmatists, the concept of a
shared nuclear force was alluring, again as much for political as strategic reasons.[47] To Bundy and the pragmatists, it seemed a tortured response to a problem that probably defied solution—"the least bad next good thing," as he has
described it. But to the extent it was ever viable, Bundy admits, "it was kept
going mainly by the skill and energy of its backers in the State Department."[48]

The political rather than the physical power of the atom lay at the center of
the MLF concept. It rested on the central assumption that, as technologies pro-
liferated, more countries would seek membership in the nuclear club. In the Foreign Policy Task Force report, Ball had warned against the danger of independent nuclear deterrents in Europe and the special problems (and opportunities)
posed by Germany. "The effects of our present policy," the 1960 Task Force report had declared, "which is to maintain tenaciously the presumed US nuclear
'monopoly,' has dangerously divided the Alliance."[49] Ball stressed that nuclear
assets were not implements of war but political instruments that might further

45. In a letter to the author (29 July 1992), Schlesinger reflected on the chasm between the
White House and the Atlantic group in the State Department: "We in the White House were much
less sympathetic with some of the Europeanists' more gimmicky proposals, like the multilateral
force."

46. Although Ball maintained excellent relations with the Kennedy White House, his relationship with McGeorge Bundy was compromised by a serious dispute over the MLF. Bundy admitted
in an interview with the author on 1 April 1967 that it caused them real problems: "George and
I had our most sustained difference over the MLF"—a remarkable statement in light of the policy
deliberations over Vietnam. On one occasion, when Rusk had let it be known in a memorandum
that he favored the concept of a multilateral nuclear arrangement, Bundy openly doubted the au-
thenticity of the State Department communiqué. In a memo to the president covering the "Rusk
paper," Bundy wrote, "The signature is the signature of Rusk, but the language is the language of
Ball," and expressed his suspicion that the under secretary took advantage of Rusk's momentary dis-
traction with other business to secure his signature on a memo, the contents of which Rusk did not
wholly endorse. Bundy wrote to Johnson, "George is pressing much too hard in a direction that does
not make sense" (McGeorge Bundy, Memorandum for the President, 28 January 1966, in NSC File,
Memos to the President, McGeorge Bundy, Box 6, Lyndon B. Johnson Library).

47. Ball was undeterred, even by his good friend the influential columnist Walter Lippmann,
who thought the MLF "was poisoning relations with France, creating a German appetite for nuclear
weapons, and persuading De Gaulle that Washington sought to break up the new rapprochement
between Paris and Bonn." See Ronald Steel, *Walter Lippmann and the American Century* (New York,
1981), 556.

48. McGeorge Bundy, interview with the author, 16 April 1992; McGeorge Bundy, *Danger and
Survival: Choices About the Bomb in the First Fifty Years* (New York, 1988), 494.

49. Stevenson report, PA-1. The report added: "There is an irony to a policy that denies atomic
information to our Allies that is known to our common enemy."

consolidate the alliance. In making his case for the idea of a shared nuclear deterrent, Ball often noted the irony of withholding from our allies technologies and delivery systems controlled by our enemies. He also regularly railed against indiscriminate proliferation. Ball's support for the MLF rested partly on the assumption that any country wanting to possess nuclear weapons badly enough ultimately would and that a multinational system of control would be desirable. Of course, he was thinking of the "German problem." "Nothing is more dangerous," he once told Kennedy, "than the bland assumption that if the Western allies gang up on Germany they can successfully hold the Federal Republic to her self-denying ordinances regarding [nuclear] weapons."[50]

Obviously moved by Ball's remonstrations, Kennedy was just as obviously unpersuaded by his conclusions. To him, the MLF seemed "something of a fake" (a "multilateral farce") so long as the United States could exercise a veto over the order to launch missiles. But the advocates of the MLF were sprinting even if the president was jogging. Finally, Kennedy's caution became an explicit component of the administration's policy. When he sent his emissaries to discuss the matter with European leaders, "he instructed them not to talk as if they were reflecting a personal preoccupation of the American President." Because he knew the MLF to be in trouble in 1963, Ball pressed Kennedy very hard. "A Germany not tied closely and institutionally to the West," Ball told Kennedy in a strongly worded memorandum, "can be a source of great hazard." The interests of the German people would have to be heard and understood. "Embittered by a deep sense of discrimination and bedeviled by irredentism, a Germany at large can be like a [loose] cannon on shipboard in a high sea." Ball argued that "Germany must play some part in nuclear defense." Additionally, the under secretary had been consistently reminding his counterparts in the French government that "the 1930s had proven the difficulty of 'keep[ing] Germany permanently in a second class position.'" All this, Ball exhorted Kennedy, "leads inevitably to the MLF."[51]

But the multilateral force, as John Lewis Gaddis has colorfully noted, "never left port."[52] Ball maintains that he regarded the plan merely as a means to an end. He was certainly not unaware of the technical and tactical difficulties associated with a multinational arrangement. But given his deep misgivings with other grandiose strategic plans that tended to exacerbate the problem of proliferation—MX and SDI to cite two schemes later strongly opposed by Ball—it seems that both the idea of nuclear control and the prospect of building on united Europe's institutional base appealed to him.

50. Ball, Memorandum for the President, 20 June 1963, p. 8.

51. Schlesinger, *A Thousand Days,* 799; Ball, Memorandum for the President, 20 June 1963, p. 14; "Memorandum of Conversations Between French Foreign Minister Couve de Murville and Under Secretary Ball, 25 May 1963," in National Security File, Box 72, quoted in Castigliola, "'The Failed Design,'" 231.

52. John Lewis Gaddis, *Strategies of Containment: A Critical Appraisal of Postwar American National Security Policy* (New York, 1982), 222.

Although perhaps not immediately, Ball was resigned to the MLF's lukewarm reception in other bureaucracies throughout the American government. After a time it seemed clear to him that, outside the walls of the State Department, there was insufficient passion to press it upon diffident Europeans. But even as late as 1966, the Atlanticists continued to believe that a multilateral system in Europe might be possible. Bundy, for one, had long before tired of the concept and believed that the European group at the State Department had become fixated on a failed idea. "I am sorry to say," he told President Johnson in January, "that this has become an obsession with George Ball, Robert Schaetzel and Henry Owen—they keep coming back to it by one means or another, and [the attached] memorandum is simply one more try."[53] In the end, Bundy was able to persuade Johnson to dump the MLF, and the proposal for a collective nuclear deterrent sponsored by the United States endured the last pang of its incremental death.

Bundy's autopsy is instructive. In the final analysis, as he has noted in his seminal study of nuclear decision making, it may be that "the MLF failed because it turned out that the underlying convictions of the decisive European Governments with respect to their relations to nuclear weapons, their relations to one another, and their relations with the United States, were all decisively different from those assumed or desired by the American supporters of the MLF." Bundy recalls "very few in the Washington of the MLF years who fully understood the commitment to national nuclear weapons that governed the policy of Britain and France." The MLF, in his eyes and Kennedy's, was interesting but not compelling. "It was one thing," he recalls, "to give limited encouragement to the European movement, but it was something else again to suppose that American proposals for the handling of nuclear weapons could themselves be a strong instrument for advancing the European idea."[54]

Not surprisingly, there are those in the Atlantic entourage who disagree with this assessment. In a fit of understatement, Schaetzel admits that "from its inception, the MLF was controversial on both sides of the Atlantic." He concedes that support for the plan in Europe was "limited," but he maintains that it was "significant." To him it was "an imaginative effort" filled with the promise of building new "organic links" in the European commonwealth. He laments that many of his counterparts in European diplomatic and defense ministries "had invested their personal prestige in the concept" and were taken aback when the plan was abruptly capsized "without consultation" by what Schaetzel sees as Johnson's "impetuous action." Since the fated MLF interlude, Schaetzel has noticed that "European leaders [are more careful about] mooring their political fortunes to unpredictable and possibly cavalier American leadership." Somewhat less sentimentally, Ball has merely relegated the MLF to "the limbo of aborted projects" and now regards it as "a manifestly absurd contrivance."[55] Maintaining that his

53. McGeorge Bundy, Memorandum for the President, 28 January 1966.
54. Bundy, *Danger and Survival*, 495, 498, 497.
55. Schaetzel, *Unhinged Alliance*, 162–63; Ball, *The Past Has Another Pattern*, 274.

role has been "enormously exaggerated," he concedes that "in retrospect, [his] preoccupation was mistaken" and that "the central assumption we were operating on was incorrect."[56]

Other students of the MLF specifically and the American politics of European integration generally have been less exculpatory. "The Europeanists in the State Department," Paul Nitze has declared, "tended to carry their enthusiasm for European integration to the point where they lost touch with their responsibility toward US interests." Conceding that there was a "significant risk" that "Communist Parties in the major European states would lead their countries into the communist camp," Nitze applauds the leadership of [Under Secretary of State for Economic Affairs] Will Clayton who, during the Eisenhower years, promoted the more benign concept of a European customs union. "The Europeanists," Nitze adds, "carried the idea of European integration beyond reason." Congress, he concludes, would never have ratified an agreement that would have permitted small nations to drag larger ones into nuclear war. When the implications of what the Europeanists were proposing came more clearly into view, Nitze maintains, they either were "fired or moved."[57]

This indictment might well be a familiar refrain to those Atlanticists who, like Schaetzel, persisted in their faith that the Grand Design—or parts of it—might be achieved. "Those of us who remained believers," he once proudly reflected, "were bound to be ridiculed, or worse, ignored. I always wore this as a badge of honor." The Atlantic partnership "was one of the really great ideas of this century." Though Ball himself concedes that the Grand Design never became more than a "figure of speech," over the years he has stubbornly refused to concede that the vision was without great merit. "If I look back with regret at events since the early 1960s," he muses in his memoirs, "it is not because I spent so much time and effort trying to advance the building of Europe, but because the effort failed. Although, God knows, American Governments have made plenty of mistakes, our encouragement of a unified Europe was not one of them. We were pursuing a worthy goal and—at the time—not a wildly unrealistic goal."[58]

56. Ball, interview, 21 July 1992. Ball has complained to the author that his "passionate attachment to the MLF has been grossly overstated." When the remark was shared in a conversation with McGeorge Bundy, it prompted a smile and raised an eyebrow (Ball interview, 6 April 1986; Bundy interview, 1 April 1987).

57. Hon. Paul H. Nitze, letter to the author, 14 July 1992.

58. Schaetzel interview, 2 August 1992; Ball, *The Past Has Another Pattern*, 222.

# 15

## Kennedy's View of Monnet and Vice Versa

### *Walt W. Rostow*

~

When John Kennedy became president, Jean Monnet was an authentic postwar hero to most of the American foreign policy establishment and a wartime hero as well to those who knew of his role in setting U.S. war production goals in 1941 and in unifying the French in Algeria in 1943. With American help, his postwar plan to modernize the French economy had not only succeeded, but its very existence in 1946–1948 provided an important element of credibility to the case for the Marshall Plan. Monnet had then gone on to perform as architect of the Coal and Steel Community, Euratom, and the Rome treaties, bringing about, among other things, a historic Franco-German reconciliation.

Some instinct told Monnet: "The institutions must be set up by the beginning of 1958. Soon, it will be too late."[1] His explicit concern at the time was the possible abstention of the German socialists in the Bundestag vote on the Rome treaties. That did not happen; but de Gaulle came to power in June 1958 out of the dynamics of the Algerian crisis. Monnet's Action Committee continued to keep and articulate the faith, and Monnet never lost hope, although the patience he cultivated and counseled was difficult for this man who reveled in translating ideas into action. But the looseness of political affairs in the Fourth Republic, which had permitted Monnet to maneuver into a central role in French domestic, and then foreign, policy had given way to a tighter system dominated by a man with a quite different view of the destiny of France and Europe.

Nevertheless, when Monnet came to Washington in the spring of 1961, he found a president surrounded by a battalion of his friends: some reaching back to his wartime years in Washington such as Acheson, McCloy, and George Ball, others, to the days of the French modernization plan (like David Bruce) or to other postwar occasions. Then there were the Europeanists in the State Department who had shared Monnet's vision of Europe and were, like him, for a moment—but only a moment—cast down by the failure of the EDC.

But Kennedy was not simply a creature of those gathered around him. Since his formative trip to the Middle East and Asia in 1951 his primary focus had

1. Jean Monnet, *Memoirs* (Garden City, N.Y., 1978), 424.

been on the developing regions, about which an American policy consensus had not yet formed and where, he came to believe, the fate of democracy would be decided. When, for example, Kennedy defined in ten chapters of his *Strategy of Peace* (1960) the "Areas of Trial" ahead in foreign policy, eight came to rest on specific problems in Asia, the Middle East, Africa, and Latin America. There, too, he had his most serious policy differences with the Eisenhower administration and with a foreign policy establishment he felt was narrowly Europeanist in perspective.

Nevertheless, when he came to the White House in 1961, Kennedy was instinctively in favor of European unity and an Atlantic partnership for all the usual reasons Americans looked benignly on that outcome: the palpable succession of tragedies European fragmentation had brought upon its peoples over the centuries climaxed by the still fresh memories of World War II; the immediate advantages of European unity in the Cold War struggle against Moscow; and, somewhere from deep in the American past, the instinct that continental unity was the right answer for others as well as for ourselves. And, as we shall see, a bit later, all this was heightened by another, more urgent, domestic consideration.

But as Monnet noted in discussing Kennedy, "To be the greatest power in the world is a lonely and dangerous business."[2] Kennedy's decisions in foreign policy could not be governed by a single criterion; and his loyalty to the European connection had, occasionally, to be diluted.

In an engaging irony, Monnet helped resolve such a conflict of criteria for Kennedy. (Incidentally, I tell this story with the enthusiastic encouragement of Robert Schaetzel, with whom, over the years, I have shared its irony.) The clash of criteria Kennedy had to settle arose as preparations went forward in anticipation of Japanese prime minister Hayato Ikeda's visit to Washington of 21–22 June 1961. The debate was between those who regarded the OECD as inherently an Atlantic club of culturally similar nations and those who believed it should be a club for the more advanced industrial nations in general. Functionally, neither aid, trade, nor monetary affairs could rationally be conducted without Japan as it was emerging in the 1960s. Moreover, some of us felt it urgent that, as Japan moved from the trauma of defeat, occupation, and isolation into roaring prosperity, it ought to be brought more fully into the work of the global community. It was clearly on its way to world stature. It was unnatural for Japan to be locked up in bilateral diplomacy with the United States. I argued with Kennedy and my working colleagues the case for supporting full Japanese membership in the OECD on these grounds. The Europeanists in the State Department, who generally found my views congenial, were troubled. Jean Monnet was in town, and they thought he might bring me back to an uncorrupted Atlantic view. I was invited to discuss the matter with him and some of my State Department friends in Bob Schaetzel's office. When the case for Japanese membership was laid before him, Monnet, who had never lost interest in Asia

2. *Ibid.*, 462.

since his work as a young man in China, supported Japanese membership. The matter was settled, of course, by Kennedy, who finally observed that if we needed a purely Atlantic club, beyond NATO, we would have to create another organization.

One should, perhaps, add that Monnet was never greatly impressed with international organizations that merely generated "cooperation" among nation-states, not integration. OECD's membership was, for him, not a prime issue.

Kennedy lived in a world where not only Ikeda but also de Gaulle, Macmillan, and many others were inescapable daily realities. For example, Kennedy went against the advice of his Europeanists (including me) at Nassau in December 1962 by granting the United Kingdom missiles for its Polaris submarines, cutting across a simultaneous plea by the Action Committee for a Franco-British settlement "in accordance with the fundamental principles of the European Community." Monnet regarded the Nassau deal as a "very grave" matter. It certainly provided de Gaulle a splendid rationale for his 14 January 1963 press conference in effect vetoing British membership in the European communities. But, on the evidence, de Gaulle was not then in a mood to accept British membership in any case. Secure in the wake of the outcome of the Cuban Missile Crisis and the French referendum of 28 October 1962, de Gaulle was about to engage in a series of captious experiments in disruption beginning with the Franco-German Treaty. Monnet and the Action Committee helped render the treaty harmless and, indeed, constructive, but not in the way de Gaulle intended.[3] The corrective device was a preamble to the treaty asserting the primacy of NATO and the Atlantic connection, a preamble inserted and accepted by the Reichstag. De Gaulle went on to overplay his hand abroad and gradually lost control of affairs at home.

For Kennedy, however, the most urgent case for supporting European unity related to his second most acute anxiety. The first was evidently his fear that the Cold War might trigger, through some tragic unintended sequence of events, the use of nuclear weapons. After all, in presiding over the closely related Berlin and Cuba crises of 1961–1962 Kennedy saw through the Gettysburg of the Cold War. The second was the deterioration of the American balance-of-payments toward the end of the 1950s, yielding a negative current account balance in 1959. Kennedy's economists (and Johnson's) were somewhat casual about this turn of events. They looked to devaluation of the dollar and floating exchange rates as means of reconciling an expansionary domestic policy with a viable balance-of-payments position.[4] It wasn't that easy. Kennedy understood that the sharp decline in the U.S. trade surplus from over $6 billion in 1957 to about

---

3. *Ibid.*, 457–58, 467–68.

4. Monnet shared, incidentally, Kennedy's sense that the emerging balance of payments was a kind of Jeffersonian "fireball in the night." He wrote to Adenauer in November 1959: "We must realize that there has been a fundamental change in the world economic situation. The American balance of payments has gone into deficit. If this situation grows worse, I need not describe what the results would be for the whole of the West and for ourselves in particular." *Ibid.*, 463.

$1 billion in 1959 was rooted in the relative rise in productivity of Western Europe and Japan in the course of the 1950s. This perception, heightened by episodes of gold withdrawals from U.S. reserves that found their way into the 1960 presidential campaign, underlay Kennedy's active support—indeed, insistence—on wage guideposts linking money wages to productivity increases; his wage-price restraint deal with Walter Reuther and David MacDonald, union leaders in the automobile and steel industries, led directly to Kennedy's thirty-six-hour war with the steel industry when United States Steel broke the mutually understood price guideline. This concern lay behind his executive and legislative initiatives for accelerated depreciation guidelines. Kennedy also installed an assistant secretary for commerce responsible for formulating policies to raise the rate of productivity increase. He even pressed James Webb at NASA to spin off for the private sector something more substantial than nose-cone material that would permit the production of a kitchen pot impossible to overheat.

The balance-of-payments concern was a major factor in Kennedy's memorable interdependence speech. That speech is usually linked to advocacy by Monnet and the Action Committee of a generalized Atlantic partnership between the United States and a united Europe, including especially the Action Committee's declaration of 26 June 1962.[5] And I have no doubt Monnet's indefatigable advocacy played a role in the crystallization of Kennedy's policy at Philadelphia. But there was a more proximate catalyst.

When I went to work at the State Department, Kennedy kept open a channel of communication, with the understanding that everything sent to him would go simultaneously to Rusk. In June I sent several memorandums on European policy to Kennedy. And upon his return from a trip to Mexico, I talked at some length with him about these memorandums late in the morning of 2 July. We discussed the whole complex of ties across the Atlantic.

He observed that in the 1950s the United States had spent its time collecting nuclear bombs, while Europe had been rounding up gold. What was needed was some way for Europe to assume increased responsibility for the state of the world economy, thus reducing the burden carried by the United States; and the United States would have to find ways of sharing with the Europeans the responsibilities of decision in nuclear matters. The heart of it, he thought, was that if there was a single political authority in Europe, he could work out an arrangement for joint control over nuclear matters. But Europe was split: "I'm the President of the United States, but who's the President of Europe?" We talked about the proposal for a multilateral nuclear force within NATO, and he probed at why Bonn might be interested when, clearly, he could not surrender to Bonn the right to fire American weapons.

We canvassed, as well, the problems in aid, trade, and money.

One memorandum he had read suggested that the concept of an across-the-board partnership between the United States and Europe might be the subject

5. See, for example, *ibid.*, 466–67.

of a major address by the president or secretary of state. Kennedy concluded by saying that he had to make a speech on 4 July at Philadelphia; he would like to make it on this international theme rather than in a more conventional patriotic style: would I send a draft over to Sorensen as soon as possible? That afternoon my deputy Henry Owen and I put our heads together and fulfilled his instruction.

A key passage in Kennedy's speech, clearly related to his balance-of-payments–productivity anxiety, was this:

> We believe that a united Europe will be capable of playing a greater role in the common defense, of responding more generously to the needs of poorer nations, of joining with the United States and others in lowering trade barriers, resolving problems of commerce, commodities, and currency, and developing coordinated policies in all economic, political, and diplomatic areas. We see in such a Europe a partner with whom we can deal on a basis of full equality in all the great and burdensome tasks of building and defending a community of free nations.[6]

In effect, Kennedy was advocating a united Old World to restore balance to the New. But the text of Kennedy's citation for the Presidential Medal of Freedom, delivered by Lyndon Johnson in December 1962, suggests that Kennedy also understood the grandeur of Monnet's achievement in broader terms: "Citizen of France, statesman of the world, he has made persuasion and reason the weapons of statecraft, moving Europe toward unity and the Atlantic nations toward more effective partnership."[7]

For Monnet the years after 1958, when de Gaulle came to power, were, in many ways, frustrating. He had somehow managed without a political base for much of the time since 1914—and continuously since 1940—to be close to the center of affairs. With de Gaulle's accession to power, he could only fight a holding action on the periphery with the Action Committee. That committee represented the abiding center of European politics, and its continued highly articulate existence was an important steadying force, holding fast to a vision that transcended the short-run vicissitudes of French, British, and German politics. In the phrase of one of Monnet's chapters, it was "a time of patience." But when de Gaulle was succeeded by Georges Pompidou—and British membership in the communities came gradually back on the agenda—Monnet was over eighty. British entry seemed assured when he retired in 1975, but, as he recognized, in a wholly natural process, the role of the Action Committee waned in the 1970s.

6. *Public Papers of the Presidents of the United States: John F. Kennedy, 1962* (Washington, D.C.: 1963), 538.

7. *Public Papers of the Presidents of the United States: Lyndon B. Johnson, 1963–1964* (Washington, D.C., 1965), I, 33.

In the sequence that began with de Gaulle's return to power in 1958, the brief period of Kennedy's presidency was for Monnet an interval of hope, touched with a strand of magic. Writing of Kennedy's death he evoked a White House "where civilization and a sense of greatness had reigned for two short years."[8] A Washington with a cavalcade of old friends who, in one way or another, shared his dream was part of it. But from his first meeting with Kennedy, Monnet was struck by his acute mind, his dynamic impact on Washington, and a vision as broad as Franklin Roosevelt's. And despite de Gaulle's looming presence, there was the substance of the Kennedy Round and on 4 July 1962 the striking affirmation of deeply rooted American support for a united Europe including Britain and for the Atlantic partnership.

I arrived in Paris on the morning of that day, to attend a meeting of the Atlantic Political Advisory Group (APAG), a NATO committee of foreign office planners. On my return, I circulated a memorandum reporting a considerable range of conversations, including Monnet's extremely hopeful view of the track ahead:

> Monnet has not been more cheerful or in better form for a long while. He believes the British will get in; that they will enter the European political process; and that we shall develop a nuclear partnership in which Germany is treated on an even-handed basis. His interpretation of the de Gaulle-Adenauer talks is as follows:
>
>     a) They have accepted UK membership;
>
>     b) They are now worried about the British camp-followers rather than Britain (Ireland, Norway, Denmark);
>
>     c) They want to solve the problem of political organization before the little fellows are in;
>
>     d) They will consult British but are searching for a formula which would permit the major powers (France, Germany, Britain, and Italy) to make policy without excessive dilution from those who merely want the economic advantages of the Common Market and a sense of being in the club. Monnet agrees this is a real and crucial issue. (My microcosmic experience of APAG convinces me that they are right and we'd better begin to think ahead about NATO organization.)
>
> On nuclear policy Monnet thinks we should stick to our stance and let things unfold slowly.
>
> On aid and trade we should keep the pressure on steadily but expect gradual results.
>
> On monetary policy we must move fast and he believes that if the matter is raised to a high enough level—well above GECD Committee Three—the major European countries will play for two reasons: first, they all have a stake in the stability of the dollar and the health

---

8. Monnet, *Memoirs,* 472.

of the US economy; second, they all have a stake in the maintenance of US military strength overseas. But the deal must be in such terms and at a level where these considerations are brought to bear.

As a final note on Monnet, he made the interesting comment that, at a reception for Adenauer, de Gaulle had taken him aside and said his own views and those expressed in the recent Monnet Action Committee memorandum were "not far apart."[9]

I don't suppose Monnet, in the wake of Kennedy's interdependence speech, was ever so optimistic again, with Nassau, Rambouillet, and de Gaulle's January 1963 press conference just down the road.

Monnet's evaluation of Kennedy on the day of the latter's funeral reaches beyond European and Atlantic matters down to the roots of the American relation to Europe during the Cold War. Monnet was invited as a friend of the Kennedy family as was I, since only the secretary of state and under secretary were there officially. Friends for seventeen years, Monnet and I made common cause. Returning from the funeral we repaired to the Occidental Restaurant. It had been for all of us an intensely emotional, draining day. Monnet had his first martini, he told me, in twenty-five years.

Conversation turned to de Gaulle's statement at the airport in Paris as he was leaving for Washington. He was asked: "Why are you going?" He replied: "The French people demand that I go."

Monnet went on: "De Gaulle was right. The French like all Europeans have lived with two fears: that the United States would get us into a nuclear war; or that the United States would make a deal with the Russians over our heads, at our expense. Kennedy turned back the Russians without war in the Cuban crisis, and he moved immediately towards peace with the Test-Ban Treaty. He was everything the French wanted in an American President. De Gaulle was right: he had to go." Perhaps all this lay behind Monnet's report in his *Memoirs* of a Paris taxi driver who said to him: "Monsieur, we have just lost a President."[10]

9. From a memorandum to Foy Kohler, assistant secretary for Europe, 9 July 1962.
10. Monnet, *Memoirs*, 471.

# 16

# Dean Acheson and John Kennedy: Combating Strains in the Atlantic Alliance, 1962–1963

## Douglas Brinkley

By early November 1962 President John F. Kennedy's handling of the Cuban Missile Crisis was regarded by most Americans as a diplomatic triumph.[1] But this nerve-racking success in the realm of superpower relations had a deleterious effect on relations with the European allies. While Americans were transfixed by the attempted installation of offensive nuclear missiles a scant ninety miles from their shores, Charles de Gaulle was forcing Europeans to face critical issues in their relationship with each other and with the superpowers. Former secretary of state (1949–1953) Dean Acheson, considered by many to be the father of NATO, would play an important, if unintended, part in the fierce debate over the direction of European relations.

Unhappy with Kennedy's display of erratic brinksmanship during the Cuban episode, Acheson was, nevertheless, relieved to have the October missile crisis over and done with. He spent late November completing two articles and polishing an address to be delivered at West Point on 5 December, a speech that would prove the most controversial of his postsecretarial years.

General William C. Westmoreland, the superintendent of the U.S. Military Academy at West Point, had invited Acheson to deliver the keynote address at a student conference on U.S. affairs. Acheson, who constantly received invitations to speak at colleges and universities, declined, he said, out of "sheer laziness." General Maxwell Taylor then intervened on Westmoreland's behalf. "Although I know that you must receive many invitations of this kind, I hope your busy

Much of the research and writing of this essay first appeared in my political biography *Dean Acheson: The Cold War Years, 1953–71* (New Haven, Conn., 1992).

1. The following abbreviations are used in the notes:

| | |
|---|---|
| DGAPP | Dean G. Acheson Personal Papers |
| HSTL | Harry S. Truman Library, Independence, Mo. |
| JFKL | John F. Kennedy Library, Boston, Mass. |
| NSF | National Security Files |
| PAF | Post-Administration Files |
| SD/WHA | State Department and White House Advisor |

schedule will permit you to accept this one," Taylor wrote Acheson. "I think it fair to say that this annual event has attained a considerable reputation, and, with the theme of 'Atlantic Community,' it would be a forum particularly appropriate for an address from Dean Acheson."[2]

Acheson could not bear to say no to Taylor, who was one of the few men in Washington whom he unhesitatingly admired. He responded, "When you ask me to do it, that is something different."[3] So it was that Acheson found himself at West Point delivering a speech titled "Our Atlantic Alliance: The Political and Economic Strands."

For the most part, the speech was vintage Acheson, a call for strengthening NATO and working toward a true Atlantic partnership. Midway through his address, however, Acheson pointed a finger at the country he saw as a spoiler:

> Great Britain has lost an empire and has not yet found a role. That attempt to play a separate power role—that is, a role apart from Europe, a role based on a "special relationship" with the United States, a role based on being the head of a "commonwealth" which has no political structure, or unity, or strength, and enjoys a fragile and precarious economic relationship by means of the Sterling area and preferences in the British market—this role is about played out. Great Britain, attempting to work alone and to be a broker between the United States and Russia, has seemed to conduct policy as weak as its military power.[4]

This excerpt, transmitted to England the following day, immediately was front-page news. The British were outraged, and the volcanic public outcry that ensued seemed out of proportion to the nature of the speech. "I wonder who the unsung reportorial genius was who read through the whole speech and found that paragraph to cable to London," an irritated Acheson wrote Arthur Schlesinger, Jr., in the midst of the controversy. "He ought to have a substantial raise."[5]

The notoriety of Acheson's speech in British newspapers and the "anguish," in diplomatic jargon, it caused at the Foreign Office and at Admiralty House (the temporary headquarters of Prime Minister Macmillan) forced the State De-

2. Maxwell Taylor to Dean G. Acheson, 27 July 1962, Ser. 1, Box 30, Folder 385, in DGAPP.

3. Dean G. Acheson to Maxwell Taylor, 30 July 1962, *ibid.* Because Acheson was not acquainted with Westmoreland, his invitation did not carry the same weight as the request from Taylor, whom Acheson knew and respected. For the Acheson-Taylor alliance during ExCom, see Dino A. Brugioni, *Eyeball to Eyeball: The Inside Story of the Cuban Missile Crisis* (New York, 1991) 240–44.

4. Dean G. Acheson, "Our Atlantic Alliance: The Political and Economic Strands," speech delivered at the United States Military Academy, West Point, New York, 5 December 1962, rpr. in *Vital Speeches of the Day,* XXIX (1 January 1963), 162–66.

5. Dean G. Acheson to Arthur Schlesinger, Jr., 31 January 1963, Ser. 1, Box 28, Folder 359, in DGAPP. Schlesinger, who was in England, had sent Acheson a clipping of Selwyn Lloyd's commentary from the Sunday *Telegraph.*

partment on 7 December publicly to underscore two points. First, despite his sometime role as presidential adviser, Acheson on this occasion had spoken as a private citizen. Second, the general thrust of Acheson's discussion—support for British entry into the European Economic Community, increased economic co-operation by all Western nations, and a buildup of conventional military power in Europe—conformed to official State Department policy. Press Secretary Pierre Salinger added that President Kennedy had had no prior knowledge of the tenor of Acheson's speech.[6] Kennedy himself never publicly condemned the speech, but he approved a press release that said: "U.S-U.K. relations are not based only on a power calculus, but on [a] deep community of purpose and long practice of close cooperation. Examples are legion. . . . 'Special relationship' may not be a perfect phrase, but sneers at Anglo-American reality would be equally foolish."[7]

British pride had been too deeply wounded to be placated by State Department disclaimers. "He had stung us and we were temporarily numb," Acheson's close friend Sir Oliver Franks recalled.[8] Some British newspapers resorted to ad hominem attacks. The *Daily Express* denounced the American's "stab in the back." The *Sunday Times* hypothesized that Acheson's "tactless commentary" derived from America's success during the missile crisis, which must have "gone to his head." The *Daily Telegram* noted that Acheson, who was always "more immaculate in dress than in judgment," was "extremely unlikely ever again" to hold high office.[9] The *Spectator* ruefully wrote: "In this transitional period . . . we have a right to ask that our friends should not make matters worse. It is the nature of nations diminished in power to feel humiliated when the fact is called to their attention." The *Economist* alone refrained from blaming Acheson, saying his speech merely "sparked off what has always been the most disturbing feature of postwar Conservatism's inferiority complex; namely, the feeling that when in travail, it is an appropriate reflex to turn anti-American."[10]

Many of Acheson's British friends—for example, Sir Anthony Eden, Lord Patrick Devlin, Noel Annan, Desmond Donnelly, and Lord Frank Stowe-Hill—could not understand why Acheson had spoken so critically of their country and were concerned that his words would exacerbate anti-U.S. feeling throughout

6. State Department telegram, 7 December 1962, in NSF Countries, Box 170A, "UK 12/6/62," JFKL. See also Max Frankel, "Acheson Speech Irks British; U.S. Terms Criticism Minor," *New York Times,* 7 December 1962, p. 1.

7. See McGeorge Bundy to Robert J. Manning, 7 December 1962, in NSF, Box 170A/34, JFKL. The statement is also quoted in David Dimbleby and David Reynolds, *An Ocean Apart: The Relationship Between Britain and America in the Twentieth Century* (New York, 1988), 255.

8. Lord Oliver Franks, interview by Douglas Brinkley, Washington, D.C., April 1989.

9. Quoted in David Nunnerley, *President Kennedy and Britain* (London, 1973), 1. Nunnerley provides a fascinating account of the collapse of Anglo-American relations during the Kennedy years. Also see Andrew J. Pierre, *Nuclear Politics: The British Experience with an Independent Strategic Force, 1939–1970* (New York, 1972), 225.

10. "New Power Arising," *Spectator,* 14 December 1962, p. 920; *Economist* quoted in Pierre, *Nuclear Politics,* 225.

the United Kingdom. Acheson defended himself in a letter to Sir Frederick Leith-Ross: "Since both the *Times* and the *Telegraph* have printed my speech in full, you have seen that I did not deliberately start out to cause pain to my friends. In fact it was with great surprise that I found that a quite subsidiary sentence had been taken from a speech to a student conference, causing even the unflappable Mac [Harold Macmillan] to flap."[11]

The most galling phrase was "Great Britain has lost an empire and has not yet found a role." David Ormsby-Gore, the British ambassador to the United States at the time and an old friend of the president's, was asked by the press what he thought of Acheson's remarks. The ambassador replied that many of its points were "much in line" with official British policy. Acheson, he pointed out, was pro-British; his record spoke for itself.[12] David K. Bruce, the American ambassador in London, worked assiduously behind the scenes to calm Whitehall, emphasizing that except for the one unfortunate line, Acheson's speech was merely a reaffirmation of official Anglo-American foreign policy.[13]

Acheson had not foreseen the negative repercussions: "It had not occurred to me that a speech to a student conference would go ricochetting around the world in this way, nor furthermore, that the paragraph held the variety of meanings which seemed to be distilled from it," he wrote Arthur Schlesinger, Jr. "Doubtless I should have known better." But Acheson meant what he said and never publicly apologized for his remarks.[14]

Unfortunately for Acheson, who was hoping the ruckus would subside quickly, Harold Macmillan had concluded that Acheson's comments had denigrated "the will and resolution of Britain and the British people" so thoroughly that they required an official response. Although he understood that Acheson's remarks had placed Macmillan in an uncomfortable position, President Kennedy personally telephoned the prime minister to persuade him not to get drawn into a public debate that could only further damage Anglo-American relations.[15]

Macmillan decided he could not heed JFK's advice. He rebuked Acheson, in the form of a letter to the British public, printed in all the leading British newspapers, for committing "an error which [had] been made by quite a lot of people in the course of the last four hundred years, including Philip of Spain, Louis XIV, Napoleon, the Kaiser, and Hitler." He answered Acheson's assertion that Britain's "attempt to play a separate power role" was "about to be played out" by saying this applied to the United States and every other country in the West

11. Dean G. Acheson to Sir Frederick Leith-Ross, 16 January 1963, Ser. 1, Box 19, Folder 238, in DGAPP.

12. Quoted in Frankel, "Acheson Speech," New York *Times.*

13. See, for example, Robert M. Hathaway, *Great Britain and the United States: Special Relations Since World War II* (Boston, 1990), 75.

14. Dean G. Acheson to Arthur Schlesinger, Jr., 14 January 1963, Ser. 1, Box 28, Folder 259, in DGAPP.

15. Drew Middleton, "Macmillan Rebukes Acheson on Speech," New York *Times,* 8 December 1962, pp. 1, 8, Nunnerley, *President Kennedy and Britain,* 1–2.

as well. "The doctrine of interdependence," the prime minister declared, "must be applied to in the world today if peace and prosperity are to be assured."[16]

Macmillan also charged that Acheson had misdescribed the British Commonwealth as a sentimental organization without political structure, unity, or strength. "Mr. Acheson," the prime minister said, "seems wholly to misunderstand the role of the Commonwealth in world affairs." He feared that Acheson's denigration of Britain's world status would add to his government's difficulties in obtaining membership in the EEC.[17]

In retrospect, one can see that Acheson's speech received considerably more attention than it warranted because of the aspersion cast on the idea of the "special relationship" between the United States and Great Britain. "In his speech Acheson said quite rightly that Britain had lost her old role and was seeking a new one," recalled Sir Howard Beale, Acheson's friend and the Australian ambassador to the United States during the Kennedy years, "but in that inimitable way he sometimes uses in expressing words, he had given an impression quite unwittingly, which deeply hurt the feelings of the British people."[18]

To strike a blow at the special relationship was to attack the time-honored conventions of the Anglo-American relationship. Although many politically sophisticated Britons conceded that Acheson had said nothing that they themselves had not said privately, they were still angry that the former secretary of state made such remarks in a public address. Acheson accepted this criticism. "Macmillan came pretty close to saying the same thing when he said recently, as quoted by the *Washington Post*, that 'Britain could not expect to play a great power role in the new condition of the world,'" he wrote Francis Miller, special assistant to the Bureau of Educational and Cultural Affairs in the Department of State. "But they are British and I, an alien. While they may justify my *Position*, I doubt, alas, if they justify my stating it."[19]

There was widespread speculation as to what motivated Acheson's remarks. Many attributed them to American cockiness in the aftermath of the missile crisis, although "cocky" is hardly the way Acheson felt. Others thought Acheson

16. Published letter to Lord Chandos, 7 December 1962, reprinted in Harold R. Macmillan, *At the End of the Day, 1961–1963* (London, 1973), 339. Macmillan's statement was a reply to a letter he had received from Lord Chandos (president of the Institute of Directors and former Conservative cabinet member), Sir Louis Spears, and Sir Robert Renwick, requesting that the prime minister seek a disavowal from Acheson before he met with Kennedy in the Bahamas on 19 December.

17. *Ibid.* The British Foreign Office also wired Macmillan's statement to Dean Rusk as an official government telegram (8 December 1962, in NSF Countries, Box 170A, "UK 12/6/62," JFKL).

18. Sir Howard Beale, interview, 16 April 1964, in JFKL, Oral History Program. Beale recalls that he was in England when the furor over Acheson's remarks hit the London papers: "I spent the next few days in England defending him and when I came back, I took him to task and asked him why I should have to defend him! He told me it was one of those inadvertent things; he had thought the words he used were all right, some of his people had read the speech and saw nothing wrong—it occurred to nobody that it could be interpreted in any way wrong."

19. Dean G. Acheson to Francis Miller, 24 January 1963, Ser. 1, Box 20, Folder 255, in DGAPP.

was a mouthpiece for President Kennedy, who was showing a typical Irish-American disrespect for Britain. The *Daily Mirror*, which had the largest newspaper circulation in Britain, emphasized that connection in an editorial in which it characterized Acheson as a key presidential adviser. The author noted that Britain had been "written off" by another American in 1940, "by a man who told Roosevelt we didn't have any hope in hell in Hitler's war." "That man," the editorial continued, "was President Kennedy's father—the rich, faint-hearted Mr. Joseph, the American Ambassador to the Court of St. James in the days of Dunkirk."[20]

Not only had Acheson's ill-chosen words upset the British, who believed themselves consigned to a marginal role by Washington since the Suez war, but they had also raised questions about President Kennedy's political motivations. Some suspected that Kennedy had prodded Acheson into making the West Point speech as an attempt to damage Macmillan's government. These speculations were off the mark. Kennedy preferred the Conservative Macmillan, who favored—if somewhat reluctantly—British entry into the EEC, over the neutralist Labourites. He had no desire to hurt the Macmillan government. Asked years later by a graduate student whether he had been prodded by the Kennedy administration into making the speech, Acheson replied, "Nobody prods me, I prod myself."[21]

On both sides of the House of Commons, reaction to the speech was also strong. The Labour party, led by Hugh Gaitskell, was slowly turning from the notion of joining the Common Market to pursuing a neutralist course. Labour interpreted pronouncements like Acheson's statement that Britain's future lay with Europe as interference in British domestic affairs. It was not Acheson's charge that Britain had not yet found a role in the post-1945 world order that irritated them. The source of their anger was Acheson's timing. His remarks—made just as Britain was experiencing a difficult transition period vis-à-vis Germany, France, and other EEC members—weakened the country's bargaining position.[22]

There were exceptions to the prevailing critical view of Acheson's speech. "Your words of praise for the unfortunate West Point speech lost in the hurricane of British flap touched me and reassure me that, after all, it had a kernel of thought," a grateful Acheson wrote to Henry Kissinger, at that time a professor at Harvard. Other friends offered their support. "Congratulations on your address at West Point and the worldwide attention which it aroused," wrote General Maxwell Taylor, the man who had recruited Acheson to deliver the speech.

20. Quoted in Middleton, "Macmillan Rebukes Acheson," New York *Times.*
21. Quoted in Cecil Ellis Vaughn, "A Comparison of the Foreign Policy Viewpoints of Dean Acheson as Secretary of State and as Elder Statesman" (Master's thesis, University of Miami, 1967), 88–89.
22. Frankel, "Acheson Speech," New York *Times.* See also Nunnerley, *President Kennedy and Britain,* 1–13; and Miriam Camps, *Britain and the European Community, 1955–1963* (Princeton, 1964), 463–65.

"You gave the cadets and their colleagues strong meat for their intellectual molars," Felix Frankfurter wrote from the hospital, concerned about the clamor Acheson's speech had created. Acheson told Eugene V. Rostow, "[Frankfurter] has been very much exercised at the British press attacks on me, and worries a great deal about how to ensnare the Establishment so that we may subtly arrange for my reinstatement as a friend and not Public Enemy No. 1."[23]

Acheson's West Point speech is a useful benchmark for reevaluating the common criticism of Acheson as too pro-British. In 1970 Chester Bowles tagged the former secretary of state as "one of the greatest Prime Ministers Britain ever had."[24] Many of Acheson's harshest critics, historians as well as his contemporaries, have given far too much weight to Acheson's Anglophilia; time and again Acheson has been seen, wrongly, as "more British than the British." This misperception stems from confusing appearance with substance. Acheson may have been brought up like an English gentleman, may have looked like an English gentleman, but in reality he was a hard-nosed American pragmatist concerned primarily with enhancing his country's power and prestige abroad. There is no doubt that Acheson had a taste for British goods and style and an admiration for certain aspects of British political institutions, but there is no evidence that this admiration ever came at the expense of American interests.[25]

The historian Gaddis Smith has concluded that what Acheson admired most about Britain was its empire. In Smith's view, Acheson wanted to create in the post–World War II period a loosely knit American empire that would replace Britain's declining commonwealth. Acheson envisioned a global Monroe Doctrine—minus the Soviet sphere of influence—with the State Department emulating the role of the British Foreign Office as administrative overseer and protector.[26]

Acheson's debunking of the special relationship in his West Point speech was not an isolated, impulsive epigram. The statement is consonant with his longstanding views. From the time of the first postwar loans, Acheson always was

23. Dean G. Acheson to Henry Kissinger, 7 January 1963, Ser. 1, Box 18, Folder 236, in DGAPP; Taylor to Dean G. Acheson, 7 December 1962, Ser. 1, Box 30, Folder 385, *ibid.;* Dean G. Acheson to Eugene V. Rostow, 13 December 1962, in David S. McLellan and David Acheson, eds., *Among Friends: Personal Letters of Dean Acheson,* (New York, 1980), 240–41. Acheson began to refer to himself in letters as "Public Enemy No. 1 in England." See, for example, Dean G. Acheson to McGeorge Bundy, 13 December 1962, Ser. 1, Box 4, Folder 51, in DGAPP.

24. Chester Bowles, second interview, 1 July 1970, in JFKL, Oral History Program.

25. For discussions of Acheson's supposed Anglophilia, see Douglas Brinkley, "Dean Acheson and European Unity," in *NATO and the Founding of the Atlantic Alliance and the Integration of Europe,* ed. Francis H. Heller and John R. Gillingham, (New York, 1992); Lawrence S. Kaplan, "Dean Acheson and the Atlantic Community," in *Dean Acheson and the Making of U.S. Foreign Policy,* ed. Douglas Brinkley, (New York, 1992); and "The Diplomat Who Did Not Want to Be Liked," *Time,* 26 October 1971, pp. 19–20. For a superb evaluation of Anglo-American ties, see Christopher Hitchens, *Blood, Class and Nostalgia: Anglo-American Ironies* (New York, 1990).

26. Gaddis Smith, *Dean Acheson,* The American Secretaries of State and Their Diplomacy, ed. Robert H. Ferrell and Samuel Flagg Bemis (New York, 1972), 416.

among the first in Washington to counsel rebuffing British requests for special concessions. Acheson always felt Britain was a uniquely important partner of the United States, but this belief was accompanied by the recognition that it was an unequal partner and that "unique did not mean affectionate."[27]

Acheson's wariness was demonstrated in 1950, when he discovered that certain British Foreign Office and American State Department diplomats were drafting a paper defining the two countries' "special relationship." He immediately ordered all copies of the "wretched paper" destroyed. He thought that formalizing a privileged British position with the United States would perturb other allies, annoy the American public, and give "[Senator Joseph] McCarthy . . . proof that the State Department was a tool of a foreign power." No doubt constrained by his official position, Acheson did not call into question "the genuineness of the special relationship" but instead argued that "in the hands of the troublemakers" the joint paper "could stir up no end of hullabaloo, both domestic and international."[28] In 1962 Acheson, no longer secretary of state, could take the gloves off and pummel the special relationship directly.

Near the end of his life Acheson got to the nub of his concern. "I've always thought that the special relationship was something which grew out of our past history and the fact that we spoke the same language, and that we had, to a very large extent, the same interests," he admitted. "That there was nothing basically political about it and that perhaps it was a mistake to talk about it at all."[29] Although one would be hard-pressed to explain why the grand Anglo-American collaboration of the World War II was not "political," Acheson's criticism seems to be of sanctifying the special relationship.

A British friend once suggested to Acheson that if he favored a special relationship with another country it was West Germany, but Acheson emphatically denied this. "Please don't think I 'prefer' the Germans," Acheson protested. "No such suggestion can be found in the [West Point] speech; nor is it in my mind."[30]

A corollary of overweighing Acheson's Anglophilia is undervaluing his contributions to European integration. In fact, his eye was always on the larger picture—that is, continental Europe—where a special relationship with Britain had no place and instead was perceived as an obstacle to the European Community movement. Acheson scoffed at the notion of a Pax Anglo-Americana in which Washington and London would run the world together.

One of the ironies about the West Point speech, however, was that Acheson had violated a cardinal principle of his own: never criticize a NATO ally. John F. Kennedy, whom Acheson had chastised continuously for insensitivity to the

27. Dean G. Acheson, *Present at the Creation: My Years in the State Department* (New York, 1969), 387–88.

28. *Ibid.*

29. "Hard Words from the Veteran American Statesman Dean Acheson, in Conversation with William Hardcastle," *Listener,* 19 June 1970.

30. Acheson to Leith-Ross, 16 January 1963, Ser. 1, Box 19, Folder 238, in DGAPP.

problems of NATO members, did not turn the tables on Acheson; he refused to denounce him by name or to disassociate himself from the elder statesman.

## The Skybolt Controversy and the Nassau Agreement

Late 1962 was brimming with evidence of Britain's declining influence in America: lack of full consultation during the Cuban crisis and Acheson's West Point speech were prominent examples. London was also caught in a major defense crisis triggered by the Kennedy administration's abrupt cancellation of a promised air-to-surface missile called Skybolt, a weapon Britain regarded as essential for the Royal Air Force.[31] The British now perceived America as attempting to strip it of its recently acquired independent nuclear deterrent.

The Pentagon, led by Secretary of Defense Robert McNamara and armed with Acheson's NATO review of March 1961 and his cost-effectiveness analysis ($500 million had already been spent, and he projected that the weapon would cost an additional $2.8 billion), objected to independent nuclear capabilities for the European nations; they wanted the United States to maintain its nuclear monopoly. Ninety-seven percent of NATO's nuclear weapons were under U.S. control, for the United States had maintained that it was the only member with the technical know-how to manage them properly. The military was supported by President Kennedy and other civilian advisers such as Acheson who also believed that a separate British nuclear force was superfluous, for it would duplicate what was already available for the defense of Europe and squander important resources. Therefore, shortly after the resolution of the Cuban Missile Crisis, McNamara, with the president's support, unilaterally canceled the Skybolt program, which would have provided Britain with an independent intermediate-range missile. From the American point of view, the decision was logical and cost-effective, but it was another blow to British self-esteem. Britain had developed a hydrogen bomb and exploded it at Christmas Island in May 1958. The Royal Air Force, which could penetrate Soviet airspace, thus had the capability to drop nuclear weapons. What Britain now needed was a long-range delivery system. The Skybolt missile would have allowed British bombers to attack from eight hundred miles off their target, well beyond the range of its opponents' air defenses.

Secretary of State Rusk had warned McNamara that the cancellation of Skybolt would cause the Macmillan government problems, but McNamara insisted that he would be able to iron them out with Britain's defense minister, Peter Thorneycroft. On 7 December, in the midst of the furor over Acheson's West

31. David N. Schwartz, *NATO's Nuclear Dilemmas* (Washington, D.C., 1983), 96–103, offers excellent evaluations of the decision to cancel Skybolt, the McNamara-Thorneycroft meeting, and the meeting of Kennedy and Macmillan at Nassau. Also see Pierre, *Nuclear Politics,* 224–43; Lawrence Freedman, *Britain and Nuclear Weapons* (London, 1980), 10–18; and Hathaway, *Great Britain and the United States,* 61–67.

Point speech and before McNamara had a chance to talk with Thorneycroft, the decision to cancel Skybolt was leaked to the press. When McNamara arrived in London to discuss alternative defense plans with Thorneycroft on 11 December, he was met with an outraged British public, indignant over the dual affront from the United States. Thorneycroft maintained that Skybolt had been offered to Macmillan by Eisenhower in 1960 in exchange for the use of the Holy Loch Polaris base in Scotland. Now, after Britain had canceled its own Blue Streak missile program on the strength of Eisenhower's promise, the United States was trying to renege. "This cancellation . . . went deeper than defense policy and went to the very root of any possibility of the British trusting America in defense dealings again," Thorneycroft reflected in 1966.[32] McNamara left Britain without reaching a new accord.

This new strain in Anglo-American relations gave even more importance to Acheson's speech. "I suppose it was the coincidence of some reporter's coming across the sentence at just the time of the Skybolt incident that touched off the commotion," Acheson wrote in early 1963.[33] It would be up to Kennedy and Macmillan to try to revitalize British-American ties.

On 19 December 1962, Kennedy and Macmillan held a previously scheduled meeting at Nassau in the Bahamas to discuss both the status of negotiations for Britain's entrance into the EEC and the Skybolt issue. Kennedy was met by a prime minister seething over American insolence toward his country. Macmillan, who wanted to reduce British defense expenditures without sacrificing his nation's pretensions to power, told Kennedy he could not accept Skybolt's cancellation, for this would surely dismantle his already wobbly parliamentary backing. Kennedy replied that the Skybolt program had been scrapped; the issue was not negotiable. To help the prime minister politically on the eve of British elections, Kennedy offered five Polaris missiles for British submarines on the condition that Whitehall pledge them to a NATO-wide nuclear force and not maintain an independent force of its own. Macmillan, though unhappy with the restrictions, realized that for political reasons he had to accept them; he could not go home empty-handed. After negotiating an escape clause that permitted unilateral use of the weapons in case of a national emergency, Macmillan accepted Kennedy's watered-down offer, which became known as the Nassau Agreement, to save face and to camouflage yet another blow to British pride.

The Nassau Agreement was not a diplomatic success for Kennedy, however. The pact led to the abortion of his Grand Design for Europe before it had even begun to take shape. The replacement of Skybolt missiles with Polaris submarines provided de Gaulle with a pretext for vetoing British entry into the Common Market, which he did on 29 January 1963. The Nassau Agreement, de Gaulle declared, was clear evidence that Britain was more concerned with main-

32. Lord Thorneycroft, recorded interview by David Nunnerley, 18 June 1969, p. 16, in JFKL Oral History Program.
33. Acheson to Leith-Ross, 16 January 1963.

taining its incestuous ties with the United States, including the Anglo-American nuclear partnership, than with joining the European Community. As an afterthought, Kennedy had offered de Gaulle Polaris submarines on the same terms as those accepted by Macmillan, but the general defiantly turned them down. He had not been consulted about the Nassau Agreement, so he would not accept any placating handouts from Kennedy and Macmillan.[34]

Four months after the West Point speech and the Skybolt controversy, Acheson was still embarrassed by the peculiar role he had played in the diplomatic drama. "As you have doubtless seen from the press, my purpose in life now is to make enemies," he wrote a young friend. "I shocked the British by accident, and really annoyed the allegedly phlegmatic people." [35] But the West Point speech was only one perturbation in a turbulent period of Anglo-American relations.

Britain has used the special relationship, coupled with plans for an independent nuclear deterrent, to maintain its image as a great power in a postwar order in which the United States was dominant. The question left for historians to debate is why Dean Acheson's speech stirred such a commotion. It offered no novel insights; the decline of the British Empire was obvious to everyone on both sides of the Atlantic. Nor was urging the British to reorient themselves away from the United States and toward closer integration with the European Community a startling proposition; dozens of British statesmen had been saying the same thing for years. Acheson's speech had caused a stir in Britain simply because he had said aloud the unsayable: Britain's pretensions to imperial grandeur were illusions. And the United States was no longer willing to tolerate these illusions, which were sustained by Britain's bilateral orientation. London had to realize that, in American eyes, Britain was simply another European nation. Acheson's West Point speech, followed by Kennedy's cancellation of Skybolt, had shocked the British into realizing finally that their diplomatic self-image was unrealistic. Acheson erred not in saying what he did but in saying it so bluntly.[36]

"Britain has lost an empire and not found a role" became a catchphrase to describe nearly all of Britain's postwar woes. "One of the great troubles of the remark," Acheson told the journalist William Hardcastle in an interview for the *Listener* in 1970, "one which I struggled to overcome is that you must not be epigrammatic. The first requirement of a statesman is that he be dull. That is not

34. Richard J. Barnet, *The Alliance: America, Europe, Japan, Makers of the Postwar World* (New York, 1983), 212–13. Barnet's chapter 5 offers a fascinating profile of the personal relationship of Kennedy and de Gaulle.

35. Dean G. Acheson to Michael Janeway, 5 March 1963, Ser. 1, Box 16, Folder 209, in DGAPP.

36. Nunnerley, *President Kennedy and Britain,* 3–13. For an overview of Acheson's attitude toward Anglo-American relations, see Dean Acheson's address at the 1963 conference on Anglo-American relations sponsored by the English-Speaking Unions of the United States and the Commonwealth, New York, N.Y., 1 May 1963, Ser. 3, Box 51, Folder 57, in DGAPP.

always easy to achieve. And that statement suffered from being too epigram-matic and quotable. If I'd taken twice the number of words to express it, it would have been inoffensive and recognized as true at once. Since then it has been adopted by almost every British politician, though they never have given me credit for it all."[37]

In his later years Acheson's dictum against criticizing NATO allies was hon-ored often in the breach when it came to Britain. He openly scolded London for ordering economic sanctions against the white-minority government of Rhode-sia. "Little England with a big mouth, and garnished with anti-Germanists," Acheson wrote Desmond Donnelly in 1966, "seems to describe a type which is set-up for General de Gaulle." Speaking before the American Bar Association in Washington in 1968, Acheson claimed Britain was involved in a conspiracy, "blessed by the United Nations," to overthrow Ian Smith's Rhodesian govern-ment. In 1969 he charged that economic sanctions in southern Africa were a substitute for "the war Britain lacked heart and means to fight." The British by this time had developed some immunity to Acheson's goading barbs. When asked in the House of Commons about these remarks, Prime Minister Harold Wilson responded that the charges were ludicrous. Wilson added, "Mr. Acheson is a distinguished figure who has lost a State Department and not yet found him-self a role."[38]

## French Nationalism Versus the Atlantic Partnership

President Charles de Gaulle of France was not displeased with the Nassau Agree-ment, for it served to confirm his well-established doubts about allowing Britain entry into the Common Market. The agreement showed that the special rela-tionship between the United States and Britain, the Anglo-Saxon conspiracy of which de Gaulle had complained since World War II, was alive and well. De Gaulle had begun to distance France from American hegemony in Western Eu-rope as early as September 1958, when his call for a NATO directorate in the form of a partnership among the United States, Great Britain, and France was squelched by Washington. By March 1959 he had withdrawn the French Medi-terranean fleet from NATO's command and banned American nuclear weapons in France, while simultaneously initiating an independent nuclear force (*force de frappe*).

The Cuban Missile Crisis cemented de Gaulle's conviction that an indepen-dent nuclear force was the sine qua non of a great nation. France and, for that matter, all of Western Europe could no longer rely solely on the American nu-

37. "Hard Words," *Listener,* 19 June 1970.

38. Dean G. Acheson to Desmond Donnelly, 11 April 1966, in Acheson Papers, PAF, SD/WHA, 1965–68, Foreign Aid and NATO, Folder 4, Box 88, HSTL; Acheson quoted in Robert W. Peterson, ed., *Rhodesian Independence* (New York, 1971), 122–23; Wilson quoted in "Acheson's Gibe Returns with Some English on It," New York *Times,* 23 November 1969, p. 17.

clear umbrella. Europe had to invent its own role vis-à-vis the two superpowers, and de Gaulle was determined that France lead the way with an independent foreign policy buttressed by an independent nuclear deterrent. De Gaulle also wanted to break out of the rigidities of the Cold War game and reach détente with the Soviet Union.[39]

In the forefront of those working against the tide of archaic Gaullist nationalism was Dean Acheson. Acheson was viewed as the leading proponent of the new "Atlantic partnership," the integrationist conception nourished by the persuasive power of Jean Monnet and his Action Committee for a United States of Europe (1955–1975). Stimulated by Monnet's thinking and the committee's lobbying efforts, Acheson crusaded for the Partnership—greater European political unification within a larger transatlantic framework that included British membership in the Common Market.[40] Acheson's advocacy took two forms. One depended on his direct access to the president. Whenever he had the opportunity, Acheson warned that the administration's frequent votes against European allies in the UN would weaken NATO and stall the European movement toward greater political unification. Acheson also used another avenue, his pipeline to the White House via like-minded thinkers such as George Ball. As under secretary of state, Ball, who had worked closely with Monnet on plans for the European Coal and Steel Community in the late 1940s and who later represented it and several other Common Market agencies in America, provided Acheson with a staunch integrationist ally in government. His European friends—most notably Dirk Stikker and Jean Monnet—confirmed that Ball and his young deputy assistant secretary for European affairs, J. Robert Schaetzel, were respected throughout the continent as experts on European trade policy and on the integrationist movement. So, throughout the Kennedy and Johnson years Acheson stayed in touch with both men in an attempt to influence policy and keep his thinking current.

More than anything, though, it was the persuasive power of Monnet—who met with Acheson on 3, 6, 13, and 18 March 1961 in Washington—that sparked Acheson's more visionary thinking on the future of U.S.-European relations. Acheson and Monnet were working together again to launch a new institutional initiative: the Atlantic partnership, which would unite the West by combining the two separate powers of the United States and a united Europe. Acheson suggested to the president, through George Ball, that he invite Monnet to the White

39. Don Cook, *Charles de Gaulle: A Biography* (New York, 1983), 355–72. Cook's chapter 18 explains the Gaullist vision of Europe in detail. Also see Barnet, *Alliance,* 212–16; Richard P. Stebbins, *The United States in World Affairs* (New York, 1958–1967), 94–139; and Miriam Camps, *European Unification in the Sixties: From the Veto to the Crisis* (New York, 1966), 1–28.
40. Interviews with George Ball, February 1988, Princeton, N.J.; J. Robert Schaetzel, May 1989, Bethesda, Md.; and Pierre Uri, October 1990, Hempstead, N.Y., all by Douglas Brinkley. Jean Monnet created the Action Committee in 1955 to promote European integration measures and began promoting his Atlantic partnership concept in 1959. See also Acheson-Monnet correspondence, Ser. 1, Box 23, Folder 288, in DGAPP.

House to promote his Atlantic partnership plan. This was a shrewd move; Acheson understood that such a meeting would remind Kennedy that de Gaulle spoke for only a fraction of Europeans and that the majority supported an economic and military partnership with the United States, Canada, and Great Britain. Kennedy was intrigued by the ideas of the Action Committee. In 1963 he would award the Freedom Medal to Monnet as the founder of the European Coal and Steel Community. Monnet was likewise impressed with Kennedy; his memoirs are filled with praise of the president's creative vision of the world and his strides toward achieving "an equal partnership between the United States and a united Europe."[41] Kennedy never shared Acheson and Monnet's extreme enthusiasm for an Atlantic partnership, however. He found it difficult to believe that transnational economic and military ties would in the long run prevail over narrow nationalism.

Monnet made another important three-week visit to Washington in April 1962 and began lining up appointments with highly placed friends in the Kennedy circle: Dean Rusk, Douglas Dillon, Walt Rostow, Henry Owen, McGeorge Bundy, J. Robert Schaetzel, and, of course, Dean Acheson and George Ball. Monnet was on the circuit trying to sell his vision of partnership between the United States and a united Europe. James Reston of the New York *Times* wrote of Monnet on 11 April: "He knows that there are immediate difficulties, but he assumes their solution and asks: What is the next step? And with the question he has at least started a quiet debate among some of the most powerful officials in Washington."[42] Working with Acheson at his P Street home in mid-June, Monnet put the finishing touches on a new Action Committee resolution which, given to Ball, Rostow, Owen, and Schaetzel, resurfaced in a slightly revised form in a major policy speech Kennedy delivered a week later.

In his famous declaration of interdependence speech at Independence Hall on 4 July 1962— to which at various draft stages Rostow, Acheson, Ball, Schaetzel, and Owen had contributed—Kennedy did promise that the United States would work with a united Europe to create "a concrete Atlantic partnership, a mutually beneficial partnership between the new union now emerging in Europe and the old American union founded here 173 years ago." The speech contained elements of the resolution issued during the previous week by the Action Committee. The resolution in many ways resembled the economic portion of Acheson's NATO policy review of 1961. The committee stated: "The economic political unity of Europe including Britain and the establishment of relations of equal

41. Jean Monnet, travel diary, "Voyages de Jean Monnet, 1955–1975," Monnet Papers, Foundation Jean Monnet, Ferme Dorigny, Lausanne, Switzerland; Memorandum for the President, Subject: Luncheon meeting with Jean Monnet, 6 March 1961, in NSF, Box 321, JFKL; Jean Monnet, *Memoirs,* trans. Richard Mayne (Garden City, N.Y., 1978), 472. For the Ball-Monnet relationship, see George Ball, "Introduction," in *Jean Monnet: The Path to European Unity,* ed. Douglas Brinkley and Clifford Hackett (New York, 1991); and Ball, *The Past Has Another Pattern: Memoirs* (New York, 1982), 66–99.

42. Monnet travel diary, James Reston, New York *Times,* 11 April 1961.

partnership with the United States, alone will make it possible to consolidate the West and so create conditions for lasting peace between East and West."[43] Although Acheson liked both the resolution and Kennedy's speech, since he had a hand in writing both, he cringed at the phrase "equal partnership"; as a lawyer he had seen and been engaged in countless partnerships but never one that was equal, he declared.[44] Acheson had some private qualms about Kennedy's speech; it might be a sly attempt to obtain support for the Trade Expansion Act through New Frontier rhetoric. The act, which passed that August, gave the president authority to establish what amounted to a free trade zone embracing the United States and the Common Market.[45]

A month before the West Point speech in December 1962, Acheson wrote Monnet with a litany of complaints: weakness in the West, a U.S. dollar crisis, the hollowness of the Grand Design, de Gaulle's continuing anti-British bias, the mediocrity of world leadership, the slowness of the European integration process, and the endless crises in the Atlantic Alliance that made the notion of a durable Atlantic partnership appear unrealistic. Monnet disputed these bleak assessments. But Acheson was growing pessimistic about the prospects for European integration. In a letter to J. Robert Schaetzel in April 1963, he noted that it was mandatory for Monnet to be optimistic. That was the purpose of the Action Committee: to promote all aspects of the European integration movement, to prod the Western leaders to think broadly and boldly. But although Acheson approved of its public relations activities, he thought Monnet's organization essentially weak, handcuffed by de Gaulle's obstructionism and by its own visionless bureaucratic members. De Gaulle had power; Monnet had only channels to like-minded people and could not counter the French president's continuing opposition to British entry into the Common Market. "Monnet and his people can help: they are good at organizing support for a new idea when the opponent is ignorance or inertia," Acheson wrote Schaetzel. "But they cannot lead against de Gaulle. They have no power base."[46] It had become clear to Acheson that the Atlantic partnership could not be fully developed until de Gaulle left the scene.

43. For a discussion of JFK's Independence Day speech and Monnet's Action Committee resolution, see François Duchene, "Jean Monnet's Methods," in *Jean Monnet,* ed. Brinkley and Hackett, 184–209. For the text of JFK's speech, see *Public Papers of the Presidents of the United States: John F. Kennedy, 1962* (Washington, D.C., 1963), 538. For Monnet's proposal, see "Joint Declaration, June 26, 1962," in *Action Committee for the United States of Europe: Statements and Declarations, 1955–1967* (Lausanne, Switzerland, 1988), 62–65. My understanding of the JFK-Monnet relationship comes from my interviews with J. Robert Schaetzel, May 1989; and François Duchene, October 1990, Hyde Park, N.Y.
44. Quoted in J. Robert Schaetzel, *The Unhinged Alliance: America and the European Community* (New York, 1975), 41.
45. Dean G. Acheson to Hans J. Morgenthau, 25 March 1963, Ser. 1, Box 23, Folder 289; and Dean G. Acheson to William L. Clayton, 12 April 1963, Ser. 1, Box 6, Folder 77, both in DGAPP. For a good brief discussion of the Trade Expansion Act, see Frank Costigliola, "The Pursuit of Atlantic Community, Nuclear Arms, Dollars, and Britain," in *Kennedy's Quest for Victory: American Foreign Policy, 1961–1963,* ed. Thomas G. Paterson (New York, 1989), 30–31.
46. Dean G. Acheson to Jean Monnet, November 1962; Jean Monnet to Dean G. Acheson, 23 November 1962, Ser. 1, Box 23, Folder 288, both in DGAPP; Dean G. Acheson to J. Robert Schaetzel, 1 April 1963, Ser. 1, Box 28, Folder 356, in DGAPP.

Acheson was writing out of bitter experience: on 14 January 1963, de Gaulle had stunned the Western world with the announcement that France would veto Britain's entry into the Common Market. De Gaulle gave three reasons for his decision: Britain's economic structure and monetary system differed from that of the six Common Market members, and it lacked the will to change; the current member nations had more similarities with each other than differences, whereas with Britain they had more differences; and Britain's admission to the EEC would be followed by applications from other nations, which if approved would lead to the formation of a "gigantic Atlantic Community that would be dependent on and be run by America."[47]

De Gaulle's position infuriated his Anglo-American allies, who thought him bent on undermining the Atlantic community and NATO. On 29 January, six days after signing a bilateral treaty with Germany, France entered its official veto against British entry into the EEC, the only one of six member nations to do so. These events brought to a climax a tumultuous period in postwar European history. In short order, de Gaulle had rejected JFK's Polaris submarine offer, turned his back on England, and embraced West Germany. His goal was to launch a new political alignment in Europe, based on the Paris-Bonn axis, that would counter U.S. hegemony while initiating an era of improved relations with the USSR.

Acheson believed that de Gaulle's actions had to be countered with a demonstration of unity within the Atlantic Alliance. France must be reprimanded and persuaded to reconsider British entry into the EEC. "I have been hand-holding, encouraging, advising, and prodding on both sides of the Atlantic as General de Gaulle lowered the boom with such a resounding thud," Acheson wrote John Cowles. "Although the warning was ample and clear, no one thought the worst would really happen. . . . This threat is greater than that of last October [the missile crisis] and can't be handled with a blockade—or with bandaids. I have been sounding like a combination Jeanne d'Arc and Henry V."[48] As Acheson saw it, the question was how to get de Gaulle to overcome his obsessive fear that the United States was trying to exercise control over NATO and had plans to absorb an expanded Common Market and turn France into an American satellite.

Some of Acheson's German friends asked the former secretary to contact Chancellor Adenauer personally to lobby against de Gaulle's announced veto, a tactic the State Department approved. "If anyone can affect General de Gaulle's decision you are surely that person," Acheson cabled Chancellor Adenauer on 18 January. "I urge you to dissuade him from the disastrous course of breaking off negotiations with the British on their application to the Common Market. His indicated course will destroy the unity of Europe and of the West which you have so brilliantly and patiently worked to bring close to its pinnacle."[49]

---

47. De Gaulle is quoted in Alfred Grosser, *The Western Alliance: European-American Relations Since 1945* (New York, 1982), 206–208.

48. Dean G. Acheson to John Cowles, 31 January 1961, Ser. 1, Box 6, Folder 83, in DGAPP.

49. Telegram, Dean G. Acheson to Konrad Adenauer, 18 January 1963, in Acheson Papers, PAF, SD/WHA, Box 86, HSTL. The following day Acheson wrote Truman that he had urged Ade-

Although Acheson could not dispel the chaos de Gaulle was wreaking on the alliance, he comforted himself with Jean Monnet's aphorisms that the unification of Europe could only take a step forward in an atmosphere of crisis. De Gaulle's vision of Europe, Acheson felt, held little appeal for other European nations, who would be less than enthusiastic about exchanging the French pipe dream of renewed grandeur for American military and economic strength. De Gaulle's actions had done some damage, but Acheson did not believe they would change the course of Allied policy. Acheson saw the Gaullist vision as resting on shaky grounds: one of de Gaulle's rationales for vetoing the British bid was that the six current Common Market members were not tied to an outside power by special political or military pacts. Acheson, on the contrary, "supposed that all six were tied to us or—at least equally important—that we were tied to them by the most special political and military pact in our history, one which reversed the whole course of our foreign relations since President Washington's Farewell Address— the North Atlantic Treaty."[50]

Undeterred by Acheson's efforts, de Gaulle turned his energies toward achieving Franco-German unity. On 23 January, again to U.S. shock and dismay, he had signed a treaty with Chancellor Adenauer solidifying closer economic and military ties between their two nations.[51] Acheson had known that Adenauer was concerned about the Kennedy administration's commitment to Germany and that de Gaulle had been shrewdly cultivating his fellow conservative Catholic friend, but the treaty nevertheless came as a shock. "Chancellor Adenauer made a mistake—and I think a serious one—in signing the French treaty when he did," Acheson wrote to Kurt Birrenbach, an industrialist who was a Christian Democratic party member of the Bundestag. "The Chancellor has never understood General de Gaulle's design [of French leadership in Europe] nor the undignified and demeaning role designed for him and for Germany. He has believed that his place in history would be that of the reconciler of France and Germany—a place long since occupied by Messieurs Schuman and Monnet. Neither nation has today the power, interest, or inclination to return to the futile hostilities of the past. His real role, if he but knew it, was to cement together Western Europe and North America."[52]

Since 1945, Acheson continued, the Western European countries had be-

---

nauer, by cable, "to move General de Gaulle from the disastrous course he has chartered, which, if followed, will go far to destroy the Chancellor's life work" (Dean G. Acheson to Harry S. Truman, 19 January 1961, Ser. 1, Box 31, Folder 396, in DGAPP).

50. Dean G. Acheson, "De Gaulle and the West," *New Leader*, 1 April 1963, pp. 17–22, Acheson, "The Obstacles to Partnership," speech delivered at California Institute of Technology, Pasadena, Calif., 7 March 1963, Ser. 3, Box 51, Folder 56, in DGAPP; Dean G. Acheson to Kurt Birrenbach, 19 February 1963, Ser. 1, Box 3, Folder 36, in DGAPP; rpr. in Acheson, *Among Friends*, 242–44.

51. Acheson wrote Michael Janeway that he had given his German friends "hell for the Chancellor's stupidity in signing the treaty with France on his visit to Paris" (Dean G. Acheson to Michael Janeway, 5 March 1963, Ser. 1, Box 16, Folder 209, in DGAPP).

52. Acheson to Birrenbach, 19 February 1963.

haved toward Washington like "anemia patients with a blood bank. . . . We are happy that our friends are feeling so invigorated and confident that they class the United States with a host of other countries with which they do not wish to be involved. But we wonder whether General de Gaulle really expressed a view which Germans want the Chancellor to accept?"[53] American journalists as diverse as Walter Lippmann and James Reston joined Acheson in criticizing Adenauer's action.

Adenauer did not respond to Acheson's cable until after he had signed the Franco-German treaty. Then, in a detailed two-page confidential letter, he defended his action and maintained that he had previously procured the blessing of the Kennedy administration. "In some of the reports and articles [emanating from Washington] . . . the Federal Government and I, myself, have been criticized for having signed the German-French Treaty on January 22nd," Adenauer wrote Acheson. "Well, I had informed Secretary of State Rusk when he visited me last summer that we intended to establish closer ties with France; I asked him whether the United States had any reservations in this respect. Mr. Rusk answered at the time that the United States, of course, had no reservations, that, on the contrary, they would warmly welcome a close relationship between Germany and France and that they, themselves had special ties to Great Britain." Adenauer added that when he was informed in December that the treaty would be signed, the U.S. ambassador to Bonn, Walter Dowling, again conveyed American support of the Franco-German pact. "And now, everything is supposed to be interpreted in a different way because President de Gaulle, in his press conference on January 14, made his well known remarks on the entry of Great Britain into the EEC."[54]

Shortly after the treaty was signed, President Kennedy asked Acheson for a comprehensive analysis of why the Grand Design was coming unglued before it had even gotten started and what immediate steps the administration might take to counter de Gaulle's defiance and Adenauer's ambivalence. In "Reflections on the January Debacle," the sixteen-page memo he produced, Acheson called the chancellor's statements in his confidential letter preposterous. Did Adenauer really expect him to believe that the coincidence of the treaty signing with de Gaulle's remarks was merely fortuitous? Adenauer knew full well that de Gaulle was using Franco-German rapprochement as an instrument for reducing America's influence in Europe. Acheson wrote: "One cannot say that the West has not had ample warning [in Adenauer's summer meeting with Rusk] of the French and German action, yet it has been caught unprepared and been thrown into confusion. What was unexpected was not de Gaulle's wishes and desires, but that he acted, and acted so brazenly and revealingly. And what was surprising about

53. *Ibid.*
54. Adenauer to Acheson [n.d.], in Acheson Papers, PAF, SD/WHA, January–December 1963, Box 86, HSTL.

Adenauer was that he acted so submissively in signing a treaty of Franco-German rapprochement."[55]

Acheson urged the president to apply pressure on West Germany to make a choice between the United States and France, for the treaty was immutable. To aid the Germans in understanding the long-term benefits of siding with the United States, Acheson recommended that they be provided with a written analysis of Gaullist policy and reasons why Bonn should reject it along with an in-depth prospectus of long-range political, economic, and military policies for European–North American collaboration. Acheson followed with his own detailed evaluation of the dangers posed by de Gaulle and a blueprint for strengthening the Atlantic Alliance. The most important thing, Acheson told the president, was to reassure Bonn, in writing, that the United States stood firmly behind German reunification.[56]

Although Kennedy and Rusk concurred with Acheson's main objective—eliciting German disavowal of the recently signed treaty—they were not as enthusiastic as Acheson would have liked about the quid pro quo he was recommending. But given that de Gaulle was playing realpolitik poker and Germany was the stake, Kennedy decided it was advantageous to make use of Acheson. Who better to challenge the French leader than a distinguished American statesman known throughout Europe as a stalwart of NATO and a true believer in the Atlantic partnership idea? "Any discussion we have on . . . Germany," Kennedy instructed McGeorge Bundy in early February, "should include Dean Acheson."[57]

But as the months went by, Acheson became more and more perturbed. Kennedy, he thought, was handling the crisis as he had Berlin and Cuba, by drift and indecision. "I have been carrying on a war on two fronts—one against the Chancellor in the Bundestag to minimize the damage caused by his stupidity in signing the French treaty when he did," Acheson wrote a friend in Dusseldorf, "the other, against my own government for its complete lack of perception of the intensity of German concentration on reunification and our silly dallying with Moscow over Berlin."[58]

There were also tensions over Adenauer's assertion in his letter to Acheson that Rusk had endorsed the idea of a Franco-German treaty and even had favorably compared it with America's intention to develop closer ties with Britain. Acheson thought Rusk was focused more on clearing himself of blame for the recent events than on meeting the crisis and altering its course. Instead of clearing his name, Rusk's lawyerly rebuttal of Adenauer's report of their conversation confirmed Acheson's suspicions that Rusk had made an inadvertent blunder. "I

55. Dean G. Acheson, Memorandum, "Reflections on the January Debacle," 31 January 1963, in Acheson Papers, PAF, SD/WHA, Box 86, HSTL.

56. *Ibid.*

57. Quoted in Costigliola, "Pursuit of Atlantic Community," 50.

58. Dean G. Acheson to Roger Warren Evans, 20 May 1963, Ser. 1, Box 9, Folder 115, in DGAPP.

did not refer in any way to any special relations with Britain in the context of the most general remarks about the importance of Franco-German reconciliation," Rusk wrote Acheson in an attempt to set the record straight with his former boss.[59]

Unconvinced that Kennedy and Rusk understood the urgency of getting Germany to reverse its course, Acheson, like a big-game hunter stalking his prey, pointed his pen and took aim at Charles de Gaulle, the true villain of the piece. In the January issue of *Foreign Affairs*, he published an article titled "The Practice of Partnership," which examined the problems hindering better relations between NATO allies. Acheson also supplied the White House with a detailed memorandum on how best to rattle de Gaulle's sublime self-confidence and to pressure him to terminate his plan to develop an independent French nuclear force.[60]

In early March Acheson set off for a university lecture circuit on the West Coast with the specific aim of deflating de Gaulle and his anachronistic vision of a Europe united around one dominant nation-state. At his first stop, the California Institute of Technology, Acheson did not criticize de Gaulle by name. But at a news conference following his lecture, Acheson explicitly stated that de Gaulle's vision of a Europe independent of the United States was "a mistaken policy." "We must press on with our policies," he continued. "I think [de Gaulle] will slow things up . . . but it's no cause for despair." Sooner or later, Acheson said, Britain would become in effect, if not in name, a partner in the EEC.[61]

At his next stop, the University of California at Berkeley, Acheson lashed out at the French president in no uncertain terms. He warned de Gaulle that he could not expect American military protection of a Europe that excluded American influence, although it was precisely this fantasy that undergirded the French president's notion of "a Europe from the Atlantic to the Urals" minus Great Britain. De Gaulle, buoyed by the first successful French atomic explosion in the Sahara in February 1960, envisioned a united Western Europe with conventional and nuclear power sufficient to balance the forces of Soviet-controlled Eastern Europe. But there was no possibility of actually attaining such a balance; a French nuclear force necessarily would be limited in both capacity for delivery and destructive power. In a crisis, Europe ultimately would have to rely on American nuclear supremacy. De Gaulle's fatal error lay in believing that even after banishing the American presence from Europe, he could still, when push came to shove, rely on U.S. aid if he used his small nuclear force to start a war

59. Acheson, Memorandum, 20 February 1963, and Dean Rusk to Dean G. Acheson, Feb. 3, 1963 [Private and Confidential], both in Acheson Papers, PAF, SD/WHA, Box 86, HSTL.

60. Dean Acheson, "The Practice of Partnership," *Foreign Affairs*, XLI, (January 1963), 247–60; Acheson, Memorandum, 20 February 1963.

61. Acheson, "The Obstacles to Partnership," 7 March 1963, Ser. 3, Box 51, Folder 56, in DGAPP; "Acheson Says U.S. Must Help NATO," New York *Times*, 8 March 1963, p. 3. After ten bitter years of fratricidal European infighting, Britain was admitted to the Community in 1973.

with the Soviets. Acheson characterized de Gaulle's policy as a "suicidal doctrine," for he sought the best of both worlds for his ideal Europe and assigned the worst part to America, and "it is difficult to conceive of any government in this country undertaking so unpromising a commitment."[62]

Acheson recited a list of optimal attitudes and actions for the United States. Remain confident that "the common allies" would not adopt de Gaulle's policy because it did not serve their common interest. (Europeans would realize that the United States was strong, while France was still "far from being a robust leader.") Base defense policy on an increase in conventional forces to deter Soviet expansionism into Western Europe; if the French delayed or frustrated NATO defense efforts, the United States would have to go forward "with nations able and willing to make progress." Maintain unequivocal support for German unification. Constant negotiations with the Soviets, he said, would have "seemed to Germans to edge toward increasing renegotiation of the East German regime."[63]

The next day the Elysée publicly disputed Acheson's "attack," contending that a French nuclear force would be able to prevent a Soviet invasion. The French, who viewed the tenacious Acheson as a stalking-horse for JFK, also claimed that Acheson had misinterpreted their attitude toward the alliance. De Gaulle, they insisted, believed in NATO but preferred national responsibility with the alliance to integration. Acheson's portrayal of the French position on the Common Market and on nuclear policy verged on caricature and was unworthy of serious response.[64]

France's leading newspapers had published the text of Acheson's Berkeley speech and debated the validity of its arguments. "I made the speech, in part, because of a curious modern phenomenon, the degree to which the French seem able to brainwash our correspondents in Paris," Acheson wrote Louis Halle. (He was referring to Cyrus L. ["Cy"] Sulzberger, Drew Middleton, and Crosby Noyes.) "The result is to give this country a mistaken sense of General de Gaulle's power. He has considerable capability for doing harm or to block developments, due to the vital geographical position of France, as well as to the part which France has played in the history of Europe. But compared to the United States, France is feeble. It seemed important to put de Gaulle into proportion."[65]

In his "In the Nation" column Arthur Krock remarked that Acheson's warning to de Gaulle was "not likely to produce a fundamental change in French pol-

62. Acheson, "Europe: Kaleidoscope or Clouded Crystal," speech delivered at the University of California, Berkeley, 13 March 1963, Ser. 3, Box 51, Folder 56, in DGAPP; excerpted in New York *Times,* 14 March 1963, p. 2.
63. *Ibid.*
64. Drew Middleton, "French Contest Acheson Attack," New York *Times,* 15 March 1963, p. 3.
65. Dean G. Acheson to Louis Halle, 19 March 1963, Ser. 1, Box 15, Folder 190, in DGAPP. Acheson went on to say that this brainwashing phenomenon did not happen in Bonn, London, or Rome, but that in Paris, "Cy Sulzberger, Drew Middleton, Crosby Noyes—all seemed to be putty in the hands of M. Maurois' Minion."

icy," but Krock was proved wrong, for by May the Gaullist vision no longer held sway in Europe. "I do not believe that the situation is as puzzling as the Administration appears to think," Acheson accurately noted to Truman early that May. "Germany is the present key to movement in Europe, and I think, is ready to act with us."[66]

By the summer of 1963 it was clear that most in Bonn favored the Atlanticist vision over the Gaullist one and did not want to weaken Germany's ties with the United States: the Franco-German treaty had not been a commitment between two governments but rather the final act in the passionate fourteen-year political infatuation between de Gaulle and Adenauer. On 26 June President Kennedy made the historic speech in West Berlin in which he promised to defend free Berlin from communist encroachment. His keynote phrase, "Ich bin ein Berliner," reverberated through the frenzied crowd. Shortly thereafter, the Bonn government added a preamble to the treaty with France that was widely interpreted as a reaffirmation of German ties to the United States and NATO. The Franco-German treaty slipped into oblivion, and the Kennedy administration gave a sigh of relief. At a dinner in July for French parliamentarians de Gaulle admitted he had been outflanked by the Americans. "You see, treaties are like young girls and roses; they do not last long," de Gaulle shrugged. "If the Franco-German Treaty is not to be implemented, it will not be the first time in history."[67] Although a rupture between Bonn and Washington had been averted, some commentators still believe that de Gaulle's announcement of 14 January 1963 marked the end of Kennedy's Grand Design.[68]

On 18 September 1963, Acheson spoke at the Hague before the European Movement, an organization formed in 1948 to promote European unity. Again he lashed out at de Gaulle's nationalist policies as a "lethal danger for both European and Atlantic unity" and characterized his views as "parochial nationalism."[69] Acheson's attacks on de Gaulle increased in frequency and sharpened in tone until the final crisis in 1966, when the general announced that France was pulling out of NATO's integrated military command. Acheson continued to describe Charles de Gaulle as "a great man" who "brought about a near miracle for France," but he deeply regretted and deplored "the havoc he wreaked on European unity."[70]

66. Arthur Krock, "Improbable Hypothesis for De Gaulle," New York *Times*, 15 March 1963, p. 6.; Dean G. Acheson to Harry S. Truman, 6 May 1963, Ser. 1, Box 31, Folder 396, DGAPP.

67. Quoted in Ball, *The Past Has Another Pattern*, 273.

68. See, for example, Grosser, *Western Alliance*, 208; and Robert Kleiman, *Atlantic Crisis: American Diplomacy Confronts a Resurgent Europe* (New York, 1964), 21–46.

69. See Edward T. O'Toole, "Acheson Calls Nationalism of de Gaulle Peril to Unity," New York *Times*, 19 September 1963, pp. 1, 2.

70. Dean G. Acheson to T. C. Bryant, 1 December 1970, Ser. 1, Box 2, Folder 20, in DGAPP; rpr. in *Among Friends*, 319. For Acheson's most candid complaints about de Gaulle, see Acheson, interview with the Public Broadcasting Corporation, 3 December 1967 (reels 1–3), Ser. 3, Box 53, Folder 74, in DGAPP.

## *Disenchantment with Kennedy*

By the time of the January debacle Acheson had lost all patience with the Kennedy administration's handling of both international and domestic affairs. The president continued to consult him on NATO-related matters, and in February 1963 Acheson headed a special task force on the chronic payments imbalance and dangerous outflow of gold and dollars. But Acheson was fed up with the "best and the brightest" crowd. "It seems to me interesting that a group of young men who regard themselves as intellectuals are capable of less coherent thought than we have had since Coolidge," Acheson complained to John Paton Davies. "They are pretty good at improvising, and, as Scotty Reston has observed, if we must get into trouble, it should be suddenly and unexpectedly, because they do their best with this sort of a situation. But God help us, he says, if they are given any time to think!"[71] Acheson had lost faith in McGeorge Bundy, Robert McNamara, Walt Rostow, and Dean Rusk; in his eyes George Ball and Paul Nitze, especially, had achieved the promise of their youth. "Paul Nitze's star is, I hope and believe, rising," Acheson wrote to Louis Halle. "It will be good for him, as he is not at the top of his capacity and needs to have all of it put to use. So does the country."[72]

Acheson was adamantly opposed to the administration's efforts to persuade Moscow to resume talks on a nuclear test ban, especially in the face of continuing crises in the Atlantic Alliance. He doubted Moscow's bona fides. "Rusk spreads suspicion with his futile talks with the Russians," Acheson wrote Truman, "and we continue to negotiate with ourselves in Geneva over a nuclear test ban which the Russians have no intentions of accepting." When the three-power talks (Britain, the Soviet Union, and the United States) began in Moscow with Under Secretary of State for Political Affairs W. Averell Harriman representing the United States, Acheson shuddered. Didn't Kennedy realize that the more the United States negotiated with the Soviets, the more NATO was impaired, the more Bonn worried about a bilateral Moscow-Washington deal on nuclear sharing? When the three powers signed the Limited Test-Ban Treaty on 5 August prohibiting nuclear tests in space, the atmosphere, and underwater, Acheson wondered what possible gain Kennedy expected to achieve from the deal since de Gaulle had refused to sign the treaty. Kennedy had Acheson's promise not to lobby on the Hill against ratification of the treaty—which was regarded as the most important U.S.-Soviet agreement since the 1955 accord that ended the postwar occupation of Austria—but Acheson voiced his personal lack of enthusiasm for the test ban to John Cowles the day it was signed: "The way to win the Cold War

71. Dean G. Acheson to John Paton Davies, 18 April 1963, Ser. 1, Box 7, Folder 93, in DGAPP. Davies, a senior Foreign Service officer, was one of the so-called old China hands in the State Department when Acheson was secretary. See also Dean G. Acheson, interview, 27 April 1964, 31–34, in JFKL Oral History Program.

72. Acheson to Halle, 19 March 1963.

may be difficult and unclear—though I am self-confident enough to believe that to plug away at the policies I have advocated since the end of the war will do it—but one thing seems to me as clear as day. That is that the one sure way to lose the Cold War is to lose Germany; and that the one sure way to lose Germany is to convince Germans that we are prepared to sacrifice German interests for an accord . . . with Russia."[73]

In the fall, Dean and Alice Acheson traveled throughout Europe for five weeks. Acheson spoke at three large public occasions: a conference of the Dutch European Unity group at the Hague, a session of the Bundestag, and a meeting of the German American Club in Bonn. He also spoke at informal meetings, including a private session at the Institute of Strategic Studies in England attended by more than 150 defense experts from around the world, and had numerous private meetings with over a dozen high-ranking European government representatives.[74] While in Britain Acheson also tried to patch up old friendships derailed by his West Point speech. He told a friend that he found Britain in a ghastly state of decline, "moving swiftly to a Little England, almost Swedish position." France, meanwhile, was in a "nationalist, anti-American—and if we act wisely—isolated position," whereas Italy seemed wholly "self-concerned, prosperous and divided" but "hardly an international force." Only Germany, Acheson observed sadly, was subject to American influence.[75]

Before leaving for Europe, Dean Acheson had provided for Secretary of Defense McNamara a memorandum on the future of German-American relations. Acheson argued that America's policy of integrating and denationalizing Germany had achieved considerable success in the fifteen years since the creation of the FRG. At the present time the United States needed to be vigilant, for the good relations between the two nations brought about by the stability of the Adenauer era soon might be in jeopardy. Acheson pointed to "the emergence of a new German generation, untroubled by war guilt; increasing German preoccupation with the unity issue, and some doubts as to US intentions on this score; the retirement of the Chancellor and resulting vacuum in German politics; the heady example of de Gaulle's nationalism across the Rhine; and the slow down at Brussels—all contributed to make vocal those who are not in the way of grace and who believe that the Federal Republic now has a right and duty to look more to its own national interests." Acheson wrote that he did not fear "a revival

73. Acheson to Truman, 6 May 1963; Dean G. Acheson to John Cowles, 5 August 1963, Ser. 1, Box 6, Folder 83, DGAPP; rpr. in *Among Friends*, 250–51.

74. Alice Acheson, interview by Douglas Brinkley, December 1986, Washington, D.C. See also Dean G. Acheson, statement at the Institute of Strategic Studies, Cambridge, England, 20–23 September 1963, Ser. 3, Box 52, Folder 59; Dean G. Acheson, "The American Interest in European Unity," Speech delivered at The Hague, September 1963, Ser. 3, Box 52, Folder 58; and Dean G. Acheson, "Germany in the New Europe," Address to the German American Club, Bonn, West Germany, 18 October 1963, Ser. 3, Box 52, Folder 59, all in DGAPP.

75. Dean G. Acheson to Mrs. Mortimer Seabury, 29 October 1963, Ser. 1, Box 28, Folder 360, in DGAPP; rpr. in *Among Friends*, 254–55. Mortimer and Frida Seabury were friends of the Achesons in Antigua.

of the Nazi movement, but rather the emergence of a Germany whose leaders are dedicated to national goals in the same sense that de Gaulle is."[76]

If a resurgence of German nationalism actually developed, Acheson believed, it would probably end the European unity movement. The British would view Germany with suspicion and hostility; the vitality and cohesion of the Atlantic Alliance would be usurped, leaving German reunification to come about through a Soviet-German deal; and a new nationalist German government would seek independent negotiations with Moscow, as General Hans von Seeckt did after World War I. "You know my theme song only too well," Acheson wrote McNamara, "that Germany is the most important country in the world to us. It both holds, if not *the* key to Europe, at least a key, and is subject to be influenced by us in its use as the Soviet Union, France, and Britain are not."[77]

Although Acheson acknowledged that the FRG was still dependent on the United States for its security, he believed that this advantage would evaporate if the CDU was ousted from power by the pro-Gaullist Social Democrats (SPD). To keep the FRG moderate and compliant with American policies, the United States must decline to help France develop its own independent national nuclear capability and sell Germany on the MLF. This represented a reversal of Acheson's recommendation in his NATO review document of 1961. Acheson previously had been unenthusiastic about the MLF, but given the French refusal to sign the test-ban treaty, the NATO nuclear sharing proposal appeared the surest means of keeping Bonn from moving closer to de Gaulle's open arms and escaping the proliferation of national nuclear forces in Europe. Acheson was adamant about not helping France: should the United States opt to aid de Gaulle's nuclear endeavor, "it would set up an evident comparison between the independent nuclear forces which we would be helping France and Britain to achieve and the combined and *dependent* force which we would be asking Germany to join." The United States must refuse to assist France—even if this meant yet another crack in the continuation of moderate, pro-American CDU leadership in the FRG under such leaders as Ludwig Erhard, Kai Uwe von Haeel, and Gerhard Schröder.[78]

Acheson went on to analyze internal German politics. Adenauer, recently forced to resign the chancellorship because of an arrangement made in 1961 with his coalition partner, the Free Democrats, had refused to relinquish leadership of the CDU and was making life unbearable for the new chancellor, his fellow Christian Democrat Ludwig Erhard. Adenauer and Franz Joseph Strauss openly were criticizing Erhard for his cold-shoulder attitude toward de Gaulle. If nothing was done to strengthen Erhard's hand, Acheson warned, the SPD easily would win election victory in 1965. The United States must "be prepared to

---

76. Dean G. Acheson to Robert S. McNamara, Memorandum, 16 September 1963, in Acheson Papers, PAF, SD/WHA, Box 86, HSTL.
77. *Ibid.*
78. *Ibid.*

suffer the slings and arrows of an outrageous General [de Gaulle] for sometime" in order to help CDU moderates maintain control of the Bonn government. Only if they were convinced that the United States was serious about developing an MLF in Europe would the West Germans choose Kennedy's Atlantic vision over de Gaulle's European one.[79]

Shortly after Acheson returned to Washington, President Kennedy asked for his views on the political climate in Europe with Adenauer and Macmillan newly out of office. Acheson related a story. The eighty-eight-year-old Adenauer, still steaming about being pushed aside, had scolded Erhard at the end of his two-hour inaugural address. "You're only going to be in office two years," he said, "and you took almost that long to say what you were going to do." Acheson told Kennedy: "The Germans are just different from everyone else. You have to treat them differently from everybody else." Adenauer died a few months later.[80]

Later that evening Kennedy repeated his conversation with Acheson to Benjamin Bradlee, his close friend and *Newsweek*'s Washington bureau chief. "I think Acheson . . . and Clark Clifford in a different way, are the two best advocates I have ever heard," the president said. "Acheson would have made a helluva Supreme Court justice, although he was sixty-seven or sixty-eight when I had my first vacancy."[81]

Although Acheson and Kennedy had policy differences, the two admired each other, Acheson somewhat begrudgingly. "Kennedy was very impressed with Acheson," recalls George Ball. "He retained that throughout, although they would occasionally get cross-wired. Jack was a little bit afraid of Dean. After all, Jack was a very young man and Acheson a titan."[82] By spring of 1963 Kennedy had become somewhat more relaxed in his dealings with Acheson.

Acheson had been named by the Yale Club of Montclair, New Jersey, as the Outstanding Alumnus of Yale University, and a dinner was held in his honor in April 1963. Kennedy decided to have some fun with the occasion. He sent a telegram to Acheson at the dinner, praising the former secretary while at the same time getting in a few lighthearted jabs. He made reference to the honorary doctor of law degrees from Yale that had been awarded to each man in July 1962:

> As a member of the Yale Class of 1962, I am delighted to extend congratulations to Dean Acheson as he becomes the Outstanding Alumnus of Yale University. One of Mr. Acheson's own outstanding traits is his possession of an intimidating seniority, and it gives me some

79. *Ibid.* For a good short discussion of U.S.-German relations during the transition from Adenauer to Ludwig Erhard, see Hans W. Gatzke, *Germany and the United States* (Cambridge, Mass., 1980), chapter 8.
80. The Erhard inaugural story is told in Benjamin C. Bradlee, *Conversations with Kennedy* (New York, 1975), 224–25.
81. *Ibid.*
82. George Ball, interview, February 1988, Princeton, N.J.

satisfaction that a year ago we were able to receive our advanced diplomas on the same platform. . . .

As a Yale man I welcome this recognition, and as a Harvard man I want to assure Mr. Acheson of my reasonable confidence that in his new guise he will not be presiding over the decline of a first-rate power. It is fortunate for Yale that it has so long had so robust and experienced a leader as Mr. Acheson.[83]

The heavily Republican Montclair Yale Club roared with laughter at the president's telegram. "I particularly liked your attributing to me an 'intimidating seniority,'" Acheson wrote Kennedy in a handwritten thank-you note, "partly—I suppose—because innocuous characters like to imagine themselves impressively stern, but chiefly, I think, because of your own response to this alleged quality. Clearly no one is less intimidated by it than you are, and yet no one could have listened to the, perhaps, delusive certitude of my offerings over the past two years with more courtesy and close attention."[84]

When John F. Kennedy was assassinated on 22 November 1963, Acheson, along with the rest of the country, mourned. "No one knew what had happened," Acheson wrote a British friend. "We were like victims of an earthquake. Even the ground under our feet was shaking." But Acheson disputed the account of the emotional mood in America portrayed by the media. "Surely there was sorrow for the death of a brave young man and an inexpressibly gallant young widow and two utterly pathetic and heart-breaking children," Acheson wrote. But it was not the bewilderment attendant on losing a great leader, as it had been when FDR died, for Kennedy was not that. "It was fear from utter collapse of all sense of security which lay at the bottom of the emotion."[85]

Acheson wrote to Jacqueline Kennedy, praising her for acting as "a symbol to us of what this sorrowing nation should be." Her stoicism brought to the country a much-needed "belief in the nobility of the human spirit."[86]

It was this quality of grace under pressure, the ability not to complain but to bear and endure life's hardships, that Dean Acheson most admired in an individual; perhaps the same could be said of John F. Kennedy. Both also believed in courage—the courage to act boldly—but Acheson thought the debonair Kennedy only mimicked courage and was not inherently courageous like Harry Truman or himself. Acheson equally admired the ability to make firm decisions, a capacity General George Marshall called "the rarest gift given to man." He

83. Telegram, John F. Kennedy to Dean G. Acheson, 19 April 1963, Ser. 1, Box 18, Folder 223, in DGAPP.

84. Dean G. Acheson to John F. Kennedy, 6 May 1963, Ser. 1, Box 18, Folder 223, in DGAPP.

85. Dean G. Acheson, "Thoughts Written to a British Friend on the Assassination of President Kennedy," in Acheson, *Grapes from Thorns* (New York, 1972), 81–82.

86. Dean G. Acheson to Jacqueline Kennedy, 28 November 1963, Ser. 1, Box 18, Folder 223, in DGAPP.

thought that Truman had this gift [87] Kennedy was too self-conscious, Acheson declared, too worried about what others thought of him. If action was overdeliberated, it was no longer decisive. This was Kennedy's fatal flaw, Acheson believed. From the Berlin Crisis to the Cuban Missile Crisis to the collision with de Gaulle to the Test-Ban Treaty, Acheson found Kennedy's leadership wanting. Acheson acknowledged that Kennedy, like himself, wanted to beat back Soviet expansionist efforts and win the Cold War. JFK, however, was not enough of a hawk; he often turned soft when the chips were down. On a personal level, Acheson had grown to like the young president and his ironic wit. He empathized with the president as he confronted difficult decisions, and he found Kennedy's foreign and defense policies light-years ahead of Eisenhower's. But Acheson still lamented what he saw as a continuing decline of presidential leadership since the Truman-Acheson team had left government.

Acheson believed Kennedy had drifted into what most considered foreign policy successes. But at what cost? Kennedy seemed to equate averting confrontation with demonstrating strong leadership; to Acheson this represented timidity and mediocrity. The United States was the richest, most militarily powerful nation-state the world had ever seen. Its enemy, the Soviet Union, sought world domination. To Acheson's mind, there was no reason why the United States, with all its power and might, could not contain Soviet expansionism, develop an Atlantic partnership, and win the Cold War; all it would take would be single-minded resolve. But that resolve had to be undergirded by a strong, viable, and cohesive NATO and by American nuclear superiority. To Acheson, the Grand Design remained a direction rather than a policy, a prescription for the future rather than an honest-to-god program to be implemented. Kennedy, he claimed, was unable to commit himself to a real policy to unite the West beyond the veneer of exciting speeches about distant vague goals.

In trying to please the entire world community, JFK had alienated several of America's European allies while reaping nothing but headaches from the developing nations. Kennedy was afraid to make enemies of the former colonial nations, and this showed lack of courage and of a sense of priorities. Great leadership, Acheson believed, rested on knowing who your friends were and who your enemies were, and then, with persistence and determination, working systematically either to co-opt or to defeat your foes.[88]

An interview for the BBC in 1971 created yet another storm of controversy when Acheson gave a less-than-glowing assessment of John F. Kennedy. Although he was "attractive" and blessed "with real charm," Acheson declared, Kennedy was not "in any sense a great man." He explained: "I do not think he

87. Dean G. Acheson, Remarks on the Occasion of the Diamond Jubilee Celebration for the Honorable Harry S. Truman, 8 May 1959, in Acheson Papers, PAF, Speeches and Articles, 1936–1971, Box 139, HSTL.
88. Dean G. Acheson to John Paton Davies, 18 April 1963, Ser. 1, Box 7, Folder 93, in DGAPP.

knew a great deal about any of the matters which it's desirable that a chief of state or a President of the United States should know about. He was not decisive."[89] Acheson, bound to the policies and attributes of the bygone Truman era, was unable to appreciate that Kennedy had seized the mind and vision of a new generation and given it hope in America's future—even though the New Frontier rhetoric often outraced reality.

89. Kenneth Harris, "Pungent Memories from Mr. Acheson," *Life,* 23 July 1971, p. 53. Of his controversial comments on Kennedy, Acheson wrote: "Only two other speeches since I returned to private practice, I think, stirred up so much interest. My secretary tells me that two-thirds of the letters are so violently hostile and some downright scurrilous" (Dean G. Acheson to William B. Loeb, 29 July 1971, Ser. 1, Box 20, Folder 246, in DGAPP).

# 17

# Kennedy, Britain, and the European Community

## *Stuart Ward*

∼

Throughout his brief tenure in office, John F. Kennedy remained an ardent supporter of European unity.[1] The European Economic Community was seen as an exciting new experiment in European relations and formed a major pillar in Kennedy's Grand Design for the political and economic organization of the West. The Kennedy administration was equally committed to securing British membership in the Community, which was considered essential to ensuring the long-term political stability of the Continent. Harold Macmillan's EEC membership application of July 1961 was therefore warmly welcomed as a means of consolidating the steady progress of the founding "Six."[2]

Kennedy's conception of a united Europe did not, however, always correspond precisely with the designs and aspirations of his European partners. This was particularly true in the case of Britain's EEC membership bid, for which the apparent unity of purpose of Kennedy and Macmillan masked an underlying difference of view about the nature of Britain's desired role in Europe and the means by which it might be realized. Similarly, in the case of France, the Kennedy version of European unity stood in stark contrast to the European ambitions of General de Gaulle. This was no more clearly illustrated than at the time of de Gaulle's unilateral dismissal of the British EEC membership application in January 1963. The abrupt nature of de Gaulle's "veto" came as disastrous blow

1. Abbreviations used in the notes:
   CAB    Cabinet Office (PRO)
   EFTA    European Free Trade Association Archives, Geneva
   JFKL    John F. Kennedy Library, Boston
   LBJL    Lyndon B. Johnson Library, Austin
   FO    Foreign Office (PRO)
   NSF    National Security Files (JFKL/LBJL)
   POF    President's Office Files (JFKL)
   PREM    Prime Minister's Office (PRO)
   PRO    Public Record Office, London
   T    Treasury (PRO)
2. The founding member states were Belgium, France, Germany, Italy, Luxembourg, and the Netherlands.

to the Macmillan government and a major setback to the wider foreign policy objectives of the Kennedy administration. This essay examines the role of the United States in the British decision to apply for EEC membership and the difficulties of British and American policymakers in finding a common approach to the problem of de Gaulle and Europe.

~

The position of the U.S. State Department on the question of economic integration in Europe had become well established during the second term of the Eisenhower administration. Despite the economic disadvantages for the United States, the creation of the European Economic Community was considered a positive development because of the advantages of a strong political configuration in Western Europe in opposition to the Soviet bloc. The Six therefore received the full support of the United States in their endeavors to lay the foundations of a united Europe. By contrast, the Americans were far less enthusiastic about wider European trade arrangements that lacked the political commitment for greater European unity. The British proposal for a European free trade area in 1957 was regarded with suspicion by the State Department for this very reason. These feelings were shared by the French, who saw the British plan as an attempt to disrupt the progress of the EEC. Indeed, it has recently been shown that the United States played a not insignificant role in the French decision to break off the free trade area negotiations in November 1958.[3] The State Department was equally suspicious when the United Kingdom subsequently formed a smaller free trade area among the "Seven" in 1959.[4] The European Free Trade Association was seen as a purely commercial association that threatened to dilute the political cohesion of the Six.

The attitude of the United States on these issues contrasted markedly with the objectives of the United Kingdom government, which had invested a great deal of time and energy working toward a limited economic arrangement with the EEC and avoiding any political commitment. Britain had long felt unable to join the Six because of its economic and political links with the Commonwealth and because of a general unwillingness to sacrifice national sovereignty to a supranational body. Following the breakdown of the free trade area negotiations, the British continued to examine possibilities for an economic "bridge" between the EEC and EFTA, claiming that this would mitigate the political dangers of an economically divided Europe. But it became increasingly evident to British policymakers that such an arrangement was not negotiable, partly because of French opposition but also because of the well-known views of the Americans.

---

3. See R. T. Griffiths, "The End of the OEEC and the Birth of the OECD," in *Explorations in OEEC History,* ed. R. T. Griffiths (Paris, 1997).

4. The seven founding members of EFTA were the United Kingdom, Denmark, Norway, Sweden, Austria, Switzerland, and Portugal.

The American position was clearly spelled out by the U.S. under secretary of state, Douglas Dillon, during a visit to the United Kingdom in December 1959. In discussions with British ministers he left no doubt that, as far as the United States was concerned, a degree of political commitment to European unity was an essential prerequisite to any discriminatory economic agreement between Britain and the Six.[5]

Senior British ministers, including the prime minister, Harold Macmillan, were known to share the Americans' desire for strong political cohesion within NATO and regarded the development of potentially rival trading blocs in Europe with apprehension. Moreover, as the Community consolidated itself, concern mounted that the Six would develop an independent line on political and defense matters. The prospect of a strong political voice in Europe, favored by the United States, would pose a direct challenge to Britain's influence in the wider world and threaten the Anglo-American "special relationship." These fears prompted Macmillan in early 1960 to set up an interdepartmental steering committee to reexamine the various avenues open to Britain in relation to the Six. The committee, headed by Sir Frank Lee, handed down its report in May 1960, calling for fundamental changes in policy. The report recommended that Britain should abandon attempts to negotiate loose economic agreements with the Six and should instead seek full membership in the European Community. This finding was based on the assessment that special derogations could be negotiated for the problems of Commonwealth trade preferences and British agriculture, provided Britain could demonstrate a genuine commitment to European unity. Moreover, it was argued that once inside the Community, Britain could play a leading role in its development and ensure the protection of British sovereignty. It was emphasized, however, that the greatest obstacle to EEC membership might be the reluctance of the French to open the door to Britain. In his covering note to the report, Lee warned that "an essential step must be to ensure by some preliminary approach that the Six (and this really means France) would be willing to see us join or move to close association with them on terms which we could accept. To launch another initiative and receive a second rebuff would be disastrous."[6]

The problem of convincing General de Gaulle of the need to include Great Britain in the political and economic organization of Europe became a major focus of British policy planning throughout 1960. It was recognized that the support of both the United States and the Federal Republic of Germany would be essential in this regard. In discussions with Konrad Adenauer in August, Macmillan was encouraged by the chancellor's favorable attitude toward the possibility of an accommodation between Britain and the Six.[7] As far as the Ameri-

5. "Mr. Dillon's Visit: Sixes and Sevens," 8 December 1959, T234/717, in PRO.
6. "The Six and the Seven: The Long Term Objective," May 1960, 4, CAB129/102/Pt. 1, in PRO.
7. Macmillan to Lloyd, 14 August 1960, PREM11/2993, in PRO.

cans were concerned, however, it was felt that little could be achieved while Eisenhower remained in office because of the apparent lack of sympathy for Britain's special problems in coming to terms with the Community. The Eisenhower administration had gained a reputation in Whitehall, rightly or wrongly, for being shortsighted in its support for the Six, and the prospect of a new administration raised hopes for a change of heart from the Americans.

～

The inauguration of President John F. Kennedy in January 1961 did not occasion any drastic policy changes in relation to the "Sixes and Sevens" question. The official view remained that the United States would support British membership in the EEC, provided that this involved a genuine commitment to European unity rather than an attempt to weaken the political aspirations of the Six. In a report of March 1961, former secretary of state Dean Acheson emphasized the importance of a strengthened Europe to meet the growth of Soviet power and recommended that Britain should not be encouraged to remain apart from the Six because of a special relationship with the United States: "Over time, the UK might become convinced that its position apart from the continent did not constitute a promising base of power, particularly if the US was dealing ever more closely with growing strength on the continent. The US should look with favor on any trend in British thinking which contemplates eventual full membership in the six."[8]

Despite the continued hard line of the Europeanists in the State Department led by George Ball, the Macmillan government had cause for optimism about the change of administration. Whitehall officials began to report a "more pragmatic attitude" toward the United Kingdom's special economic and political difficulties in relation to the Six and a willingness to find solutions to these problems. In an early visit to Washington, Sir Frank Lee noted, "The first thing which must strike everyone is the new spirit which animates the Administration, and which seems to pervade the very air of Washington in a most exhilarating way." Lee placed great store on the constructive attitude of Ball, who "went out of his way to be friendly and cooperative, and explicitly disclaimed any tendency to be blindly pro-Six." The British also noticed a distinct change in the force of the Kennedy administration's advocacy for British EEC membership. In mid-March 1961, Ball told members of the British Embassy "almost aggressively that Britain should reverse the trend which had set in when she was driven out of Calais 250 years ago, that within five years she would be a full member of the European Community, and that, if she were to become a member, she would without difficulty become the dominant influence in the political and economic development of Europe."[9]

8. Acheson Report, "A Review of North Atlantic Problems for the Future," March 1961, p. 25, NSF/Box 220, in JFKL.

9. Lee to France, 24 February 1961, FO371/158161; "Sir Frank Lee's Personal Report on the Visit to Washington," 24 February 1961, PREM11/3284; and Caccia to Reilly, 16 March 1961, FO371/158161, all in PRO.

The British considered Ball to be an important link between the United Kingdom and France because of his close relationship with Jean Monnet. Ball's thinking about European integration had been influenced by Monnet, who shared the view that the political and economic organization of Europe would not be complete while Britain remained outside. Ball and Monnet were also of the opinion that the British tended to overestimate the problem of France.[10] During a visit to London at the end of March, Ball expressed the view that the French government would agree to United Kingdom membership, so long as the number of derogations requested from the Rome Treaty were kept to a minimum. Although he acknowledged the existence of certain elements in France that would oppose British entry, these would not prevail. This view seemed to be reinforced on 2 March, when the French foreign minister, Maurice Couve de Murville, gave a speech to the Consultative Assembly of the Council of Europe, which was interpreted in London as a clear invitation to join the Six. Couve asserted that "the Common Market was, and always remained, open to any other European country which wished to join it" and that "therein lies, for some at least, a valid possibility and without doubt the only really satisfactory solution." But these encouraging signs did not correspond with the experience of British officials during exploratory talks with the French in February and March. The talks revealed "little, if any common ground" between Britain and France on the question of possible derogations for Commonwealth trading interests and British agricultural subsidies. UK Treasury officials were forced to conclude, "We have not found the makings of a solution or a basis on which formal negotiations could be undertaken with any prospect of success."[11]

General de Gaulle's views about the future role of the European Community were revealed to Kennedy during a visit from the president of the French National Assembly, Michael Chaban-Delmas in March 1961. Chaban-Delmas had been "entrusted with a personal mission from General de Gaulle" to convey the general's ideas about the need for a fundamental reorganization of the procedures for consultation among the Western allies. He proposed that the three nuclear powers of the West, Britain, France, and the United States, should assume responsibility for the direction of the alliance and establish regular meetings so that Western policies could be "intimately coordinated." General de Gaulle was open to suggestions about the precise form of these consultations, but he was

---

10. In June 1961 Monnet told members of the British Colonial Office that the United Kingdom showed a lack of understanding of de Gaulle's position. He claimed that "de Gaulle wouldn't and couldn't object" to British membership because his views were "coloured and guided by thinking of how history would judge his actions" (Colonial Office to Macmillan, 14 June 1961, PREM11/3556 in PRO).

11. "Record of a Meeting to Discuss the Six-Seven Problem," 30 March 1961, FO371/158162, in PRO; "Assemblé consultative du conseil de l'Europe," Douzième session ordinaire, Compte Rendu Officiel, 2 March 1961, p. 716; "The Six-Seven Problem: Appreciation of the Present Situation and of Possible Courses for Future Action, Note by the Treasury," 7 March 1961, CAB134/1854 [E.S. (E) (61)1], in PRO.

certain that it would be "easy to arrange for meetings of the three chiefs of Government in a way which will not frighten Chancellor Adenauer or any other Western chief of Government." This suggestion was almost identical to de Gaulle's earlier proposal for a "tripartite directorate" of NATO, which had been rejected by Eisenhower and Macmillan in October 1958. The significance of his latest proposal, however, lay in the way he envisioned the division of responsibilities among the "Big Three." As Chaban-Delmas explained:

> The most complete coordination should exist between the three Western Powers which have responsibilities extending beyond their own borders. These are the United States, which is the leader and the greatest power of the West; the United Kingdom, which has special ties with the Commonwealth; and France. . . . General de Gaulle is working for a united Europe and is in constant touch with West Germany and the other nations of Europe. This makes France the natural channel for the coordination of policies on the continent in the same way in which the United States and the United Kingdom are the natural channels for the coordination of policies in other geographical areas.[12]

Although Kennedy skillfully evaded any commitment to this proposal, it was clear that de Gaulle's views on the political organization of Europe were far removed from the objectives of the United Kingdom and the United States. De Gaulle saw the European Community as a vehicle for reestablishing France as an independent world power, in equal partnership with Britain and the United States. His designation of continental Europe as France's "natural channel" of influence implied that Britain should remain outside the Six. This vision contrasted markedly with the conception of Macmillan, who saw Britain's role in Europe as a "bridge between Europe and North America" and a means of "binding Europe within the wider Atlantic Community."[13] Thus from the very beginning, the aspirations of Britain and France in Europe were thoroughly at odds with each other.

This central fact was not lost on Macmillan, who had spent many months considering ways and means of "coaxing" the French. As early as November 1959 it had been acknowledged that this could not be done by "fair words" alone; it would be necessary to draw out a "bigger card": "The more dramatic it is, the more essential it is to the security and prosperity of Europe, the more permanent, and the longer we can hold it in our hands, the better. It must appeal to de Gaulle, but it ought also to appeal to a number of his partners. It must have attractions for the Americans. It must be an absolute jewel."[14]

12. "Tripartite Consultation Between France, the United States and the United Kingdom," 10 March 1961, NSF/Box 70, in JFKL.

13. CAB128/35 Pt. 1, C.C. 24, 26 April 1961, in PRO.

14. Bishop to Macmillan, "Thoughts on Policy Towards Western Europe," 11 November 1959, PREM11/2985, in PRO.

For Macmillan, the "jewel" emerged in the form of Anglo-French cooperation in the development of a joint nuclear deterrent. Such an arrangement had
been in the back of Macmillan's mind from the early days of his premiership, but
it was scrutinized in detail in early 1961. The French nuclear program was central to de Gaulle's aim of restoring France's international prestige, despite the
massive strain on French resources. Although the general had never formally requested technical assistance from the United Kingdom, it was clear that any
offer from Macmillan would be extremely attractive to the French, who were still
several years away from constructing serviceable nuclear weapons. The British
Foreign Office canvassed a range of possibilities, from elevating the French to a
special position of nuclear trusteeship with the United Kingdom, or alterna-
tively, a situation in which the United Kingdom would assign its nuclear force
to a NATO command, on the condition that the French did the same.[15] This
second alternative effectively meant giving up the independent U.K. nuclear deterrent, thereby lowering Britain's nuclear position to that of the French.[16] It was
clear, however, that under no circumstances could Britain release information to
the French without American agreement because it had become virtually impossible to determine the precise national origin of any particular piece of information. These issues were examined in detail in a meeting of the cabinet at Cheq-
uers in January, in which it was emphasized that "we cannot embark on any sort
of bargain with the French at least until we know more about how the Americans feel on these questions."[17]

In April 1961, Macmillan set off for Washington for his first meeting with
the new president. The main purpose of his visit was to sound out American
opinion about the "Six-Seven Problem" and the closely related question of
French cooperation. Macmillan made clear his intention to seek membership for
the United Kingdom in the European Community, provided he could be certain
of United States support. He also raised the problem of France in this and other
areas affecting the cohesion of the Atlantic Alliance as a whole. Macmillan offered the view that "the pride of General de Gaulle, and of other very determined
men in Europe demanded that they should have some fuller share over the nuclear strength of the west," although he insisted that he was "posing a problem,
not offering a solution."[18] In reply, the Americans welcomed the suggestion that

15. Shuckberg to Macmillan, 26 December 1960; Shuckberg to Brook, 26 December 1960,
PREM11/3325, both in PRO.
16. The idea of abandoning the independent deterrent, and at the same time joining the European Community, naturally raised strong objections. Macmillan's private secretary, Philip de Zulueta, noted, "This may be the right policy, or at least the only practicable one, but if so I am inclined
to emigrate" (de Zulueta to Macmillan, 17 January 1961, PREM11/3325, in PRO).
17. Home to Dixon (Paris), 25 January 1961, PREM11/3325, in PRO.
18. "Record of a Meeting Held at the White House," First Meeting, 5 April 1961, CAB133/
244, in PRO. Macmillan subsequently outlined his thoughts in greater detail in a memorandum to
Kennedy of 28 April. He indicated that the United Kingdom would be willing to assist France, by
providing either technical information or warheads if the French could be persuaded to agree that
they would not use their strategic nuclear forces except after consultation with the United States and

Britain should join the Six and noted the similarity of U.S. and U.K. views on this matter. On the question of nuclear cooperation with France, however, the response was far from enthusiastic. The Kennedy administration had a firm policy of nonproliferation of nuclear weapons technology and was uneasy about the prospect of trading nuclear know-how for economic and political benefits. Acheson spoke strongly against the suggestion of assisting France to develop nuclear weapons because this would ultimately lead to equal treatment for the Germans. Moreover, he argued that the French would eventually realize that the expense of developing nuclear weapons and the means to deliver them were beyond their means.[19]

Macmillan's visit prompted Kennedy to initiate a reexamination of the entire question of nuclear assistance to the French. Although members of the Kennedy administration agreed fully with Macmillan's appraisal of the French problem, they could not bring themselves to agree with his ideas for a solution. Kennedy clarified his position in a letter to Macmillan of 8 May: "After careful review of the problem, I have come to the conclusion that it would be undesirable to assist France's efforts to create a nuclear weapons capability. I am most anxious that no erroneous impression get abroad regarding future US policy in this respect, lest they create unwarranted French expectations and serious divisions within NATO."[20]

This message did not come as a surprise to Macmillan, who responded by emphasizing his conviction that de Gaulle would "withhold his full cooperation until he gets some satisfaction for his nuclear ambitions." Despite Kennedy's apparently firm decision, the issue was not closed as far as the United Kingdom was concerned. Indeed, British officials were content to bide their time with what was, on balance, "a very satisfactory position." It was pointed out to Macmillan that he had avoided the danger that the Kennedy administration might satisfy French aspirations with virtually no help from Britain. It was considered essential that, if the French were to be assisted, this should be done largely at the instance and the expense of the United Kingdom. "Only in that way shall we work on de Gaulle's attitude to the United Kingdom in such a way as to facilitate a settlement of the Six-Seven problem on terms which we (and the Commonwealth and EFTA) would find acceptable. . . . In short, [we] have secured the

---

United Kingdom; to participate in tripartite arrangements for the use of these forces, including joint arrangements for the selection and allocation of targets; and to commit to NATO any tactical nuclear weapons for use by French forces in NATO. The objective was that France's nuclear capacity should develop, "not as an independent national force, but as a contribution to a joint Western deterrent held in trust on behalf of the free world as a whole." Macmillan also expressed himself in favor of discussions with France on the production of means of delivery of nuclear weapons. See Macmillan to Kennedy, Annex III, "Nuclear," 28 April 1961, PREM11/3311, in PRO.

19. "Record of a Meeting Held at the White House," Second Meeting, 5 April 1961, CAB133/244, in PRO.

20. Kennedy to Macmillan, 8 May 1961, PREM11/3311, in PRO.

President's acquiescence in our general policy without having made him a present of such cards as we hold and can still play."[21]

In the meantime, Macmillan had informed the cabinet that any further steps toward joining the European Community would depend on the outcome of President Kennedy's forthcoming visit to Paris in June. Kennedy had offered to raise the question of Britain joining the Community informally with de Gaulle, without giving any appearance of United States pressure. Macmillan agreed that de Gaulle ought not get the impression that Britain and the United States had "ganged up together to bring pressure to bear on him."[22] Nonetheless, he was eager to know whether there was any reasonable prospect of negotiating special arrangements for Britain's Commonwealth and agricultural problems with the Six. By this stage the British had received word from a range of sources that the position of the French had hardened further.[23] This impression was confirmed when Kennedy returned from Paris via London on 5 June to inform Macmillan of the outcome of his talks with de Gaulle. The general had stated flatly that the British still had "serious difficulties in joining the Community" and that they had "not yet chosen between the Commonwealth system and Common Market membership." The general's insistence that "the British must come all the way in or not come at all" was interpreted as an expression of his determination to keep Britain out. Indeed, Kennedy frankly informed Macmillan of his impression that General de Gaulle had "no particular wish to see the United Kingdom join the Six."[24]

By this time the Macmillan government was clearly running out of options. Mounting press speculation throughout the spring of 1961 had created the atmosphere of an impending announcement on the EEC question, yet little progress had been made in establishing a firm basis for successful negotiations. The growing uncertainty about Britain's intentions had led to a degree of tentativeness in business circles, as well as engendering considerable suspicion and mistrust among the Commonwealth and EFTA countries. The need to put an end to speculation seems to have forced Macmillan's hand into a public decision to apply for EEC membership. On 31 July, he formally announced his government's intentions in the House of Commons, claiming that it was "now better to bring matters to a head and to open negotiations than to postpone negotia-

21. Macmillan to Kennedy, 15 May 1961, PREM11/3311, and "The Complex: A Stocktaking," 16 May 1961, PREM11/3328, both in PRO.

22. Cabinet Minute, 26 April 1961, CAB 128/35 Pt. 1; and Macmillan to Kennedy, 28 April 1961, PREM11/3311, both in PRO.

23. See, for example, Figures to EFTA Washington Mission, 1 June 1961, UK File 20/00, in EFTA; Steel (Bonn) to Foreign Office, 30 March 1961, FO371/158162, in PRO.

24. Rusk (Paris) to State Department, 3 June 1961, NSF/Box 176, in LBJL; "Note of points made during the private discussion between President Kennedy and Prime Minister Macmillan at Admiralty House on Monday, June 5, 1961," 8 June 1961, POF/Box 127a, in JFKL; CAB128/35 Pt. 1, C.C. 30, 6 June 1961, in PRO.

tions until the omens, and in particular the attitude of the French Government, were more clearly propitious." Despite the strength of the French position, it was hoped that de Gaulle could be convinced by a combination of pressure from his partners in the Six and the possibility of political and military concessions from the United Kingdom. British strategy was summarized somewhat more baldly by Philip de Zulueta in a memorandum to Macmillan: "If we cannot bully the French we shall have to try either to persuade or bribe them."[25]

~

Kennedy responded warmly to the announcement from the United Kingdom, congratulating Macmillan on his new European initiative. The State Department, however, held strong reservations about the way Macmillan had qualified his EEC membership statement. Ball was particularly concerned about the conditional nature of Britain's application, describing it as an attempt "to slide sideways into the Common Market." By stressing the need to satisfy arrangements for all of Britain's interests, particularly the Commonwealth and EFTA, Macmillan had "raised problems that will almost certainly assure a protracted and complex negotiation." Ball was adamant that the United States could not support any merger between the Commonwealth preferential trading system and the European Common Market. To permit Commonwealth countries to have either free or preferential access to the Common Market would be extremely damaging to U.S. temperate agriculture, as well seriously distorting the whole concept of European integration. Similarly, the interests of the EFTA neutrals would have to be set to one side until the arrangements for full membership of Britain and Denmark had been completed. Thus Ball insisted that "we should not now under any circumstances agree to support, in general terms, the principle of 'association' for the neutrals."[26]

In addition to these problems, the State Department also had to deal with the awakening of the American press and public to the economic realities of the British application. The emerging agricultural policies of the Six had already raised cries of alarm among American farming groups, and the prospect of U.K. membership provoked fears of further discrimination against U.S. exports. Ball approached British officials soon after the EEC announcement, asking them to bear these sensitive issues in mind in negotiations with the Six. Despite the anticipated diversion of trade arising from British membership in the Six, however, the State Department expected that the overall effect of an enlarged European Community would be favorable to American economic interests. The stimulated growth rate of a fully integrated European market would increase demand for

25. Macmillan, Speech to the House of Commons, 31 July 1961; De Zulueta to Macmillan, 18 June 1961, PREM11/3557, in PRO.

26. Ball to Kennedy, 7 August 1961, p. 4, NSF/Box 170, in JFKL.

U.S. industrial products, thereby compensating U.S. industry for any loss of market share. Moreover, U.K. membership in the EC would tend to reduce the level of agricultural protection in Europe because of Britain's liberal trade policies.[27]

Much as Ball had feared, the negotiations in Brussels between Britain and the Six developed into a protracted debate over technical details because of the complexity of Commonwealth consultation, the difficulty of establishing a common position among the Six, and a mutual unwillingness to offer concessions. British officials also complained about the "petty and shortsighted attitude" of the French in insisting that the United Kingdom accept the French position on all points. The leader of the British negotiating team, Edward Heath, had originally hoped to complete the negotiations by the end of July 1962, but it became clear at an early stage that this schedule would have to be revised. Indeed, by mid-spring there was growing speculation that General de Gaulle might call off the negotiations altogether.[28] This view was based on an apparent hardening of the French position following the breakdown of the negotiations for political union among the Six in April. The "Fouchet negotiations" had formed a major part of General de Gaulle's broad plans for French political leadership of Europe and had been frustrated by Dutch and Belgian insistence that the United Kingdom be included.[29] In a press conference on 15 May, de Gaulle was curiously silent about the question of Britain and Europe, despite the key role of this issue in frustrating his political objectives. The British ambassador to Paris, Sir Pierson Dixon, saw this as an ominous sign and informed Macmillan of his view that "de Gaulle has now definitely decided to exclude us."[30]

U.S. Embassy officials in London were well aware of British nervousness about de Gaulle's attitude at this time. Moreover, they remained well informed about the measures that were being contemplated in the Foreign Office to shake the general's intransigence. On 17 May Ambassador Bruce received word that Macmillan might be prepared to discuss with de Gaulle "the implications for a common European defense policy of UK becoming a member of the EEC . . . which will imply the possibility of coordination of French and British defense policy in the nuclear field." The idea of an Anglo-French "nuclear trusteeship" as a bargaining chip for British entry into the Common Market had come under fresh examination in the spring of 1962 and was strongly advocated by senior ministers such as Harold Arthur Watkinson (defense), Thorneycroft (aviation),

27. Lee to France, 14 September 1961, FO371/158166, in PRO; Ball to Kennedy, 23 August 1961, NSF/Box 170, in JFKL.
28. Miriam Camps, *Britain and the European Community, 1955–1963* (London, 1964), 390; Bruce (London) to State Department, 5 April 1962, NSF/Box 170, in JFKL; *Financial Times,* 19 April 1962, p. 1.
29. See Alessandro Silj, *Europe's Political Puzzle: A Study of the Fouchet Negotiations and the 1963 Veto* (Cambridge, Mass., 1967).
30. Harold Macmillan, *At the End of the Day, 1961–1963* (London, 1973), 118.

and the prime minister himself.[31] Ironically, at this time the Kennedy administration was considering ways that Britain's own independent nuclear deterrent might be gradually curtailed.[32] Therefore, the State Department received the new developments in British thinking with a certain degree of alarm, if not surprise, especially in the light of Macmillan's forthcoming visit to the Chateau de Champs in June. Kennedy's national security adviser, McGeorge Bundy, expressed the president's concern in discussion with Ambassador Ormsby-Gore. Although the president did not take an attitude of "doctrinaire opposition" to a nuclear deal with France, he felt that it would be worth considering only if it would buy something "really spectacular" like full French cooperation in NATO as well as British entry into the EEC. Bundy revealed that the Americans had "thrown a somewhat similar fly over the General" earlier in the year, the only result being that "he had attempted to snap up the fly while turning down flat any idea of closer cooperation." The president was therefore anxious that Macmillan should bear this in mind during his talks with de Gaulle. Macmillan instructed Ormsby-Gore in reply to reassure the president "that I have no intention of doing anything foolish at Champs."[33]

Macmillan remained true to his word, and the question of Anglo-French cooperation in defense matters was discussed only in the most general terms at Champs. The prime minister's reluctance to play the "nuclear card" was based as much on divisions within his own cabinet as on pressure from the Kennedy administration. Throughout the summer of 1962 he received numerous conflicting memorandums from his colleagues on a specific proposal for Anglo-French cooperation in the development of a nuclear submarine. The proposal had been discussed in general terms by Watkinson and the French minister of defense, Pierre Messmer, on the basis that Britain would provide the know-how on the submarine and the French would develop a suitable missile. This program was intended to provide Britain and France with a successor deterrent for the 1970s. The strongest opponent to such an arrangement was Heath, who was nervous about any developments that might upset the steady progress of his negotiating team in Brussels. On the advice of his French colleagues he told Macmillan: "It is now clear that there is no question of our having to buy our way into the Common Market by cooperating with de Gaulle in the production of a nuclear deterrent. There is therefore no compelling reason for embarking on a joint programme at present." To settle the issue, Macmillan ordered a joint For-

31. Bruce to State Department, 17 May 1962, NSF/Box 170, in JFKL; Watkinson to Macmillan, "Nuclear Weapons," 12 April 1962, PREM11/3712, in PRO.

32. A National Security Council Policy Directive of 21 April 1962 stated that "over the long run it would be desirable if the British decided to phase out of the nuclear deterrent business" and that the United States should not prolong the life of the British nuclear deterrent. Cited in Richard E. Neustadt, "Report to the President: Skybolt and Nassau," 15 November 1963, p. 23, NSF/Box 322, in JFKL.

33. Ormsby-Gore to Macmillan, 17 May 1962, PREM11/3712, and Macmillan to Ormsby-Gore, 29 May 1962, PREM11/3712, both in PRO.

eign Office–Defence Ministry study to examine the various possibilities for Anglo-French nuclear cooperation. The findings of this group were submitted on the eve of Macmillan's fateful meeting with de Gaulle at Rambouillet in December: "The Committee were unable to see any fruitful possibilities of Anglo-French cooperation in any of these fields. The main general reason for this is the expressed French determination to be completely independent of any other country as regards their own nuclear deterrent . . . it follows that there is no future in pursuing this line of thought any further, still less in mentioning it to President de Gaulle."[34]

By this stage, however, Macmillan was fighting on two fronts to preserve his own nuclear deterrent in the face of the American decision to cancel Skybolt and to keep the flagging Brussels Conference alive.[35] The EEC membership negotiations had reached a deadlock on the long-standing problem of reconciling British agriculture with the Common Agricultural Policy of the EEC. Ball noted that the loss of momentum in Brussels "partly reflects the distaste of de Gaulle and Adenauer for British entry into Europe; it also reflects the negative reaction of the 'good European' members of the commission of the Common Market to a British tendency to treat the negotiations as a commercial haggle rather than a major political undertaking." The State Department became anxious to find ways of breathing life into the negotiations to ensure against their failure, but only limited options were available. The American ambassador to the EEC Commission, John Tuthill, strongly advised against direct intervention on the part of the United States because this would be resented by the Europeans.[36] Thus the Americans were forced to sit back and "continue to play the role of sympathetic observer."

It was amid this atmosphere that Macmillan went to Rambouillet to discuss these latest developments with de Gaulle. At their first meeting on 15 December de Gaulle made clear his decision to exclude Britain from the European Community. Although he did not speak of a "veto," he discoursed at length on every conceivable obstacle to British entry, emphasizing the lack of progress in the negotiations since their previous meeting at Champs in June. Although there was a certain degree of truth in his assertion that the negotiations had stalled, it seems clear that de Gaulle's objections to British membership ran far deeper. By the end of the visit Macmillan was convinced that "de Gaulle would, if he dared, use some means, overt or covert, to prevent the fruition of the Brussels negotiation." Macmillan then set off for Nassau to discuss with Kennedy the future of

---

34. "Extract from a record of conversation at the Chateau de Champs," 3 June 1962, PREM11/3712; Watkinson to Macmillan, 4 July 1962, PREM11/3712; Heath to Macmillan, "Anglo-French Collaboration: Nuclear Submarine/Missile System," 13 July 1962, PREM11/3712; "Rambouillet and Anglo-French Relations in the Nuclear Field: Memorandum to the Prime Minister," 7 December 1962, PREM11/3712, all in PRO.

35. On Skybolt, see John Newhouse, *De Gaulle and the Anglo-Saxons* (London, 1970).

36. Ball to Kennedy, 10 December 1962, and Tuthill to State Department, 17 December 1962, both in NSF/Box 170, in JFKL.

Britain's independent deterrent, in particular the substitution of Polaris missiles for the much maligned Skybolt weapons system. Macmillan curiously chose not to inform Kennedy of the full implications of de Gaulle's stance at Rambouillet and insisted that the Brussels negotiations were "wholly unconnected" with the Polaris issue. The effect of an agreement to supply Polaris to the United Kingdom would be "frankly, absolutely none."[37] The Americans, however, were more sensitive about the possible repercussions, and Ball advised the president that this might be the biggest decision he had been called upon to make. Kennedy replied, "That we get every week, George," but nonetheless he clearly recognized "grave political risks for Mr. Macmillan and serious risks also for our own policy in Europe."[38] To mitigate these risks, it was decided to offer Polaris missiles to France as well as Britain, on the condition that each agreed to assign its Polaris forces to NATO.

Macmillan accepted the offer but reserved the right to withdraw his force from NATO in case of a national emergency. De Gaulle, however, saw this as a shameful surrender of sovereignty and declined the offer on the grounds that France possessed neither the submarines to deliver the Polaris missiles nor the warheads to arm them. Instead, the general found in Nassau the perfect pretext to veto Britain's entry into the European Community. In his famous press conference of 14 January, he alluded strongly to the Polaris agreement as evidence of Britain's continued attachment to the United States and suggested that Britain might "one day come round to transforming itself enough to belong to the European Community without restriction and without reservation, placing it ahead of anything else." But he made clear his view that "England is not yet prepared to do this, and that indeed appears to be the outcome of the long, long Brussels talks." De Gaulle's announcement did not bring an instant halt to the negotiations in Brussels because the possibility that he was "thinking and speaking literally seemed rather too incredible." By the end of January, however, it had become painfully clear that his words were seriously meant; after more than a year of negotiations the Brussels Conference was brought to a close. Kennedy was all too aware of the devastating effect of de Gaulle's decision on Macmillan, and this was reflected in his message of consolation: "You will know without my saying so that we are with you in feeling and in purpose in this time of de Gaulle's effort to test the chances for his dream world. Neither of us must forget for a moment that reality is what rules and the central reality is that he is wrong and Europe knows he is wrong. . . . Moreover I count on you to let me know whenever you think we can strike a blow. And if this is an unmentionable special relationship, so much the better."[39]

37. Neustadt, "Report," 81, 89; Macmillan, *At the End of the Day*, 355.
38. Bundy's notes from the Nassau meeting, cited in Neustadt, "Report," 77.
39. Charles de Gaulle, *Major Addresses, Statements and Press Conferences, May 19, 1958–January 31, 1964* (New York, 1964), 208–22; Colegate to the Secretary General (Figures), 19 January 1963, UK File 20/00, in EFTA; Kennedy to Macmillan, n.d. [1963], POF/Box 127, in JFKL.

For Britain, the breakdown of the Brussels negotiations was clearly a monumental disaster that seriously damaged the credibility of the Macmillan government. Within the space of four years, the British had twice been publicly rejected by General de Gaulle, leaving their carefully constructed European policy in tatters. For the Kennedy administration, the assessment of these events fell somewhat short of "disaster" status. Certainly for the Europeanists in the State Department who had worked tirelessly to promote British entry such as George Ball and J. Robert Schaetzel, the veto came as a bitter disappointment. The question of whether it represented a "failure" of U.S. policy, however, was open to question. In the aftermath of the breakdown, the State Department examined the issue of whether a different approach might have brought about a more favorable result. It was concluded that there was "nothing wrong in the basic structure of our purpose and no great choice which we should clearly have made differently." Nevertheless, errors in "tactics and timing" were acknowledged: "Our messages to de Gaulle were not always perfectly framed; our lectures to NATO have been sounder in logic than in sweet persuasiveness; . . . our faithful affection for Jean Monnet has made us optimistic when we might better have been cautious." This view was not shared by the British Defence Ministry, which continued to feel that American refusal to permit a nuclear deal with de Gaulle was the ultimate cause of the breakdown. Peter Thorneycroft insisted to the Americans: "You never could and never will get de Gaulle into nuclear collaboration with *you*. It is too transatlantic. He means it when he says he will not let France down. It is we who can bring him into collaboration, with us and so with you. . . . You must tell us we can carry our technology across the Channel . . . if you had proposed it we'd be in the Common Market now and France would be in the Alliance."[40]

It is difficult to cast judgment on this question because Macmillan never made an offer of nuclear collaboration and de Gaulle never asked for one. What remains clear, however, is that de Gaulle had two closely related foreign policy objectives: to raise his country to the status of an independent nuclear power and to establish France as the political center of a united Europe. There is no evidence to suggest that de Gaulle ever considered trading one of these objectives for the other; both were vital components of an indivisible whole. De Gaulle's rejection of the Polaris offer is an important clue in this regard. Kennedy's offer was genuine, and Ambassador Bohlen in Paris had been instructed to examine the problems of warheads and means of delivery in discussions with the French government. De Gaulle was told that "no possibilities were excluded, all relationships were open for discussion" and that the offer was "a beginning, not an end."[41] But de Gaulle rejected the offer outright before these details could be

40. Memorandum for the President, "The U.S. and de Gaulle: The Past and the Future," 30 January 1963, NSF/Box 116a, in JFKL; Neustadt, "Report," 108.
41. Neustadt, "Report," 105.

John Newhouse (Author of "De Gaulle and the Anglo Saxons")
Leopoldo Nuti (Cantania)
Helge Pharo (Oslo)
Anthony Sampson (Author of *The Anatomy of Britain*)
John Waldron (Jean Monnet Council)
Stuart Ward (European University Institute)
Thomas Zoumaras (Truman State University)

## Acknowledgments

Three institutions working together made this volume possible: the John F. Kennedy Foundation (Boston), the European University Institute (Florence), and the Eisenhower Center at the University of New Orleans (UNO). Most of the papers included here were delivered at an October 1992 conference held in Florence under the direction of Richard T. Griffiths. His assistant, Stuart Ward, did more than anyone to ensure that the fine papers became essays in this edited volume. The excellent assistant director at the Eisenhower Center, Annie Wedekind, did a magnificent job of checking facts and answering last-minute queries for Louisiana State University Press. She was assisted by Matthew Ellefson and Michael Edwards of the Eisenhower Center, who earned our deep gratitude for logging numerous weekend hours to get this manuscript ready for publication. Charles Daly at the Kennedy Foundation not only paid for the Florence conference but offered his wisdom and guidance on numerous occasions; we're all grateful for his leadership, professionalism, and unwavering sense of humor. A very special mention is due two former American ambassadors—J. Robert Schaetzel and William vanden Heuvel—who provided the intellectual rationale for holding the Florence symposium in the first place. In addition, we retain an enormous sense of debt to McGeorge Bundy, who served as a consultant to this volume, helping the contributors answer a steady flow of questions pertaining to the Kennedy era.

We would also like to thank Louisiana State University Press, particularly Maureen Hewitt, assistant director, and editor Donna Perreault. Trudie Calvert served ably as the manuscript's copy editor.

The Eisenhower Center for American Studies at Metropolitan College of UNO was founded in 1983 by Stephen E. Ambrose and serves as a research institute dedicated to the study and preservation of American history and leadership. The Center's projects include scholarly conferences, the maintenance and growth of the World War II oral history archives, the Majic Bus educational program, and twentieth-century American literature projects. None of this would be possible without the continued enthusiastic support of Chancellor Gregory M. St. L. O'Brien and Dean Robert L. Dupont, and we give them special thanks.

# Index

ACDA. *See* Arms Control and Disarmament Agency (ACDA)

Acheson, Dean: and Cuban Missile Crisis, 8, 288; and Berlin Crisis, 18; on German-American relations, 30, 311–13; and NATO, 54; and Portugal, 149–50, 155–56, 160; and Angola, 155–56, 160, 163; and balance-of-payments crisis, 178; and European colonialism, 272*n*30; and Monnet, 281, 300–302, 304; Anglophilia of, in West Point speech of, 288–96, 294*n*23, 298; Skybolt controversy and Nassau Agreement, 296–99; and Atlantic partnership versus French nationalism, 299–309; and Ball, 300; on de Gaulle, 307–309; disenchantment of, with Kennedy, 310–16, 316*n*; and Test-Ban Treaty, 310–11; trip through Europe by, 311–13; and MLF, 312, 313; and British EEC membership bid, 320

Action Committee for the United States of Europe, 264–65*n*4, 272, 283–85, 300–301, 300*n*40

Adenauer, Konrad: Macmillan on, 6; and Kennedy, 16–31, 46; retirement of, 16; advisers of, 17; and Berlin Crisis, 17–22, 39; and Berlin Wall, 19; and Western Alliance, 22–28; and danger of Soviet attack, 23–24; and de Gaulle, 24, 25, 26–27, 30, 39–40, 40*n*10; and Cuban Missile Crisis, 28; and détente, 28–31; and German reunification, 30; on East Germany, 40; and MLF, 62; and balance-of-payments crisis, 172–73; and Germany's payment of NATO-related U.S. expenses, 172–73; and "Chicken War," 257; and British EEC membership bid, 303–304, 303–304*n*49, 319;

and Franco-German treaty of 1963, 305–307; and Erhard, 312, 313

Adzhubey, Alexy, 20, 24

AEC. *See* Atomic Energy Commission (AEC)

Africa, 150–65, 178, 266*n*8, 273, 282, 299

Agriculture, 215–16, 215*n*, 217*n*11, 219, 222, 225, 229–30, 229*n*37, 232–34, 241, 251–54, 252*n*, 257, 332

Aiken, George, 91, 91*n*56, 92

Algerian crisis, 34, 45, 151, 152, 154, 281

Aluminum industry, 219*n*

Anderson, George, 85

Anderson, Robert B., 172, 173, 178, 178*n*24

Andronikov, Prince, 40*n*11

Angleton, James J., 132*n*7

Angola, 151–65

Annan, Noel, 290

APAG. *See* Atlantic Political Advisory Group (APAG)

Arms Control and Disarmament Agency (ACDA), 69, 77, 78, 79, 82, 85, 90, 92

Arms control policy, 66–72, 67*n*2, 67*n*3. *See also* Test-Ban Treaty

Athens meeting of North Atlantic Council, 55–58

Atlantic Alliance, 25, 26, 38, 47, 130, 135, 136, 288–316

Atlantic Political Advisory Group (APAG), 286–87

Atomic Energy Commission (AEC), 36, 45, 70, 71, 78, 79, 82, 87, 90, 98, 99, 101, 104, 118–19

Aubrey, H. G., 227

Azores base, 148–65

Baghdad Pact, 117

109, 110, 111; Harriman mission to Soviet Union on, 28, 29, 82–89, 94, 109–11, 310; assessment of, 66–69, 93–94, 111–13; and Kennedy, 66–69, 72–94, 100–13; signing of, 66, 95, 111, 310; historical background on, 69–72, 96–100; and Khrushchev, 70, 80, 81, 85–86, 90, 98, 100, 102, 103, 106–11; and France, 73–74; Geneva negotiations on, 77–80, 98–104; and Eighteen-Nation Disarmament Committee (ENDC), 78, 80, 86, 105, 105*n*13, 106, 108; Senate approval of, 89–93, 95, 109–10, 111; and U.S. domestic politics, 89–93; public opinion on, 91, 111; nonsignatories of, 95; signatories of, 95; withdrawal clause of, 95, 110, 111; American change in position on nuclear test ban, 97–98; text of, 114–15; and Acheson, 310, 310–11

Textile agreement/textile industry, 250–51, 250*n*21, 258, 274*n*36, 275*n*38

Thomas, Hugh, 15

Thompson, Llewelyyn, 20, 76, 82–84, 86

Thorneycroft, Peter, 296–97, 327

Thorp, Willard, 238*n*

TNC. *See* Trade Negotiations Committee (TNC)

Tobin, James, 201, 206, 207

Tokyo Round of General Agreement for Trade and Tariffs (GATT), 257*n*32, 259

Trachtenberg, Marc, 139, 146

Trade: European Free Trade Association (EFTA), 40, 318–19, 324–26, 332; and balance-of-payments crisis in Europe, 169–90, 199–200, 210–11, 217*n*11, 234, 263, 283–85; Eisenhower's policy on, 170–72; and GATT, 179, 207, 213–22; U.S. policy on exports, 200; European-American trade policies from 1961–1963, 212–34; Ball on, 219, 239, 239*nn*4–5, 240, 273–75; U.S. import duties on carpets and glass, 222–26, 222*n*19, 223*n*21; disparity issue between U.S. and EEC regarding tariffs, 230–31, 231*n*41; and "Chicken War," 231–34, 257; textile agreement, 250–51, 250*n*21, 258; and nontariff barriers

(NTBs), 253–54. *See also* Trade Agreements Act of 1934; Trade Expansion Act

Trade Agreements Act of 1934, 239*n*5, 240, 243, 246, 249

Trade Expansion Act (TEA): and Congress, 179, 223–24, 223*n*22; and EEC, 212, 228–31, 257; purpose of, 226–28; and Ball, 235, 242–44, 258, 274–76, 274*n*35; significance of, 235–36, 256–60, 273, 275–76, 302; background on, 236–40; innovative provisions of, 240–51; gaps in, 251–54; consequences of innovations in, 254–57

Trade Negotiations Committee (TNC), 214, 230, 230*n*39

Treasury Department, 100, 169, 175, 180–81, 183–85, 206. *See also* Dillon, C. Douglas

Treaty of Rome, 213*n*3, 231, 234

Triffin, Robert, 185

Trollope ploy, 122

Truman, Harry, 8, 35, 67, 67*n*2, 117, 128, 170, 303*n*49, 309, 310, 314–15

Turkey, 12, 116–28, 141, 142

Tuthill, John Wills, 265, 329

Twist Operation, 181–84

Tyler, William R., 62*n*27, 265*n*5

U-2s and U-2 incident, 5, 8, 100, 117

U Thant, 11–12, 122

United Kingdom. *See* Great Britain

United Nations, 11–12, 18, 19, 33, 78, 95*n*4, 96, 97, 150, 152, 158–59, 255

United States. *See* Congress, U.S.; Defense Department; Kennedy, John F.; State Department; Treasury Department; and other government agencies and officials

U.S. Information Agency (USIA), 84

Uruguay Round of General Agreement for Trade and Tariffs (GATT), 256, 257

USIA, 84

USSR. *See* Soviet Union

Valletta, Vittorio, 132*n*7, 135*n*14

Van Lennep, Emile, 190–91, 199–200, 202

Vernon, Raymond, 235, 242*n*, 243